THE
CELLULOID CURRICULUM

HAYDEN FILM ATTITUDES AND ISSUES SERIES

THE CELLULOID CURRICULUM:
HOW TO USE MOVIES IN THE CLASSROOM
Richard A. Maynard

THE
CELLULOID CURRICULUM

HOW TO USE MOVIES
IN THE CLASSROOM

RICHARD A. MAYNARD

*Teacher of Social Studies and Afro-American History
Simon Gratz High School, Philadelphia; Community
College of Philadelphia; Great Lakes Colleges
Association, Philadelphia*

*Films Editor and Educational Film Reviewer
Scholastic Teacher Magazine*

HAYDEN BOOK COMPANY, INC., NEW YORK

This book is dedicated to the beautiful students of
Simon Gratz High School—who made it all happen!

1   2   3   4   5   6   7   8   9   PRINTING

71 72 73 74 75 76 77 78   YEAR

FOREWORD

The Film Study people are now scattered—delightfully and often product-ively, though sometimes confusingly—among quite different philosophies and practices: film-as-art, films-to-turn-the-kids-on, film-as-another-language, film-as-one-of-the-humanities. What I haven't seen before and what seems to me so crucial in The Celluloid Curriculum is evidence of an actual course, in which the subject matter is drawn from vital experiences and concerns and questions (mar-riage, ethical issues, race relations, responsibility, the impact of war . . .), and the material, the "stuff" of the course, is films and response to films. This is not "Film Study" in any of the usual senses.

A few years ago this use of films would have sounded so visionary, not to mention impractical. But here is a teacher who is working in an inner city high school in the midst of all the problems highlighted on the front page of any big city paper, who has used films—feature films that don't last just 40 minutes and which cost rental money—to build a whole course, several courses, around the American experience in this century as seen through those films. Each chapter, each suggested unit, seems so right, so reasonable, so worth trying that one is carried along in a blend of curiosity and growing conviction that this approach makes remarkable educational sense.

The book is a gold mine for teachers. Maynard knows films, for one thing. But he knows them from more perspectives than those of the movie buff. He knows them as wrought, lit, and shaped experiences, part of the social scene of the immediate past (beginning, say, around 1915) and the present, as vital forces in our lives, as things that have affected the way people see themselves and other people and the world outside the front door.

But the book's richness is not only in its knowledge of film as art, enter-tainment, social force and reflection of actualities and fantasies in our world. If a book can have a perceiving ear, this one has: an ear for a student's concerns, worries, questions, his eagerness to wrestle with problems he can take seriously. The ear is equally perceiving of the teacher's concerns, his desire for "relevancy," and his need for specific strategies and materials to try out and develop and incor-porate into his own style and that of his class.

Finally, the book moves with ease and helpfulness in and out of print and film, in and out of thoughtful and searching sociological and critical materials that illuminate the topics and questions raised by the films.

Any chapter here could take a teacher and his class into a valuable partner-ship experience in learning, using part or all of Maynard's ideas, questions, and suggested films, and going beyond them into something students and teachers create for themselves.

David Mallery
Director of Studies
NATIONAL ASSOCIATION OF INDEPENDENT SCHOOLS

v

CONTENTS

INTRODUCTION
The Medium as the Method

When I was a high school student, I used to look forward to the days when my teachers would show movies. Movies were a regular part of the educational repertory of many of my teachers, and they would show them to the class to introduce, illustrate, or conclude a unit of study. Friday was usually movie day. What could be more perfect for teacher and students alike than a cinematic experience to celebrate the closing of a tedious week of education? The teacher could rest his voice—and also his feet—after four days of intensive lecturing. And the students—well, movies in class gave us a chance to catch up on our sleep, eat potato chips, and sit and discuss the weekend's coming events. As for the events taking place on the screen, which ran the gamut from a 20-minute version of the colonists vs. the Indians in *Drums Along the Mohawk* (to illustrate American frontier history, naturally) to Walt Disney's *How to Catch a Cold* (which I somehow managed to see about once a year from elementary school to twelfth grade), they were more one-dimensional than the printed pages of textbooks. But they were fun. At least we didn't have to concentrate.

As I look back on my adolescence and reflect on how little turned me on in school, I keep thinking about movies. Why was it that I never paid a blessed bit of attention to any film ever showed in school, and yet on most weekends paid to see motion pictures for pleasure and entertainment? Certainly the kinds of things I was shown in school helped tune me out. But once I remember an assembly program in the tenth grade where about 700 students were shown the *Caine Mutiny,* and even then I recall spending that two-hour period doing a hundred other things instead of paying attention to the screen. In school, for me, the medium was definitely not the message.

Recently my experience as a teacher of both high school and college students has convinced me that motion pictures represent a significant, vital, cultural force in our society. They are a good part of our literature, our art, our sense of humor, our conscience—a mirror of ourselves. Using films extensively in my own classroom has taught me the value of the motion picture medium as a teaching device. Films and television condition our socialization process. The classroom, a major socializing agent, therefore, has a responsibility to use them to provide the kinds of meaningful experience students are now crying out for.

Many school are changing their libraries into instructional materials centers. The very latest in audio-visual technology (carousel projectors, cassette recorders, portable video tape machines, Technicolor 1000 projectors, etc.) is becoming standard equipment for most schools. Film-appreciation and film-making courses have also been added as valid new curricula. Yet somehow, despite all of the technical innovations, English and history classes continue to function as traditional, textbook-oriented subjects where the media, at best, still serve purely as audio-visual aids. And, at worst, they sit in the teacher's closet and gather dust.

In the school system in which I am now teaching, huge television studios are used to tape classroom lectures from the local educational channel. Twenty-five or thirty film projectors circulate among classrooms showing standard educational pap (even *How To Catch a Cold* is still around). And kids still learn what they have to from books.

I don't blame teachers entirely for the abuse of these materials. Part of the problem rests with the kids themselves. Students, in my experience, do not automatically tune in to the media. When shown in the traditional classroom setting, films can be quite boring. Kids have seen the school as a rigid structural environment for so long that they actually believe this is the way it should be. Ask them sometimes their concepts of school. They may not like it, but they have a pretty good idea of what it's supposed to be. "School is books." "School is a teacher 'teaching'." "School is writing and listening."

Films have no legitimacy in such an environment. Many educators will argue that they are good audio-visual aids (and voice savers), but few will concede that they are literature, or art, or social document. At this moment in my own Social Studies department, there is a hot debate between those who want to spend a newly acquired grant of funds on films (such as old television documentaries like the *Biography* series) to illustrate or supplement concepts, and those, like myself, who wish to spend the money on films around which entire conceptual units can be built.

Students have sat through (or slept through) so many dull films that they probably couldn't care less what we purchase. A few years ago, one of my students returned to school after a week's absence and asked what she had missed. I told her that the class had seen *Dr. Strangelove* and discussed its importance in relationship to man's callous lack of responsibility for his fellow man. "Oh, is that all? So long as I didn't miss too many notes."

Celluloid Curriculum is about how to use motion pictures effectively in the classroom. It is designed as a handbook for enlivening a curriculum by giving movies the educational legitimacy they have so long deserved and helping teachers find exciting new methods of communicating with kids. Having experimented with this kind of teaching for some time now, I have discovered two effective ways of using films. The greater part of this book is an illustration of these two basic methods of teaching with films.

The first method, and in some ways, the most traditional, subordinates films to certain basic conceptual themes. In this way, the film is used as a piece of literature designed to present a particular phase of the study. For example, a class in political science studying the concept of power might read Machiavelli's *The Prince* and George Orwell's *Animal Farm*. That same class could be doubly enriched if it also saw *Citizen Kane* and *Privilege* and then discussed the subject based on *all* of the materials analyzed. Films used in this way are not simply motivators or visual aids, but have legitimate status as equal parts of the study along with books. This kind of thematic approach lends itself very well to entire courses of study in English and the social studies. In Part I of the book, I have suggested several conceptual units (Sex Education, Law Enforcement, Black Studies, Ethical Problems, Social Problems, etc.) that use films as key literary sources, in some cases along with books and in others as the only classroom materials.

The second method of teaching with films that has worked for me makes use of movies as primary classroom sources. This involves a direct study of the films themselves for their historical and social content. I am not talking about technical cinematic study. Despite its increased popularity, relatively few teachers (including myself) are either die-hard movie buffs or experts on cinematic technique. What I am proposing is that teacher and students look at films for the ideas they communicate. For example, a class can study Western movies, examining how they perpetuate a basic myth about American society, and why that myth (and the Western film) is so popular. Or, the class can analyze the history of the Great Depression by watching *Dead End, The Grapes of Wrath,* and *Forty-Second Street* as reflections of the 1930s. Or it can study the stereotyped portrayal of Blacks throughout screen history and examine the reasons behind it. Or, it can analyze the propaganda of *Triumph of the Will*; the attitude towards war in *The Guns of Navarone*; the imperialism of *Gunga Din*. In Part II of this work I have presented several classroom units demonstrating this kind of historical and social analysis of films (The Black Stereotype, Images of Africa, Interpretations of War, Movies as History, etc.).

I have already indicated my belief that motion pictures can revitalize curriculum. Part of this book contains some of my own classroom experiences in learning to develop better methods of teaching. The rest of the book contains detailed suggestions in maintaining this format. Although the "suggested" unit chapters are loaded with more films than one teacher could possibly use (even if he had an unlimited budget), they are based on either what I have taught or plan to teach. I have tried to make this my criterion throughout the book—to cite only the kinds of things I myself would teach in the classroom. I could not have written this book otherwise.

Most of the films recommended for study in the conceptual units are fulllength features. Although I have listed several excellent short subjects, I believe that features, which were made originally to entertain people, are the most neglected films educationally. In my experience educators raise fundamental objections to them like: "They are too long for the class period and the roster cannot be extended," "They too often deal with 'extra' material for commercial appeal (sex, violence, etc.), which is not suitable for the classroom (particularly recent films)," "They are too expensive to rent," etc.

In the final section of the book, designed as a practical information guide, I have tried to deal with these complaints and others like them. Only the last (money) can really sabotage a good program, and though I have no panaceas, I have offered some possible solutions.

The Celluloid Curriculum is designed as a detailed introduction to the types of methods of film study explained here. We plan to follow it with a series of classroom unit-texts containing many of the supplementary reading materials suggested throughout the various chapters of this book. Thus far, either completed or in the planning stages, are unit-texts on *The Black Man in Film, Images of Africa on Film, Cinematic Views of the Great Depression,* and *War Propaganda on Film.* Available for use with each unit-text will be a 30-minute 16-mm extract reel, presenting key scenes from films discussed in the unit. These reels will be produced and distributed by Films Incorporated of Wilmette, Illinois. These student anthologies can be used in classrooms where the teacher has accepted the principles of the celluloid curriculum and wishes to provide specific reading materials for his students to accompany screenings. How useful such materials can be should become evident after reading this book.

ACKNOWLEDGEMENTS

A work of this kind could not be possible without the cooperation and encouragement of a great many people. I would therefore like to personally thank the following people:

Professional film educators: David Sohn, Curriculum Consultant for the school district of Evanston, Ill.; John Culkin, Director of the Center for Understanding Media; Frank McLaughlin and Charles Faucher, editors of *Media and Methods Magazine*; and David Mallery, Director of the National Association of Independent Schools.

Educational colleagues: Marcus Foster, Superintendent of Schools for Oakland, Calif. and formerly Principal of Simon Gratz High School, Philadelphia; Dr. Frederick Holliday, Principal of Simon Gratz High School; Herman Steinberg, Social Studies Department Head, Simon Gratz High School; Richard Robinson, English Department Head, Simon Gratz High School; Arthur May, friend and colleague who assisted me with my research; Dr. Robert DeHahn, Director of the Great Lakes Colleges Association; and Dr. Barry Grossbach, History Department Chairman, Community College of Philadelphia.

Film industry leaders: Donald Johnjack, Films Inc.; Andrew Sager, Walter Reade Films; Walter Dauler, Audio-Brandon Films; John Whitesell, Warner Brothers; Leo Dratfield, Contemporary-McGraw-Hill Films; Frederick Wiseman, Zipporah Films; David Picker and Miss Peggy Fisher, United Artists; Miss Regina Cornwall, formerly of the Museum of Modern Art; and Stanley Leshner, National Football League Films.

Special thanks also must go to Bill Cook and Bob Boynton of Hayden Book Company for their faith in me and all of the assistance they gave me with my manuscript.

Finally I would like to acknowledge the members of my family who had so much to do with guiding me through the long summer of 1970—my wife, Lorrie, who lived every minute of this manuscript with me; my son, Jeffrey, who spent part of the first year of his life trying to understand why he couldn't play with all of his daddy's papers; Gene Maynard, my father, who instilled in me a love and appreciation for movies; and finally, Mrs. Helen Goldberg, my mother-in-law, who diligently typed and corrected my manuscript.

RICHARD A. MAYNARD

PART I

Bringing the Subject to Life–

Film as an Independent Part of the Curriculum

Towards a Celluloid Course of Study–
A Memoir

A few years ago I wrote an article about how I experimented with the required course of study for high school senior social studies by using films to introduce or supplement the basic required material (sociology, economics, and government). The films, real high-quality stuff like *Dr. Strangelove, A Thousand Clowns, Lord of the Flies,* and *Twelve Angry Men,* made the classes far more interesting and gave me a new sense of enthusiasm for teaching.[1] But there were problems. I was showing feature films in classes that were supposed to run 40 minutes each and I either had to bring kids in early, or keep them late (imagine all the enemies I must have made), or show the films a reel at a time over a three- or four-day sequence. (This, I might add, was not too bad a solution, given my alternatives, but many of my peers and my department chairman insisted that four days to show a film was "wasting time.") In addition, I had my students read supplementary paperback books on themes similar to the films in order to provide as many experiences as possible. This time I got flack from English teachers who were planning to use books like The Crucible and Invisible Man later in the year and whose thunder I was stealing. Indeed one English teacher sternly criticized my interpretation of a work of literature and told me to stick to my own subject, which was history. To make matters worse, the money that funded my program from a special grant was used up. By the end of that first year, despite my successes in the classroom, it really looked as though my course, for all the publicity I gave it in my article, was doomed.

No doubt many teachers who have performed similar innovative experiments have experienced setbacks like this. It's always the same story: "Your program is great. Now let's get back to business as usual." For me "business as usual" had to be based on that fantastic "experiment." I had seen those films—commercial, entertaining, exciting, sexy pictures—stimulate more discussion, inspire more creative writing, motivate more reading, and build up better teacher-student rapport than any educational text, device, or gimmick in existence. I could not go back to a lecture, textbook-oriented classroom. Not anymore.

[1] For details of this experience see Maynard, Richard A., "The Social Studies and Media," **The Social Studies**, vol. 60, December 1969 pp. 327-329. Reprinted in Films Deliver: Teaching Creatively with Film. Edited by Schillaci, Anthony, and Culkin, John M. New York: Citation Press, 1970.

Fortunately, I had a principal who could move mountains and his enthusiasm for new projects was responsible for getting the school a sizable private grant for curriculum revision.[2] Part of that money was given to me to build up a course of study using films more extensively than ever. Indeed, there would even be enough money to build a school film library. The biggest problem, money, was solved.

Still nothing could be done about the roster. The school was overcrowded and run on two six-period shifts. The first shift began at 7:50 a.m. and ended at 12:05. The second started at 12:15 and ran until 4:30. Periods were shorter than ever, and there were no rooms available to keep kids late to see films. (Can you imagine asking anyone on that first shift to come in early?)

For the most part, I realized that the films would have to be split on a day-by-day basis and I had learned to live with that. One class, however, was to have some additional benefits. With the cooperation of the English and math departments, we scheduled one group of college-bound kids to four straight periods in the same room (social studies, math, and English, with the last two alternating as double periods). In this way, the three teachers could borrow time from each other for lengthy projects (like film showing). After two years of this, I estimate that I must owe the English and math departments about 600 hours. We also hoped that English and social studies could be merged into a kind of humanities program, where kids would read the same literature and see the same films, but each teacher would deal with them according to subject. (If this seems awfully provincial, and it does to me, keep in mind that the schedule and the academic departments of most schools are remarkably inflexible. I considered myself lucky to be able to show films in their entirety to at least one class, and I wasn't about to start subverting the entire system.)

What I am now about to present is a kind of montage of the high points and low points of two years' involvement with a new kind of course of study. Although it is still based on the preformulated social studies curriculum (as dictated by the Pennsylvania State Department of Instruction), some very special things happened, mostly because the films changed the environment of the classroom. Students and teacher learned together.

The standard high school sociology curriculum guides "strongly recommend" beginning the subject with an analysis of cultural anthropology. Textbook material on this subject (in the ones I've seen, anyway) is deadly boring: definitions, terms to learn, more definitions, questions at the end of chapters. I was convinced that I could improve on that, and so I bought a paperback set of an old college favorite of anybody who's ever taken a survey course in anthropology—Ruth Benedict's <u>Patterns of Culture</u>. Written over 30 years ago, this classic on the relativity of behavior patterns in various cultures was responsible for deflating many of the ethnocentric biases of social scientists and led to a genuine objective study of world cultures and of mankind as basically one people. It is a great book, but most high school kids hate it. The vocabulary is old

---

[2] I should note here that I teach in one of those so-called inner-city schools that is 100 per cent Black and where the dropout rate is very high. I do not, however, want to overstate this. Despite the obvious problems in a school like mine, the classroom functions like anywhere else, for better or worse. Emphasis is more on academic success in the "traditional" sense. Curriculum building, therefore, is designed to sharpen skills and prepare kids for higher education and courses of study like mine are applicable to students in any "average" school system.

fashioned and pretentious; it lacks maps, charts or visuals (it's tough for most kids to visualize where the island of Dobu is), and it's long.

What a way to start a course! After one week with <u>Patterns of Culture</u> and a few of my inspiring lectures, the class was ready to lynch me. Then I showed the first film *Circle of the Sun.*

For some strange reason this beautiful yet tragic short film never gets much publicity in the film guidebooks or journals. A National Film Board of Canada production, it deals with the dying culture of the Blood Indians of northwest Canada. The Bloods, an agrarian tribe, base their entire ceremonial system on the worship of the sun. All of their rituals involve prayer to the sun as the provider of all life, and on their clothing and their houses are countless drawings of the great shining object. In all prayer sessions the people sit in a circle to emulate the sun. Pete Standing Alone, a young Blood who has left the reservation to find work as an oil driller and a cowboy (irony?), returns annually to attend a special religious festival of the sun. Pete tells us (he is the film's only narrator) that he continually comes home, but he has never really learned the significance of any of the ceremonies. Only the old Bloods know the real meaning and they will not reveal it. Thus the young feel alienated, since they can't participate in the rituals, and the old refuse to share their religious knowledge with the young. As the film ends, with the sun setting, we see that Blood culture is truly dead. An old Indian heartily praying to the sacred sun is wearing sunglasses.

Suddenly the class began to realize what anthropologists mean when they talk about cultural genocide. The Blood Indians of *Circle of the Sun* provided us with a living case study. The kids spent days talking about how Blood culture changed and why some cultures have been swallowed up by Western technology. The film motivated the first genuine class discussion on anthropology.

Recognizing a good thing, I followed this up with another documentary film— the feature-length *Dead Birds.* This truly remarkable motion picture, one of two case studies done by Harvard's Peabody Museum,[3] documents the cultural complexities within what has been popularly labeled a "primitive" society—the Dani people of central New Guinea. The film, with a bare minimum of narration, and not a single Western value judgement, objectively records the life style of a people whose entire existence centers around a perpetual war with their neighbors. No one seeing this film could ever label the Dani "savages" (a term that Benedict whole-heartedly condemns). Their humanity and compassion for each other is brilliantly captured by the cameras.

The kids seemed to genuinely like this film. They began to apply the tenets of <u>Patterns of Culture</u> to it by studying various elements of Dani civilization. They scrutinized the religious, familial, and technological "patterns" and actually worked as anthropologists—which is exactly what a film like *Dead Birds* demands from those who see it.

To conclude this unit (which was now running over schedule because of the depth of the film discussions) I added a most unusual film, the likes of which I doubt has ever been shown in a high school class (or a serious film study class

---

[3] The other film, **The Hunters,** about a group of Kalahari Bushmen on a hunt for a giraffe is equally good at depicting objectively the life style of a unique culture. It can be used effectively instead of **Dead Birds,** or better yet, along with it. See the Filmography for details of acquiring both.

From the motion picture **Dead Birds.** Courtesy of Contemporary-McGraw-Hill Films.

for that matter). I showed *Mondo Cane.*

Many people have questioned my selection of a film that critics have condemned as sensationalistic garbage. *Mondo Cane* is, of course, unabashedly sensationalistic in its attempts to prove that universally men are savages, whether they are New Guinea "primitives" or Western "sophisticates." Its director, Gualtiero Jacopetti, was once, I believe, the editor of an Italian exposé magazine, and he seems expert at arranging sordid, horrifying scenes (such as a New Guinean woman suckling a pig, a custom when a child is born dead). The musical score (including the popular song *More,* which one student interpreted as a perfect theme for a film of so many excesses) is deliberately hammy with all those violins and drums to stir emotion. And there are some obviously staged scenes, including a "pagan" feast with "savages" devouring a pig, but wearing such "civilized" matter as wrist watches and sunglasses. It is the antithesis of scientific anthropology. It is Margaret Mead gone amok.

Yet for a few important reasons *Mondo Cane* was a very effective part of the unit. First of all it is undeniably commercial—a complete surprise to students who have just viewed two very studied documentaries. Therefore, it was very entertaining, and at the same time it gave the class a chance to develop its anthropological skills. One by one its unscientific value judgements and flashily edited sequences came under fire. A student protested that he could make a film in which everyone looked savage simply by arranging the scenes selectively. Others were quick to point out that anthropologically many of the so-called savage rituals were merely bits and pieces of the entire cultural pattern and were all perfectly explainable. (The scene showing a woman suckling a pig is meant for shock effect, when actually a ritual like this is common in parts of the South Pacific, where a pig is valued almost as much as a man since it is the major source of food. Indeed a similar situation is described in *Dead Birds* without value judgements. The class was quick to make that comparison.) In a negative, yet very significant sense, *Mondo Cane* brought out the anthropologists in them.

I must defend showing it for another reason. Sensationalistic and anti-intellectual as it is, there is a very human quality about *Mondo Cane.* I realize this seems contradictory, but the film itself is a contradiction. Interspersed with all of the fancy edited garbage are frighteningly realistic flashes of the inhumanity of our own society. One scene that haunts my memory even now is that of the animal life on the island of Bikini, where the first H-bomb tests took place. Birds lay eggs that will never hatch, and some birds who have lost their instinct to fly actually live underground. And a sea tortoise who struggles to lay her eggs, has lost her sense of direction and vainly attempts to find the sea. She walks in an endless circle until she dies as the camera frames her futile path. These scenes pose fundamental questions about the horrors our human technology can inflict and how "savage" indeed we may be.

One other scene in this grab bag of a movie makes up for all of its other ineptitudes. To my knowledge, it is the only film released commercially that shows the operation of an amazing cultural phenomenon—the cargo cult. Prior to the showing of the film, in a lesson on how cultures affect each other, I read to the class from a standard anthropology text about a group of New Guinea "primitives" who discovered the cargo airplanes of the British and claimed they were their ancestors as great birds who have come to carry them off. (The Dani people of *Dead Birds* have a similar belief.) These people have left their highland homes and set up quarters near the air field. Here they erected wooden replicas of the planes as religious symbols and pray to their gods to release them from the white infidels so the planes can carry them to heaven. This is a rare example of a technological concept from one culture serving as a metaphysical object to another. *Mondo Cane,* in one of its rare unstaged sequences, captures this on film. It is the last scene in the film and the one that generated the most discussion.

To conclude the unit I asked the class to write about how much alike men were despite vast cultural differences. Using Benedict and the three films as sources, they demonstrated anthropological sophistication greater than mine. I lectured very little during this unit, and I learned a great deal.

The second unit in the course dealt with the sociological concept of norms in a society. I realized that I would have to teach concepts like norms, morés, and folkways, as well as conformity and deviation. This, of course, meant some lecturing. For class reading I selected Sinclair Lewis' Babbitt, perhaps the best-known portrait of conformist behavior in its worst sense. (I must add that the kids read this reluctantly. Although it may be the best American sociological novel of all time, high school seniors insist that it is "jive".)[4]

Realizing that the initial material was rather dry, I immediately showed a short film called *Time Piece*. Made by Jim Henson (of the Muppetts of *Sesame Street* fame), this eight-minute series of images flashing through the mind of an uptight "Joe-suburbanite" is riotously funny. Sitting in a hospital bed, a man hears the thumping of his heart and suddenly imagines himself out on the street fighting traffic, watching women, hurrying to the office, working at his dull job, watching women, and so on. He is confused, sexually frustrated. We see his wife, who looks like the "before" half of the Geritol commercial, and his images of her as a sex partner. One scene copies the famous eating-seduction sequence of *Tom Jones*. Insecure (images flash by of his neighborhood changing—a Black kid on a pogo stick, later a gorilla), he is truly a victim of our success-oriented times. The only dialogue in the film is our hero's weak cry of "help" as he subsequently sees his head on a food platter, on a dollar bill, and finally in a toilet about to be flushed. If the film sounds crazy, it is. And its images turned the class into amateur psychoanalysts. I have never seen a short film generate so much discussion. The kids insisted upon seeing it again and again. Each time they caught another symbol of the problems of a "Babbitt." The film, I believe, tele-scopes Babbitt's sad existence into a brief, but meaningful, experience.

After discussing *Time Piece* and Babbitt, we turned to view the nature of non-conformity in our society. For the next readings, the class chose between Hunter Thompson's Hell's Angels and Tom Wolfe's Electric Kool-Aid Acid Test. Both portray types of group nonconformity.

While they were reading these, I showed a film which I now regret using, *Conformity*, one of those pseudo-sociological CBS television documentaries made in the early 1960s. (Another was *The Detached Americans*, which holds up slightly better.) Narrated in tongue-in-cheek style by Harry Reasoner, it attempts to show how Americans over-conform to the point that individuality and creativity are stifled. It dwells comically on what it calls the "herd" instincts in our society. Although a few of its points are valid, I would not show it again. Made in 1963, it is already dated. A film has to be pretty absorbing for kids not to joke about the low hemlines of the dresses and the actors dancing the twist. Also it has a very preachy quality, lecturing that if we continue in this single-minded conformity, we will end up like those you-know-what Russians. The kids didn't care for it much and neither did I. (It is one of the few films I showed that I had not seen before.)

There are many films dealing with nonconformist behavior. Indeed, this seems to be a favorite theme for today's film-makers. (With the great success of *Easy Rider, Alice's Restaurant,* and *Five Easy Pieces,* it's becoming "the thing," i.e., conformist to make movies about nonconformists.) I had plenty to choose from

---

[4] There is a film version of the novel, made in 1934, starring Guy Kibbee, available from Audio-Brandon Films. However, it is merely a typical Depression comedy using Lewis' characters and would be of no use as a substitute for the novel.

in determining what to show. I used three films, similar in theme, but very different from each other, to illustrate various types of nonconformity and what motivates it. Since the class was reading about group behavior (Hell's Angels and the hippies), the films concentrated on individual behavior.

From the motion picture **Loneliness of the Long-Distance Runner.** Courtesy of Walter Reade, Inc.

Tony Richardson's *Loneliness of the Long-Distance Runner* is perhaps one of the most popular classroom films ever made. There are several good study guides for it, including one put out by its distributor. It has also been run on television many times. Yet, not one kid had seen it before, and its surprise ending retained its significance. The film is British and the dialogue is heavily cockney, but kids

seemed to pick it up right away, since its hero, Colin Smith, is a universal identification figure for rebellious youth. Colin, the delinquent, robs a bakery and is
sent to a reform school. (We see his entire background through a series of
beautifully edited flashbacks.) At school, the "guvnor" (headmaster), a typical
liberal-type (in the worst sense), hopes to channel Colin's aggression by letting
him run in a long-distance race against a public school. The youth runs, and after
we see his entire life flash before him, he stands defiantly at the finish line,
smiling and refusing to win. His rebellion is complete. (I must add that even the
most sophisticated students get caught up in the urge to cheer him to win. And
some in the classroom actually hissed at the screen when he refused.) Colin had
broken one of the mores of our society—he refused to play to win.

Most of the class contrasted his behavior to Babbitt's. Colin's rebellion, which
would undoubtedly lead to greater punishment, was, nevertheless, open and
emotionally liberating. This contrasted perfectly with Babbitt's bumbling attempt
at a backstreet romance. Some students, however, insisted that Colin's rebellion
was impractical and self-defeating, and at least Babbitt's deviation was more
realistic.

Sidney Lumet's *The Hill* really moved me when I saw it in a theater a few
years ago. I was impressed with the toughness of the dialogue, the grim power
struggle between the sergeant major and his staff sergeant, and the fine acting
(especially Ossie Davis). It seemed like a good film to use in a unit like this,
since it was about the most conformist institution imaginable—a military prison.
Somewhere in the North African desert, the British army has set up a prison for
men who've disobeyed while in the field. The purpose of the prison is to "break"
the men of their deviant ways and send them back to the front as "good
soldiers." It is run by a tough, but honest sergeant major, who despite being out-
ranked by two weakling officers, is the real power in the place. He has devised the
perfect means of breaking men's wills—a 30-foot hill of sand that men are forced
to climb in full gear time after time in the blazing hot sun. The plot involves the
sergeant's sincere belief in his job (to serve his army) being undermined by a
brutal, sadistic staff sergeant. It also deals with five "deviant" soldiers who are to
be the victims of the hill, their efforts to save themselves (particularly Sean
Connery as a sympathetic former sergeant major who's seen the futility of war),
and their ultimate, ironic failure.

The film got a mixed response from the class. It certainly made its point
about the evils of total conformity, and it was exciting. But many could not
understand the dialogue of the film. Though directed by an American, it is
uncompromisingly British, and the clipped military accents were hard to follow.
Some of the girls in the class found it too brutal, and the discussions were not
as enthusiastic as with *Loneliness of the Long-Distance Runner*.

The last film in the unit was one of the best I have ever shown, *Lonely Are
the Brave*. This story of a modern cówboy, symbolically trapped by the
technology of an automated age and his attempts to escape it, has a tremendous
appeal in the classroom. The kids identify and actually cheer for John W. Burns
(played, for a change, with restraint by Kirk Douglas), who breaks out of jail
(after breaking in to see a friend!) and outwits a mechanized posse (he shoots a
helicopter from the sky), as he and his half-wild horse ride off to freedom. The
kids also sympathize with his reluctant pursuer, a tired sheriff surrounded by

conformists and yes-men (played by Walter Matthau), who secretly longs for the cowboy to get away. And then, in supreme irony, cowboy and horse are struck down on a rainy highway by a truck full of toilet fixtures. Is there any place in our society for a nonconformist? Must his fate be destruction? Is his only purpose in film and literature to provide *us* with the vicarious experience of breaking norms? *Lonely Are the Brave* raised such questions.

Discussions followed on all the films and Babbitt. I looked at the calendar. I knew that things were running over schedule, and good conformist that I was, I initiated a new subject. (I am more reluctant to be so "cover-the-course" conscious now.)

A standard course in sociology requires additional units on social stratification and minority group relations. I seriously considered teaching a detailed film-oriented section on social class. I did obtain a paperback set of Vance Packard's Status Seekers, which reads very well as pop sociology and contains pieces of many notable studies on social class. In their English class the kids were reading James M. Barrie's The Admirable Crichton, a great satirical defense of social classes in the English tradition.

There was a problem in this unit that I should have anticipated. There just aren't many decent films around on the subject of social class. The British have done a few, *Room at the Top* being a good example. But Status Seekers was about the American system, and *Room at the Top* is indigenously British. Another British film, Joseph Losey's *The Servant,* seemed at first to be a reasonable source to pair with The Admirable Crichton (since it deals with a lower-class butler's subversion of his decadent master, forcing the two actually to reverse roles). However, seeing it on television for the first time just before I was ready to order it, I realized it wasn't quite what I needed. Well made and acted, it was certainly worth seeing as a kind of modern horror story, but there was almost no development of the servant's motives for his evil schemes, and to pin them on social class differences would really be stretching things.

Films dealing with the American stratification system were not much help. Kitty Foyle is one of the most famous novels of the "girl from the wrong side of the tracks can't fit in our society" genre, but the film is an old soap opera. *A Place in the Sun,* the noted film version of Dreiser's An American Tragedy, could be useful, though it raises far more issues than social class differences. To limit any analysis of it to this one topic would be to abuse it. So I taught the unit with Packard's book. It wasn't bad really, but the class was impatient for another film.

The final sociological unit dealt with race and minority groups. Once again films were a crucial part of the development of the subject. A few students were assigned to read the section of Gordon Allport's classic The Nature of Prejudice on the "authoritarian personality." In reporting to the class, they listed a few of the traits most common to people who were extremely prejudiced (i.e., authoritarian): belief in absolutes (no compromise), extremely moralistic, unswervingly right (everyone else is wrong). I then showed the National Educational Television film *Where is Prejudice?* The film is a documentary record of a week-long sensitivity session involving 12 middle-class college students (of all races and ethnic groups) who maintain they are not prejudiced. Little by little, as they talk about their personal feelings, the students reveal that they are all highly prejudiced, and the film brutally records their personal interplay. Towards the end, one of the students turns out to be very close to the "authoritarian" in the study. He announces that because of his absolute faith in God he will survive, and all those who believe otherwise are ". . . going to eternal condemnation, and this whole world is going with you." The film ends shortly after this with the student participants sitting, staring at each other in horrified silence. Tom Lehrer's satirical song *National Brotherhood Week,* which opened the film on a note of humor, closes it grimly.

This is an amazing motion picture. I first saw it on television on *NET Journal* a few years ago, and I remember then how stunned I was by it. My class was equally taken with it. First of all, it gave them a chance to analyze the prejudiced behavior of the students and to detect which one might be an "authoritarian" personality. But more important than that, the film acts as a kind of mirror into one's own soul, and that agonizing silence which is part of the film's conclusion carries over into the classroom. Unlike the other films I had shown, this one left the class in a kind of a stupor. There was no urge to discuss the material, just a long, soul-searching (at least that's what I like to think it was) silence.

As I have stated earlier, my students are Black and highly conscious of the new sense of awareness permeating their community. A great deal of the rest of this unit was spent discussing racism, civil rights, and Black power. Being White and an outsider, this was a difficult area for me, and I tried to tread softly, remaining as nondirective as possible. The class read Ralph Ellison's brilliant novel The Invisible Man, which deals with a symbolically invisible Black man's search for an identity in a White society. It is a basically pessimistic comment on the alternatives for Blacks in our culture.

To contrast Ellison's hero's invisibility, I showed *Nothing But a Man.* I hoped that the kids would see in this film about a Black man and his wife struggling for a decent existence in rural Alabama, that a Black man, if determined, could maintain his sense of identity.

Nothing But a Man is perhaps still the only realistic treatment of Blacks on the screen. The film's hero (played by Ivan Dixon) finally accepts his responsibilities as a man (after White bigotry nearly pushes him to the brink of deserting his wife) by staying in a town where he has become an outcast and fighting for his rights. Still he has few alternatives beyond this.

The class responded in anger. "So what if he went back to his wife? What else was there to go back to? No job. No life. He's a fool, a sucker. Why didn't he move North? Or revolt?"

This unit had no nice neat conclusion.

The next part of the course dealt with the American economic system. This is supposed to be a textbook-oriented study of economic principles and, frankly, it is the most notoriously boring part of any social studies curriculum. I did use a text here to cover an overview of our capitalistic economy. Since part of the course dealt with consumer economics, I was able to use NET's excellent documentary *The Poor Pay More.* Though slightly dated (it was made in 1966 and recommends a truth-in-lending law, which now exists), the film touches on all of the economic problems of the poor. Its most relevant conclusion is that most of the means used to exploit the poor (high interest rates, lengthy installment arrangements, etc.) are institutionalized. The entire economic system works to keep poor people poor. The film raises some excellent questions about discrimination against the poor in retail prices and quality of merchandise. Many students did optional investigatory reports on whether the film's conclusions were still true. In most cases the kids reported that they were.

Later in the study of economics, we came to the unit on supply and demand. After discussing the classical law of supply and demand, I challenged the class (and the economic principle) by saying: "In a society like ours, with its advanced technological capacity, demand for most basic human wants needn't exist. We can produce an endless supply of goods if we wish. The reasons we don't is to maintain the price system."

This was hotly debated with students arguing both sides. Then, to illustrate my point, I asked them how we could create artificial demand. How could we make people believe they needed certain goods and services enough to pay for them? I then assigned Vance Packard's book <u>Hidden Persuaders</u> about the subtleties of advertising. The book is psychologically exaggerated, and somewhat dated (1958), but the kids love it. It is a fabulous introduction to elementary psychology.

To update it, I made copies of an article from a July 1968 issue of *Time* magazine on television commercials today. And then, for a grand finale, I showed the 1967 award-winning commercials. We looked at about three a day, analyzing the psychological implications of each. Again and again, I asked the class: "What is being sold, besides the product?"

The commercials proved to be a mirror of our age: imperialism ("El Exigente—the most demanding man in Latin America." One of the kids called him an Uncle Tom); middle-class "Americana" (Kodak's "the way you look tonight"—a blonde, blue-eyed small-town girl leaving for her prom. Her date looks more like her twin brother); sex appeal (Eastern Airlines in Acapulco with alternating shots of go-go girls, male cliff divers, and jet planes taking off); and so on. What started out as an exercise in economics became a primer in social psychology. (One kid insisted on interpreting the semantics of Pepsi's "Come Alive" slogan.)

The final part of the course was supposed to deal with law and government. By now I was far behind my department's timetable, and I must admit that I really rushed things towards the end.

I began a unit on power and propaganda using Orwell's <u>Animal Farm</u> and Shakespeare's <u>Macbeth</u> as readings. I then showed *Citizen Kane,* which the class really liked. (It is one of the few old films (1941) that transcends time.) But sadly, the semester was slipping out from under me. I had to cover all of the basic data on the American political system, and I realized the necessity of that. Films on American government are either inept or far-fetched. I just couldn't see show-ing pot-boilers like *Advise and Consent* or *The Best Man* to illustrate how the system works. And I wasn't about to use the stuff the school board circulates like *Our State House in Action* or *Meet Your Mayor.* Not with the cinematic standards I'd set.

The next thing I knew, it was all over. Graduation practices, senior trip, post high school orientation—all cut into class time. The year ended with a whimper instead of a bang. I had to cancel *12 Angry Men* and *Paths of Glory,* which I'd hoped to use in a unit on the definition of justice. There just wasn't time.

Looking back on these experiences, I realize that teaching had become some-thing new to me. I lectured less, the class discussed more, and I discovered that personally I could be a lot more effective by guiding rather than directing. It is true that in terms of selecting the films and readings I called the shots. I was still in control of the classroom. But once I turned on that projector, things were different. My students and I were on a new, common ground. We were sharing an experience together. We had begun to communicate.

STUDENT BIBLIOGRAPHY AND FILMOGRAPHY[5]

Anthropology

Book

BENEDICT, Ruth. Patterns of Culture. Boston: Houghton Mifflin, 1959.

Films

Circle of the Sun. 30 minutes. Color. National Film Board of Canada Production, 1960. Rental or purchase from Contemporary-McGraw-Hill Films.
Dead Birds. 90 minutes. Color. Peabody Museum, Harvard University, 1963. Rental or purchase from Contemporary-McGraw-Hill Films.
The Hunters. 90 minutes. Color. Peabody Museum, Harvard University, 1958. Rental or purchase from Contemporary-McGraw-Hill Films.
Mondo Cane. 105 minutes. Color. Directed by Gualtiero Jacopetti (Italian-English narration), 1962. Rental from Audio-Brandon Films.

Norms of Society (Conformity)

Books

*LEWIS, Sinclair. Babbitt. New York: Harcourt Brace Jovanovich, 1949.
*THOMPSON, Hunter. Hell's Angels. New York: Random House, 1967.
*WOLFE, Tom. The Electric Kool-Aid Acid Test. New York: Farrar, Straus and Giroux, 1968.

Films

Time Piece. 8 minutes. Color. Directed by Jim Henson, 1965. Rental or purchase from Contemporary-McGraw-Hill Films.
Conformity. 49 minutes. Black and white. CBS Television Production, 1963. Rental or purchase from Carousel Films.
Loneliness of the Long-Distance Runner. 103 minutes. Black and white. Directed by Tony Richardson (British), 1962. Rental from Walter Reade 16.
The Hill. 122 minutes. Black and white. Directed by Sidney Lumet (British), 1965. Rental from Films Inc.
Lonely Are the Brave. 107 minutes. Black and white. Directed by David Miller, 1962. Rental from Universal 16.

---

[5] Those entries in the bibliography which are asterisked indicate that the book also appears in paperback. To find the publishers for the paperback versions, see Books in Print, 1970. New York: R. R. Bowker Co., 1970.

Alternative Films

A Thousand Clowns. 105 minutes. Black and white. Directed by Fred Coe, 1965.
A good film version of the play of the same name. Deals comically with a
TV writer who will not tolerate the disgusting conformity around him.
Somewhat overplayed by Jason Robards. Rental from United Artists 16.
Cool Hand Luke. 129 minutes. Color. Directed by Stuart Rosenberg, 1967. Great
film, with Paul Newman in top form as a chain gang rebel who refuses to
swallow the system. George Kennedy as a fellow prisoner won an Oscar
for supporting actor. Rental from Audio-Brandon Films or Twyman Films.

Social Class

Book

*PACKARD, Vance. The Status Seekers. New York: McKay, 1959.

Films (none actually shown)

Room at the Top. 116 minutes. Black and white. Directed by Jack Clayton
(British), 1958. Rental from Walter Reade 16.
A Place in the Sun. 120 minutes. Black and white. Directed by George Stevens
(based on Theodore Dreiser's novel An American Tragedy), 1951. Rental
from Films Inc. The original film of Dreiser's novel *An American Tragedy*
made in 1932 by Josef Von Sternberg (originally the great Serge Eisenstein
was to have directed it), is available for rental from Universal 16.
The Servant. 115 minutes. Black and white. Directed by Joseph Losey (British),
1963. Rental from Audio-Brandon Films.
Still a Brother. 90 minutes. Black and white. Directed by William Greaves and
William Branch (narrated by Ossie Davis), 1967. An over-long but interesting appraisal of the Black middle class in the tradition of E. Franklin
Frazier's famous study Black Bourgeoisie. Rental or purchase from
Contemporary-McGraw-Hill Films.

Race and Minority Groups

Books

*ALLPORT, Gordon W. The Nature of Prejudice. Reading, Mass.: Addison-Wesley,
1954.
*ELLISON, Ralph. The Invisible Man. New York: Random House, 1952.

Films

Where Is Prejudice? 60 minutes. Black and white. Directed by Dick McCutcheon,
1967. Rental or purchase from NET Film Service. An excellent study guide
and a transcript of the dialogue are also available.
Nothing But a Man. 92 minutes. Black and white. Directed by Michael Roemer,
1963. Rental from Audio-Brandon Films.

Alternative Film

Pressure Point. 95 minutes. Black and white. Directed by Hubert Cornfield, 1961.
    Black psychiatrist vs. American Nazi. Good case-study approach to under-
    standing prejudice. Rental from United Artists 16.

Economics

Book

*PACKARD, Vance. <u>The Hidden Persuaders</u>. New York: McKay, 1957.

Article

"And Now a Word About Commercials," *Time Magazine,* July 12, 1968, pp. 55-60.

Films

The Poor Pay More. 58 minutes. Black and white. NET Productions, 1966.
    Rental or purchase from NET Film Service.
Award Winning Television Commercials—1967. Color and black and white.
    Rental or lease from American TV Commercials Festival. Other reels of
    commercials are available for inexpensive rental from the Museum of
    Modern Art.

Power and Revolution–
A Sample Unit

About a year after I had started my celluloid-oriented curriculum, a very "hip" student approached me with the kind of challenge that makes a teacher's ears burn nowadays: "Hey, Maynard. You know that movie course you're teachin', the one with the commercials an' stuff. It ain't relevant!"

I knew it had to come, the most popular cliché of our times was to be leveled at me. And by a kid who wasn't even in my class. I challenged him, asking him to define his terms and on what he based his opinions.

"Today's youth, particularly Black youth, has to know about the mechanics of power. The nitty-gritty on how to get some and hold on to it. Ain't that what society's all about? Ain't that the reason for revolutionary cats like me? Your class is a lot of jive. You wouldn't have the guts to face the real stuff in that class. Revolution and guerila warfare is where it's at."

I couldn't answer him. I believed what I was teaching was "relevant" and I wasn't going to patronize him by playing the guilty liberal for not complying with his wishes. I also wasn't about to sow the seeds of my own destruction. Guerila warfare indeed!

Yet, to this day, that kid's statement still haunts me. In these troubled times when our youth is forced into the tactics of confrontation to achieve power, and when it begins to talk in terms of revolution (i.e., total institutional changes), what better place is there than the classroom to discuss the implications of all the rhetoric. What I am about to propose is a unit of study for social studies or English classes dealing with the acquisition of political and social power, the means of sustaining it, and the role of revolution in a society where power is concentrated in the hands of a few.

Many motion pictures have dealt with themes like these (and capitalized on them, as in dreary Hollywood products like *Getting Straight* and the *Strawberry Statement*). Consequently films can be used to present the complexities of the issues from different points of view.

Stokely Carmichael and Charles V. Hamilton in their book Black Power: The Politics of Liberation in America accept as a definition of political power "The psychological control over the minds of men."[1] Whether you agree with the

---

[1] This definition they attribute to Hans Morganthau author of Politics Among Nations. New York: Alfred Knopf, 1966, p. 29.

definition or not, it seems to represent a consensus among the revolutionary young that political power in our society is psychologically oppressive. It, therefore, seems reasonable for a class to deal initially with the pros and cons of the issue.

At this point the teacher could assign something appropriate as a class reading. There are several paperback versions of Machiavelli's classic guidebook on political power <u>The Prince</u>, and it might well serve the needs of class discussion illustrating the timelessness of the issue. Or, in a class in English literature, Shakespeare's <u>Julius Caesar</u> might be in order, for a similar kind of example.

Whatever the class chooses to read, the film literature in this area is rich. Although, as I've indicated, film-makers have tended to exploit the subject, and most of the motion pictures dealing with it do so negatively. Still, let the class examine some of them.

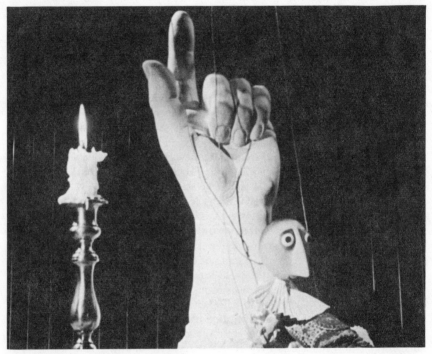

From the motion picture **The Hand.** Courtesy of Contemporary-McGraw-Hill Films.

An excellent introductory film would be *The Hand,* directed by Czech animator Jiri Trinka. This brilliant short film (19 minutes) is so complex and visually compelling that it is difficult to summarize and needs to be seen for a total appreciation. A meek puppet who makes flowerpots is suddenly terrorized by a human hand. At first the hand is polite and friendly, and the puppet accepts it until he sees what fate the hand has in store for him. The hand insists that the puppet obey its will. He refuses, chasing the hand away, but it constantly returns, using all manners of persuasion: the mass media (television, newspaper, and telephone), sexual seduction (it dresses up like a woman), and ultimately, force. The puppet is captured and tied to strings, forced to carve a huge statue of the hand. Somehow he manages to escape and runs back to the safety of his house, locking out the hand by nailing all the doors and windows. Ironically, in his panic, the puppet upsets one of his flowerpots, which falls on his head and kills him. In the last scene, the hand, now dressed in a black glove, pins a medal on the dead body and gives a rigid hand salute (Nazi-style).

By this time the class should be highly perplexed and inquisitive (as the reader must be from my description of the film). What does it all mean? What do the puppet and the hand represent? The individual victimized by the state? The oppression of freedom by an autocratic government? A parody on fascism, or communism, or American "democracy?"

I'm not sure I know the answers to these questions myself. Still, the film is a useful introduction to this kind of unit. It raises crucial questions about man's relationship to the powers that control his destiny, and it provokes a great deal of discussion. (The teacher may or may not want to relate the film to its Czech origin (1965) and go into why such a film could not be made in Czechoslovakia today. Personally, I wouldn't, since this might limit the discussion to too narrow a topic.)

There are many feature films dealing with case studies in power, both political and individual. Futuristic films about the all-powerful state inhibiting individualism tend to be the weakest and least convincing sources a teacher could use. The film version of Orwell's 1984 follows the novel closely but it moves very slowly and lacks cinematic punch. The class might be better off reading the book.

Francois Truffaut's film of Ray Bradbury's Fahrenheit 451, about a rigid, anti-intellectual society that burns books, is slightly better, though the subject side-tracks too often to a confusing romance between the hero (Oscar Werner) and his mistress (Julie Christie), who looks exactly like his wife (also Julie Christie).

Probably the best futuristic portrayal of a monolithic, all-powerful state is Peter Watkins' film *Privilege*. Told in semi-documentary style (reminiscent of Watkins' famous *The War Game*), *Privilege* tells the story of how the English government of the future uses a boyish pop-singer named Stevie Shorter to harness and control the emotions of the younger generation. Stevie is the government's mechanical man, programmed to lead the masses into conforming to the right principles at the right time.

The film has a frightening opening scene in which Stevie Shorter is escorted on the stage of a mobbed theater and put into a cage. His captors, dressed in police uniforms proceed to beat him brutally as he sings "set me free." The raging audience is then unleashed on the police, avenging Stevie. An off-screen narrator calmly explains the effectiveness of controlling the environment to channel such hostile emotions. The entire event has been staged.

Later the government uses Stevie to lead a massive religious revival to get the population to conform totally to the tenets of God and country. Naturally, it succeeds. The film concludes with Stevie's attempted rebellion and its failure because the people won't accept him as an ordinary human being.

This film is far from perfect (as critics in 1967 harshly indicated), but it is timely, exciting, and loaded with commentary on the future power of governments and the means at their disposal to exploit people. It certainly fits that definition of "psychological controls" and it raises crucial questions about our own society.

American film-makers have been most successful in dealing with the power theme when concentrating on the careers of individuals. The screen version of Robert Penn Warren's All the King's Men won a few Oscars, and it does present the semi-historical use of a demagogue in the person of Willie Stark (Huey Long). This film is still interesting (and for me much better than the book) despite its age (1949).

Elia Kazan's *A Face in the Crowd* (1957), about a hillbilly singer who becomes a public idol (even in the political sense), is another frightening look at the rise of a potential demagogue. Lonesome Rhodes (Andy Griffith) rises to power through his ability to sell his personality on television. This film was one of the earliest to predict potential impact of the TV medium and its message is very timely when considered along with Joe McGiness' provocative book The Selling of the President 1970.

The most fascinating portrait of individual power a teacher can show is still Orson Welles' *Citizen Kane* (1940). Having used it in many of my classes, I can testify to its timeliness and relevance. Welles' portrait of ruthless editor Charles Foster Kane (based on the career of William Randolph Hearst) is so well known, I won't summarize it here. If the film is shown along with, say, *Privilege* and *The Hand,* it presents excellent questions for discussing the nature of power. Certain key questions will come immediately to mind: Is Kane like the hand in his efforts to control everything around him? Is his use of his newspaper similar to the exploitation of the mass media by the state in *Privilege*? Although Kane's own political ambitions were thwarted by a scandal, could he have been a potential dictator? Are there elements in our society that indicate that a Charles Foster Kane could succeed today? Could "the hand" symbolically be representing someone like him?

Naturally any class seeing *Citizen Kane* will want to talk about its cinematics, its unconventional means of story-telling, and its actors. But as a portrait of the extremism of power, it is second to none.

There are other cinematic possibilities in a unit like this. The teacher of Shakespeare could make use of film versions of Richard III, Macbeth (actually there are three alternatives here, including Akira Kurosawa's Japanese version *Throne of Blood*), or Julius Caesar. All of these films deal with the quest for power and would make excellent conversation pieces next to *Citizen Kane* or *Privilege* (or both).

The motion picture based on William Golding's Lord of the Flies also raises some interesting questions on the subject. Is force a better means for governing a society than reason? The power struggle between Jack (the forceful) and Ralph (the rational) is beautifully conveyed in this exciting film, which never achieved the acclaim it so thoroughly deserved. The relationships between the children are richly drawn, and all of the fable quality, as well as the "savage" philosophy of the book has been brought to life on the screen. The film works very well in the class-room, particularly among kids whose reading skills would ordinarily put such a complex novel off limits. It certainly applies well in a unit like this one, since it reduces power relationships to their simplest terms. I highly recommend it.

At this point the teacher could start to tie the various readings and films together. He may wish to pursue them further, questioning whether or not power corrupts the individuals who attain it. Or, he may wish to move on to an analysis of a society (which may or may not be our own) in which too many share in too little of the power. Hence, the legitimacy of revolution.

From the motion picture **Citizen Kane.** Courtesy of Films Inc.

Revolution is a word that stands out in today's rhetoric. Whether one accepts the standard dictionary definitions (a complete overthrow of a political system; a complete institutional change in a society), or the more complex analysis of Frantz Fanon (who interprets it as the political and mental liberation of oppressed people from tyranny[2]), the very term ignites an emotional storm in our contemporary society.[3] The task of the teacher in presenting the concept should be to remove himself from the emotions of the issue and act as a catalyst presenting the questions, not answers. Is a revolution—a total institutional change in a society—a solution to the problems of that society? Historically, in societies that have undergone revolutions, have the resulting changes been, indeed, for the better? Is revolution caused by an unequal distribution of political power, economic power, or both? Do the revolutionaries of one generation become the new oppressors of the next? Will a political and social revolution in America solve our outstanding problems like poverty, racism, and militarism? These are the kinds of questions a unit like this should address itself to.

From the motion picture **Lord of the Flies.** Courtesy of Walter Reade, Inc.

Students should be exposed to some introductory reading on the subject. A good idea might be to prepare a "revolutionary" reading list, including works by

---

[2] Fanon, Frantz. The Wretched of the Earth. New York: Grove Press, 1965, **passim.** Available in paperback.

[3] In his classic analysis of the subject, historian Crane Brinton comments on the wide range of definitions of the term revolution and all of the emotional ramifications attached to them. Brinton, Crane. Anatomy of Revolution, revised ed. New York: Random House, 1957, pp. 3-5.

Thomas Paine, Karl Marx, Frantz Fanon, Eldridge Cleaver, and other advocates of total revolution. In this way the students can get directly into the polemic of revolution and then exchange each other's readings through discussion.

In the meantime the teacher can prepare to show three films on the subject, which present it in all of its complexity.

The first film is the animated version of George Orwell's classic Animal Farm, which really captures the spirit and flavor of Orwell's satirical condemnation of revolution, particularly the Russian Revolution. Snowball, Napoleon, Boxer, and all of the other animals in Orwell's ideological barnyard come brilliantly to life. The film works extremely well with reluctant readers who are "hooked" by it initially because it is a cartoon. Gradually they become aware of the seriousness of its theme, and although they may never think of reading the book, they become experts on Orwellian political thought. The film, of course, follows the outline of the novel, showing the animals of Manor Farm in rebellion against their human exploiters, only in the end to be subverted by their leaders, the pigs, who become the new tyrants. Orwell's animal revolution goes full cycle and it points out the futility of revolution. The film does make some alterations in the plot, particularly at the conclusion. In the book, when Benjamin, the donkey, looks at Napoleon and the other pigs and sees men's faces, the story ends, symbolizing the hopelessness of the cause. The film alters this and shows the animals resorting to open rebellion against the pigs, signifying some hope. If the film's ending seems too soft, the teacher can point out the alternative of the book, and the class can discuss which is more effective.

By now the students have read some pro-revolutionary work and have seen Orwell's condemnation of revolution. This would be an excellent time to show what is perhaps the greatest film about revolution ever made, *The Battle of Algiers.* Made by the Italian Director Gillo Pontecorvo, the film details in semi-documentary style the violent struggle of the Algerian Liberation Front (FLN) against the French to end colonial rule. The film expertly presents the cause of the revolutionaries, showing the European animosity toward native Algerians, the ghetto-like conditions of the Casbah, the lack of Muslim religious freedom (effectively demonstrated by showing a secret wedding between two devout Algerians), and the brutal assassination of political prisoners by the French.

The violent struggle is then documented step by step. The FLN attempts to discipline the Algerians by outlawing liquor, drugs, and prostitution. Its members destroy bars and even shoot the local whoremaster. All of this illustrates the total unity and singleness of purpose needed in a revolution.

The French respond with a curfew and then plant a bomb in the Casbah, killing many. The FLN retaliates, blowing up three crowded areas in the French quarter. Women and children are slaughtered on both sides. The FLN then calls a general strike for eight days to demonstrate Algerian national unity to the United Nations, even though during the strike, the French military commandant is able to single out the leaders of the movement. One by one he tracks them down, and through brutal interrogation he crushes their movement. Yet at the end of the film (skimming the historical details), the Algerian people spontaneously rebel with the spirit of their martyred leaders.

There are many noteworthy reasons for showing this film. First of all, it presents a brutally realistic picture of a violent revolution, without the glamorous rhetoric. It shows the pain on both sides, and the French, while clearly the oppressors, at least come out of it looking human. (The military Commandant, Colonel Mathieu, makes a moving speech in which he explains the nature of his duty and why he will not accept the label of fascist. His plea should make a fascinating point for discussion, both on the film and the subject in general.)

Despite the underscored objectivity of the film, it is still the best pro-revolutionary statement I have seen. Frantz Fanon, a Black psychiatrist from Martinique, whose work became the ideological proselytizer of the Algerian movement (and since his death of the "third world" revolution), would, no doubt, have been pleased with it.

From the motion picture **Viva Zapata.** Courtesy of Films Inc.—20th Century Fox.

To conclude the unit, there is one other useful film that has something to say about revolution, Elia Kazan's *Viva Zapata,* with Marlon Brando in the title role. *Viva Zapata* is neither pro- nor anti-revolution. It deals with the effects of revolution on the men who participate. The strength of this film rests with the skillful acting of Brando as Zapata—the simple, illiterate Mexican peasant who was cast in the role of general. Zapata is not a man of great force; in fact, he constantly rejects leadership, but his desire to feed his people, the poor Indians of southern Mexico, motivates his involvement. As the revolution progresses (or regresses), we see Zapata change. He becomes hardened and brutal, even to the point that he must kill an old comrade. His character is made more meaningful because of two other figures in the film. One is his fun-loving brother (Anthony Quinn), who abuses his new power and becomes a greedy tyrant. The other is a professional revolutionary (chillingly played by Joseph Wiseman), who advocates revolution for its own sake and who ultimately sows the seeds of Zapata's destruction.

The film also details the Mexican Revolution (1910-1918) with reasonable historical accuracy, portraying such figures as Diaz, Madero, Huerta, and Villa. It has flaws. John Steinbeck's dialogue is overly profound and philosophical, and this tends to detract from the film's realism. But no unit on revolution could be complete without it. It raises questions where *Animal Farm* and *The Battle of Algiers* provide answers. And, in an issue like this one, who really has the answers?[4]

The teacher can conclude the unit by attempting to tie all of the elements on power and revolution together through some conceptual essay. Perhaps a quotation from a well-known political document could be interpreted, having students make references to all the films and readings.

A unit like this one is highly teachable. The films compress many literary experiences into a shorter more digestable form and enable teacher and students to cover a much broader area of information. This is an example of "relevant" education.

STUDENTS' BIBLIOGRAPHY (A REVOLUTIONARY READING LIST)

*CLEAVER, Eldridge. Soul on Ice. New York: McGraw-Hill, 1968.
*——. Post-Prison Writings and Speeches. Edited by Sheer, Robert. New York: Random House, 1969.
DEBRAY, Regis. Revolution in Revolution. New York: M R Press, 1967.
*FANON, Frantz. Black Skin, White Masks. New York: Grove Press, 1967.
*——. A Dying Colonialism. New York: Grove Press, 1967.
*——. Toward the African Revolution. New York: Grove Press, 1968.
*——. The Wretched of the Earth. New York: Grove Press, 1965.
GUEVARA, Che. Diary of Che Guevara. New York: Grove Press, 1968.
*MANNONI, O., Prospero and Caliban. The Psychology of Colonization. New York: Praeger, 1967.
*MAO TSE TUNG. Mao Tse Tung: An Anthology of His Writing. Edited by Fremantle, Anne. New York: New American Library, 1962.
*MARX, Karl. The Communist Manifesto. New York: Monthly Review Press, 1964.
*MEMMI, Albert. The Colonizer and the Colonized. New York: Orion Press, 1965.
*MILLS, C. Wright. Listen Yankee. New York: Ballantine Books, 1960.
*PAINE, Thomas. Common Sense and Other Political Writings. Edited by Adkins, Nelson F. New York: Liberal Arts Press, 1953.

---

[4] I must note that although cinematically **Viva Zapata** is fairly straight stuff (no razzle-dazzle camera technique, etc.), whenever I show it, students applaud at the end. This indicates its power.

FILMOGRAPHY

Power

The Hand. 19 minutes. Color. Directed by Jiri Trinka (Czechoslovakian), 1965. Animated. Rental or purchase from Contemporary-McGraw-Hill Films.

1984. 91 minutes. Black and white. Directed by Michael Anderson, 1956. Rental from Audio-Brandon Films.

Fahrenheit 451. 112 minutes. Color. Directed by Francois Truffaut, 1967. Rental from Universal 16 or Twyman Films.

Privilege. 104 minutes. Color. Directed by Peter Watkins (British), 1967. Rental from Universal 16.

A Face in the Crowd. 100 minutes. Black and white. Directed by Elia Kazan, 1956. Rental from Charlou Productions.

All the King's Men. 109 minutes. Black and white. Directed by Robert Rossen, 1949. Rental from Audio-Brandon, Swank Films, or Twyman Films. Note: The rental on this film is usually inexpensive.

Citizen Kane. 119 minutes. Black and white. Directed by Orson Welles, 1940. Rental from Films Inc., Janus Films, or Audio-Brandon Films.

Macbeth. 105 minutes. Black and white. Directed by Orson Welles, 1948. Much maligned in its time, Welles' *Macbeth,* despite its low budget (made at Republic Pictures, using old sets from westerns) and some third-rate supporting acting, is the most exciting film version of the play. Rental from Audio-Brandon Films.

Macbeth. 107 minutes. Color. Directed by George Schaefer, 1961. This version was originally made for television's *Hallmark Hall of Fame* program. Filmed on location in Scotland, it stars Maurice Evans and Judith Anderson as the bloody couple. I like the Welles' version better. Rental from Audio-Brandon Films.

Throne of Blood (Macbeth). 105 minutes. Black and white. Directed by Akira Kurosawa (Japanese), 1957. English subtitles. Rental from Audio-Brandon Films.

Richard III. 155 minutes. Color. Directed by Laurence Olivier (British), 1956. Rental from Audio-Brandon Films.

Julius Caesar. 121 minutes. Black and white. Directed by Joseph L. Mankiewicz, 1953. This version, starring Marlon Brando as Antony, holds up quite well. Rental from Films Inc. There is a very low-budget version of *Julius Caesar* around, with Charleton Heston (before he became a star) which I have not seen, but have been told is poorly done. A new, spectacular version has recently been released, also starring Heston. Complete with nudes and a more "adult" interpretation (at least according to a recent *Playboy* spread), this film might not be available for the classroom for some time.

Lord of the Flies. 90 minutes. Black and white. Directed by Peter Brook (British), 1963. Rental from Walter Reade 16.

Some Other Possibilities: Documentaries

Blood on the Balcony. 92 minutes. Black and white. Directed by Pasquale Prunas (Italian), 1963. English narration. A vivid documentary on the rise and fall of Benito Mussolini. Rental from Audio-Brandon Films.

Mein Kampf. 119 minutes. Black and white. Directed by Edwin Leiser (Swedish), 1961. English narration. Documentary on the rise and fall of Hitler's Germany. Interesting film for highlights of the tyranny, but very sensationalistically done. Rental from Audio-Brandon Films.

The Twisted Cross. 58 minutes. Black and white. NBC TV's *Project 20* Series, narrated by Alexander Scourby, 1956. A brief documentary on Hitler's rise and fall containing many excellent film clips. Purchase or rental from Contemporary-McGraw-Hill Films.

Rise and Fall of the Third Reich. 107 minutes. Black and white. Xerox-ABC Television, narrated by Richard Basehart, 1968. Film version of William L. Shirer's great book. Excellent documentary. Rental from Films Inc.

Revolution

Animal Farm. 75 minutes. Color. Directed by John Halas and Joy Batchelor (British), 1954. Animated. Rental from Contemporary-McGraw-Hill Films.

The Battle of Algiers. 125 minutes. Black and white. Directed by Gillo Pontecorvo (Italian), 1968. English subtitles. Rental from Audio-Brandon Films.

Viva Zapata. 113 minutes. Black and white. Directed by Elia Kazan, 1952. Rental from Films Inc.

Other Interesting Possibilities

Ten Days that Shook the World. 68 minutes. Black and white. Directed by Sergei M. Eisenstein (Russian), 1928. Silent. Eisenstein's official film made on the tenth anniversary of the Bolshevik revolution is really a grand satire on the Kerensky government. It is very funny and not at all revolutionary. Use this to show how a revolutionary society reminisces. Rental from Audio-Brandon Films.

If . . . . 111 minutes. Color. Directed by Lindsay Anderson (British), 1969. A highly original, heavily symbolic look at today's student rebellion against "irrelevant" false values. Staged in the setting of a British boy's boarding school, *If . . .* brutally and comically is truly a film for today's youth. Rental from Films Inc.

Burn. 115 minutes. Color. Directed by Gillo Pontecorvo (Italian), 1970. This film, which was a commercial failure, is destined to be known as Pontecorvo's "other" movie. The fictitious account of a Caribbean slave rebellion, *Burn* has much in it to suggest it could have been a masterpiece like *The Battle of Algiers.* However, it appears to have been edited through a meat grinder. For an interesting piece of speculation on why this revolutionary film went wrong, see Pauline Kael's review of it in *The New Yorker,* vol. 46, November 7, 1970, pp. 159-162. Rental from United Artists 16.

Another World: Black America and the White Middle Class–
A Film Un-Festival

After 300 years of cultural "invisibility" in America, it's finally happened–it's "in" to be Black. Black studies programs in colleges are rapidly becoming standardized in the academic world. African clothing, Afro hairdos, and soul food are part of the national mainstream. Leonard Bernstein has a cocktail party for the Black Panthers. Sidney Poitier is a top-grossing movie star. And Flip Wilson does suntan oil commercials. Black, is, indeed, beautiful.

As a teacher in a Black school, with some knowledge of Afro-American history, I too have attained a new legitimacy in society. I am consulted by predominantly White school districts on integrating curriculum effectively. I am called upon to speak publicly at suburban educational and civic conferences on race relations. And I have appeared on a local radio show as an "expert" on Black America. Somehow, despite my White middle-class socialization, I am looked upon by my peers as special.

There is something basically sickening about all this White preoccupation with Blackness. It's all so superficial, so patronizing. None of the suburbanites I visit really understands the nature of American racism. I don't think all the lectures on African history or Black Power are going to change us (White America) very much. Indeed, the very existence of those suburbs demonstrates how insincere the interest really is.

What I am about to propose is a kind of crash course for understanding (or at least realistically facing) Black America. I call it a film "un-festival," because it involves a very painful process of watching the problems of Blacks and then facing the causes of those problems. The films involved hold up a kind of a mirror to White America, and there's nothing very festive about that.

A unit of this kind should begin with a film that is very Black, as far removed from White society as possible. In this way the viewers see the situation from a distance, without (for the moment) any personal involvement. In the meantime, some background reading can be done as an introduction to spell out all of the issues. Charles Silberman's excellent Crisis in Black and White is an ideal introductory source, although it could use some updating (much has happened in race relations since 1964).

For an initial film I recommend *Malcolm X: Struggle for Freedom*. This Grove Press release is simply a filmed interview with the now martyred father of Afro-American nationalism. It was made a few months before his death in early 1965, and it serves as a good polemic on the needs of Black Americans for an ethnic identity. Malcolm was the precursor of the militancy of today and he has a kind of mystique among Whites, who largely ignored him while he was alive. This film, therefore, defines the issues in the struggle for Black awareness, and Whites can look at it objectively, since, after all, Malcom is advising *his* people.

Another excellent choice to open this unit (or to use with *Malcolm X*) is NET's *Color Us Black*. This remarkable documentary was made in early 1968 at Howard University during a student sit-in. Hardly objective, the film takes the side of the students, allowing them to do much of the actual narration. The students demand that Howard be "relevant" to the needs of Black society. Their views are demonstrated by their own rhetoric as well as by some skillfully edited scenes involving well-known Black personalities like Claude Brown (author of Manchild in the Promised Land and a Howard graduate), who claims the school is too conscious of copying White institutions. One shocking sequence involves the career of Dr. Nathan Hare, a militant sociologist fired by Howard for taking part in an anti-draft demonstration, who has become a professional prize fighter. Dr. Hare's anger is demonstrated in his ring skill as he floors his White opponent in the first round.

The second half of *Color Us Black* includes a student-made film on Black awareness, which shows, symbolically, the termination of an interracial romance so that the young Black man involved can return to his people ("You can't fight the man if you're livin' with his woman," he asserts). The background of this segment is provided by a speech by nationalist Ron Karenga, which is used as the young man's conscience. The whole thing is quite effective.

Color Us Black presents a contemporary statement of the effects of Black power on the young. White Americans who see it cannot miss the spirited independence and anger of its theme. Yet it is still Blacks speaking to Blacks (i.e., "their" problem).

Another possibility that could be useful at the beginning of this unit is the unusual *Now Is the Time*. Originally made for a local television station in Philadelphia, this film is now available nationally. Stars Ossie Davis and Ruby Dee recite the words of Black poets and writers who have commented on the injustices of American society (Langston Hughes, Countee Cullen, James Baldwin, etc.). In the background, shots are shown of Black students marching angrily on the Philadelphia Board of Education. The message is that the young Afro-American will not tolerate the conditions that Mr. Davis and Miss Dee are describing. The film ends on a very shocking note. A Philadelphia "freedom school" for preschool Black children (ages 18 months to 5 years) is shown. The adult instructor, John Churchville, is indoctrinating the kids in pride in Blackness, and self-defense. His hope is to give them an emotional armor against the dehumanization process White America will inflict upon them. (He teaches them to reject the terms "boy," "nigger," "Negro," "flunky," etc.—all of which are demeaning.)[1]

White audiences, who after reading Silberman should be somewhat sensitized

---

[1] This same "school" was later filmed by CBS Television for its film **Black History: Lost, Stolen or Strayed**, which I will deal with elsewhere.

to the issues, may still be quite shocked by this ending: "What are *they* trying to do? Teaching children to hate." The film is frightening and it raises crucial questions about the deep polarization between the races.

After showing one (or all) of these, the nature of the films should be altered to concentrate more on the actual problems Blacks face, i.e., the reasons for all the anger in the first three films.

A valuable reading for this part would be Claude Brown's realistic memoir Manchild in the Promised Land. Brown documents the Black life style, from rural poverty to urban poverty, and the kinds of values that come from such a life. His book is great because it is not a typical rags-to-riches success story. The Claude Brown who "makes it" at the end is still the same individual who ran dope and pimped and did anything else he could to survive. His personality is unaltered and that lack of resolution opens up new insights to White Americans seeking to understand problems confronting Blacks.

The best film to show here is Shirley Clarke's devastating *The Cool World*. Based on the novel by Warren Miller, it documents a few days in the life of Duke Custis, a 15-year-old gang member in Harlem. The film opens with a Marcus Garvey type figure preaching to the members of the Black community about how the "White devils" have destroyed the humanity of Afro-Americans. Ominously he sets the stage for the tragic story to follow. (A similar figure was used in the Pulitzer Prize-winning play *The Great White Hope* as the symbolic conscience of Black America, though the role was badly diluted in the film version.)

In the next scene Duke and some other boys board a school bus where a patronizing White teacher is taking his class on a trip to Wall Street. The bus slowly moves downtown, the teacher pointing out the sights to his class. "Here is the highest rent district in New York. And that's the famous Plaza Hotel. Did you ever see anything so beautiful?" When they get to Wall Street, he asks the kids if they remembered to take their "Own a Share of America" pamphlets.

Gradually the story focuses on Duke. He is intelligent and loyal to his friends and family (a mother and a fanatically religious grandmother). He has one dominant goal in life: he wants to own his own "piece" (revolver). Off screen his voice explains the value of the piece ("To revive the boppin' days and make me the coolest man on the block"). The local adult crime boss, Priest, will sell it to him, not because of the profit involved but to "make a man" of Duke.

The rest of this astonishingly realistic film focuses on Duke's quest for the piece. The viewer is literally saturated with images of Black poverty and frustration (a junkie gang leader who can't grow up; Duke's mother complaining about the roaches and rats; a not quite 15-year-old whore who didn't realize the ocean was only as far away as a subway ride to Coney Island). In one scene we see Duke help an old friend, Hardy, chase away some rival gang members. Hardy is an athlete. He's got scholarship offers. He'll make it. Yet as he and Duke talk, we see that intellectually both of them are on the same high plain. Hardy wants his education. Duke wants his piece. Why?

The film finally ends when Duke, unable to get the piece, rumbles with the other gang and stabs its leader to death. The police come, beat him savagely, and take him away.

I have seen the reaction this film leaves with people, particularly Whites. They are stunned. For almost two hours they have confronted another world—an alien world of filth, poverty, and crime. They have gotten to know and sympathize with a kid whom society will label a brutal killer. What made Duke kill? What made the gun so valuable to him? What real alternatives do kids like Duke have? Why is the gang so significant? What has it all got to do with being Black?

Seeing this film (which for obvious reasons never had much of a theatrical run when it was released a few years ago) is a new experience for most Whites. It forces them to confront the society behind the headlines, which they have never seen (or weren't willing to see) before.

Another film, similar to *The Cool World* in its realism, is *The Jungle,* a short reenactment of Black gang life made by an actual street gang. While it lacks the polish of the Shirley Clarke film (which is more than understandable), it is an equally effective statement on the gang culture and the frustrations of Blacks trapped in ghetto conditions.

Of course, the gang structure is only one phase of the problem, and a good film to balance it is *Nothing But a Man.* I have noted elsewhere the simple, yet very moving human statement this film makes. It, too, is highly effective at forcing Whites to face up to the conditions confronting Blacks. (It's a pity that commercial film-makers continue to capitalize on the White interest in Blackness by turning out slick evasive products like *The Lost Man, The Landlord,* and *Halls of Anger.* Films as honest as *The Cool World* and *Nothing But a Man* are rare.)

There are two other highly effective celluloid documents on ghetto life. The CBS TV program *The Tenement* is now available commercially. Documenting the every-day lives of Blacks trapped because of lack of education and unemployment in a dreary Chicago slum, it has an awesome impact on those who see it. The most tragic segments are the interviews with the residents, many of whom optimistically dream of "better times" to come.

Who Do You Kill? was originally part of one of the most intelligent dramatic series on television (that's why it lasted only one season) *East Side/West Side.* Starring George C. Scott as a social worker, this episode deals with a Black couple from Harlem (James Earl Jones and Diana Sands) whose infant is fatally bitten by a rat. I can't visualize any White American, even the most racially biased, being unmoved by it.

Hopefully, after seeing at least one of the above films on ghetto life, the students have moved from asking "Why are they so angry?" to "Why are conditions so miserable?" Two special films can effectively bring the unit to a close. I strongly recommend that both be shown, since they are quite different from each other.

No Hiding Place is another episode from the *East Side/West Side* series. A White middle-class suburb (Maple Gardens) is confronted with what many communities consider a terrible crisis—it is about to be integrated. Chuck Baxter is an educated, liberal man. He seems outwardly pleased that the Black family is going to be his next-door neighbor, and he chastises his Southern-born wife for not totally sharing his feelings. Chuck then calls Neil Brock (George C. Scott), a social worker and old friend, to come into the community and help quash the fears of the residents that their property values will fall if the Blacks move in. Meanwhile, a ruthless real estate agency is trying to create a seller's panic by warning that the community will turn into a slum.

There are some oversimplifications in the plot, but certain things ring sadly true. The Black couple, it turns out, are both educated, articulate people. Chuck and his wife really like them. But in the midst of the seller's panic, the deepest feelings of racial animosity are finally displayed. In order to keep the neighborhood economically stable, each resident who sells has promised to allow those who are staying in the community to find a buyer, thus undercutting the "blockbusting" realtors. The Black couple finds a buyer for a home, and this forces Chuck Baxter into a crucial battle with his conscience. His neighbors introduce him to a Mr. Adams, an old, self-educated gentleman, who has money but little of the "social values" of White middle-class Americans. Chuck suddenly becomes apprehensive, demonstrating a fear of Mr. Adams. "He's not the same," he asserts. Chuck must come to grips with his own anti-Black feelings. As George C. Scott puts it: "He'll accept a White Negro, but not a Black one."

The film ends with Chuck's alienation of his Black neighbors and his ambivalence in deciding whether he, too, should move.

This is the only film I have ever seen where most of the crucial issues dividing Blacks and Whites are dealt with: social class, property value, false liberalism, and institutional racism. (Chuck has a legitimate economic fear that if his property does lose money he will be in deep financial trouble since the "system" has him in debt up to his ears.) How many Whites seeing a film like this can identify with Chuck Baxter? How many, despite their liberal philosophies, would act similarly in that situation? The film begins to hold up a mirror that says—evaluate yourself.

The last film in the un-festival (I think by now that title is more understandable) has almost nothing to do with Blacks. It is a film exclusively about White middle-class America. Frederick Wiseman's *High School* is one of the most controversial documentaries ever made. Some educators and film critics applaud it as a superb and accurate essay on the failure of our educational system. Others, particularly teachers, claim it is biased, deceptively edited negative propaganda. (I saw the film with a teachers' group recently, and this was the major reaction.)

High School is an unnarrated film about a White middle-class academically excellent school in Philadelphia. The camera, which is anything but objective, takes the viewer on a grand tour of an antiseptic, irrelevant, dehumanizing prison. A guidance counselor chastises a girl in front of her parents for wanting to become a beautician. A faculty disciplinarian growls at a boy who feels he has been unfairly punished by a teacher: "When you are addressed by someone older than you are in authority, it's your job to respect and listen . . . . What you should have done is showed some character. We're out to establish that you can take orders."

A social studies teacher, who looks sincere enough, is trying to teach his all-White class about racial tolerance. He asks who would join a club with Negro members. Immediately he adds, to insure sincere class response, "There's no right or wrong answer." An English teacher recites "Casey at the Bat," for herself apparently, since her class appears to be doing anything but listening. Another teacher sets up a discussion, and then interrupts the students as they grope for words. The camera catches the emptiness of it all; the boredom, the apathy. The kids of *High School* are taught to conform. They are not committed to anything except the success-oriented society their teachers, parents, and community seem to value so highly.

The film ends with the principal reading a letter from a young alumnus about to enter battle in Vietnam. He has promised all of his military insurance to the school if he is killed. He asserts that his greatest lesson from his years there is that he is "only a body" dedicating himself to a higher cause. The principal's voice concludes the film. "When I read this," she says tearfully, "I know we are doing a good job."

High School, it can be argued, is designed to show only the negative aspects of White, middle-class education. Certainly this is true. But the film-maker has captured a fundamental fact about the nature of White America—its lack of human commitment. The high school is merely a symptom. Its graduates will be the dominant power group in America in a few years. Are they prepared to solve the basic problems confronting America? What is their sensitivity to the problems of Duke in *The Cool World* or the Chicago families of *The Tenement.* Are they the ones Malcolm X and the angry Howard students have marked for open race war?

High School is the final piece in this un-festival. It is the mirror for White Americans to gaze into and determine whether they like what they see.[2]

BIBLIOGRAPHY[3]

*SILBERMAN, Charles. Crisis in Black and White. New York: Random House, 1964.
*KNOWLES, Louis L., and Prewitt, Kenneth, Eds. Institutional Racism in America. Englewood Cliffs, N.J.: Prentice-Hall, 1969.
*CARMICHAEL, Stokely S., and Hamilton, Charles V. Black Power: The Politics of Liberation in America. New York: Random House, 1968.
*MALCOLM X, and Haley, Alex. Autobiography of Malcolm X. New York: Grove Press, 1965.
*BROWN, Claude. Manchild in the Promised Land. New York: Macmillan, 1965.
GRIER, William H., and Cobbs, Price M. Black Rage. New York: Basic Books, 1968.
SILBERMAN, Charles. Crisis in the Classroom. New York: Random House, 1970.
*THOMAS, Piri. Down These Mean Streets. New York: Knopf, 1967. The Puerto Rican Manchild in the Promised Land. Very absorbing.

FILMOGRAPHY

Malcolm X: Struggle for Freedom. 22 minutes. Black and white. A Grove Press presentation, 1966. Purchase or rental from Grove Press Films.
Color Us Black. 58 minutes. Black and white. Directed by Dick McCutcheon, 1968. Purchase or rental from NET Film Service.
Now Is the Time. 32 minutes. Black and white. W C A U Television (Philadelphia, Pa.), 1968. Rental from Anti-Defamation League of B'Nai Brith; purchase from Carousel Films.
The Cool World. 104 minutes. Black and white. Directed by Shirley Clarke, 1964. Purchase or rental from Zipporah Films.
The Jungle. 25 minutes. Black and white. Produced by the 12th and Oxford Streets Corp., Philadelphia, Pa. Rental from the 12th and Oxford Streets Corp.

---

[2] I must note that I am a graduate of the school portrayed in the film.
[3] Read these in order during the unit, preferably before each film.

Nothing But a Man. See citation in Chap. 1.

The Tenement. 40 minutes. Black and white. CBS TV News, 1967. Rental from Anti-Defamation League of B'nai Brith; purchase from Carousel Films.

Who Do You Kill? 51 minutes. Black and white. Talent Associates Production (*East Side/West Side* series), 1963. Purchase from Carousel Films; for rental, check local sources, including libraries.

No Hiding Place. 51 minutes. Black and white. Talent Associates Production (*East Side/West Side* series), 1963. Rental from Anti-Defamation League of B'nai Brith or Mass Media Ministries; purchase from Carousel Films.

High School. 75 minutes. Black and white. Directed by Frederick Wiseman, 1969. Purchase or rental from Zipporah Films.

Other Possibilities

A Time for Burning. 58 minutes. Black and white. Directed by William C. Jersey and Barbara Connell, 1966. A distillation of four months in the life of Pastor L. William Youngdale who attempted to integrate the all-White Augustan Lutheran Church in Omaha, Nebraska. The film points out all of the problems involved in true integration. One particular segment involves the angry, but logical, statements of a Black militant barber named Ernie Chambers. Purchase or rental from Contemporary-McGraw-Hill Films or the Anti-Defamation League of B'nai Brith.

The Dissenters: Daniel Watts. 30 minutes. Black and white. National Educational Television, 1968. An interview with the militant editor of *The Liberator.* Watts angrily comments on race war, Black Anti-Semitism, and Black power. Not very cinematic, but powerful. Purchase or rental from NET Film Service.

The Way It Is. 60 minutes. Black and white. National Educational Television, 1967. A devastating documentary on the problems of a ghetto junior high school. Especially recommended for people removed from the educational field. Purchase or rental from NET Film Service.

Confrontation: Dialogue in Black and White. 35 minutes. Black and white, 1967. An actual dialogue between Blacks of all philosophies and similar Whites. Pay particular attention to the overall lack of communication. Rental only from NET Film Service.

Diary of a Harlem Family. 20 minutes. Black and white. Public Broadcast Laboratory, 1969. A brutal look at the plight of a Black family in Harlem seen through the still photographs of Gordon Parks. Purchase or rental from NET Film Service.

The World of Piri Thomas. 60 minutes. Color. National Educational Television (narrated by Piri Thomas), 1969. The author of *Down These Mean Streets* conducts a tour of "el barrio" (Spanish Harlem). He is an excellent spokesman for the growing anger among poor Puerto Ricans. Purchase or rental from NET Film Service.

Dutchman. 55 minutes. Black and white. Directed by Anthony Harvey (from the play by Leroi Jones), 1967. Not everyone, White or Black, can tolerate the angry polemic of Leroi Jones in any form—play, poem, or essay. Here for the first and only time, a Jones play has been filmed, capturing all the terror and bitterness of the original. A White woman sexually taunts a young Black man on a subway. After initial resistance, he yields to her, whereupon she murders him. Symbolically, this is Jones' view of relations between the races. Whether the viewer agrees or not, in a unit like this one the shock value has a sensitizing effect. Rental from Walter Reade 16 Films.

Crime and Punishment: The Criminal, the Police, and the System–
A Classroom Unit on Film

The next-to-the-last sequence of Frederick Wiseman's vivid editorial-documentary *Law and Order* contains a very effective (and somewhat unfair) gimmick. Until this point the film has brutally documented the conflicts between petty criminals (a prostitute, a wife-beater, a teenage thief, a juvenile gang, a drunk) and the police. It has concentrated on the futility of law enforcement in the face of the sad social conditions that foster this type of crime. Then, suddenly, a scene has been edited in from what appears to be a totally different context. Richard Nixon, campaigning for the presidency in 1968, is shown giving his famous "Law and Order" speech:

> "Crime is going up . . . . 43% of the American people are afraid to walk the streets at night . . . . I pledge to you new leadership to bring back respect for law and order in this great country of ours."

Obviously this scene is meant to comment on the typical politician's opportunistic oversimplification of a crucial issue. In this context, Mr. Nixon comes out looking like a seedy villain. I have indicated that this gimmick is somewhat unfair. Both political candidates in 1968 made such speeches (as do most politicians today) and singling out Mr. Nixon merely demonstrates the film-maker's disregard for him. Nevertheless, gimmick or not, it is very effective. The film has thoroughly demonstrated the complexities of criminality and law enforcement, and any standard oversimplification of the issues does, indeed, look ridiculous.

How do we, as teachers, cope with the topics of crime and correction in our classes without falling victim to standard clichés about law and order (or, as some liberals like to add, law and order "with justice")? Crime is a tremendous problem in our society. Many young people have already had contact (as participants or victims) with it. Then, too, there is the rapidly developing norm among youth (particularly since the campus demonstrations) that the police are "pigs." I remember a class discussion where one of my students announced he was thinking about doing police work after graduation, and the entire class turned on him and shouted "pig."

I would like to see extensive classroom study of criminology and law enforcement through the use of a number of motion pictures. However, I must add a cautionary note. No commercial film deals with the complexities of this subject adequately. Movies are made to have popular appeal, and often in dealing with this subject, they have tended to either romanticize criminals and police or paint pictures of them so evil that they are beyond human recognition. Therefore, I suggest that films in this area be used merely as eyeopeners, as motivators of further study, discussion, and research. The films I am about to recommend can achieve this limited purpose.

Finding a good student text for this unit is also difficult. Standard criminology textbooks are too technical and become too quickly dated. Most popular works on subjects like crime, police work, and prisons are either moralistic sermons, polemics, or idealistic condemnations. One book I can recommend (and one which I intend to use with my own classes) is Congressman James H. Scheur's To Walk the Streets Safely, a brief but logical analysis of the nature of "predatory" crime and how society can effectively deal with it. I like this book for its recognition of the social conditions that breed crime and its compassionate attitude towards solutions. I think students will be similarly impressed with it, and it can serve as an effective background reading.

A unit like this should begin with a classroom analysis of criminal behavior. What constitutes crime? What motivates it? Is it ever excusable?

Hundreds of movies have been made about criminals. The famous gangster genre of the 1930s (*Little Caesar, Public Enemy,* etc.) can best be studied as an intrinsic part of the Depression era, and I will discuss it later in that context. Hollywood has made several "historical" gangster films, looking back on the 1920s and 1930s with nostalgia, with films varying in quality from *Babyface Nelson* to *Bonnie and Clyde.* But these deal little with the sociological problem of crime today.

The best way to begin examining the nature of the criminal would be to study the juvenile offender as a demonstration of the initial motives for antisocial behavior.

National Film Board of Canada's short film *You're No Good* (starring Michael Sarrazin) is an excellent portrait of a young man about to commit his first crime. Eddie is a fatherless high school dropout, who desperately needs status. He steals a motorcycle, and his imagination starts to wander. He sees himself being pursued by the police, running away with his girl to a tropical paradise. The film concentrates on Eddie's thoughts, and the viewer becomes increasingly aware of the youth's sad existence and his motives for the crime. At the end his guilt possesses him, as he imagines the police pursuing and trapping him. Faced with no other recourse, the bewildered young man discusses his problem with a social worker as he awaits the police.

You're No Good is very effective cinematically. The flashbacks of Eddie's home life reveal his frustrations and past failures. The fears of his conscience (over and over he hears, "They're after you, Eddie") are vivid portraits of a youth possessed by guilt. Eddie is a potential criminal (the title of the film infers that), but he is also a boy with deep personal problems. Stealing becomes an outlet for him. Students will want to discuss his motives and, possibly, the alternatives a kid like Eddie has. The teacher might want to inject some comment like "Once he commits a crime, regardless of his personal motives, he becomes a danger to society and must be stopped." The sympathies of students with Eddie might not tolerate such a harsh condemnation. Thus they are committed to discussing how the youth can be rehabilitated.

I have already mentioned Shirley Clarke's film *The Cool World* for its candid portrayal of a Black juvenile gang. This film would work well in this unit, since it thoroughly demonstrates the mentality of juvenile delinquency. It also raises some questions about the responsibility for such crime with the characterization of Priest, the neighborhood's adult criminal. Priest is a local hustler, a graduate of the gangs. He can provide the kids with many of the stimuli for violence (everything from dope to guns), as well as an image of success in the "professional world." Yet Priest is ruled by the White syndicate, which eventually destroys him.

The character of Priest, in his relationship to Duke, the young gang leader, and the White-dominated "organization" indicates the complexity of criminal associations, even with juvenile delinquents. How much juvenile crime is caused by the influence of illicit alcohol or drugs? What is the source of these poisons? What is the responsibility of organized crime for petty street crime? *The Cool World* provides some glimpses into the total society of the criminal.

The rehabilitation of juvenile offenders has been a subject for many commercial films. Audiences like to see the bad kid learn the error of his ways and reform. Yet the only film of this genre that has ever had a lasting impression on me is the old documentary (1948) *The Quiet One.* Directed by Sidney Myers, with narration written by the noted film critic James Agee, this film traces the existence of Donald, a ten-year-old Black child, confronting poverty and frustration in the tenements of Harlem. Donald's hostility leads him to vandalism for an outlet, and as a result he is sent away to the Wiltwyck School for delinquent boys. Ultimately (after much difficulty, including an attempt to run away), the boy shows signs of being rehabilitated. The film is quite moving and is used often in the training of teachers and social workers for its insights on the futility of ghetto life and the hostility that produces criminal behavior.

An interesting parallel to *The Quiet One* is Claude Brown's brutally frank memoir Manchild in the Promised Land. Brown's early life was much like Donald's, and he too was sent to Wiltwyck School. His portrayal of the school is much different from the film's, and although he dedicates his book to the place, it obviously had no such effect in reforming him. Students could read Brown's book after they see *The Quiet One* and make this comparison.

Having examined some examples of juvenile criminal potential, the class should turn its attention to the personality of the hardened criminal. An interesting way to approach this would be to screen a most unusual film, Claude Lelouch's *To Be a Crook.* Essentially, this is a satirical comedy about four young Frenchmen who after seeing countless American gangster pictures and westerns decide to embark on a life of crime. They quit their jobs and go into training, mastering physical self-defense, marksmanship, safecracking, and all of the big-time criminal skills. Their first caper is the theft of a pack of chewing gum, followed by the kidnapping of a streetwalker's dog. It's all quite funny, and their big-time kidnapping of a movie star, who turns out to be a stand-in, is hilarious. The film ends on a violent, downbeat note, which is against its humorous grain and not very effective. But its commentary on the glorification of crime, of the status and attraction it has for youth, is bitter and thought-provoking. Beyond the comedy is a portrayal of many of us who identify with criminals (or movie "criminals") as an escape from the dull nature of every-day life. Students usually get a great deal out of this unusual film, and it can serve as a good introduction to the study of adult criminal behavior.

There are a few films documenting the personalities of criminals in sufficient depth for this type of study. Professional thieves and gangsters are portrayed in such dimension in John Huston's classic melodrama *The Asphalt Jungle,* even if they are somewhat over-romanticized. The Sterling Hayden portrayal of a "pro" who'd like to retire and Sam Jaffe as an aging intellectual gang member are particularly worthy of discussion. Students can try to deduce from the vivid characterizations the motives that brought these men together. They can also analyze why audiences sympathize with them and whether films like *The Asphalt Jungle* tend to romanticize criminals too much.

Perhaps the best known in-depth portrait of contemporary criminals is Truman Capote's book In Cold Blood. The film version of that work, written and directed by Richard Brooks, is almost equal to it. Concentrating on the union of two sad individuals, Perry Smith and Dick Hickock, it probes their backgrounds through vivid flashbacks (much more is shown about Smith than his partner) to demonstrate their potential for the brutal murders they are about to commit. The first two-thirds of the film are excellent. The audience lives with the two protagonists and identifies with them, deploring their act (the murder of an entire family for a non-existent box of money), but at the same time is compassionately aware of their psychological motives. The film collapses somewhat after the killers are apprehended into a wishy-washy plea against capital punishment. Although the closing scene of Smith's execution is moving, it doesn't seem to fit into the general mood of the earlier sequences. Still *In Cold Blood* is the kind of film that can work very well in a unit like this. It documents criminal activity realistically and with understanding.

From the motion picture **In Cold Blood.** Courtesy of Columbia Pictures.

Screen portraits of murderers have long been very popular (which is something to ponder over), and several actors have come into prominence for their cold-blooded killer roles (Richard Widmark in *Kiss of Death,* Alan Ladd in *This Gun for Hire,* etc.). Few of these have any value in this unit since they lack depth, but there is one film about a murderer which lends itself perfectly to this kind of study. Denis Sanders' *War Hunt* is a fairly recent low-budget, little-known film which was buried as a second feature in drive-ins. Ostensibly about a military patrol during the last days of the Korean War, *War Hunt* is really the psychological study of a murderer. A young, introverted soldier (John Saxon) becomes a hero by going on mission after mission, killing the enemy silently with a stiletto. When the cease-fire comes, he is upset and refuses to accept it, even to the point of sneaking out at night to kill enemy guards. To compound matters, he has adopted a Korean orphan boy who is beginning to emulate his foster father's behavior.

This is a frightening film that raises questions about the legitimacy of murder and murderers in war time. The killer is stopped by a conscience-ridden officer in the end, but it is not unreasonable to assume that many like him were trained in the fine art of killing in the military, and the skill could have some transfer in civilian life.

Whatever cinematic portraits of criminals a teacher uses in this unit, there is one film that is absolutely necessary. Alfred Hitchcock's *The Wrong Man* is one of the great director's least recognized masterpieces. The film, in semi-documentary style, traces the true story of Manny Balestrero, a musician, who was mistakenly accused of robbery. Manny (played by Henry Fonda) is arrested by the police and put through a dehumanizing nightmare of interrogation (underplayed, with the detectives speaking in monotone voices), fingerprinting, and standing in the line-up. In the months awaiting trial, his wife goes insane from shock and insecurity. In the end he is released, but the damage to his life has been irreparably done.

The point of *The Wrong Man* is that this predicament could happen to any of us. The web of circumstantial evidence, the dutiful zeal of the police, and the man's lack of confidence in himself are all presented with realistic impact. The film is positively frightening. It can be an effective transition from the study of the criminal to an analysis of the nature of law enforcement. Students should be asked to put themselves in Manny's position and in the position of the police. How can we prevent a recurrence of incidents like this?

Studying the role of the police as law enforcers may be the most difficult classroom activity. Here is a matter that really generates the generation gap. As I've already indicated, it is becoming a norm among most kids that the cops are "pigs"—evil men who persecute the downtrodden and the young while letting the real criminals (the industrial pollutors, the war-hawk politicians, etc.) go free. Of course, this is a dangerous generalization and the students should be given an opportunity to study the actual duties of the police and the problems involved in pursuing them.

Hollywood has made many pro-police films, some of which are quite skillful. The original *Naked City* was a good, realistic look at a police department in action (as were many of the episodes in its television series counterpart). Unfortunately, I have not been able to locate it in 16-mm form. Three recent films come to mind as reasonable depictions of police as dutiful human beings. One is the very popular *In the Heat of the Night*, which presents the teaming up of a Black Northern cop (Sidney Poitier) and a White Southern police chief (Rod Steiger). Despite the racial implications (which have little to do with the straight police work) and the super-character of the Black cop (nobody is that right, that often), the film does present the police as fair human beings.

Don Siegel's *Madigan* (with Richard Widmark and Henry Fonda) is a more complex film about a big-city police department. The cops are human (one is even crooked), they make mistakes, but they certainly are not portrayed as "pigs."

Bullitt with Steve McQueen as a hip San Francisco cop who isn't quite sure he likes his job has been one of the most popular movies in recent years. Although its emphasis is on fast action and an absurd plot, the character of detective Bullitt is thoroughly interesting. Kids seeing it will probably want to discuss why more cops aren't like him.

Maybe a film like one of those above is necessary in the unit; maybe not. One thing is clear though; the class needs to discuss the significance of a police force and the fundamental need for it. The teacher should raise questions about recent restrictions on police power, such as the dismissal of confessions as evidence in court and the requirement to inform all suspects of their constitutional rights. (Congressman Scheur's book has an excellent explanation of this.) Unfortunately, the only film that has so far approached these issues has been *The Detective* with Frank Sinatra. And that was so badly made, so vulgar and inept, that it would be useless in the classroom.

There are a couple of films, made some years ago, that raise questions about the necessity of limiting some police powers. William Wyler's screen version of the play Detective Story could be useful here. Detective McCloud is a good cop. He is honest, conscientious, and tough with criminals. He is, however, possessed with a desire to destroy criminals beyond the limits of his duty. The film is fascinating in the first half as McCloud (Kirk Douglas) reveals his feelings about his work and how they developed. His partner, Lou, is more humane and is an excellent contrast to the semi-psychopathic McCloud. The early part of the film raises all of the key questions about the limits of police power. McCloud is obsessed with breaking criminals, but it is obvious that the ones he taunts (especially a seedy abortionist) are despicable characters. The impact of the film is lessened by the contrived involvement of the detective's wife with the abortionist and McCloud's inability to grant mercy even to her. In the end he risks his life unnecessarily because he realizes his lack of compassion.

Despite its plot contrivances, I recommend *Detective Story* for the classroom. It is well directed and exciting, and its examination of the police is highly relevant.

A portrait of police power run amok is presented in Orson Welles' *Touch of Evil.* Welles plays a power-mad police chief in a southwestern border town. This film is significant since it presents the policeman as a criminal, and although overstated, the potential for such villainy always exists in a society where police play such an important role.

To conclude this phase of the unit, Frederick Wiseman's *Law and Order* is ideal. I have already indicated Wiseman's editorializing and his selectivity in editing. However, this documentary on the Kansas City police force is not anti-police. It demonstrates, in typical Wiseman style (no narration, only the voices

of the participants are heard), the rotten job the police have to do. They are
society's garbage men, forced to punish the poor souls who are victims of poverty
and lack of education. If cops are brutal (and in some scenes they are extremely
so), it is because their job is brutalizing.

From the motion picture **Law and Order.** Courtesy of Zipporah Films.

The last scene of the film really demonstrates the dilemma of being a policeman.
A young Black man has come to see his wife (whom he is separated from) and
his children. He arrives to find his wife in bed with a stranger. He demands that
the man leave the house, and his wife calls the police. The cops tell the husband
to leave. He complains, stating his problem. An officer replies, "O. K., but there's
nothing we can do about that." One of them suggests the man get a lawyer, file
for divorce, and gain custody of his children. He responds that he has no money.
The police then tell him to leave. "There's nothing we can do." The camera
focuses on the man's tearful eyes. All of his anger and frustration are revealed.
Once again the voice of the policemen, "There's nothing we can do." The man
turns and runs away. The police get into their car and leave.

What will happen to that man? What about his children? *Law and Order*
shows the police as human beings trapped in one of the most difficult jobs society
has ever created.

The unit could end here. The class has examined the criminal and the enforcer,
and the societal forces affecting each of them. However, law enforcement doesn't
end at this point, and some study of trial and punishment would bring this to a
more logical conclusion.

Courtroom dramas are very popular on stage and screen. Indeed, some of the best have been transferred from one medium to the other. Although such dramas are highly entertaining (my own favorite is Billy Wilder's film of Agatha Christie's Witness for the Prosecution), most of them are overly slick and superficial. Like films about American politics, courtroom dramas merely use the framework of the justice system to provide contrived entertainment. Surprise endings are the stock in trade of this genre. I am reluctant to recommend any film of this type, since none really suits the purpose of the unit. Otto Preminger's *Anatomy of a Murder* is a reasonably accurate depiction of trial procedure and the dialogue has a realistic ring to it. However, it is basically a sordid case being tried involving murder and rape, and like most Preminger films, it is overly sensationalistic.

The best films about our court system are those concerning the role of the jury, rather than the entire trial. Sidney Lumet's *Twelve Angry Men*, about the deliberation of a jury on the fate of a "culturally-deprived" young man, is well known, and I will not summarize it here. Despite a tendency to sacrifice reality for long, dramatic speeches (like Lee J. Cobb's breakdown towards the end in which he reveals he has identified the defendant with the son he despises), *Twelve Angry Men* is a valuable classroom film.

An excellent motion picture to use with it is NET's study *Justice and the Poor*. This documentary portrays the double standard of justice we have regarding the poor. The relations with police, the difficulty in obtaining bail, and the lack of qualified lawyers demonstrate the serious problems in our legal system. How many of the people depicted in this film will actually benefit from the compassion of juries like the one in *Twelve Angry Men*? Films like this, which demonstrate how many of the poor are sent to jail, raise questions about who the criminals really are.

Prison films present the same kinds of problems for this unit, since they too have oversimplified the issues. No prison film to date has effectively dealt with the loneliness of confinement, the mental and sexual pressures of life behind bars. The best of this group is *The Birdman of Alcatraz,* the true story of Robert Stroud who killed two men (one a prison guard) and spent most of his adult life behind bars. Stroud is known for his contributions to the study of and care for birds, as well as his refusal to allow confinement to break his soul. Burt Lancaster gives an excellent portrayal of Stroud and the film is a serious critique of our prison system. Still it does not confront enough of the issues, and since Stroud is rehabilitated, it is not a typical example of a system that tends to harden criminals, not reform them. A good student text to follow this up with is Dr. Karl Menninger's detailed critique of our penal system The Crime of Punishment.

I don't know of any film that actually defends capital punishment. A teacher searching for objectivity in this area will be hard pressed to find it. Indeed, most books on the subject condemn it. It might be useful for the teacher to play devil's advocate here, since some of the criminals the class studied earlier (Smith and Hickock, Priest, the killer from *War Hunt*) needed to be removed from society. Is killing them the answer?

The best film I have ever seen on this subject is NET's short film *Life on Death Row*. Dialogues with prisoners framed against art sketches of prison life depict the futility of their existence. The words of the convicts are read by actors, but this does not detract from the reality and the horror of life on death row. One of them admits his guilt, but ponders over what good it would do for him to die.

Robert Wise's *I Want to Live* (with Susan Hayward) is the story of the first woman ever executed in the gas chamber, and it includes the horrifying scene of Miss Hayward's last moments. This film, however, shows its age, with its bland assumption that the woman was innocent without effectively establishing a case against her in the courtroom scenes. It therefore looks ridiculous for her to be executed after such a mockery of justice. The trial is simply not believable.

The famous French film *We Are All Murderers,* which brutally condemns capital punishment, is available for classroom use. It is very one-sided, but devastatingly persuasive in its portrayal of four men awaiting the blade of the guillotine. I recommend it, but certainly not for the squeamish.

The purpose of this unit is to give a class a chance to examine elements of law and order in our society. Some of the films I have sketched should provide impetus for further reading and research. They can add a new dimension to the study of criminology if used correctly.

BIBLIOGRAPHY

SCHEUR, James H. *To Walk the Streets Safely.* Garden City, N. Y.: Doubleday, 1969.

*BROWN, Claud. *Manchild in the Promised Land.* New York: Macmillan, 1965.

*MENNINGER, Karl. *The Crime of Punishment.* New York: The Viking Press, 1968.

FILMOGRAPHY

You're No Good. 28 minutes. Black and white. National Film Board of Canada Production, 1965. Purchase or rental from Contemporary-McGraw-Hill Films.

The Cool World. See citation in Chap. 3.

The Quiet One. 68 minutes. Black and white. Directed by Sidney Myers (narration written by James Agee), 1948. Rental from Contemporary-McGraw-Hill Films.

To Be a Crook. 110 minutes. Black and white. Directed by Claude Lelouch (French), 1965. English subtitles. Rental from Twyman Films or Hurlock Cine World.

The Asphalt Jungle. 112 minutes. Black and white. Directed by John Huston, 1950. Rental from Films Inc.

In Cold Blood. 133 minutes. Black and white (cinemascope print available). Directed by Richard Brooks, 1967. Rental from Columbia Cinematheque.

War Hunt. 81 minutes. Black and white. Directed by Denis Sanders, 1962. Rental from United Artists 16.

The Wrong Man. 105 minutes. Black and white. Directed by Alfred Hitchcock, 1957. Rental from Warner Brothers 16.

Madigan. 101 minutes. Color. Directed by Don Siegel, 1968. Rental from Universal 16.

In the Heat of the Night. 109 minutes. Color. Directed by Norman Jewison, 1967. Rental from United Artists 16.

Bullitt. 113 minutes. Color. Directed by Peter Yates, 1968. Rental from Warner Brothers 16.

Detective Story. 103 minutes. Black and white. Directed by William Wyler (from the play by Sidney Kingsley), 1951. Rental from Films Inc.

Touch of Evil. 95 minutes. Black and white. Directed by Orson Welles, 1958. Rental from Universal 16.

Law and Order. 81 minutes. Black and white. Directed by Frederick Wiseman, 1969. Rental from Zipporah Films.

Anatomy of a Murder. 161 minutes. Black and white. Directed by Otto Preminger, 1959. Rental from Audio-Brandon Films, Twyman Films, or Swank Films.

Twelve Angry Men. 95 minutes. Black and white. Directed by Sidney Lumet, 1957. Rental from United Artists 16.

Justice and the Poor. 60 minutes. Black and white. NET Production, 1968. Purchase or rental from NET Film Service.

Birdman of Alcatraz. 146 minutes. Black and white. Directed by John Frankenheimer, 1962. Rental from United Artists 16.

Life on Death Row. 9 minutes. Black and white. Public Broadcast Laboratory, 1968. Purchase or rental from NET Film Service.

I Want to Live. 120 minutes. Black and white. Directed by Robert Wise, 1958. Rental from United Artists 16.

We Are All Murderers. 113 minutes. Black and white. Directed by Andre Cayatte (French), 1957. English subtitles. Rental from Audio-Brandon Films.

Other Possibilities

Rebel Without a Cause. 111 minutes. Color. Directed by Nicholas Ray, 1955. The late James Dean became the hero of American youth in the mid-fifties with this compassionate movie about alienated teenagers. The film shows its age, but the psychological motives for the delinquency of middle-class kids are still quite timely. And Dean's acting holds up well. Rental from Audio-Brandon Films, Twyman Films, or Swank Films.

The Hoodlum Priest. 101 minutes. Black and white. Directed by Irvin Kershner, 1961. A powerful film about a tough priest who opens a half-way house for the rehabilitation of young criminals. It is based on the life of Father Charles Dismas Clark of St. Louis, where it was filmed. Don Murray as Father Clark and Keir Dullea as a young criminal who won't reform are excellent. This film presents a possible new dimension in law enforcement— the church. Rental from United Artists 16 or Swank Films.

The Killing. 83 minutes. Black and white. Directed by Stanley Kubrick, 1956. This early film of the well-known Kubrick is very similar in theme to *The Asphalt Jungle*. Sterling Hayden almost repeats his role of the earlier film as a sullen, but expert thief. Rental from United Artists 16.

Hard Contract. 107 minutes. Color (cinemascope print available). Directed by S. Lee Pogosten, 1968. This film was debunked by critics as pretentious when it was released, but although far from perfect, it has a very original theme. A professional killer (James Coburn) is sent on a job to the French Riviera. He is likable, even moral, except for his profession. By focusing on sidelights like Vietnam, the Middle East, and Biafra (the camera dwells on TV newscasts and newspaper headlines), the film attempts to demonstrate society's parallel to the murderer. An interesting film, if not a wholly successful one. Rental from Films Inc.

Breathless. 89 minutes. Black and white. Directed by Jean-Luc Godard (French), 1961. English subtitles. Godard's first film about a young hoodlum (Jean-Paul Belmondo) who kills a policeman without much motive and hides out with his American girlfriend. The film is all style, with little dramatic substance, supposedly a takeoff on American gangster films. But it does raise questions about audience identification with a criminal. Belmondo is extremely likable, despite his callous crime. Rental from Contemporary-McGraw-Hill Films.

The Brotherhood. 98 minutes. Color. Directed by Martin Ritt, 1968. There are no really good American films about organized crime. This recent movie has some interesting things to say about the Mafia, but it is basically a sentimental portrait of the generation gap among gangsters. Starring Kirk Douglas. Rental from Films Inc.

Compulsion. 103 minutes. Black and white (cinemascope print available). Directed by Richard Fleischer, 1959. This film version of Myer Levin's fictionalized account of the famous Leopold-Loeb case is reasonably good. The two youths are shown plotting their "super murder," although their motives are never too clear. Their apprehension and betrayal of each other is interestingly filmed, as is their well-known trial (with Orson Welles as Clarence Darrow). Rental from Films Inc.

Marriage as an Institution–
A Unit on Sex Education for the Social Studies and English Classes

Sex education courses in high schools, at least the ones I've observed, generally fall into two categories. The first, for females, revolves around the physiological makeup of the sexes and the perils of premarital pregnancy. Methods of birth control are dealt with, but in the end, students learn that there is just no substitute for chastity. For boys, sex education generally means the husky gym teacher's ultra-frank lectures on society's pro-male double standard for premarital fun and games. (In Frederick Wiseman's film *High School*, a gynecologist gives a similar "hairy" lecture to an all-male assembly and coming from him, the locker-room rhetoric is obscene.)

This kind of classroom instruction occurs (and belongs) in the hygiene class. Teaching about the physiological nature of sexual behavior may best be left to those sexually segregated classes where student problems and questions can be dealt with as frankly as possible. My complaint about such classes is not that they are necessarily bad, but that even at best they are limited. There seems to be an automatic assumption in such courses that human sexual problems cease to exist with the great panacea, marriage. The institution of marriage is one of the subjects that is least considered in the typical high school curriculum. If and when it is discussed, beyond the hygiene class, it is a part of home economics, where the emphasis is on the domestication of women. (I have yet to see a good coeducational program studying the institution of marriage in all its complexities.)

I believe that such subject matter should be a relevant part of the social studies and English curricula. In these classes, which are, hopefully, discussion oriented, students can examine the nature of our marital patterns in a variety of ways. And they can do it objectively. The curriculum I am about to propose naturally involves the viewing of a number of motion pictures concerning various aspects of marital relationships. If shown in the context of a planned sex education program using good supplemental readings, these films can help students examine the dynamics of the most basic institution in any society.

To plan such a course of study, the teacher needs to find a good, comprehensive book to serve as a supplementary text. I can recommend two books that can work in this capacity. Robert O. Blood, Jr. and Donald M. Wolfe's Husbands and Wives: The Dynamics of Married Living is one of the best-known sociological studies on marriage and standard reading in many college classes. Somewhat dated now (1960), particularly in its use of statistics, it nevertheless provides a detailed coverage of the numerous aspects of the marriage institution (courtship, infidelity, child rearing, divorce, etc.). And it is available in paperback.

Vance Packard's books, despite their tendency toward oversimplification, are always popular among high school students. The Hidden Persuaders and The Status Seekers are two of his works that have brightened my classroom in the past. Packard's newest book The Sexual Wilderness: The Contemporary Upheaval in Male-Female Relationships is also a comprehensive study of the total subject and it is more recent (1968) than the Blood and Wolfe book. The early chapters involving the "new morality" may anger students, since they definitely put Packard at the wrong end of the generation gap. (He is zeroing in on the "new" promiscuity of youth and seeking an explanation for it.) However, the later chapters are rich with detailed information on the dynamics of marriage, and as usual, they are well written.

No book (as I have so often pointed out in this work) can substitute for the impact of films in this type of study. Therefore, after assigning the necessary reading, the teacher can begin to program the order of his cinematic presentations.

The films in this study should be divided in a manner similar to the text: starting with patterns of courtship, followed by an examination of the relationships of various couples, the impact of divorce, and the supposed deviancy of bachelorhood and spinsterhood.

A good introductory film would be the National Film Board of Canada's documentary *Courtship and Marriage*, in which the courting customs of four cultures (Canadian, Sicilian, Hindu, and Iranian) are examined. The film focuses on four couples from these cultures and the differences (and similarities) in their preparations for marriage. A film like this is very useful in building a discussion on the wide range of courtship customs around the world. An interesting supplement to this would be to have the class read an excerpt from Ruth Benedict's Patterns of Culture on the mating patterns of the Dobu of the South Pacific. In this culture the young man establishes his manhood by "sleeping around" with the various eligible females. His day of betrothal comes when the mother of the girl he is with catches him and stands in the doorway accusingly.[1]

If the class thinks the various courtship customs are strange (especially Benedict's Dobuan), this would be an appropriate time to delve more deeply into our own mating behavior. The National Film Board of Canada (which is really far ahead in its production of valuable sex education films) has a few short pieces that point out some of our courtship problems. In *The Game,* a male high school student is challenged by his peers to "make it" with a girl. Feeling his manhood threatened, he does pursue a girl in his class whom he eventually succeeds with. Although he later feels guilty about his affair, his friends insist on discussing his conquest, as if to gain some vicarious experience from it. *The Game* points out our own double standard in male-female relationships, where the girl's reputation is forced to suffer. (A similar film *The Merry-Go-Round* can be used instead to deal with the same general theme.)

Probably the best film for teenagers about our premarital standards is

---

[1]An interesting parallel to this is described by James Joyce in his short story The Boarding House. Joyce was commenting on the Irish system of courtship when he wrote this tale of Mrs. Mooney, the landlady, catching her daughter at just the right time with a bachelor boarder. Husband hunting in Dobu is not so far removed from this. Students might enjoy reading the story as a follow-up to Benedict's piece.

Phoebe: The Story of a Premarital Pregnancy. As the film opens we see Phoebe, a high school girl, experiencing a serious emotional problem. Later, through flashbacks, we realize that she believes she is pregnant. The film does not resolve itself. Phoebe anticipates the reactions of her parents and boyfriend, but we never see her actually confront them. It ends forcing the viewer to consider and discuss her alternatives. Whatever happens, it should be clear to the class that the "courtship" of Phoebe is not exactly atypical in our society.

There are other cinematic alternatives in studying courtship patterns. One might be to take a look at such behavior among older people: unmarried, divorced or widowed. The feature-length film *Marty* won several Academy Awards in 1955 and presents a realistic look at the romance of a past-30, homely, shy man and a lonely, timid woman. There is something sensitive and beautiful about *Marty* that makes it worth seeing for any purpose. But, it is especially useful here as a vivid look at the courting patterns of the other side of the generation gap.

Another interesting film that could be used at this point is *Middle of the Night*. Based on a play by Paddy Chayefsky (who wrote <u>Marty</u>), this story of an over-50 widower in love with a woman half his age is extremely well done. Films like this could easily be mawkish or syrupy, but *Middle of the Night* is, in a sociological sense, very realistic. The pressures of family, the loneliness of middle age, and the sexual insecurity that is so much a part of our society, are all dealt with in this rewarding film.

Marriage, itself, has been the basis for countless motion pictures, and it is not my purpose to survey the film literature on the subject. I am recommending that kids examine a few marital relationships on film, which present various problems and yet contrast with each other. After viewing these, the class can compare the relationships and discuss alternative solutions to the problems they see.

George and Martha of Edward Albee's celebrated play <u>Who's Afraid of Virginia Woolf</u> are hardly the couple next door. Their vulgarity, drunkeness, and painfully destructive parlor games make them stand out as one of the most neurotic couples in dramatic literature. Yet, despite all of the overkill tactics and blue language, the marital relationship of George and Martha (and that of their younger guests) is so interesting and complex that it deserves the sociological analysis of students. The motion picture version (directed by Mike Nichols and brilliantly acted by Elizabeth Taylor and Richard Burton) heightens the dramatic impact and puts the viewer closer to the emotional terror than was ever possible on the stage. Indeed this film is rich in analytical data for students.

The plot of *Who's Afraid of Virginia Woolf* is well known, and I will not summarize it here. But there are certain key scenes that underscore the seriousness of the problems of George and Martha. Martha has created an imaginary child, a 16-year-old boy. Although her husband repeatedly warns her against bringing up the subject, she describes the boy to their guests. Gradually, as she and George set out on the path of destroying each other (he almost strangles her after constant taunting about his failures in life; she tries to seduce their male guest to show George that she'll stop at nothing), the child becomes the focal point of their conflict. George, in a final piece of revenge, gets his wife to describe their son, and then announces the boy has been killed. Martha becomes hysterical, claiming he can't break the rules. Their lives are intertwined in a series of sadistic games.

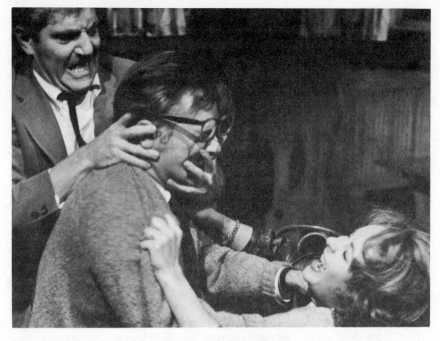

From the motion picture **Who's Afraid of Virginia Woolf.** Copyright © 1966 by Warner Bros. Pictures, Inc.

I heartily recommend this film for high school viewing. I know the objections to it (its profanity, its explicit sexuality), and I am willing to admit it is all over-dramatized. But students will be fascinated by it, and their analyses of the suffering of George and Martha would be an excellent starting point in examining the problems of married couples. Albee's characters are a veritable textbook on marital problems (childlessness, impotency, promiscuity, loneliness, etc.). Why did Martha create an imaginary child? Why did she throw herself at their male guest? Why was George so sure the destruction of the child was perfect revenge? What were some of the causes of George and Martha's love-hate relationship?

Later, after some other examples are viewed, the class can return to the characters of *Who's Afraid of Virginia Woolf* for comparison.

I don't know how kids will react to John Cassavetes' film *Faces.* After being exposed to the slick camera work and fluid editing of *Who's Afraid of Virginia Woolf,* they will probably be shocked by the endless painful scenes that seem to run forever. *Faces* is a difficult film to sit through. (I remember seeing it in a theater, feeling very uncomfortable.) It is so close to life, so totally realistic, that it is like no other cinematic experience.

A middle-aged man, Richard Frost, announces to his wife that he's leaving her. No single incident has prompted his action; it is a combination of the "little things" over the years which made him feel empty. After he leaves to stay with a prostitute, his wife goes out and picks up a rather repulsive young man in a night club. She brings him home and they make love. In the morning her husband returns to find his wife has attempted suicide. The young man, who actually saved her life, fearfully runs away.

Faces is much more than the few incidents I have described here. It is the most realistic examination of the marital institution ever filmed. If *Virginia Woolf* was overdramatized and poetic, *Faces* is terrifyingly real and painful. Mr. and Mrs. Frost are people we know, and their problems result from a basic lack of communication born out of years of loveless marriage. Students will want to analyze the husband's apparently sudden decision to throw it all away. What could cause all of their years together to crumble so swiftly? Why did Mr. Frost return home the next morning, and why (after what he had done) was he so upset to find his wife with another man? Why did she attempt suicide? Wasn't her affair justifiable?

This film is long and depressing. I recommend it only if the class is looking at several other films on the subject. Cassavetes' cinematic style is so far removed from typical commercial film-making, that kids may want to discuss it more than the subject matter. By all means the teacher should allow plenty of time for this.

Another possibility in a unit like this is the recent commercial success *Two for the Road,* starring Audrey Hepburn and Albert Finney. Here we meet the Wallaces, young, wealthy jet-setters. On board a plane they sit glaring in every direction but at each other. Joanna Wallace thinks of how they met, and gradually through a series of skillful flashbacks their 12 years of marriage are exposed. We see them meet and fall in love as penniless tourists in France. After they marry they continue to travel, since he is an architect working from place to place. The film's director, Stanley Donen, has arranged each flashback to show a different trip at a different stage of their marriage. Mark Wallace becomes successful, wealthy, bored. After they have a child, he travels alone and drifts from affair to affair. Later Joanna too has a romantic interlude with the brother of a friend. Yet in the end, after viewing all of the stages of their marriage, we find that they still love each other: as they exchange profanities in the last scene, they do so lovingly.

Two for the Road is commercially slick and highly entertaining. Its cinematic style, at first a puzzle as the flashbacks overlap, is ultimately beautiful. Students should enjoy the film simply as entertainment. However, the marriage of Mark and Joanna Wallace is quite different from that of George and Martha or the Frosts. The Wallaces are still young and, with all their problems, still communicating. Also, we have seen their marriage from the beginning and watched the vacillation of their relationship. Students could probably plot a graph of the ups and downs in their life together. It would be quite easy to evaluate their problems in terms of growing success, as if (according to an old literary cliché) there were some negative correlation between wealth and happiness. But I don't think that kids will dismiss the subject that simply. The film is loaded with meaningful dialogue that can serve as a springboard for a discussion on marriage. At one point, after several years together, Mark tells his wife he enjoys sex more with her now, "when it means less." What are the implications of such a statement? Are George and Martha or the Frosts likely to make similar statements?

The Wallaces of *Two for the Road,* of course, are not typical people. They are too rich, too far removed from the lives of most of us. But their relationship is fascinating, and it serves as one more analytical example for students investigating the stability of the institution of marriage.

An excellent addition to all of the examples studied so far would be to examine the marital relationship of a Black couple. Social scientists have pointed out that in our society the Afro-American male has been forced by discrimination into a less significant economic and social role in marriage. Consequently his relationship with his wife and family is hampered by his inability to dominate. The class should be assigned to read some appropriate analysis of the Black family and the role the male is forced to play. A good choice would be the chapter entitled "Acquiring Manhood" in the book Black Rage by two prominent Black psychiatrists.[2]

Unfortunately, there aren't too many commercial films that have dealt honestly with Black men and women, particularly on a sexual level. I have already mentioned the remarkable *Nothing But a Man.* This film realistically dramatizes the relationship between a Black man and his wife. It describes their courtship, their deep love for each other, and the serious problems confronting them. Duff Anderson, the husband, has been openly contemptuous of the racist rule in a Southern town. As a result, he is jobless. Gradually his problem leads him to self-pity, and in one scene he strikes his wife. Later, after seeing his father die an alcoholic, he decides he will face up to his responsibilities (including the adoption of his illegitimate child) and make amends with his wife.

The class should discuss the Andersons' marital problems in terms of the general comparison with the other couples they have seen, and then deal with the uniqueness of their situation because they are Black.

Though not as effective as *Nothing But a Man,* the marriage of the Youngers in the film version of Lorraine Hansberry's A Raisin in the Sun is worthy of a similar discussion. Walter Lee Younger (portrayed by Sidney Poitier) faces even more difficult problems than Duff Anderson. He must do menial work for a living; he dreams of creating a profit-making business; and his household is dominated by his mother. This film is a valuable look at Black family life, though its theatrical plot (contrived around the spending of an inheritance), clearly puts it second to *Nothing But a Man.*

There is a film dealing with the problems of interracial marriage—Larry Peerce's *One Potato, Two Potato.* Describing the romance and marriage of a White divorcée and a Black man, the film is realistic and honest. The love affair is believably acted by Barbara Barrie and Bernie Hamilton, and the film has much to say about interracial tolerance. Toward the end, however, it tends to lapse into sentimentality as the woman's ex-husband returns to gain custody of their eight-year-old child. Still the marital relationships, between the woman and both her current Black husband and her ex-White husband, are worthy of classroom analysis.

There are many motion pictures about marital infidelity. Many of them have capitalized on popular interest in the subject, and trash like *Strangers When We Meet, The Chapman Report,* and *The Sandpiper* is the standard result. Films like these have no place in the classroom in a study of marital stability, since they simply don't approach the problem with any depth. (I must add that they would be valuable in a study of what motivates popular taste.)

One film that evaluates the nature of infidelity much more deeply than others of the genre is Agnes Varda's *Le Bonheur,* which describes a happily married man, deeply in love with his wife, who meets and has an affair with an attractive young woman. Soon he discovers that he is equally in love with both women, and he tries to explain this to his wife. The rest of the film is highly melodramatic, with the wife ultimately committing suicide and the husband marrying his lover.

---

[2]Grier, William H., and Cobbs, Price M. Black Rage. New York: Basic Books, 1968, pp. 55-74.

Students may or may not accept the contrivances of the plot or Miss Varda's poetic rendering of the story. Indeed, my own description of it sounds awfully corny. But *Le Bonheur* raises an interesting question about the nature and meaning of love. Is it possible to be equally in love with two people? Can our society permit such a relationship? In a unit as comprehensive as this one, some discussion of our culture's concept of love is necessary. And, too few motion pictures (or novels) have dealt with it on the level of *Le Bonheur*.

Now that the students have examined some examples of marital relationships (and, remember, the films I have described are only suggestions), the problem of divorce can be analyzed. In either of the recommended texts (Blood and Wolfe or Packard), there is detailed information on legalities of divorce and the effects on family stability. As a follow-up to the readings, an ideal film would be the satirical comedy *Divorce American Style*. This brutally funny film provides a thorough examination of all of the problems involved in a divorce. It documents the dissolution of a 17-year marriage and the burdens placed on the husband (Dick Van Dyke), especially the outrageous alimony that drives him to the brink of poverty. Another man, in a similar financial fix (Jason Robards), attempts to marry off his ex-wife to whomever he can find to free himself from supporting her. And with razor-edged humor, the film describes the effects of divorce on children, who become confused about their relationships with their parents. In one particularly funny scene, a child refers to his mother's suitor as "uncle daddy."

Despite a contrived ending reuniting the couple, *Divorce American Style* raises some important sociological questions about the effectiveness of divorce. Wouldn't most of the couples examined earlier have been better off divorced? Why are divorces so difficult to obtain if so many couples are incompatible? The class could also examine why the satirical treatment is so effective. Obviously divorce as it exists in our society is not much of a solution for a bad marriage.

There are several other films on the subject of divorce, but most of them are tear-jerking melodramas. The film version of Neil Simon's hit play The Odd Couple (with Jack Lemmon and Walter Matthau), although pure entertainment, has some interesting things to say about the effects of divorce on husbands suddenly forced to live alone. Oscar and Felix develop, in effect, a sexless marital arrangement, with each one assuming an appropriate role. Their relationship may be worthy of some discussion.

Having examined several examples of the patterns of courtship, marriage, and divorce, the students should spend some time discussing the alternative of bachelorhood. The stability of our society is based on the family unit, and, therefore, an unmarried male or female is something of a deviant.

The swinging, promiscuous, but ultimately lonely and empty existence of a bachelor is beautifully documented in *Alfie*. Michael Caine plays *Alfie,* a man fearful of responsibility who spends his life casually jumping from bed to bed without ever making a single commitment to another human being. We see his illegitimate son, whom he ultimately rejects by refusing to marry his mother; his affairs with several women, including a nasty abortion he arranges for a married woman he has impregnated; and in the end his rejection by a woman who has turned him out for a younger man.

Alfie is a good film for young people, its explicit sexual content notwithstanding. It openly deals with the emptiness of being alone and in its own way, it is a great advertisement for marriage.

The female counterpart of *Alfie* can be found in John Schlesinger's film *Darling* (for which Julie Christie won an Oscar). The heroine is a conniving female who destroys a marriage, only to desert her lover for fame and popularity. (She ends up marrying a prince.) *Darling*'s plot is too farfetched, and I have already seen students rebuff this film, which was so heavily praised a few years ago. Still it can provide an interesting companion piece for *Alfie* with its description of a swinging, mod female (and it is much better than such recent efforts in this genre as *Poor Cow* and *Joanna*).

From the motion picture **Rachel, Rachel.** Copyright © 1968 Warner Bros.—Seven Arts, Inc.

Hollywood has made so many films about old maids, one would think the American movie-going public must be exclusively made up of them. Personally, I can't sit through another film about a poor sex-starved, over-30 school teacher (why must they always be school teachers?) groping for her first romance. Yet, in a unit on marriage, some attention must be paid to the loneliness of unmarried females. *Rachel, Rachel* has a plot that comes right out of the formula of old-maid romances. But the beautiful, subdued acting of Joanne Woodward and the fluid direction of Paul Newman make this just about the best film around on the loneliness of the woman who has lost hope of finding a mate. It can be used as a good counterpiece to *Alfie*.

Studying the institution of marriage through films can be a very negative experience. One thing most of the motion pictures I've described have in common is that they are all problem oriented. Courtship is a problem, marriage is a problem, divorce is a problem, living alone is a problem. . . . This is also true of the literature and drama on the subject. A good way to bring things to a conclusion would be to discuss why so much of our marital patterns is interpreted so negatively.

In the recent highly successful Broadway musical *Company,* a 35-year-old bachelor asks his married male friends how they feel about their lives. Their answer is a song, appropriately titled *Sorry-Grateful,* which both criticizes and cheers married living. The students might benefit from hearing this song before they embark on their concluding analyses. With a subject so complex as this, the ambivalence of the song title may be the most accurate interpretation of our marriage institution there is.

STUDENTS' BIBLIOGRAPHY

Texts

*BLOOD, Robert O. Jr., and Wolfe, Donald M. Husbands and Wives: The Dynamics of Married Living. New York: Free Press, 1960.
*PACKARD, Vance. The Sexual Wilderness: The Contemporary Upheaval in Male-Female Relationships. New York: McKay, 1968.

Supplements

*BENEDICT, Ruth. Patterns of Culture. Boston: Houghton Mifflin, 1939, 1959.
*GRIER, William H., and Cobbs, Price M. Black Rage. New York: Basic Books, 1968.

Recording

Company. Original cast album. Columbia Records, 1970. Produced and directed for the stage by Harold Prince. Book by George Furth. Music and lyrics by Stephen Sondheim.

FILMOGRAPHY

Courtship and Marriage. 60 minutes. Black and white. National Film Board of Canada Production, 1965. Purchase or rental from Contemporary-McGraw-Hill Films.
The Game. 28 minutes. Black and white. National Film Board of Canada Production, 1965. Purchase or rental from Contemporary-McGraw-Hill Films.
The Merry-Go-Round. 23 minutes. Black and white. National Film Board of Canada Production, 1966. Purchase or rental from Contemporary-McGraw-Hill Films.
Phoebe: The Story of a Premarital Pregnancy. 29 minutes. Black and white. National Film Board of Canada Production, 1964. Purchase or rental from Contemporary-McGraw-Hill Films.
Marty. 91 minutes. Black and white. Directed by Delbert Mann, 1955. Rental from United Artists 16.
Middle of the Night. 118 minutes. Black and white. Directed by Delbert Mann, 1959. Rental from Audio-Brandon Films or Twyman Films.
Who's Afraid of Virginia Woolf. 129 minutes. Black and white. Directed by Mike Nichols, 1966. Rental from Warner Brothers 16.

Faces. 129 minutes. Black and white. Directed by John Cassavetes, 1968. Rental from Walter Reade 16.

Two for the Road. 111 minutes. Color (cinemascope print available). Directed by Stanley Donen, 1967. Rental from Films Inc.

Nothing But a Man. See citation in Chap. 1.

A Raisin in the Sun. 127 minutes. Black and white. Directed by Daniel Petrie, 1961. Rental from Audio-Brandon Films, Twyman Films, or Swank Films.

One Potato, Two Potato. 92 minutes. Black and white. Directed by Larry Peerce, 1964. Rental from Twyman Films or Swank Films.

Le Bonheur. 85 minutes. Color. Directed by Agnes Varda (French), 1965. English subtitles. Rental from Janus Films.

Divorce American Style. 109 minutes. Color. Directed by Bud Yorkin, 1967. Rental from Audio-Brandon Films.

The Odd Couple. 105 minutes. Color (cinemascope print available). Directed by Gene Saks, 1968. Rental from Films Inc.

Alfie. 115 minutes. Color (cinemascope print available). Directed by Lewis Gilbert, 1966. Rental from Films Inc.

Darling. 122 minutes. Black and white. Directed by John Schlesinger, 1965. Rental from Audio-Brandon Films.

Rachel, Rachel. 104 minutes. Color. Directed by Paul Newman, 1968. Rental from Warner Brothers 16.

Other Possibilities

The Bachelor Party. 93 minutes. Black and white. Directed by Delbert Mann, 1957. Another realistic dramatization by Paddy Chayefsky (<u>Marty</u> and <u>Middle of the Night</u>) about a night on the town for five men attending a bachelor party. Each of them reveals his deepest emotions as the evening progresses. One, a confirmed bachelor, turns out to be the unhappiest of all. A poignant statement on the importance of marriage. Rental from United Artists 16.

Marriage Italian Style. 102 minutes. Color. Directed by Vittorio De Sica (Italian), 1964. English subtitles. A highly entertaining comedy-drama with Sophia Loren and Marcello Mastroianni, this is also an interesting look at a marriage. The mistress of a wealthy businessman traps him into marriage by pretending she is dying. She has lived with him for years and given him three sons, whom she wants to make his heirs. When the man realizes he has been tricked, a series of uproarious incidents occur. Gradually he realizes he loves her, after all the bickering, and courts her like a schoolboy. Rental from Audio-Brandon Films.

The Subject Was Roses. 107 minutes. Color. Directed by Ulu Gosbard, 1968. This film version of Frank Gilroy's Pulitzer Prize-winning play has little cinematic impact. (It is merely a filmed play.) Still it presents a good sociological treatment of a middle-aged couple's problems. Extremely well acted by Patricia Neal, Jack Albertson, and Martin Sheen. Rental from Films In

The Savage Eye. 67 minutes. Black and white. Directed by Ben Maddow, Sidney Myers, and Joseph Strick, 1960. An intriguing semi-documentary about a lonely divorcée in Los Angeles. Rental from Audio-Brandon Films.

The Pumpkin Eater. 110 minutes. Black and white. Directed by Jack Clayton (British), 1964. This film is about one of the world's unluckiest women— three marriages and eight kids. Though it borders on soap opera, *The Pumpkin Eater* still provides a penetrating look at the effects of divorce on women. Anne Bancroft is superb as the heroine. Rental from Audio-Brandon Films, Twyman Films, or Swank Films.

The Family Way. 115 minutes. Color. Directed by Roy Boulting (British), 1967. A very good portrait of a young couple unable to consummate their marriage. Forced to live with the wife's parents because of a housing shortage, cheated out of their honeymoon by a crooked travel agent, they really start off their marriage on the wrong foot. The film treats their predicament comically, yet believably. The acting is also very effective with Haley Mills (of all people) and Hywell Bennet as the couple. Rental from Audio-Brandon Films.

Only Two Can Play. 106 minutes. Black and white. Directed by Bryan Forbes (British), 1963. An extremely funny satire on marital infidelity, starring Peter Sellers. I recommend this as the comic equivalent to *Faces*. It is also worthy of discussion for its own satirical examination of sexual frustration in marriage. Rental from Columbia Cinematheque.

Diary of a Mad Housewife. 94 minutes. Color. Directed by Frank Perry, 1970. A vivid look at the exasperating life of a woman enslaved by marriage. The film makes many important statements about the burdens our marriage system puts on women, but its message is blunted by its stereotyping of males as boorish egomaniacs. Rental from Universal 16.

Who Is Responsible?
The Ageless Question

I have never seen a film as effective and powerful in the classroom as Alain Resnais' *Night and Fog*. Although the narration of this short documentary is entirely in French (with English subtitles), its message penetrates the mind and conscience of even the most reluctant viewer. The film opens with a placid country scene (in richly textured color). Grass blows gently in the breeze across a deserted railroad track. In the distance stand a few buildings, also it appears, deserted. An off-screen narrator ponders over what may have been here in the past. The scene shifts. The film is now black and white, with a grainy newsreel quality. The time is 1933. The place—Germany. The event—the rise of Adolph Hitler. Little by little the pace of the film picks up. Still photographs show massive deportations of Jews and "aliens." The concentration camps are born.

In scene after scene the film-maker assaults his audience with shocks. Photographs of nude inductees (humiliation); human beings labeled, numbered, uniformed, medically experimented with as guinea pigs (sterilized, castrated, or mutilated), and physically enslaved. The operating room, the execution block, the gas "showers" (where in the concrete ceiling there still remain the markings left by the fingernails of those who realized their fate), and the crematoriums are shown in what has become a grand tour of hell.

It is the last part of the film that provides the most gruesome impact. We see the camps as they are liberated by the Allies. Prisoners stare into space in disbelief. Bodies are displayed that were meant to be made into soap. A mountain (literally) of human hair stands ominously before us. Captured Kapos (Nazi guards) carry human heads to ditches for burial. But most shocking of all is the great "clean up." Huge bulldozers push tons of human flesh and bone (like piles of dirt) into cemetary trenches.

On the stand at Nuremberg the Kapos, the officers, and the bureaucrats all plead the same—"I am not responsible."

The scene shifts. The film is in color again. The same placid landscape we saw at the beginning has returned. The narrator closes with the question of *Who* is responsible.

Any teacher who shows this film to his class must be prepared for the reaction. Often I have seen students (boys as well as girls) rush out of the room nauseous before the conclusion. Screams during the last few minutes are common. So is laughter—a nervous, defensive kind of laughter. But most of the time, kids just sit and stare. The horror they have just seen is simply unimaginable.

58

How is a teacher to use a film of this kind? It is programmed to be shocking, building to its horrifying conclusion. Some history teachers might read a catalog description of it and use it as a visual aid when covering World War II. (Teachers on my own faculty have used it this way.) But *Night and Fog* wasn't made to be a visual aid. It is a statement about man's responsibility to his fellow man and it chooses a horrifying example from recent history to make its point.

To use a film like this correctly, a teacher needs to have some greater objective than a mere lesson in history. My first suggestion would be for teachers to read the scenario of the film before they show it. It is accessible in English.[1] Although the film's subtitles are not really necessary for the viewer to grasp its meaning, it is best that the teacher know exactly what the real issues are. I further recommend that the teacher duplicate for his class the last paragraph (which I have reprinted).

Night and Fog

"The crematorium is no longer in use. The devices of the Nazis are out of date. Nine million dead haunt this landscape. Who is on the lookout from this strange tower to warn us of the coming of new executioners? Are their faces really different from our own? Somewhere among us, there are lucky Kapos, reinstated officers, and unknown informers. There are those who refused to believe this, or believed it only from time to time. And there are those of us who sincerely look upon the ruins today, as if the old concentration camp monster were dead and buried beneath them. Those who pretend to take hope again as the image fades, as though there were a cure for the plague of these camps. Those of us who pretend to believe that all this happened only once, at a certain time or place, and those who refuse to see, who do not hear the cry to the end of time."

Class discussion should now be based on the fundamental question that *Night and Fog* asks. "Who is on the lookout . . . for the executioners? Are their faces really different from our own?"

The options at the teacher's disposal are now many. A repertory of related films would effectively follow through with the unit's basic theme.

There is another film on the concentration camps with a similar philosophy, National Film Board of Canada's *Memorandum*. This film follows a group of former camp prisoners (now Canadian citizens) on a 24-hour pilgrimage to the remains of the camp at Bergen-Belsen. During their journey, the film traces over much of the same ground as *Night and Fog*. Interviews with survivors, old film clips of camp life, off-screen commentary about official "murder by memorandum" all have a similar numbing effect on the viewer. I recommend the use of *Memorandum* only if *Night and Fog* is unavailable. The two films shown together are perhaps too much for any audience to bear. And, *Night and Fog*'s statement, it seems to me, is profound enough.

It might be a good idea at this point to shift the events away from the concentration camps entirely. An excellent animated short film *The Hangman*, based on a poem by Maurice Ogden, would be appropriate. A hangman arrives in a mythical town and erects a scaffold on the courthouse lawn (beneath an inscription on the courthouse wall that says "Discite justitiam monti"—ye who have been warned, learn justice).

The hangman then selects his first victim, an alien. No one in the town objects,

---

[1] Printed in Hughes, Robert, Ed., Film, Book 2: Films of Peace and War. New York: Grove Press, 1962, pp. 234-255.

hoping this will be the executioner's only victim. But, he announces, this was just "to test the rope." He has really come after "he who serves (him) best." One by one people are called to the gallows: a Jew, a Black man, and then each citizen of the town. The visual images become horrifying as the gallows takes root in the ground. At last the town's sole survivor is summoned, since in his apathy, he was, indeed, the one who served the hangman best. Although the theme may be somewhat oversimplified, the film has great visual impact, and its statement about man's responsibility to his fellow man is very clear.

Were the people of Germany, who closed their eyes to the horror of the concentration camps, symbolically represented in *The Hangman*? This might be a logical follow-up question after seeing both films. Still, to really do justice (I mean this in the total sense) to these ideas, the theme must be discussed further.

Stanley Kramer's *Judgment at Nuremberg* was a major commercial success in 1961. Hailed by some critics as "bold," "powerful," and "a clarion call for justice;" and denounced by others as "commercial oversimplification" and, as one critic put it, "an all-star concentration camp drama, with special guest victim appearances."[2]

Here is a film that combines all of the strengths and weaknesses of an American-made "social" drama. I happen to think its basic premise, that of a society being forced to assume some collective responsibility for its leaders' misdeeds, is a good one (as did the Allied nations at Nuremberg in 1946-47. Isn't this what our disgruntled youth is clamoring for today over our involvement in Vietnam?). Therefore, its story of a judge compelled to pass sentence on a German judge who has backed up policies of Nazi injustice as "duty" is a valid one. But the film's all-star cast (Spencer Tracy, Richard Widmark, Marlene Dietrich, Judy Garland, Montgomery Clift, and Burt Lancaster (of all people, as the defendant German judge), detracts from its message. It becomes a who's who—aren't they wonderful actors—kind of thing.) Only Maximillian Schell, then a relative unknown in this country, as Lancaster's defense lawyer is really convincing—and he is arguing for duty to country *above* any higher law.

Despite its shortcomings and its length (186 minutes) *Judgment at Nuremberg* should be shown in classrooms discussing the theme of responsibility. It raises all of the important issues, and it too makes use of those German concentration camp films. Most important, it purports, like the Allied nations at the end of World War II, that men are sometimes responsible to some higher, human law than that of their country.[3]

By this point the class should be sufficiently keyed up about the inhuman horror of the Nazis and the apathy of the German people. The teacher should now move the question of responsibility in a somewhat different direction.

Discussion of *our* commitment to others can also be stimulated by programming a few significant motion pictures.

The Japanese film *Children of Hiroshima* (or *Children of the Atom Bomb* as

---

[2] For a summary of critical appraisal of the film, as well as a bitter condemnation of it, see Kael, Pauline, Kiss Kiss Bang Bang. New York: Bantam Books, 1969, pp. 255-256.

[3] The teacher may thoroughly disagree with this and the film can be discussed for its failure to make a case for "higher law." As I've indicated, Maximillian Schell's defense of national law is extremely well presented.

it is known in Japan), based on the book by Arata Osada, is available for class-rooms. Although somewhat sentimentalized, it describes with accurate brutality the notorious air raid and the impact on a few surviving children. Told through flashbacks seen through the eyes of a school teacher in the early 1950s, it is a powerful statement against nuclear war. Even more significant, however, is that it raises similar questions about *our* responsibility to those human ideals we condemned Germany for not having.

An interesting companion film to this might be Akira Kurosawa's *I Live in Fear,* which tells the story of an old man who has lived through the nuclear holocaust of World War II, but is later obsessed with the fear that Japan is again doomed for atomic destruction. (He has heard of the American H-bomb tests in the Pacific in the early 1950s.) He tries to sell all of his belongings and move his family to the "safety" of Brazil, but he fails. The family will not go, even though he burns down his own factory to show how deeply he feels. He is later committed to a mental institution, where he remains at the film's conclusion. The old man's fears should make for fascinating discussion on one of the effects of our nuclear age.[4]

What are the parallels between the Nazi death camps and the bombings at Hiroshima and Nagasaki? Was our action more justifiable? How *much* more? Have we committed crimes against humanity? Can we too be put on trial?

The kids will obviously want to discuss these issues. Some may have already read John Hersey's Hiroshima (or it could be assigned, for further study).

The teacher can now conclude the unit by showing another film. I must advise that one of those recommended below should be enough, since all are totally explicit about the ramifications of nuclear holocaust, and in a unit like this one, too much overkill would be ineffective.

Stanley Kubrick's *Dr. Strangelove: Or How I Learned to Stop Worrying and Love the Bomb* is an ideal choice to conclude with. Outrageous and brutally satirical, this film is the greatest warning to a nuclear society I have ever seen. A mad general, appropriately named Jack D. Ripper, has unleashed an unauthorized atomic attack against the Russians (who have recently installed a doomsday device that, when detonated by nuclear bombs, has the power to blow up the world). We are then faced with an assortment of weird characters: an ineffectual President named "Muffley"; the superpatriotic commander of the attack force, Major "King" Kong; Buck "Turgidson," head of the joint chiefs of staff; and the sinister scientific genius, ex-Nazi, U. S. military advisor, Dr. Strangelove. Nothing is sacred in this masterpiece of horror. All heroic and nationalistic clichés are destroyed. It is howlingly funny, but in the end (as the doomsday device goes off and the music in the background plays "We'll meet again, who knows where, who knows when"), an awful emptiness hits the viewer. What have we been laughing at?

I have used *Strangelove* in the classroom and can testify to its impact. When the second thoughts begin to hit the kids, they start to question how much of it could really happen, and what can they do to prevent it.

---

[4] Analyses of both Japanese films is available in detail in the excellent study by Anderson, Joseph L., and Ritchie, Donald, The Japanese Film: Art and Industry. New York: Grove Press, 1960.

From the motion picture **Dr. Strangelove.** Courtesy of Columbia Pictures.

As an alternative to *Dr. Strangelove,* one could show the film version of the best-selling book <u>Fail Safe</u>. Sidney Lumet (a very skilled director) has filmed it without satire. It is a grim, straightforward account of what might happen if a mechanical failure occurred in our defense system, sending planes, accidentally, on a mission of nuclear destruction. The President in this film (played by Henry Fonda) is an intelligent, competent man (in contrast to the comical idiot in the Kubrick film) and as he grapples with possible solutions, the audience identifies with him. The kids might not buy the film's conclusion, where since Moscow has been leveled by bombs, we agree to similarly destroy New York to prevent a spread of the disaster. An interesting point for discussion might be to list all of the alternatives a President may have under such circumstances.

One other motion picture could effectively conclude this unit, though I caution anyone showing it to see it first. Peter Watkins' *The War Game* (which won an Academy Award a few years ago) was originally commissioned to be made as a television program for the British Broadcasting Company. After one screening of the film, the company decided it was too gruesome for showing on commercial television.

Constructed as an acted documentary, *The War Game* begins by focusing on the reactions of the British people to the crisis of possible nuclear attack. Emergency evacuations away from urban centers begin. Shelter space is scarce and people are reluctant to put up and feed evacuees at their own expense. (The off-screen narrator asserts that all of the problems displayed in the film are based on the actual situation as it exists today regarding protection against nuclear attack.)

From the motion picture **The War Game.** Courtesy of Contemporary-McGraw-Hill Films.

Sirens blow. The actual attack has come. The blinding flash, the heat, the shock bursts, the mammoth explosions, all are shown. People walk across the screen blinded, burned, and mutilated. It is a horrifying sight. Soon the crisis worsens, since due to lack of hospital space, "hopeless" casualties are to be shot.

Weeks after the actual bombings, the other effects begin to take toll. People become apathetic and inert. Rats, disease, looting, and hunger riots have become commonplace. The narrator asks, "Would the survivors envy the dead?"

The most horrifying thing about *The War Game,* though all of the action was obviously simulated, is that everything in it is based on the actual experiences of survivors of Hiroshima, Nagasaki, and the fire bombings in Dresden, Germany.

The question at the end of *Night and Fog* comes back to haunt us. "Who is on the lookout from this strange tower to warn us of the coming of new executioners? Are their faces really different from our own?"

The teacher and class that begin a study of the horrors of the concentration camps and the "guilt" of the German people, need, it seems to me, to be examining the question of human responsibility in the total sense. The films described here help provide that very necessary self-evaluation.

FILMOGRAPHY

Night and Fog. 31 minutes. Color and black and white. Directed by Alain Resnais (French), 1955. English subtitles. Purchase or rental from Contemporary-McGraw-Hill Films.

Memorandum. 58 minutes. Black and white. Directed by Donald Brittain and John Spotton (National Film Board of Canada), 1966. Purchase or rental from Contemporary-McGraw-Hill Films.

The Hangman. 12 minutes. Color. Directed by Les Goldman (narrated by Herschel Bernardi), 1964. Animated. Purchase or rental from Contemporary-McGraw-Hill Films.

Judgment at Nuremberg. 186 minutes. Black and white. Directed by Stanley Kramer (screenplay by Abby Mann), 1961. Rental from United Artists 16.

Children of Hiroshima. 93 minutes. Black and white. Directed by Kaneto Shindo (Japanese), 1953. English subtitles. Rental from Audio-Brandon Films.

I Live in Fear. 103 minutes. Black and white. Directed by Akira Kurosawa (Japanese), 1955. English subtitles. Rental from Audio-Brandon Films.

Dr. Strangelove: Or How I Learned to Stop Worrying and Love the Bomb. 93 minutes (a perfect classroom length). Black and white. Directed by Stanley Kubrick, 1964. Rental from Columbia Cinematheque.

Fail Safe. 111 minutes. Black and white. Directed by Sidney Lumet, 1964. Rental from Audio-Brandon Films, Contemporary-McGraw-Hill Films, Twyman Films, or Swank Films.

The War Game. 49 minutes. Black and white. Directed by Peter Watkins (British), 1966. Rental from Contemporary-McGraw-Hill Films.

Other Possibilities

The Hole. 15 minutes. Color. Directed by John and Faith Hubley (voices of Dizzy Gillespie and George Matthews), 1962. Animated (Academy Award winner). An interesting little film of two construction workers discussing the possibilities of accidental nuclear war while working underground. Rental from Audio-Brandon Films.

Hiroshima Mon Amour. 88 minutes. Black and white. Directed by Alain Resnais (French), 1959. English subtitles. No doubt many readers must be raising some eyebrows since I left this well-known film out of the context of the chapter. The lyrical love story of two victims of World War II (a Japanese man who survived the bomb and a French woman who had loved a Nazi soldier) takes place in contemporary Hiroshima, with flashbacks demonstrating the symbolic relationship of the lovers to this place. Somehow, despite a few realistic scenes of the survivors of Hiroshima, the message of the film is too often muddled by the dreary romance. Resnais (who, remember, made *Night and Fog*) was hailed for his direction of a moving and unusual film. That was in 1959. Today it doesn't seem as effective. Rental from Audio-Brandon Films or Contemporary-McGraw-Hill Films.

Ladybug Ladybug. 81 minutes. Black and white. Directed by Frank Perry (screenplay by Eleanor Perry), 1963. The Perrys' follow-up to *David and Lisa,* was withdrawn right after its release in 1963. I have not seen it, but an expert like David Mallery claims this tale of the reaction of school children to an atomic alert is both quite frightening and highly significant. Rental from United Artists 16.

A Matter of Ethics–
A Cinematic Study of Ethical Problems

In the little known film *The Savage Innocents,* Inuk, an Eskimo (played by Anthony Quinn), offers a Christian missionary the hospitality of his home. When the missionary refuses to eat a plate of live worms, an Eskimo delicacy, Inuk is deeply offended. Trying again to be a good host, the Eskimo, according to the custom and tradition of his culture, offers to share with his guest a most prized possession, his wife. The missionary, shocked by such a "savage" gesture, refuses, declaring Inuk a sinner. Unable to interpret his guest's anger as anything but insult, the Eskimo strikes and accidentally kills him. Later in the film, a White policeman apprehends Inuk for committing murder, while the Eskimo insists that

From the motion picture **The Savage Innocents.** Courtesy of Films Inc.—Paramount Pictures.

his action was justified. The missionary, he argues, had deeply offended his home and family. "The man was *rude!*"

The Savage Innocents raises a significant moral question. When the customs of two cultures differ so fundamentally, which takes precedence? Which culture is morally right? What are the guidelines for determining "right" and "wrong"? Are they universal or relative? Are they rigid or flexible? Are they supernaturally determined or human controlled?

Courses in the philosophy of social ethics are offered on virtually all college campuses. High school students too are given ethical problems to deal with in literature and poetry (What are Hamlet's moral obligations, for instance?). Indeed in a dynamic society like ours, where technological change is always more rapid than political, economic, and social change, the classroom is an ideal place to discuss crucial issues in terms of an individual's ethical obligations.

The material I am about to present raises some key questions about man's concepts of right and wrong and whether it is possible to establish some universal code of ethical behavior. Standard units on ethical theory are supposed to be too complex for the average high school student. Such units are generally definition-oriented and a great deal of time is spent differentiating between philosophical ideals such as hedonism, utilitarianism, altruism, etc. If a teacher desires to begin in this way, I have no objection, though it isn't really necessary. The ethical theory unit I have in mind is geared to all students, from the brightest to the semiliterate. Naturally it is based on motion pictures, which act as an intellectual equalizer in presenting complex ethical issues to students of all academic ability levels. Such a unit can fit into any area of English or the social studies. Literature is loaded with novels and dramas on the question of universal right and wrong. Classes reading Hamlet or Arthur Miller's All My Sons should be confronted with films that raise further questions on the nature of man's ethical behavior.

In the social studies, questions of moral responsibility and human commitment constantly come up in discussions on war, ecology, race relations, and economic power. The point is that a teacher can use films to foster discussion on ethical problems with any students in virtually any given classroom situation.

The films I have chosen to illustrate this aspect of teaching are, of course, only suggestions. The teacher can select one or two to suit his purposes. I have divided the films into four categories of study for convenience. The first series deals with unsolved ethical problems. Each film here illustrates a situation where men exhibit no concept of right and wrong, living in a state of almost pure apathy. Such films should provide motivation for students to think of possible solutions.

The second category of films shows individuals forced to make decisions based on what they believe is "right." The purpose of such films is to get students to analyze the validity of these decisions, and, if possible, to provide alternatives to them.

The third group of films I have included present ethical problems in terms of "religious" morality. The individuals in these films base their "right" decisions on some "higher authority," maintaining that in the end man's fate rests on certain universal, spiritual principles beyond his control.

The concluding category deals with ethical behavior in a relative sense. That is, "right" and "wrong" are determined by men themselves according to the needs of their specific cultural environments. Unfortunately, I know of only one motion picture that adequately applies here—*The Savage Innocents,* which I used in the introduction.

Giving students a chance to discuss ethical questions in these four contexts runs the philosophical gamut in this area. The use of films allows all students to study these important concepts. Studies of ethical problems are relevant and needn't be limited to the definition-oriented college course. Suggested here is a means of opening up this curriculum.

APATHETIC SOCIETY—MEN WITHOUT ETHICS

An ideal introduction film to orient students in the philosophy of ethics is *The Detached Americans*. Originally a television documentary and now a little dated (although not nearly as much as its predecessor *Conformity*), this short film still makes a sufficient statement about the alarming trend in our society toward public apathy. It uses several contemporary examples of situations where individuals should have demonstrated concern for others but opted to ignore the problems instead. The famous Kitty Genovese case where 38 people stood by while a woman was beaten to death is cited as a horrifying incident of people not wanting to get involved. *The Detached Americans* touches on many cases of current public apathy, everything from the Genovese case and others like it to institutionalized racism (society ignoring the plight of poor Blacks). Although some of its simulated man-on-the-street interviews (using actors) are awkward, the contrivance doesn't detract from the points made about the growing problem of noninvolvement as a public norm. Are we, as the film points out, becoming an amoral people?

Students should examine some extremes of individual behavior of this kind and analyze what motivates them. The character of Saul Nazerman (Rod Steiger) in *The Pawnbroker* exemplifies a man existing without outward commitment to any moral standards. As he peers out through the barred window of the teller's cage of his pawnshop at the dregs of humanity who must sell him their last possessions, he shows not the slightest bit of compassion. When his young Puerto Rican assistant asks what he believes in, Nazerman replies, "Money. There is no God or anything. Only money. I believe in money!"

The Pawnbroker as a cinematic character study is second to none. Nazerman's motives for his callous attitude are demonstrated through a series of sudden flashbacks that become longer and more explicit as the film progresses. His life in a Nazi concentration camp has thoroughly embittered him. His family was murdered, and he was forced to watch the guards rape his beautiful young wife and use her as a prostitute. (This scene is triggered in his mind when a Black prostitute bares her breasts in front of him. Her nudity shocks his memory as he sees his wife's naked image in front of the Nazis.)[1]

Nazerman's lack of ethics gradually becomes understandable. His horrible experiences in the concentration camp have conditioned his behavior. Late in the film he begins to show some remorse as his memories haunt him. He confesses to a well-meaning female social worker that the wall he has built around himself has begun to crumble. Having acted as a front man for a Harlem gangster for years, he can no longer cooperate upon discovering that one of the gangster's "businesses" is prostitution (remembering his wife). He then demonstrates his desire to die,

---

[1] The explicit nudity in **The Pawnbroker** is highly pertinent to its dramatic development. The film cannot be used effectively without this scene. I will discuss the possibilities of using it inoffensively in the classroom in Part III.

trying to provoke the gangster into killing him. It doesn't work. Towards the end of the film some young hoodlums try to rob him. Seeking to use them as his executioners, since he can't bring himself to commit suicide, he refuses to give them any money. His disillusioned young assistant, who had planned the robbery, suddenly feels guilt-stricken and tries to stop it. He is shot. Old Nazerman stands over the youth's body unable to show emotion as the sound of police sirens fills the air. He gets up and walks over to his desk, staring at the large needle he uses to pin receipts to. The pawnbroker raises his hand and heavily drops it on the needle. He holds his bleeding hand, crying out in pain as the film ends.

Nazerman's apathy has infected his personality. His only solution was to force pain upon himself, as if to see if he still was capable of some kind of feeling.

The Pawnbroker is a superb classroom film, particularly in this context. Saul Nazerman's character provides a textbook for a discussion on ethical concepts. Is our society capable of producing others like him? Is forceful dehumanization, like that of the concentration camps, a major reason for a breakdown in ethics? Is the plight of ghetto life and poverty equally dehumanizing? Does it bring about similar results? Is Saul Nazerman a prototype "detached American," or is his an extreme case unrepresentative of our society's general apathy? What lessons can be learned from studying the pawnbroker's dilemma?

Two other films approach the problem of societal apathy in a much different way. Michaelangelo Antonioni's *Blow-Up* is an intense, symbolic treatment of an individual without a sense of right and wrong. The nameless protagonist of the film (very few of its characters have names) is a successful photographer. He is young, affluent, and egotistical. His latest project is a series of pictures taken for a book while spending a night in a flophouse for derelicts. The shots are indeed brilliant, capturing the agony of life on the skids. Yet he is only interested in the quality of his photographs, never mentioning the human subjects. As he emerges from the flophouse at the beginning of the film, a car full of young people in clown makeup passes him, cheering loudly. He waves to them as the film's audience sits mystified about the nature of such a scene.

Later while walking through a park the photographer sees a man and woman holding hands in the distance. Intruding on their privacy, he starts to photograph them. When the woman confronts him and asks for the pictures, he arrogantly refuses. "Why can't you leave people in peace?" she implores. "I can't help it if there's no peace," he replies.

The woman and another man follow him home. While her companion hides, she visits the photographer, offering herself to him if he gives her the prints. Taking advantage of the situation, he hands her a roll of film, which, it turns out, is blank.

Curious about the woman's concern, the photographer develops the film, making a series of blow-ups of each print and studying them. Gradually he notices that the man she was with in the park was shot by someone hiding behind a bush. Most of the details of the crime are revealed through the blow-ups of his pictures. It is clear that he has witnessed a murder being committed.

Thus far the film has shown a thoroughly unlikable individual who apparently lacks all sense of moral commitment to anything or anyone. Now, confronted with the responsibility of doing something about the crime he has seen, the photographer allows himself to be sidetracked so often that his opportunity for action dwindles away. He starts to call his agent to tell what he's seen, but ends up romping in bed with two teenage girls instead. Later he does return to the park, and seeing the body is still there, again starts out to find his agent to "show him." (Not once does he demonstrate any concern in calling the police.) On his way he sees a rock concert in progress and watches the crowd attack the singers in adulation. Joining them, he grabs a piece of a performer's smashed guitar, flaunting it triumphantly at the mob of screaming youths. Finally, remembering his destination, he leaves and arrives at a party where he finds the agent. Instead of insisting that they go to the scene of the crime, however, the photographer joins the party and gets "high" on marijuana. Awaking the next morning, he runs to the park only to find that the body has disappeared. As he stands there gazing at the grass, the car full of clown-faced youths reappears. Two of them begin to play an imaginary game of tennis, without rackets or ball, while the others watch intently, turning their heads from "player" to "player." The photographer joins in and when one of them asks him to retrieve the invisible ball, he picks up some air and throws it to them. Suddenly a pained expression lights his face. His eyes drop, as if he's realized his entire existence is make-believe. The scene closes as the photographer appears smaller and smaller on the screen until he virtually disappears.

From the motion picture **Blow-Up.** Courtesy of Films Inc.—MGM.

Much of the symbolism in *Blow-Up* is obscure, and the film does move at a very slow pace. But it is a fascinating portrait of an individual, and perhaps a society, without a concept of ethics. Students will want to discuss all of its cinematic complexities. And they should analyze whether the film is a representation of our society. Is the detachment of the photographer symbolic of an apathetic trend among us? What motivates his behavior? What can be done to alter it? Why did the film's director include the opening and closing scenes of the clown-faced youths? Whom are they supposed to represent? Why are so many of the people nameless?

The very title of the film, *Blow-Up* (an enlargement of a photograph to examine its details), may symbolize a "blow-up" of the increasing apathy of our own society. No unit on ethical problems could be complete without this remarkable motion picture.

The second film that examines our society in a somewhat similar way is Haskell Wexler's *Medium Cool.* When initially released, this film was publicized as a drama about the confrontation between protesting youth and the police at the Democratic Party National Convention of 1968. While it does have some extraordinary footage of those events, *Medium Cool* is about a great deal more than rebellious youth. Its protagonist is a handsome young television cameraman, who is in several ways similar to the photographer in *Blow-Up.* His major interests in life seem to be "getting some beautiful pictures" (as he puts it), and maintaining a hyperactive sex life. In the opening sequence, he and his sound man arrive at the scene of an auto accident where a woman has been badly injured. After recording the wrecked car and victim from several angles, he matter-of-factly states, "I guess maybe we ought to call an ambulance."

From the motion picture **Medium Cool.** Courtesy of Films Inc.—Paramount Pictures.

As the film progresses, the cameraman is drawn into the mainstream of the crucial events in Chicago in 1968. Going to record an interview with a Black cab driver who honestly returned $1000 accidentally left in his back seat, the "hero" is confronted by the Black man's neighbors. In the best simulated scene involving current Black awareness I have ever witnessed, the ghetto residents "tell it like it is" to the cameraman, forcing him to report a story about the despicable conditions of their environment.

Later he gets involved with a poor White woman and her son from Appalachia, whom he develops affection for. And, in the film's climax, he witnesses the violence of the Chicago confrontation. When it appears he has finally learned some human compassion, he is killed in a traffic accident. In the final scene, photographers stand over his body callously snapping pictures.

To what extent are the selfish concerns of the cameraman symbolic of public attitudes? Are the young, as demonstrated by the downtrodden students of the Chicago confrontation, the only members of our society who have commitment to a moral sense of right and wrong? Had the cameraman's experiences with our deep contemporary problems altered his detachment? To what extent? How does he resemble the photographer of *Blow-Up*? How does he differ?

Although the ending of *Medium Cool* is something of a let-down (I for one would have liked to know just how "humanized" that cameraman had become), the film is a vivid statement about our contemporary society.

A teacher using *Medium Cool* and *Blow-Up* in this unit can really "turn on" his students. These two films relate extremely well to young people by providing crucial questions about the nature of our existing society and the needs for change. Tragically, in the commercial distribution, both films were given "adult" labels and some theaters denied young people access to them. Neither film is the least bit offensive, however, and in a later chapter I'll discuss how they might be used in the classroom despite the controversy surrounding them. As portraits of the ethical problems of contemporary society, they are second to none.

A TIME TO STAND: INDIVIDUALS AND ETHICAL DECISIONS

Units on ethical behavior invariably examine decision-making on the basis of what is "right." Our society's moral code has almost made a cliché out of this concept. Many works of literature and films thematically center on the protagonist's desire to make things "right."

The teacher can use certain films to serve as examples of ethical decision-making. Each film presents an individual with a moral dilemma and how he resolves it. The students can then discuss his solution and, possibly, ethical alternatives to it.

There are several well-known commercial movies that can be used to illustrate individual, ethical decision-making. In *High Noon* (a prototype Western), marshal Will Kane can leave town with his new bride and never have to confront the vengeful Miller gang, which is on its way to destroy him. Yet Kane (Gary Cooper) feels a moral commitment to stand his ground and fight it out, even though the entire town he has struggled for years to protect has forsaken him. Students seeing *High Noon* should discuss the implications of the marshal's decision. Is it heroic or foolish? Since it is based on physical confrontation (an ultimate shoot-out), is its moral that violence is a legitimate means of settling a problem? To what extent is Kane's decision to stay and fight a reflection of our society's ethical norms? By using *High Noon*, a teacher can present a complex philosophical problem for discussion.

In the film *On the Waterfront*, Terry Malloy (Marlon Brando) decides to "do the right thing" by providing testimony against his peers in the longshoremen's union who have murdered a disloyal member. Terry's decision ultimately comes from knowing that his friends were wrong to have committed murder. Thus he courageously opposes them, despite threats to his own life. At the end of the film, however, Terry seeks out the union boss and in a ferocious fist fight, defeats him. Is this also part of his ethical commitment? Does his ultimate reliance on violence comment about our society's ethical values? This point is particularly interesting, since the final resolution of "right" in most films results from a violent confrontation with the forces of "wrong." Students should discuss this in light of our society's constant involvement in wars. Is our sense of right and wrong conditioned by our ability to use physical force?

Another classroom approach to this subject of individual ethics would be to examine films where acts of conscience signify the downfall of the protagonist. In such situations, ethical decisions become sacrificial.

The Hustler is a film that students relate to very well. Its realistic situations, centering around the career of a callous professional pool hustler, honestly portray life (students generally can see right through pretentious themes). "Fast Eddie" Felson (Paul Newman) is selfish and ambitious through much of the film. But when his racketeer promotor viciously rapes the woman he loves, Eddie becomes bent on challenging the system he has so long been a part of. At the end of the film he wins an important match knowing that it will anger the racketeer and prevent him from playing big-time pool again. He has made his sacrifice by doing what's "right," and he emerges as a heroic figure.

In *Requiem for a Heavyweight*, washed-up fighter "Mountain" Rivera (Anthony Quinn) is betrayed by his selfish manager (Jackie Gleason), who has gambled away all of the boxer's money. In the end, Rivera, out of a pathetic loyalty to his manager, enters a wrestling ring (a most demeaning situation for a former boxing contender) in an Indian costume. The fighter has sacrificed his professional dignity to protect his manager from the gangsters to whom he's in debt. Rivera, unlike the protagonist in *The Hustler*, does not emerge heroically. His ethical decision is based on compassion for a lesser man than himself, and he might be considered a fool. An interesting classroom activity would be to compare the sacrificial decisions of the two characters and how they relate to audiences. "Fast Eddie" emerges triumphant, while "Mountain" Rivera is pathetic.

There are other films that demonstrate individual ethical decisions based on a commitment to what's "right," and I'll discuss some of them in the filmography. The point students should keep in mind throughout this unit is what determines the nature of being "right." This is a fundamental principle of ethical theory.

"HIGHER LAW": INDIVIDUAL DECISIONS AND UNIVERSAL ETHICS

A study of this kind should devote some time to the question of religious morality. The basic philosophical priorities of the teacher and the nature of his class (a parochial school situation might quite naturally devote most time to this area) should determine how much weight to allot here. Unfortunately, the film literature is not as rich in this area, since most "religious" films (*King of Kings, Ben Hur, The Greatest Story Ever Told, The Robe*, etc.) have been commercial spectacles rather than sagas of faith.

Sophocles' ancient classic Antigone has a superb film counterpart. Since few translations of this play are adaptable for high school students, the film version (English subtitles) vividly provides the essential moral experience. The eternal question of heroine Antigone's obedience to man's law (the King's edict not to bury the bodies of her treasonous brothers) or to spiritual law (that the souls of all men must be laid to rest in the soil) is beautifully dramatized in the film. After seeing it, students can discuss Antigone's recognition of a law higher than man's and the validity of her choice. Supplementary readings by Thoreau or Martin Luther King, which relate to the same subject, would be ideal here, since the concept of "higher law" is a deeply ingrained part of our ethical concepts.

Another excellent film dealing with ethics in terms of higher law is the screen adaptation of Robert Bolt's play A Man for All Seasons. The ethical decision made by Sir Thomas More to morally oppose Henry VIII's divorce is not part of any conflict or dilemma. More's faith in God and his unflinching commitment to Catholic law dictates that he must condemn the King's action. Here is a man who has consciously sacrificed himself because of that higher law. He believes absolutely. Naturally the film portrays him sympathetically and uses his sacrifice as an example of man's tenacious faith in what is "right." Students will probably want to discuss Sir Thomas More's behavior beyond the context of the film, and some may even wonder if it smacks of fanaticism. Isn't another one of our society's ethical norms based on our faith in the necessity of compromise? What morally determines the limits of compromise? How is man to know when higher law takes precedence?

RELATIVE ETHICS: "RIGHT" IS DETERMINED BY THE CONDITIONS OF THE SOCIETY

Antigone and *A Man for All Seasons* imply that there is an ultimate moral code of behavior for all mankind. *The Savage Innocents,* which I summarized at the beginning of this chapter, is based on a true incident. In Eskimo culture the offer of a man's wife to "laugh" with is a deeply valued more. In our culture, which sanctifies a monogomous union of man and wife and labels deviation from it as adultery, the Eskimo custom would be a sin. Yet the fact is that ours is a world of vastly diverse cultures and the patterns of ethics in them vary considerably. Right and wrong in the anthropological sense are purely relative. A film like *The Savage Innocents* (I wish there were others as provocative) must ideally conclude any unit on ethical theory. Its conclusions should be weighed against those of the films in the other categories. To what extent do the ethical decisions so valued in our culture apply to other cultures? Are there any universal ethical norms that can be applied to mankind interculturally? If there are none, does it mean that ethics have no true value in governing man's behavior? Does this justify the society portrayed in *Blow-Up*?

Clearly these are questions that students love to grope with. Teachers can't teach a cut and dried course in what is ethical and what is not. The subject is far too complex for that. The use of films as the developing curriculum source provides dynamic, relevant discussion data. And, as teachers, what more can we ask of our materials?

FILMOGRAPHY

The Detached Americans. 33 minutes. Black and white. W.C.A.U. Television
Productions (Philadelphia), 1965. Purchase from Carousel Films; check
local film exchanges for rental and libraries for free loan.

The Pawnbroker. 116 minutes. Black and white. Directed by Sidney Lumet, 1965.
Rental from Audio-Brandon Films.

Blow-Up. 108 minutes. Color. Directed by Michaelangelo Antonioni (British-
made), 1967. Rental from Films Inc.

Medium Cool. 110 minutes. Color. Directed by Haskell Wexler, 1969. Rental
from Films Inc.

High Noon. 85 minutes. Black and white. Directed by Fred Zinneman, 1952.
Rental from Audio-Brandon Films, Contemporary-McGraw-Hill Films,
Twyman Films, or Swank Films.

On the Waterfront. 108 minutes. Black and white. Directed by Elia Kazan, 1954.
Rental from Audio-Brandon Films, Contemporary-McGraw-Hill Films,
Twyman Films, or Swank Films.

The Hustler. 135 minutes. Black and white (cinemascope print available). Directed by Robert Rossen, 1961. Rental from Films Inc.

Requiem for a Heavyweight. 85 minutes. Black and white. Directed by Ralph
Nelson, 1962. Rental from Audio-Brandon Films, Twyman Films, or
Swank Films.

Antigone. 88 minutes. Black and white. Directed by George Tzavellas (Greek),
1962. English subtitles. Rental from Audio-Brandon Films.

A Man for All Seasons. 120 minutes. Color. Directed by Fred Zinneman, 1967.
Rental from Columbia Cinematheque (at a very expensive rate).

The Savage Innocents. 89 minutes. Color (cinemascope print available). Directed
by Nicholas Ray, 1961. Rental from Films Inc.

Other Possibilities

All My Sons. 94 minutes. Black and white. Directed by Irving Reis, 1948. Arthur
Miller's morality play about a likable family man whose factory is producing faulty airplane parts raises some interesting questions about double
standards of ethics. Unfortunately the film version is slow moving and talky.
Edward G. Robinson is excellent as the man in question, however. Rental
from Universal 16.

The Angry Silence. 95 minutes. Black and white. Directed by Guy Green
(British), 1960. An exciting film about an ordinary laborer who courageously opposes his union by refusing to strike. In return for his stance, his
fellow workers "send him to Coventry" (refuse to recognize or speak to
him) and a couple of roughnecks beat him so badly that he loses an eye.
Though the film has some provocative things to say, its believability is
marred by making the union's position totally unsympathetic. It seems the
shop steward is getting his orders from an "alien" source and this detracts
from the ethical dispute between an individual and a union. Rental from
Audio-Brandon Films.

The Apartment. 125 minutes. Black and white. Directed by Billy Wilder, 1960.

Billy Wilder's award-winning comedy has something to say about the ethics of the business world. A spineless clerk lets philandering married executives take their girls to his apartment, hoping this will get him promoted. His ultimate personal involvement with his boss' mistress forces him to take an ethical stand. Rental from United Artists 16.

Billy Budd. 123 minutes. Black and white. Directed by Peter Ustinov (British), 1962. Melville's classic tale of a "perfect" young seaman's accidental murder of an evil officer and his subsequent trial and execution was supposed to symbolize a Christ figure. Peter Ustinov's film stresses all of the moral questions of the story, but falls down in the end when Captain Vere (Ustinov) gives his explanation for finding Billy guilty. The final part of the film is too vague and unrealistic. Students I've shown it to can see no point in having Billy executed, though Melville's novel did make it an ethically complex decision. Rental from Audio-Brandon Films or Hurlock Cineworld.

Edge of the City. 85 minutes. Black and white. Directed by Martin Ritt, 1957. This film is very similar to *On the Waterfront*, except for its racial theme. At the end, the portagonist must "put things right" by viciously beating the man who murdered his friend. A useful film for discussing the violent ethic. Rental from Films Inc.

The Fixer. 132 minutes. Color (cinemascope print available). Directed by John Frankenheimer, 1968. This film version of Bernard Malamud's book about a Jew wrongly accused of ritual murder is very powerful. Based on a true incident in Czarist Russia, the film tells the story of a nonreligious Jew's acquisition of faith as a form of strength while being persecuted in prison. His growing faith and his determination not to confess falsely in spite of the consequences can be compared to Sir Thomas More's stance in *A Man for All Seasons*. Rental from Films Inc.

General Della Rovere. Black and white. Directed by Roberto Rossellini (Italian), 1960. English subtitles. Vittorio De Sica portrays an amoral, cowardly confidence man during World War II, who is forced by Italian partisans to impersonate a recently killed heroic general. Gradually the man begins to live his role and he emerges a dignified, moral hero. An interesting, well-made film about how situations shape men's behavior. Rental from Walter Reade 16.

Hamlet. 152 minutes. Black and white. Directed by (and starring) Laurence Olivier (British), 1950. Hamlet's inability to carry out his commitment would make for an excellent comparison with the photographer's predicament in *Blow-Up*. This film version of the play powerfully underscores the dilemma of a man's inability to act. Rental from Walter Reade 16. (*Note:* I have not seen the recent film version starring Nicol Williamson, which is available from Learning Corp. of America.)

I Confess. 95 minutes. Black and white. Directed by Alfred Hitchcock, 1953. A movie about a priest who hears a murderer's confession, which he is obligated to keep silent even though he is later accused of the murder himself, sounds perfect for a unit in ethical problems. Unfortunately, though the film raises a number of discussion-worthy issues about faith and "higher law," it is marred by some romantic complications regarding the priest's former fiancée. A series of flashbacks explaining her involvement in the case detract from the central ethical theme. Still it is worth showing in the classroom. Rental from Warner Brothers 16.

The Incident. 101 minutes. Black and white. Directed by Larry Peerce, 1966. This pretentious film about a group of people terrorized in a subway by two young hoodlums is supposed to be a commentary on the callousness of our times. The predicament is an interesting one, and the apathy of the victims parallels the situations in *The Detached Americans,* but the corny subplots (each individual's life is revealed) and phony dialogue detract from the reality of the situation. I suppose it could be used in a unit on society without ethics, but *The Detached Americans* says more on the subject in less time. Rental from Films Inc.

King and Country. 86 minutes. Black and white. Directed by Joseph Losey (British), 1964. The military equivalent to *Billy Budd* about the sacrifice of a kindly, stammering young soldier accused of desertion. The film concentrates on the plight of the soldier (Tom Courtenay) and his lawyer's attempt to convince superiors not to convict him. Similar in theme to Stanley Kubrick's *Paths of Glory,* which I deal with in Chap. 11, *King and Country* is more of a condemnation of the military than a morality play. But its central figure so resembles Billy Budd as a Christ image that the two films might be effectively shown together. Rental from Audio-Brandon Films.

La Dolce Vita. 180 minutes. Black and white. Directed by Federico Fellini (Italian), 1961. English subtitles. This film is perhaps the best portrait of an amoral society ever made. Its story of the wasteful life of a once-talented writer involved in the decadent "sweet life" of the idle rich is a brilliant intellectual exercise. Marcello (Marcello Mastroianni) wanders from party to party and bed to bed seeking some satisfaction from life. Offsetting his adventures are a series of religious symbols created by director Fellini to demonstrate the meaninglessness of such an existence. The reason I hesitate in recommending this brilliant film is that its tremendous length (three hours) would make it difficult to show in a classroom. Still it could be very effective in a unit with *Blow-Up* and *Medium Cool* if the time to screen it can be arranged. Rental from Audio-Brandon Films.

Little White Crimes. 28 minutes. Black and white. National Film Board of Canada Production, 1967. An interesting short film about business ethics. Concentrating on the rise of an all too typical young executive, it demonstrates his selfish attitudes and conniving methods to get to the top. This film can serve as a useful motivational source for a discussion on the need for some standardized business ethics. Purchase or rental from Contemporary-McGraw-Hill Films.

The Spy Who Came in From the Cold. 110 minutes. Black and white. Directed by Martin Ritt, 1965. A slow-moving, but provocative film about the lack of ethics in international relations. An Allied spy is used to destroy a Communist East German official. The problem, however, is that the Communist is a better human being than the man the Allies hope to put in his position. Richard Burton plays the doomed British spy used as the lever for these maneuverings, who realizes there can be no right or wrong in the business of espionage. An interesting film for discussing the flexibility of our ethical standards. Rental from Films Inc.

Teaching about Social Problems—
A Survey of
the Cinematic Material

A high school teacher must truly be a jack-of-all-trades. Invariably during a semester some crisis arises either within the school itself or in our society at large when the teacher, regardless of his subject field, must deliver that timely, logical, moral lesson explaining the crisis in all its complexity and offer the students creative solutions for it. How many of us, in our social studies, or science, or art classes have groped for something inspirational and exemplary to say when some students are caught with drugs or alcohol on school grounds? A simple "not nice" or "dirty" just doesn't cut very deeply with teenagers. And, how many of us have had to take time to answer kids' questions about causes of violence, police brutality, poverty, and so on? Are we qualified to answer them? When the principal, or the school nurse, or the precinct sergeant tell us to use class time to discuss the evils of vandalism, drugs, or gangs, can we adequately communicate with our students? More and more, we are expected to, and speaking for myself, this task is becoming impossible. I know kids shouldn't take drugs, but I don't have the medical information at my fingertips that can be sufficiently persuasive. Nor am I qualified to lecture on remedies for poverty, hunger, sexual deviation, mental illness, or racism. Yet I am constantly asked to deal with precisely these social problems, and I don't think I am alone in my frustration.

The only concrete suggestion I can make for teachers like myself in such situations is to make use of the vast body of motion pictures that effectively deal with social problems. The purpose of this chapter is to survey the film literature in the various areas of social problems. This chapter's format is more like an extended filmography than an actual classroom unit. I'm assuming that teachers most often have to deal with these problems in terms of a few specific lessons; consequently lengthy readings and discussions won't easily fit. What I hope to do is provide lists of alternate films dealing with specific social problems. The teacher can use one of these (or more) to develop his lesson, and in most cases to present much of the descriptive information on causes and effects.

My division of the "problems" is strictly arbitrary. I have eliminated race relations, crime and law enforcement, and violence since they have already been dealt with at length.

The films listed in all the categories are, in my opinion, the best available. I certainly hope they can come to the aid of teachers who are constantly being pressed for "all the answers."

77

THE EMOTIONAL PANACEAS: ALCOHOL AND DRUGS

Over the years, numerous commercial films have been made to dramatize the horrors of various forms of addiction. Many of these have been "pot-boilers" designed to give an actor a tour-de-force as an agonized lush or junkie. There are, however, several useful short films in this area and a few features that effectively document the totality of the problem.

Alcoholism

Short Films

Alcoholism and the Family: The Summer We Moved to Elm Street. 28 minutes. Color. National Film Board of Canada Production, 1968. Another superbly dramatized piece from the Canadian Film Board, this film documents the life of a nine-year-old girl whose family is constantly moving from neighborhood to neighborhood because of her father's drunkenness. The film is less about the causes of alcoholism than its effects on the family, particularly children. Since the dilemma is seen through the eyes of the little girl, the impact is quite moving. Purchase or rental from Contemporary-McGraw-Hill Films.

David: Profile of a Problem Drinker. 29 minutes. Black and white. National Film Board of Canada Production, 1966. If possible this film should be used with *The Summer We Moved to Elm Street,* since it does document the motivation behind an alcoholic's behavior. David Spear is a respectable man with a good job, a family, and a home. All of this becomes threatened because of his alcoholism. I like this film because, although it does show David receiving medical help in the end, it isn't preachy or condescending. Rental or purchase from Contemporary-McGraw-Hill Films.

To Your Health. 11 minutes. Color. Directed (and animated) by Philip Stapp, 1956. An animated cartoon made for the World Health Organization, which cleverly demonstrates how some drinkers can become alcoholics. Purchase or rental from Columbia Center for Mass Communications. Also check local film sources for rental and libraries for free loan.

Feature Films

Days of Wine and Roses. 117 minutes. Black and white. Directed by Blake Edwards, 1962. For me this is a devastating portrait of the horrors of alcoholism. J. P. Miller's screenplay and the great acting of the stars are tremendously effective. Joe Clay (Jack Lemmon), a comical, happy-go-lucky public relations man, meets and falls in love with a beautiful secretary (Lee Remick). He drinks heavily; she, not at all. Gradually the constant social drinking dictated by his job (and his perpetual rationalization for his unethical work) drives Joe toward addiction. In typical alcoholic fashion, reflecting his basic loneliness and insecurity, he drives his wife into joining him in binge after binge. Soon the two of them become compulsive alcoholics. Scene after scene demonstrates the horror of their plight. (One particular sequence has Lemmon trying to find a bottle he has stashed in a plant in a green house.

Unable to remember where he put it, he hysterically tears the place apart.) In the end he has tried to reform through Alcoholics Anonymous, while she can't bear the thought of stopping. *Days of Wine and Roses* is particularly effective in the classroom since it is so commercial. It starts out as a typical Jack Lemmon comedy with the courtship and marriage of the couple. Thus it becomes twice as horrifying to watch their ultimate degradation. There are some flaws in the film. Motivation isn't always clear, and time sequences change confusingly, but it is still an awesome film. Kids will not easily forget it. Rental from Audio-Brandon Films.

The Lost Weekend. 101 minutes. Black and white. Directed by Billy Wilder, 1945. This is perhaps the best known film portrait of an alcoholic and Ray Milland won an Academy Award for his portrayal. The film still has much raw power despite its age, but it says little about the causes of the problem. I recommend it only if the teacher uses a descriptive short film first such as *David: Profile of a Problem Drinker.* Otherwise, it is merely a good, emotional melodrama. Rental from Museum of Modern Art or Universal 16.

I'll Cry Tomorrow. 117 minutes. Black and white. Directed by Daniel Mann, 1955. The film version of actress Lillian Roth's autobiography was very popular when it was released in 1955. Susan Hayward narrowly missed winning an Oscar (drunk roles as they say in Hollywood are "sure-fire" winners for actors). Somehow it seems stylistically dated and stereotyped as the down and out actress struggles back through the help of Alcoholics Anonymous. Students still may be taken with it; I don't know. The acting holds up, and the star's motives for drinking, while somewhat oversimplified, are shown. Rental from Films Inc.

Drugs

Short Films

The Losers. 31 minutes. Black and white. CBS TV Productions (New York), 1966. A provocative documentary on the perils of all forms of drugs (marijuana, pep pills, goof balls, and heroin). The film leaves many questions unanswered however, and some follow-up research on the part of students should be necessary. Purchase from Carousel Films; for rental or free loan check local film sources and libraries.

Hooked. 17 minutes. Black and white. 1966. One of the better films available on narcotics addiction with a narrative provided by interviews with actual junkies (there is no off-screen narrator). The addicts describe how they become "hooked," the lengths they have gone to to get money for drugs, and the anguish of their condition. *Hooked* is very effective at motivating discussion. Its brevity, however, is a problem, since the issues are not penetrated in much depth. Purchase or rental from Churchill Films.

Drugs in the Tenderloin. 52 minutes. Black and white. NET Productions, 1967. A typically excellent NET documentary, this film explores the world of both addicts and users of hallucinogenic drugs in San Francisco's "Tenderloin" district. Much of it is seen through the eyes of an anti-poverty worker who describes the motives for the extensive use of drugs by the young people in the neighborhood. Most of the dialogue is highly candid. Purchase or rental from NET Film Service.

Monkey on My Back. 29 minutes. Black and white. National Film Board of
Canada Production, 1957. This short film should not be confused with the
sensationalistic Hollywood movie of the same title (which fictionalized the
biography of ex-fighter, ex-addict, Barney Ross). *Monkey on My Back* is
the first-person memoir of a Canadian drug addict, Dick Smith, who
describes his life as a junkie. This film can be used very well with *Hooked*
to provide additional depth in understanding the motives for using
narcotics. Purchase or rental from Contemporary-McGraw-Hill Films.

From Pot to Psychedelics. 32 minutes. Black and white. NET Productions, 1967.
This is an informative study of the controversial nature of drug use (or abuse).
It includes several interviews with "hip" users of hallucinatory drugs, medical
people, and "guru" Timothy Leary. Purchase or rental from NET Film
Service.

LSD: Lettvin vs. Leary. 51 minutes. Black and white. NET Productions, 1967.
This well-known debate between Dr. Timothy Leary (pro) and psychologist-
physiologist Dr. Jerome Lettvin (con) on the hazards and effects of LSD
has the advantage of presenting students with all sides of the controversial
issue. I must add that the logical Dr. Lettvin makes a much more appealing
case against the drug. Purchase or rental from NET Film Service.

Professor Lettvin Tuned In. 90 minutes. Black and white. NET Productions, 1968.
The sequel to the Lettvin-Leary debate, this film focuses on Dr. Lettvin's
candid answers on drug use to questions from an audience of young people.
The film is quite effective in its appeal to youth that drugs merely dull
their judgement in a world so badly in need of it. However, it runs too long,
and I recommend that teachers using it select one reel only to prevent a
saturation effect on the class. Purchase or rental from NET Film Service.

The Circle. 57 minutes. Black and white. National Film Board of Canada Production, 1965. An excellent, candid documentary of the rehabilitation of
addicts at Daytop Village in Staten Island, New York. Parts of this are very
harrowing, demonstrating the difficulty in becoming unhooked. Purchase
or rental from Contemporary-McGraw-Hill Films.

Feature Films

Like the commercial movies about alcoholism, films about drug addicts have
generally sensationalized the problem in order to give some key actors emotionally charged roles. Therefore, films like *Monkey on My Back* and *Synanon* are of
little or no value here. I have only seen three feature films that effectively deal
with drug problems, not counting Sidney Lumet's film of Eugene O'Neill's autobiographical play Long Day's Journey into Night, in which Katherine Hepburn
portrays the mother addicted to morphine. Naturally this drama is about much
more than the drug problem.[1] The three valuable features are as follows:

The Connection. 103 minutes. Black and white. Directed by Shirley Clarke, 1962.
This film version of Jack Gelber's notorious play was released with difficulty
in this country because of its use of the word "shit." However offensive this
might be to some ears, this word is used constantly by addicts to refer to

---

[1] **Long Day's Journey into Night.** 136 minutes. Black and white. Directed by
Sidney Lumet, 1962. Rental from Audio-Brandon Films.

heroin. *The Connection* does not compromise in language or portrayals in presenting a brutally realistic look at a group of junkies. Using a film-within-a-film technique (a patronizing film-maker is allegedly filming a group of addicts waiting for their "connection"—their fix). The addicts describe their problem, some quite humorously but with a tragic undertone. Although the film slips into absurdity on occasion, and there is a weak performance by the actor who plays the heartless pusher, it is one of the most realistic dramatizations of addicts I have seen. Rental from Audio-Brandon Films.

A Hatful of Rain. 107 minutes. Black and white. Directed by Fred Zinneman, 1957. This well-known film of the Broadway hit has withstood age extremely well. It documents with painful agony the life of a former war hero, whose harsh wounds forced a physiological need for drugs. His plight, and that of his wife and understanding brother who spends all of his money trying to pay off the drug pushers, is brilliantly dramatized. The acting by Don Murray as the addict and Anthony Franciosa as his brother is excellent. Students could screen this along with *The Connection* to demonstrate the existence of various types of addiction. Rental from Films Inc.

The Man with the Golden Arm. 119 minutes. Black and white. Directed by Otto Preminger, 1955. This is probably the most famous film ever made about narcotics addiction, with Frank Sinatra in his greatest role. It deals little with the causes of the problem and concentrates instead on the personal life of a junkie trying desperately to reform. It is valuable only as a portrayal of the horror of addiction, but I think it has definite classroom potential to motivate discussion on the causes of addiction. I have not been able to locate a 16-mm distributor of this film.

MENTAL ILLNESS AND RETARDATION

Many documentary films in this area tend to be very clinical and technical in their approach. Such films might be excellent training materials for employees of mental health clinics, but they are not well suited to the high school classroom. Consequently I have limited the listings to a few films that have a wide audience appeal.

Short Films

Breakdown. 40 minutes. Black and white. National Film Board of Canada Production, 1964. This is a dramatized film of a young woman who goes through a severe schizophrenic breakdown. It documents the disintegration of her personality, her treatment in a decent mental hospital, and her road to ultimate recovery. Discussion can be oriented around all aspects of the problem, since the film is quite comprehensive. Purchase or rental from Contemporary-McGraw-Hill Films.

One in Every 100. 60 minutes. Black and white. NET Production, 1968. A depressing but detailed documentary comparing the situations in two centers for the training of the mentally retarded in Canada and England. The film stresses the overcrowded and understaffed conditions that exist in such institutions, but it also demonstrates the compassionate teaching techniques used to train retarded children. Purchase or rental from NET Film Service.

Feature Films

David and Lisa. 94 minutes. Black and white. Directed by Frank Perry (screenplay by Eleanor Perry, from the novel by Dr. Theodore Isaac Rubin), 1962. This film is perhaps the most commercially successful screen treatment of mental illness. David is highly intelligent but deeply paranoid. He fears a human touch, believing it can be lethal. Lisa is almost mute, speaking only in phrases that rhyme. The story of their relationship and the therapy they work on each other is beautifully told. Clinically speaking, students can comprehend David's emotional disturbance more clearly than Lisa's, since the film reveals more about him. Still this is a superb classroom motion picture. Rental from Walter Reade 16.

The Snake Pit. 108 minutes. Black and white. Directed by Anatole Litvak, 1948. The shocking impact this film had in its day is well known. The sensation-alistic melodrama of a woman suffering from inhuman treatment in a mental institution is still (sadly) all too possible today. Olivia DeHavilland's shrieking performance holds up well and the film can be used as an accompaniment to Frederick Wiseman's *Titicut Follies* to show how little things have changed. Rental from Audio-Brandon Films.

The Three Faces of Eve. 91 minutes. Black and white (cinemascope print available). Directed by Nunnally Johnson, 1957. Joanne Woodward won an Oscar with her brilliant portrayal of a woman with three totally different personalities. The semi-documentary style of this true story is very effective. I recommend it particularly for discussion of the motives behind Eve's triple self. Rental from Films Inc.

Fear Strikes Out. 100 minutes. Black and white. Directed by Robert Mulligan, 1957. Anthony Perkins as baseball player Jim Piersall in the excellent dramatization of the athlete's struggle with mental illness. This film is a graphic and detailed portrait of a human being's psychotic agony. Karl Malden as Jim's domineering father is very believable as a prime cause of his problem. Rental from Films Inc.

A Child Is Waiting. 104 minutes. Black and white. Directed by John Cassavetes, 1963. This film about the teaching of retarded children in a special school should be a lot better than it is, especially considering the performances of the youngsters. Although it makes some poignant statements about the needs of the mentally retarded, it too often leans towards sentimentality. Judy Garland's portrayal of an overly compassionate teacher doesn't help much. Still this is one of the few commercial films ever to tackle such an important subject. Rental from United Artists 16.

Freud. 140 minutes. Black and white. Directed by John Huston, 1962. This has to be one of the most underrated films of all time. Montgomery Clift does a splendid job as the great psychologist in his early years, probing the sexual relationship to psychoses. *Freud* can serve as an excellent motivator for any unit on mental health, as well as an exciting view of history. Rental from Universal 16.

The Titicut Follies. 80 minutes. Black and white. Directed by Frederick Wiseman, 1968. A devastating look at the treatment of the mentally ill. Frederick

Wiseman's editorial documentary style (*High School* and *Law and Order*) dwells on the dehumanization of the inmates of the Massachusetts State Institution at Bridgewater. It is almost impossible to describe this place. The patients, of course, are pathetic. The psychiatrists and the guards appear more as tormentors than aids. Often Wiseman lets his camera and sound equipment run beyond speech, particularly in the case of the inmates whose sad, frightened facial expressions are all too clear. The title of the film comes from a talent show put on by the patients—but the real "show" is the tragic environment of the asylum. As one critic commented after seeing *Titicut Follies*—it "tells you more than you could possibly want to know, but no less than you should know. . . ." Rental from Grove Press Films.

SEXUAL DEVIATION

Short Film

The Homosexuals. 45 minutes. Black and white. CBS Television Production, 1968. This is the only documentary for television I have ever seen about a surprisingly large part of our population. The film covers many aspects of homosexuality, using interviews with doctors, religious leaders, law enforcement officials, and homosexuals themselves. Although it doesn't explain enough about the causes of homosexuality (is it biological or mental?), it presents a candid, detailed look at the problems of sexual deviants in our society. Purchase from Carousel Films; check local sources for rental and libraries for free loan.

Feature Films

The Mark. 127 minutes. Black and white. Directed by Guy Green (British), 1961. A remarkable film about a man who had been convicted of molesting a ten-year-old girl (actually he was convicted of intent to molest since he stopped short of the act), and his rehabilitation through psychiatry and sexual adjustment. The delicate subject matter is handled tastefully as the film concentrates on the psychological problems that motivated the man's desire for female children. The acting is superb with Stuart Whitman as the disturbed man, Rod Steiger (with an Irish accent) as his psychiatrist, and Maria Schell as the woman who teaches him the value of normal love. I cannot recommend it highly enough. Rental from Walter Reade 16.

The Collector. 119 minutes. Color. Directed by William Wyler (British, based on John Fowles' novel), 1965. One can interpret this film simply as a horror story—timid, but deranged young man kidnaps a pretty girl, taunts her, and ultimately murders her. Or, it can be viewed as a study of psychotic behavior. I would rather discuss the nature of the kidnapper in terms of his sexual maladjustment. He does not seduce his victim, likening her to a pretty butterfly in his collection. What could have motivated his feelings toward her or others of the opposite sex? This frightening movie doesn't answer these questions, but students seeing it might want to try. *The Collector* is certainly about a most unusual sexual deviant. Rental from Columbia Cinematheque.

Victim. 100 minutes. Black and white. Directed by Basil Deardon (British), 1961.
  A suspense film about blackmail and homosexuality might not seem like
  good classroom fare. However, *Victim* is a surprisingly honest treatment of
  the problems faced by homosexuals. A lawyer who had once had a homosexual relationship with another man attempts to destroy a blackmail ring,
  even at the risk of his own reputation. This film is totally honest about the
  problems facing homosexuals, yet it is tastefully constructed. At a time
  when film-makers are exploiting this hitherto "taboo" subject, *Victim* is an
  example of the way it should be handled. Rental from Janus Films.

The Fox. 110 minutes. Color. Directed by Mark Rydell (based on the novel by
  D. H. Lawrence), 1968. Compared to most of the sickening portrayals of
  lesbianism (*Therese and Isabel, Beyond the Valley of the Dolls,* etc.), the
  relationship between Anne Heywood and Sandy Dennis as two "friends"
  living together on an isolated farm is handled sensitively and believably. The
  story of a man entering their lives, reviving heterosexuality in one and
  destroying the other, is also handled well. Certainly discussions on homosexuality (male and female) are no longer off limits in classrooms, and a
  film such as *The Fox* can provide some insights and raise some significant
  questions. Rental from Warner Brothers 16.

The Boys in the Band. 110 minutes. Color. Directed by William Friedkin, 1970.
  The film version of Mart Crowley's hit play is the most explicit documentation of male homosexual behavior on the screen. Its language is offensive,
  but realistic, and its characters are pathetically believable. Certainly no
  study on the topic could be complete without it. Rental from Swank Films.

OLD AGE

The problems of the aged in a society as dynamic as ours are often disregarded.
The film literature on this crucial subject is seriously limited. Even noncommercial
documentaries are far too few.

Short Films

Aging. 30 minutes. Black and white. NET Production, 1966. A frank, yet optimis-
  tic look at growing old in our society. The film sees the family as the prime
  caretaker of the aged, revitalizing the role of the grandparent. Purchase or
  rental from NET Film Service.

Old Age—The Wasted Years. 60 minutes. Black and white. NET Production, 1967.
  A detailed study of the retired American, pointing out the economic problems and lack of opportunity confronting old people. Purchase or rental
  from NET Film Service.

Old Age—Out of Sight, Out of Mind. 60 minutes. Black and white. NET Production, 1968. This is one of the hardest documentaries to sit through. It
  exposes the conditions of institutions for the aged, particularly the nursing
  homes, which are sadly inadequate. Interviews with geriatric physicians and
  welfare officials indicate how truly bad conditions in such institutions are.
  Very depressing. Purchase or rental from NET Film Service.

Feature Films

Make Way for Tomorrow. 92 minutes. Black and white. Directed by Leo McCarey,
1937. It is possible to look at this film about an elderly couple forced by
economic conditions to live with their married children as simply a portrait
of the problems of the Depression. However, seeing it on television recently,
I was most impressed by the timelessness of its dramatization of the problems
of the old. It is a very honest movie. Rental from Museum of Modern Art.

The Shameless Old Lady. 95 minutes. Black and white. Directed by Rene Allio
(French, based on a story by Bertholt Brecht), 1966. English subtitles. This
is a charming, whimsical film about a 70-year-old woman who decides after
the death of her husband to devote herself to a life of good times and fun.
She ends up shocking her married children, who expect her to act like a
woman her age. Though not especially realistic, *The Shameless Old Lady*
makes some appropriate satirical points about society's expectations for the
aged. Rental from Walter Reade 16.

Umberto D. 89 minutes. Black and white. Directed by Vittorio De Sica (Italian),
1955. English subtitles. One of the saddest movies, this is a bitterly realistic
character study of a nearly penniless, lonely old man. This very moving film
truly communicates the problems of the aged in our society. Rental from
Audio-Brandon Films.

The Whisperers. 105 minutes. Black and white. Directed by Bryan Forbes (British),
1967. Dame Edith Evans portrays a lonely, poor old woman on the verge of
senility (she fears everyone around is whispering about her). Although the
film declines into maudlin melodrama (with the reunification of the old
woman and her wastrel husband after years of separation), Dame Edith gives
a frighteningly real portrayal of the tragedy of old age in our society. It is
significant, I feel, that the film was a financial failure when released. How
many of us want to see movies on this subject? Rental from United Artist 16.

POVERTY

In the past decade, the American mass media have done more to demonstrate
the needs of the poor than any time since the Great Depression. Countless films
have been made for television, many in the great "muckraking" tradition, to
attack the complacency of affluent viewers. Thus the short film literature in this
area is rich, and I have selected some of the best for suggestions. Feature films, on
the other hand, with the exception of the examination of the lives of derelicts in
Midnight Cowboy, have not dealt with the subject much. All of the good motion
pictures dealing with poverty as a social problem (like *Our Daily Bread* and *Grapes
of Wrath*) were made during the 1930s, and I will deal with them in the unit on
the Depression.

Short Films

Hunger in America. 54 minutes. Color. CBS Television Production, 1968. To me,
this is the most devastating documentary ever made for television. When
it was originally shown, my classes spent a week discussing its implications

and following the McGovern Senate hearings on the Department of
Agriculture's food distribution plan. The film documents the unbelievable
problems of hunger and malnutrition facing poor White tenant farmers,
Black sharecroppers, Mexican Americans, and a group of Navajo Indians.
Its impact is ferocious, and no one watching it can go away unmoved.
Purchase from Carousel Films. Check local film sources for rental, or
libraries for free loan.

The Cities and the Poor. 2 parts (60 minutes each). Black and white. NET Production, 1968. A detailed study, including many first-hand interviews with
people in government on the sad condition of urban poverty in this country.
The film concentrates on the cities of Los Angeles and Chicago, indicating
the situations in both (particularly the absence of any decent welfare system)
are typical of most of our urban centers. Purchase or rental from NET Film
Service.

The Tenement. See citation in Chap. 3. A candid, tragic look at life in a Black
Chicago slum.

Uptown: A Portrait of the South Bronx. 27 minutes. Black and white. Produced
by Herb Danska Film Services for Lincoln Hospital Mental Health Services,
1965. A brief, but touching look at an urban poverty cluster. The sound-
track is made up of the residents' voices (no off-screen narration), expressing
their frustrations and their hopes. This is a very revealing statement about
the nature of poverty. Purchase or rental from Contemporary-McGraw-Hill
Films.

The Poor Pay More. See citation in Chap. 1. A revealing film study of the economic
discrimination against the poor.

The Welfare Revolt. 60 minutes. Black and white. NET Production, 1968. *NET
Journal's* documentary on the grass roots organizations in poor communities
struggling for a uniform, decent welfare system. The film effectively portrays
the frustrated voices of the poor and their demands for human treatment.
Purchase or rental from NET Film Service.

On the Bowery. 65 minutes. Black and white. Directed by Lionel Rogosin, 1956.
A classic documentary (winner of international awards) on the problem of
the derelict. The cameras follow three men living in New York's skid row
as they drift through their daily routine. One of the few really honest films
on this subject. Rental from Contemporary-McGraw-Hill Films.

The Marshes of "Two" Street. 29 minutes. Black and white. K V I E Television
(Sacramento, Calif.), 1969. A penetrating cinematic study of a skid-row
neighborhood in Sacramento, with all of the "types" one might expect there.
However, the subject is treated compassionately and the film implies that
some of the responsibility for such social plight goes beyond the unfortu-
nates it portrays. Purchase or rental from NET Film Service.

Appalachia: Rich Land, Poor People. 59 minutes. Black and white. NET Production, 1968. This is one of the most detailed films on the economic plight
of the poor Whites of Appalachia. Focusing on a town in Eastern Kentucky,
the film demonstrates the obsolescence of the coal mining economy and the
lack of a substitute resource. It also presents the plight of a people with
little education or job skills. Purchase or rental from NET Film Service.

Christmas in Appalachia. 29 minutes. Black and white. CBS TV Production, 1965.

A sad, ugly film about the poor of Whitesburg, Kentucky, celebrating Christmas. The film is a bitter look at a depressed community. Try showing it at Christmas time. Purchase from Carousel Films; check local film sources for rental and libraries for free loan.

Feature Film

Hunger. 115 minutes. Black and white. Directed by Henning Carlsen (Swedish), 1966. English subtitles. I almost hesitate to recommend this film about a writer starving to death during a depression in 1890. I have not seen it (I don't know if I could sit through it), but critics indicate it is a graphic description of the decline of the human spirit due to physical hunger. Per Oscarsson won international recognition for his portrayal of the starving man. *Hunger* might be best used to indicate parallels existing in our own society. Rental from Audio-Brandon Films.

Movies and Literature

In virtually every book on film, it is almost obligatory that a chapter on films as literature be included. Somehow educators seem to think that movies as extensions of great novels or plays represent the most valuable use of the medium. Not long ago, a very "hip" English teacher colleague of mine asked me how he could obtain 16-mm prints of *To Kill a Mockingbird, The Good Earth,* and *The Red Badge of Courage.* When I asked him why he had chosen these three, he explained that his students would be reading them in class and he wanted the films for "reinforcement."

Unfortunately, his attitude is all too typical among so many so-called "film teachers." Using films as reinforcement is the very weakest way a teacher could take advantage of the medium. It betrays a lack of faith in film—almost like saying that movies are merely pictures of the prose of a novel, and everybody knows that prose is more valuable.

It is for reasons like this that I at first hesitated to include a chapter on films and literature. I am fearful that teachers will use the cinematic versions of novels and plays that I list here exactly the way my colleague did—to put finishing touches on literature. Therefore, before I begin my list of cinematic versions of print for classroom study, I feel compelled to make a case for some more extensive use of films in the English class than reinforcement.

The film version of a novel or play has for me two basic functions in the classroom. The first of these is as a legitimate substitute for the work of literature. I can see the eyebrows raising already, as if I had just uttered some unspeakable profanity. How can movies substitute for the great prose of a Dickens, or a Hemingway, or (heaven forbid) a Shakespeare?

My answer to such anticipated questions is that in many cases they cannot. However, the teacher of literature needs to set certain classroom priorities. What can my students read, within their ability level? How can I broaden their interests their literary horizons? What do I want them to take away from a work of literature—the beauty of the style or the thematic content? Do I want my class to study one work by a particular author or survey a wide range of his literary output?

Obviously films can answer some of these questions. There have been many great novels and plays made into movies. Some have turned out poorly in this transition, others have been admirably preserved by film, and a few have actually improved because of it. The teacher who has a class of reluctant readers, with limited literary horizons, and who is more interested in content than style, can choose a film from the wide variety of decent literary adaptations available. The major criterion for this teacher's selection should be: Does the film capture the literary essence of the book or play? If it does, then show it. I have already mentioned that the animated film of George Orwell's Animal Farm can make semi-literate students experts on Orwellian philosophy, which they could never begin to read. Sinclair Lewis' Elmer Gantry is lengthy and difficult for reluctant readers, but the film version is fast moving and spirited. Despite certain plot alterations and character changes from one medium to another, there can be no doubt that the film has adequately portrayed the "spirit" of Lewis' work. Why not use the film instead? An eleventh grader forced to read Melville's Moby Dick will probably neglect it until the night before the test and then rush through a college outline synopsis of it—or worse yet the Classic Comic Book version. After all, how many 16-year-olds care about old whaling stories, even if this one is supposed to represent a microcosm of mankind? But show John Huston's exciting, thought-provoking film and much of the symbolic flavor of the novel is impressed on that kid (despite the cinematic and literary shortcomings it may have). Again, it is the priority of the teacher that counts—what do you want your students, even your worst students, to get out of literature?

From the motion picture **Moby Dick**. Courtesy of United Artists.

The second use of films based on novels and plays that I recommend will, no doubt, have more appeal to even the most traditional English teacher. The transmedia study is an interesting and unique way of surveying literature. By this I mean have students read a novel or play and then show the film version of it—not for the purpose of reinforcement, however. The film should be viewed and noted for the ways it treats its prose equivalent. How does the plot change? How are the characters portrayed? In what ways does the cinematography complement or substitute for the descriptive passages of prose? How has the fluid action of the film "opened up" the action of the novel or play? Does the film communicate the attitudes of the author? Does the film distort them? Does it in any way improve on the text?

The transmedia method is a wonderful way to present in-depth literary study in any classroom. It gives students (and their print-bound teachers) the full value of the written work and recognizes the film as a legitimate literary source as well.

The following lists include titles of films based on novels and plays that I have not previously mentioned in the context of this book. All of these could substitute for their literary equivalents if necessary, and they would be excellent for transmedia studies. Works like The Grapes of Wrath, A Raisin in the Sun, etc., cited elsewhere in the book, should, of course, be considered in this context as well.

One final note for teachers of literature. There are two useful books that can serve as further guides in this area. They are:

*BLUESTONE, George. Novels into Film. Berkeley: University of California
    Press, 1957. A very complicated, sometimes ambiguous study on the trans-
    ition from print to celluloid. Nevertheless, it is the only major source of its
    kind.
*SHERIDAN, Marion C. *et al.* The Motion Picture and the Teaching of English.
    New York: Appleton-Century-Crofts, 1965.

NOVELS ON FILM

Listed here are films based on novels that I feel relate to high school students. I realize that there are competent film versions of Wuthering Heights, Pride and Prejudice, and The Last of the Mohicans, but forgive my sacrilege if I say I fully understand why kids dislike them so, and therefore see no reason to discuss them here. Thank goodness there's no film version of Silas Marner!

East of Eden. 115 minutes. Color. Directed by Elia Kazan, 1955. One of John
    Steinbeck's worst novels has been transformed into an exciting, meaningful
    film. Based on only the last third of the book (concentrating on the rivalry
    between Adam Trask's sons), Paul Osborne's script transcends most of the
    heavy-handed biblical analogies and concentrates on personal relationships
    and standards of value. The acting of the late James Dean still looks remark-
    ably good. I recommend a transmedia study here to demonstrate how a film
    can improve on a work of literature. Rental from Audio-Brandon Films,
    Twyman Films, or Swank Films.
Moby Dick. 116 minutes. Color. Directed by John Huston, 1956. Critics have
    severely knocked this film because of the miscasting of Gregory Peck as

Captain Ahab, but that seems very little reason not to show it. Peck is quite good actually, and the script is an intelligent rendering of the mood of Melville's complex novel. As I have indicated, this film will attract more students to the ideas of the author than having them read the book. Rental from United Artists 16.

From the motion picture **The Informer.** Courtesy of Films Inc.

The Informer. 100 minutes. Black and white. Directed by John Ford, 1935.
　　Liam O'Flaherty's short novel is good reading, and John Ford's film, despite its age, is still exceptional viewing. The dilemma of divided loyalties faced by Gypo Nolan is excellent discussion material. An ideal, timely way to use *The Informer* would be to screen it along with the recent reworking of its theme for the Black Power film *Uptight*. Rental of both films from Films Inc.

The Good Earth. 138 minutes. Black and white. Directed by Sidney Franklin, 1937. One of the best film versions of any novel ever made. The characters of Pearl S. Buck's work come brilliantly to life in this beautiful film that just doesn't seem to date. Last year I observed a tenth grade humanities class discussing it. They were studying China at the time, and they responded to the film as enthusiastically as to any exciting new movie. The teacher who absolutely must have the whole novel covered may be annoyed that the film concludes with Oolan's death, which occurs before the book ends. (I heard one teacher register such a complaint.) But nothing can detract from the beauty and power of this exceptional film. Rental from Films Inc.

Elmer Gantry. 145 minutes. Color. Directed by Richard Brooks, 1960. Sinclair Lewis' religious charlatan has been cleaned up for the screen, and the book's plot has undergone several alterations. But this film is so exciting and brilliantly acted (with Burt Lancaster, who reached his professional peak in the title role and has been playing it ever since) that students will be awed by it. Much better than the book. I wish there were a similar screen equivalent to Babbitt. Rental from United Artists 16.

The Sun Also Rises. 129 minutes. Color (cinemascope print available). Directed by Henry King, 1957. I have never seen a totally satisfactory film of Hemingway's works, but this comes reasonably close. The essential mood of the novel is captured with beautiful filming in France and Spain. Tyrone Power is very good as the impotent Jake Barnes, although the casting of Ava Gardner as the nymph-like Brett Ashley (with a passion for bullfighters) and Errol Flynn as the drunken Mike Campbell is a bit too realistic for comfort. Rental from Films Inc.

For Whom the Bell Tolls. 156 minutes. Black and white (the original version was in color but the 16-mm prints are not). Directed by Sam Wood, 1943. This was once considered a great film of a fine novel, but somehow time has begun to wear on both of them. I saw the film again recently and the dialogue (which closely follows the book) sounded pompous and unrealistic. Maybe this work of Hemingway's should be relegated to a historical look at the leftist idealism of the late 1930s. Rental from Universal 16.

Far from the Madding Crowd. 169 minutes. Color (cinemascope only). Directed by John Schlesinger (British), 1966. Critics disliked this visually beautiful film of Thomas Hardy's bloodless novel, but it's really quite good. The trials and tribulations of Bathsheba (Julie Christie) border on soap opera, but that's the novel's fault. The film gives it all some life and believability; and anything that can do that to Thomas Hardy can't be all bad. Rental from Films Inc.

David Copperfield. 133 minutes. Black and white. Directed by George Cukor, 1935. Old, old, old! Teenagers don't exactly identify with this story, and I don't know if this antique film will help much. Personally, I really like it, especially after seeing that mangled television movie version recently with an all-star cast. Nobody can play Micawber like W. C. Fields. But I still don't know if kids will like it. And, on second thought, what's so great about the book anyway? Rental from Films Inc.

Great Expectations. 115 minutes. Black and white. Directed by David Lean (British), 1947. A very well acted film (with John Mills, Alec Guiness, Jean Simmons, and Finlay Currie) based on Dickens' noted novel. This is the kind of film that is such a respectable treatment of a work of literature that it could easily substitute for it. Rental from Walter Reade 16.

Oliver Twist. 116 minutes. Black and white. Directed by David Lean (British), 1948. My favorite Dickens work and one which is still heavily used in secondary schools has been accurately adapted in this film. It is so accurate, in fact, that the anti-Semitic tone of the novel through the character of Fagin (played by Alec Guiness) prevented the film from getting much distribution in this country. The depiction of the slum conditions of Dickens' London is excellent and provides a good lesson in the history of social reform. This is a useful film, affording the teacher many opportunities to discuss the broader implications of its story and theme. Rental from Janus Films.

A Tale of Two Cities. 120 minutes. Black and white. Directed by Jack Conway, 1935. Or 117 minutes. Black and white. Directed by Ralph Thomas (British), 1958. Both films are reasonably good adaptations of Dickens' anti-revolutionary novel. (I wonder how kids react to it today?) Unless you have a passion to hear Ronald Coleman's" . . . far, far better thing I do . . ." the British film is almost as good, film purists to the contrary. Rental of the American (1935) version from Films Inc. British version from Walter Reade 16.

Lord Jim. 154 minutes. Color. Directed by Richard Brooks, 1955. The works of Joseph Conrad are usually difficult for students to read, yet they are rich in meaning. *Lord Jim* has much to say about man's responsibility toward others in terms of conscience and commitment. The motion picture adaptation is beautifully filmed (made on location in Cambodia) and well acted by Peter O'Toole as the conscience-stricken Jim. Often the film oversimplifies the plot, but it is so visually gripping and faithful to the essence of the novel that it can easily be substituted for the book in classrooms. I highly recommend it. Rental from Audio-Brandon Films, Twyman Films, or Swank Films.

Outcast of the Islands. 93 minutes. Black and white. Directed by Carol Reed (British), 1953. I have never read this novel by Joseph Conrad, and I don't know if it is used much in classrooms, but the high critical acclaim for this film indicates that the adaptation is excellent. I saw it on television recently and was impressed with it simply as a motion picture. Rental from Walter Reade 16.

The Rocking Horse Winner. 91 minutes. Black and white. Directed by Anthony Pellissier (British), 1950. D. H. Lawrence's eerie short story about a little boy who mysteriously picks winning race horses while playing on his rocking horse is brilliantly adapted by this film. The film retains the suspenseful mood of the story, tracing it to its tragic end, while also adding depth to the major characters, making the events more believable. This is excellent material for a transmedia study. Rental from Janus Films.

Sons and Lovers. 103 minutes. Black and white (cinemascope print available). Directed by Jack Cardiff, 1960. This beautiful cinematic version of D. H. Lawrence's novel alters some of the basic story line, in many ways improving it. The film vividly captures the feeling of life in a poor coal mining town and the acting, particularly by Trevor Howard and Wendy Hiller, is superb. Since this film stands up so well on its own, it would be ideal for a transmedia study, having students note the delicate changes from novel to motion picture. Rental from Films Inc.

The Innocents (based on Henry James' novel The Turn of the Screw). 92 minutes. Black and white (cinemascope only). Directed by Jack Clayton, 1962. This is the perfect film for a transmedia study. Henry James' weird novel about a governess protecting two children from a couple of ghosts leaves the reader wondering whether the ghosts are real or the woman is mad. The film version implies that the governess (Deborah Kerr) is an aging and prudish religious fanatic, but the suspense is, nevertheless, pulsating. Students should study the film in relationship to its literary counterpart. Rental from Films Inc.

Tom Jones. 127 minutes. Color. Directed by Tony Richardson (British), 1963. Henry Fielding's sexy, funny period piece comes brilliantly to life in this great movie. College classes studying the novel should see the film to demonstrate how good a cinematic adaptation of literature can be made when the film-maker understands the subject. In secondary schools, why read the book when the film tells it all so well? Rental from United Artists 16.

O. Henry's Full House. 117 minutes. Black and white. Directed by Henry Hathaway, Howard Hawks, Henry King, Henry Koster, and Jean Negulesco, 1952. This is a surprisingly good compilation of five of the best O. Henry short stories (The Cop and the Anthem, The Last Leaf, The Clarion Call, The Ransom of Red Chief, and The Gift of the Magi). Each episode is handled by a skilled director and competent "star" cast (Charles Laughton, Marilyn Monroe, Richard Widmark, Oscar Levant, David Wayne, and others) and is introduced by the late John Steinbeck appearing on screen. I saw this film recently for the first time, and I was impressed by the skillful adaptation of some of America's favorite short stories. Rental from Films Inc.

The Red Badge of Courage. 69 minutes. Black and white. Directed by John Huston, 1951. A very good film of Stephen Crane's short anti-war novel about the Civil War, which for some reason was considered a failure when it was first released. Film critic Lillian Ross in her behind-the-scenes book Picture (New York: Holt, Rinehart and Winston, 1952) explains what went creatively wrong with the film. This is an interesting work on the complexities of film-making, but it really isn't necessary for teachers using *Red Badge of Courage*. The film is good enough as it is. Rental from Films Inc.

To Kill a Mockingbird. 129 minutes. Black and white. Directed by Robert Mulligan, 1962. Harper Lee's book is so popular in high schools and reads so well that using the film isn't really necessary. Even in a transmedia study, the film is such an exact interpretation of the book that I would use it only for students with severe reading or motivational problems. Rental from Universal 16.

Ship of Fools. 150 minutes. Black and white. Directed by Stanley Kramer, 1965. Here is a film that has taken a well-written, best-selling novel and changed much of it beyond recognition. Katherine Anne Porter's novel was a bitter portrait of a group of despicable people en route to Germany in 1933. The film's screenplay (by Abby Mann) softens many of the characters and greatly changes the meaning of the story. Still, the film is quite good cinematically and excellent for a transmedia study. Rental from Twyman Films or Swank Films.

The Young Lions. 167 minutes. Color (cinemascope print available). Directed by Edward Dmytryk, 1958. This is another example of a film that greatly alters the characterizations of the novel on which it is based. In Irwin Shaw's book, the character of Christian, the German, becomes more and more despicable as the story progresses. But in the film, as interpreted by Marlon Brando, the German is humanized and grows disgusted with Nazism.

Although the film is slow-moving and heavy-handed at times, it is worth
studying with the novel to examine the significant differences in interpretation. Rental from Films Inc.

The Ugly American. 120 minutes. Color. Directed by George H. Englund, 1963.
The popular Lederer and Burdick novel about the failures of American-Asian
policy is still timely and the film is a moderately successful treatment of the
theme of the episodic book. Concentrating on the sincere but fumbling
American ambassador (well played by Marlon Brando), the film conveys
the book's warning reasonably well. It is no substitute for the novel, but
can be used effectively with it in a transmedia study. Rental from Twyman
Films, Swank Films, or Universal 16.

The Trial. 118 minutes. Black and white. Directed by Orson Welles, 1962. No
works of literature are more fascinating for me than the obscure masterpieces of Franz Kafka. I have often assigned The Trial to my students, who
also find it fascinating. A few years ago I ordered the film version, even
though it was one of the few things by Orson Welles I had not seen. I
assumed that if he made it, despite some negative reviews, at the very least
it would stimulate some hot discussion. Then at the last minute, I had to
cancel it due to lack of funds (a problem I deal with in the last section of
the book) In preparing this book, I have seen the film, and I was seriously
disappointed. It's not that Welles doesn't capture the essence of the Kafka
theme—he does. But the film is so slow moving and poorly acted (particularly Anthony Perkins, who is usually very competent, as Joseph K), that I
cannot recommend it except for those interested in how a cinematic literary adaptation can go wrong (which is a legitimate classroom activity).
Rental from Audio-Brandon Films. *Note:* There is a film version of Kafka's
The Castle. 90 minutes. Color. Directed by Rudolph Noelte (German),
1969. Dubbing in English. This stars Maximilian Schell, but I haven't seen
it and hesitate to recommend it because of my experience with *The Trial.*
Apparently Kafka is very hard to adapt. Rental of *The Castle* from Walter
Reade 16.

The Caine Mutiny. 125 minutes. Color. Directed by Edward Dmytryk, 1954.
Herman Wouk's popular novel has been made into a superior motion pic-
ture, beautifully acted by Humphrey Bogart, Jose Ferrer, and Van Johnson.
This film is useful in a transmedia study alongside the novel and Wouk's
successful play The Caine Mutiny Court Martial. Rental from Audio-Brandon
Films, Contemporary-McGraw-Hill Films, Twyman Films, or Swank Films.

Mr. Roberts. 123 minutes. Color. Directed by John Ford and Merwyn LeRoy,
1955. This excellent film is really based on the successful Broadway play,
but it can also be compared to Thomas Hegan's series of episodes that
comprise his novel. The story, in any form, has much to say about man's
relationship to authority and can well be used in some larger conceptual
unit. And, it is still very, very funny. Rental from Twyman Films or Swank
Films.

The Harder They Fall. 109 minutes. Black and white. Directed by Mark Robson,
1956. I don't know if students read Budd Schulberg's bitter novel about
corruption in boxing, and in the larger sense, life. The film version is
excellent, with Humphrey Bogart in his last role as a fight promoter battling

with his conscience. Students interested in Schulberg's style and who have read <u>What Makes Sammy Run?</u> (of which there is no film) should see this as a further sampling. Rental from Audio-Brandon Films.

True Grit. 128 minutes. Color. Directed by Henry Hathaway, 1969. While not exactly a great work of literature, the novel has a charm reminiscent of Mark Twain and is currently being read in high school English classes. The film can be a useful source, since it shifts the central interest from the teen-aged heroine to the aging U. S. marshal. Naturally this is due to the bigger-than-life figure of John Wayne in the role. Students reading the book would benefit from seeing the film as an example of how the presence of a single performer can change the emphasis of the story. Also the film is visually beautiful and one of the most entertaining Westerns of all time. Rental from Films Inc.

The Heart Is a Lonely Hunter. 124 minutes. Color. Directed by Robert Ellis Miller, 1968. Paperback copies of Carson McCullers' novel about a compassionate deaf-mute are already being used in eleventh-grade English classes in my own school. The film version is a reasonably literal interpretation with Alan Arkin as the mute, Mr. Singer. Though both novel and film may be overly sentimental for some, Miss McCullers' work has long been neglected in literature courses. The film is an example of a great respect for the novelist's style. Rental from Warner Brothers 16.

An Occurrence at Owl Creek Bridge. 27 minutes. Black and white. Directed by Robert Enrico (French), 1962. <u>And</u> *Chicamauga.* 33 minutes. Black and white. Directed by Robert Enrico (French), 1961. The mystical, Civil War short stories of Ambrose Bierce are always exciting reading. These two films based on them are brilliant examples of cinematic literary adaptation. The French director Robert Enrico has captured the spirit and anti-war mood of the tales and has created films that communicate them virtually without dialogue. Both films are highly recommended for fascinating transmedia study. Purchase or rental of both from Contemporary-McGraw-Hill Films.

Champion. 90 minutes. Black and white. Directed by Mark Robson, 1949. This film is based on a short story by Ring Lardner. Using the basic story as a framework, the film expands the narrative about the decline of a selfish boxer into an analysis of corruption in society. This, too, would be ideal for a transmedia study to demonstrate how cinema can be used to expand and open up literature. Rental from Audio-Brandon Films or Swank Films.

Catch 22. 120 minutes. Color. Directed by Mike Nichols, 1970. Joseph Heller's brilliant anti-war novel has been made into a most unusual film. Screenwriter Buck Henry has adapted it faithfully, but his script virtually assumes the viewer has read the book. The film can be used effectively in a transmedia study, with discussion centering on whether it should be able to stand as a separate entity from the novel. Not yet available in 16 mm.

The Yearling. 135 minutes. Color. Directed by Clarence Brown, 1946. Marjorie Kinnan Rawlings' novel has become a classroom standard, particularly in junior high schools. Frankly, unless the teacher has no other books at his disposal for "reading exercise," the film is every bit as good as the novel. Why not show it and have the kids read something else? Rental from Films Inc.

Afterthought

I realize that Mary McCarthy's sex-oriented novel The Group is not exactly classroom fare, and I have few expectations that it will ever be. But anyone interested in a fascinating transmedia study (perhaps in a college film course) would benefit from reading it first and then seeing director Sidney Lumet's colorful film version. As a follow-up to both, students should read critic Pauline Kael's essay "The Making of the Group," in her book Kiss Kiss Bang Bang (New York: Bantam Books, 1968, pp. 83-124). Miss Kael's analysis of the director's alteration of the novel and her criticism of it raise all kinds of questions about artistic license in cinematic adaptation. Both the book and the film may be "trash," but that, too, is a legitimate part of our culture and deserves some classroom attention. *The Group.* 150 minutes. Black and white. Directed by Sidney Lumet (screenplay and adaptation by Sidney Buchman), 1966. Rental from United Artists 16.

PLAYS ON FILM

In my zeal to destroy some of our meaningless educational "sacred cows," I have already noted my opinion that the plays of William Shakespeare should not necessarily be taught for their own sake. When a kid asks why he has to read "that stuff" and a teacher responds that "everyone reads it" or "because it's great," the teacher ought to retire because he really doesn't know his subject (or his kids). If Shakespeare is great (and *some* of it is), then it is because of its rare ability to deal with timeless human problems. To demonstrate this timelessness, teachers might use the plays in conceptual units where they can be integrated into some meaningful context. I have already suggested that *Macbeth* and *Julius Caesar* can serve as portraits of man's selfish quest for power, and *Hamlet* poses relevant questions about ethics and personal psychology. Naturally these plays can also be studied for their impact as drama and their fascinating stagecraft. But let's drop all that meaningless stuff about Shakespeare for Shakespeare's sake. Talk about widening the generation gap . . . .

There are other Shakespearian plays on film that capture the essential drama and benefit by being opened up beyond the confines of the stage. Listed here are a few that English teachers can find relevant use for:

Henry V. 137 minutes. Color. Directed by Laurence Olivier (British), 1945. This may not be one of Shakespeare's most meaningful plays, but it's a whale of a spectacle. Olivier made this version, which features the Battle of Agincourt, during World War II, using horses borrowed from Irish farmers and a papier maché crown. The film did much to uplift the spirit of Britons immediately after the war, demonstrating that art could not be defeated.[1] Students could view it in this context, or simply as a splendid outdoor adaptation of a reasonably entertaining play. Rental from Walter Reade 16.

Othello. 92 minutes. Black and white. Directed by Orson Welles, 1955. Or *Othello.* 116 minutes. Color. Directed by Stuart Burge (adapted by and

---

[1] For an illuminating discussion on the making and significance of this film, see Crowther, Bosley, The Great Films. New York: Putnam, 1967, pp. 165-168.

starring Laurence Olivier), 1966. Students who read the play about the
jealous Moor should see both of these films for a thorough transmedia
study, since they are so vastly different from each other. The Welles film
abridges much of the play and opts for fascinating visual effects. The
Olivier version, in contrast, is almost the complete text and rather stagebound. Students will also want to discuss the interpretation of the role of
Othello, particularly Olivier's, which borders on a hysterical imitation of
Mantan Moreland. Rental of the Welles' film from Contemporary-McGraw-
Hill Films; Olivier's from Warner Brothers 16.

Romeo and Juliet. 138 minutes. Color. Directed by Renato Castellani (British),
1954. This is still the best available version of Shakespeare's famous
romance, filmed in lovely color in Verona (with a young Laurence Harvey
and Susan Shentall). Rental from Walter Reade 16. The old American film
of *Romeo and Juliet* (126 minutes, black and white. Directed by George
Cukor, 1936), is one of those MGM all-star things, with Leslie Howard and
Norma Shearer, and it really looks its age. Except for John Barrymore's
Mercutio, the acting is laughable today. Still, for nostalgists, it is available
for rental from Films Inc. The best film of *Romeo and Juliet* is Franco
Zeffirelli's 1968 hit, but it is not yet available for classrooms. Teachers
interested in transmedia study could have a field day with *Romeo and
Juliet.* There are two film versions of the ballet adaptation, one done by the
Bolshoi Theater Group of Moscow (96 minutes, color); the other with
Margot Fonteyn and Rudolph Nureyev and The Royal Ballet (124 minutes,
color). Both are available for rental from Audio-Brandon Films. Also, for
this kind of study, a teacher could use the recent musical West Side Story
for an updating of the romance. (*West Side Story.* 151 minutes. Color.
Directed by Robert Wise, 1961. Rental from United Artists 16.)

The Taming of the Shrew. 122 minutes. Color (cinemascope print available).
Directed by Franco Zeffirelli, 1966. I don't know why anyone would want
to take this bit of Shakespearean trivia seriously, but the film version
(despite its critical failure) with Elizabeth Taylor and Richard Burton looks
good and moves at a zesty pace. Rental from Columbia Cinematheque.

Electra. 110 minutes. Black and white. Directed by Michael Cacoyanis (Greek),
1963. English subtitles. Euripides' classic tragedy is magnificently filmed
in its actual setting, the ruins of ancient Mycenae. Irene Papas is brilliant
in the title role. The film retains all of the tragic flavor of the play, but
supplements it with outdoor action and the creative use of the camera.
Rental from United Artists 16.

Phaedra. 115 minutes. Black and white. Directed by Jules Dassin, 1962. Students
who read Euripides' ancient tragedy Hippolytus and Seneca's or Racine's
adaptation Phaedra are aware of the shifting from one character to another
as the central tragic figure. This updated film version of the latter plays
would be ideal for screening by students. Although Jules Dassin's film has
its shortcomings, it is a rare example of a modern interpretation of an
ancient play. Rental from United Artists 16.

The Sea Gull. 142 minutes. Color. Directed by Sidney Lumet, 1968. The plays
of Anton Chekov are long and talky and consequently don't film very well.
This movie with a large, international cast (James Mason, Simone Signoret,

David Warner, and Vanessa Redgrave) presents the entire play nicely photo-graphed in color. However, somehow it drags on endlessly. Students reading several of the playwright's works may be interested in this adaptation, but it won't have much appeal otherwise. Rental from Warner Brothers 16.

Becket. 148 minutes. Color (cinemascope print available). Directed by Peter Glenville, 1964. This popular film version of Jean Anouilh's play, with Richard Burton and Peter O'Toole, is exciting and well acted. Every time I see it, however, I find it more pretentious and annoying. It isn't really about the Middle Ages. It isn't really about Archbishop Becket's act of faith (the film merely pays lip service to this). It isn't really about anything, except a bitchy relationship between two men. Students can screen it without read-ing the play (which it improves upon) and discuss the characterizations since they are its content. Rental from Films Inc.

Cyrano De Bergerac. 112 minutes. Black and white. Directed by Michael Gordon, 1950. With a film version this close to the text of the play and so well acted (Jose Ferrer won an Oscar in the title role), there is no reason for students to read it at all. Seeing the film is enough. Rental from Audio-Brandon Films, Twyman Films, or Contemporary-McGraw-Hill Films.

A View from the Bridge. 110 minutes. Black and white. Directed by Sidney Lumet, 1962. Playwright Arthur Miller has never been fully satisfied with any of the film versions of his work, and I tend to agree except for this one. Capturing the somber, tragic mood from Miller's play, the film's location on the New York waterfront sufficiently removes it from the confines of the stage. The story, about a good-natured dock worker who unconsciously loves the young niece he has raised as a daughter, has all the elements of classical Greek tragedy. Rental from Walter Reade 16.

The Crucible. 113 minutes. Black and white. Directed by Raymond Rouleau (French), 1958. English subtitles. Jean-Paul Sartre's adaptation of Arthur Miller's anti-McCarthyist play on the Salem Witch Trials alters its meaning considerably. This film cannot be used instead of the play, but might be useful in a transmedia study examining the French interpretation of a uniquely American work. Rental from Audio-Brandon Films.

Death of a Salesman. 111 minutes. Black and white. Directed by Laslo Benedek, 1951. Arthur Miller's most famous play is not a particularly good film. Although it is faithful to the text, the movie version is heavy-handed and slow moving. Much of the tragedy of Willie Loman comes across as melo-drama. Have kids read the play, period. Rental from Audio-Brandon Films or Twyman Films.

The Miracle Worker. 107 minutes. Black and white. Directed by Arthur Penn, 1962. William Gibson's play is standard reading in English classes where I teach, and the film is a perfect transformation from one medium to another. The drama of Helen Keller and Annie Sullivan is heightened by some brilliant camera work. This film would also be useful in teacher train-ing. Rental from United Artists 16.

The Little Foxes. 116 minutes. Black and white. Directed by William Wyler, 1941. Lillian Hellman's play about a vicious, social climbing Southern family is still very timely, attested to by a recent successful revival on Broadway. The film also transcends its age by presenting a brutally accurate interpretation of the play. The acting, particularly Bette Davis as the evil Regina, holds up extremely well. Rental from Films Inc.

From the motion picture **The Miracle Worker.** Courtesy of United Artists.

Inherit the Wind. 127 minutes. Black and white. Directed by Stanley Kramer, 1960. This film, based on the historical play about the Scopes' Monkey Trial of 1925, is more than a reenactment of history (indeed, it takes quite a few liberties with the facts of the case). It is, instead, an interesting statement on man's right to define his relationship with God in his own way. Spencer Tracy and Frederic March are splendid as the fictionalized Clarence Darrow and William Jennings Bryan, respectively. Rental from United Artists 16.

The Prime of Miss Jean Brodie. 116 minutes. Color. Directed by Ronald Neame (British), 1969. This recent play has been adapted into a splendid film, if you like stories about neofascist, old-maid school teachers. Maggie Smith is excellent in the title role, and the European locales of the film sufficiently remove it from being stagebound. Although it is a reasonably good adaptation of a play, I'm not sure *The Prime of Miss Jean Brodie* will be of much interest to kids. Rental from Films Inc.

Tea and Sympathy. 122 minutes. Color (cinemascope print available). Directed by Vincent Minnelli, 1956. Robert Anderson adapted his own play for the screen, and the result is a sensitive film about the heterosexual awakening of a young man of questionable masculinity. Deborah Kerr is just great as a professor's wife who convinces him of his manhood. This film is so tastefully made and believably acted that it belongs in classrooms for study, in both the dramatic and the sociological senses. Rental from Films Inc.

A "Way-Out" Suggestion

Peter Weiss' weirdo play The Persecution and Assassination of Marat as Performed by the Inmates of the Asylum of Charenton Under the Direction of the Marquis De Sade doesn't read very well (it takes an hour just to get through the title). The recent film version, however, captures all of the absurdity, comic horror, and strange wisdom of the amazing drama. It features the original cast and the text remains intact, except for the ending, which is even more hideous. If a class is studying current trends in drama, this film is a must. *Marat/Sade* (as it is most commonly and affectionately known). 115 minutes. Color. Directed by Peter Brook (British), 1967. Rental from United Artists 16.

PART II

The Movie as the Message–

*Film as a Historical and
Social Object of Study*

10

The Western:
A Mirror of Our Age?–
A Classroom Memoir

In the Introduction of the book I stated my belief that film should be studied as a social entity, as a true extension of ourselves. So far, in all of the units discussed, I have not yet used the medium in exactly this way. Films, I hope I have demonstrated, can serve as remarkable supplements, but outside of pure cinematic analyses, how can teachers use them as "pure" subject matter?

My first experience using films in this way was perhaps my most rewarding as a teacher. Several years ago, my department was trying to work out various units in sociology, since this was the first year the subject was to be taught. For advanced classes, such as my college-bound "humanities" group, this was no problem. They had the skills, it was argued, to grasp the sophisticated concepts of "traditional" sociology. But the other kids, the "average" classes and the "slows" (at my school, where the student body is 100 percent Black, academic tracking is not considered discriminatory), were not supposed to be equipped to grasp such high-level material. (I sometimes wonder who believes all of this academic labeling stuff, anyway.) Each department member was, therefore, given additional flexibility to prepare "relevant" sociological data for his nonadvanced classes. Silly as this must seem (and it does to me), it gave me an opportunity to break in a new stage of film study without the usual reprimands about deviating from the prescribed curriculum.

I decided to take an aspect of our popular culture and explore it with the kids by analyzing why it is popular, why we enjoy it, and how it relates to other forms of behavior in our environment. This kind of study can apply to virtually any subject—humor, religion, sex, violence, etc.—when we examine how the mass media convey it. I chose the Western film because of its immense enduring popularity (the first motion picture to tell a story, *The Great Train Robbery*, was a Western), and because I believe the values it portrays are deeply ingrained in the American social structure. My design was to expose the students to some of the reality of the history of our westward expansion from the post-Civil War period until the official close of the frontier in the mid 1890s. I would then present them with the myth of the cowboy image as portrayed in several Western movies. As a follow up, students would have to explain why the myth was created and what purpose it served the contemporary society.

The class I chose to try this with was labeled as academically "average," which meant the range of student abilities ran from college level achievement to semi-literacy. (Schools with ability tracking systems are notorious for dumping any new admits and recently returned truants into "average" classes, which is a commentary on their definition of "average".) It also had the largest enrollment of any of my classes—38 students, and it met first period (7:50 a.m.). First-period classes at my school are always the largest since it is taken into account that very few will show up. Attendance in such classes is poor and lateness is taken for granted. I was, therefore, doubly anxious to try the unit with this group to see if it would have any effect on improving attendance or curbing lateness.

I began by forming a team of five students (volunteers) to gather materials on the reality of Western history. As I brushed up on my facts (a teacher's reading list appears at the conclusion of this chapter), the kids found several good pictorial histories of the West, and with a borrowed macrolense camera, made slides of the photographs in the books. The pictures captured the somber, barren nature of the Western terrain, as well as the weather-beaten faces of the real pioneers, cowboys, cavalrymen, and Indians.

The kids followed this by tape-recording some authentic Western music and several ballads about the destruction of the Indian, including Johnny Cash's *Drums* and Buffy St.-Marie's *My Country 'Tis of Thy People You're Dying.*

I decided to lecture as little as possible, presenting the material by putting much of the interpretive burden on the students. Therefore, except for one note-taking session at the very beginning on the cattleman's West and the reasons for the extinction of the long-horned steer, I never gave a formal lecture. To illustrate the reality of Western history, the class read the last chapter of O. E. Rolvaag's classic on the pioneers Giants in the Earth. In this chapter, the book's "hero," Per Hansa, finally loses his struggle with the environment he has fought so long and hard to conquer. He freezes to death in a blizzard. The chapter is entitled "The Great Plains Drinks the Blood of Christian Men and Is Satisfied."

The students also read the last chapter of Phillip Durham and Everett Jones' The Negro Cowboys on the West as fiction. This described how Western heroes like Owen Wister's The Virginian were created at the expense of leaving out the contributions of Black Westerners. Since the Virginian was to become the proto-type Western hero (Southern born, tough, but noble at the core), Blacks would merely remind us of part of his less heroic nature. Therefore, although many Afro-Americans participated in the westward movement, they never (until recently with the rise of Jim Brown as an "actor") shared in its romantic mythology. The class also read a reprint on the contributions of actual Black Westerners from the April 1969 issue of *Negro History Bulletin.* Curiously, though I made a thorough search, I could find no film that accurately presented the factual history of the West in documentary fashion.[1]

---

[1] I must note that Contemporary-McGraw-Hill Films does have a documentary from NBC TV's **Project 20** series called **The Real West.** This film, while loaded with excellent accurate photographs of the times, is narrated with nostalgia and gross over-glorification by Gary Cooper, who did more to perpetuate the myth on the screen than any actor except John Wayne. Banjo music and heroic phrases permeate the film, and at the end Cooper, appropriately in the last public appearance before his death, salutes the myth with this decree: "It was rough and rugged and full of hardship, but wouldn't it be fun to start all over again." I didn't use the film, but I realize now it would be perfect to illustrate how deeply the mythology goes.

While they were getting into the readings, I asked the students to state their preconceived notions about what the "real" West was like. Many responded that they were ignorant of the extent of Black participation. Per Hansa of <u>Giants in the Earth</u>, they argued, couldn't possibly star in a Western film. His life had no "action." He didn't even carry a gun. One of the things that surprised me most about their responses was their inability to conceive of winter on the great plains. Many commented that they had never seen it snow or even rain in a Western film, and some argued that it shouldn't, since this would deter the action.

To follow up the readings, I distributed the following quotations I had collected contrasting myth and reality about the West. They included statements from people like Frederick Jackson Turner, Hollywood's John Ford, and Black militant Eldridge Cleaver. We spent two days discussing which of them may or may not be realistic descriptions.

"American democracy is . . . the outcome of experiences of the American people in dealing with the West."

Frederick Jackson Turner—Historian (1903)

"The Great Plains Drinks the Blood of Christian Men and Is Satisfied."

O. E. Rolvaag—<u>Giants in the Earth</u> (Chapter 4)

"Go West young man . . . if you strike off into the broad, free West, and make yourself a farm from Uncle Sam's generous domain, you will crowd nobody, starve nobody, and . . . neither you nor your children need evermore beg of Something to do!"

Horace Greely—Editor of the *New York Tribune* (1867)

"But hurrah for Lane County [Kansas], the land of the free,
  The home of the grasshopper, bedbug and flea,
  I'll sing loud her praises and boast of her fame
  While starving to death on my government claim."

Popular Pioneer Song (1887)

"He loved the trackless wilds, rolling plains and mountain solitudes of our land . . . and has stood as a barrier between civilization and savagery, risking his own life to save the lives of others."

From <u>Deeds of Daring: The Story of Buffalo Bill, the Monarch of Bordermen</u> (a bestseller of 1879)

"I propose that I shall prosecute the war with vindictive earnestness against all hostile Indians, till they are obliterated or beg for mercy."

Colonel George A. Custer (1876)

"I am tired of fighting. Our chiefs are killed. Our old men are dead. Our young men are dying. It is cold and we have no blankets. The little children are freezing . . . Hear me, white chiefs, I am tired . . . I will fight no more . . . forever.

Chief Joseph of the Nez Percé Tribe (1877)

"He is America's Robin Hood. He never fails to distribute his stolen loot among weeping widows about to lose their homesteads. Old men receive his coat in the freezing cold with tearful thanks."

A contemporary description of Jesse James

"WANTED FOR MURDER AND ROBBERY"
JESSE JAMES
DEAD OR ALIVE
$25,000 REWARD

St. Louis Midland Railroad (1876)

"The country needs heroes . . . When the legend becomes a fact . . . show the legend!"
John Ford—Director of over 50 Western films

"The emerging shape of a new world order, and the requisites for survival in such a new world, are fostering in young whites a new outlook. They recoil in shame from the spectacle of cowboys and pioneers—their heroic forefathers whose exploits filled earlier generations with pride—galloping across a movie screen shooting down Indians like Coke bottles."
Eldridge Cleaver, Soul on Ice (1968)

"It's life's illusions I recall,
I really don't know life, at all."
Popular song (1969)

Then I showed the first film, National Film Board of Canada's *Corral*. This brief portrayal of a cowboy breaking and taming a horse did not cause any tremendous enthusiasm among the students. They had seen cowboys break horses hundreds of times on film. (One student said it looked like an extended Marlboro commercial, as indeed it does.)

We began to discuss why they had seen this so often and whether it had any application to the behavior and "action" of Westerns in general. We then explored it as a theme of man combatting nature and always coming out a winner. In Giants in the Earth, Per Hansa was defeated by nature; how many others were like him? Why do Westerns always show man's conquest?

I followed this by having the students present the slides they had taken of the "real" West. The kids were particularly amazed when they got a look at the real pictures of some of the legendary "heroes." Billy the Kid looked like something out of Oliver Twist. And when Calamity Jane was shown, there was a unanimous "Who's he?" Geronimo certainly didn't look like a ferocious savage (he appeared to be about five feet tall). And when slides were shown of other Indians, the students played the tape recording of Johnny Cash and Buffy St.-Marie. Sympathy for the Indians grew, and the class continuously raised questions on the nature of the cavalry and Indian scouts as "exterminators."

It was now time to present the myth. I was able to acquire some funds for rental of feature films from another school project which, though adequately funded, had not been fulfilled (more on this and other sources of funds later). I ordered four feature-length Westerns: *She Wore a Yellow Ribbon, Left-Handed Gun, Ride the High Country,* and *Lonely Are the Brave.* In addition, I assigned the class to watch *Shane,* which was to be shown on television the following week. (I got about 75 percent response on this, which is not bad for a TV assignment.) Each film was to present a particular aspect of the myth: the cavalry, the outlaw, the lawman, the gunfighter, and the cowboy. Each was a quality product from Hollywood with high production values and competent actors. My hope was that by now the students would be able to see beyond the myth and challenge the reasons our society values such portrayals. Then problems arose.

I had no way of showing full-length features in that first-period class. We were together only 40 minutes a day. I couldn't ask them to come in earlier (though by now attendance had greatly picked up and lateness was becoming less of a problem), and although many expressed willingness to stay after school, there were no available rooms. My only choice was to show a reel of a film a day, but that would take weeks. How do you explain to the administration that you're going to use three periods this week to screen *The Left-Handed Gun?* They might bend a little if you were showing a film of a Shakespearian play or *Little Women,* or some other acceptable "literary" thing—but *Left-Handed Gun,* you've got to be kidding.

I yielded to pressure and agreed to show only one reel of each film (except *Lonely Are the Brave,* which I did show in its entirety over a three-day span), choosing the reel that showed most evidence of the myth.

In the meantime I showed a CBS TV *Twentieth Century* program called *The Western Hero,* which had excerpts from early Westerns going back to *The Great Train Robbery* with "Bronco Billy" Anderson. The class roared with laughter at the "corn-ball" antics of old cowboy stars like Tom Mix and Buck Jones, but when the film concluded with scenes from *High Noon* and an episode from television's *Gunsmoke,* they watched with serious attention. I wondered if they really were ready to analyze the myths.

The first feature was John Ford's epic on the cavalry *She Wore a Yellow Ribbon* (I showed the second reel). The students were acquainted with Ford, since they had read a paraphrased statement of his in which he advocated the creation of artificial heroes. The part of the film screened presented a tough, aging cavalry officer John Wayne (who else?) and his troop trying to escort two women to a stagecoach through hostile Indian country. In the course of the action many heroic deeds are performed. Wayne's scout is besieged by about 100 Indians and miraculously escapes by jumping from one cliff to another. A sergeant and his patrol come back from a skirmish, wounded but determined to return and "wipe out the dirty gut-eating savages." A former Confederate captain, now a private in the post-Civil War cavalry, is buried wrapped in a Confederate flag to the tune of "Dixie." All of this is played on the authentic background and visual beauty of the Monument Valley of New Mexico and accompanied by nostalgic choral music ("Yo ho ho, she wore a yellow ribbon . . .").

The class was then asked to compare this to the slides they saw of real Indians and cavalry, and what they had read. The discussions were fascinating and, frankly, I barely said a word. Some complained that since much of the cavalry was Black, the "heroism" depicted should have shown Black troopers. Others argued that the Indians were stereotyped and deliberately made to look savage. One young man indignantly protested that the point was that this was all false heroism anyway, since it meant glorification of the destruction of the Indian. One thing was clear, John Ford's cavalry generated a good deal of hostility.

The next feature was *The Left-Handed Gun,* a fictional biography of Billy the Kid. I had hoped to contrast the heroic depiction of the outlaw (as a kind of Robin Hood—all of our "successful" outlaws, even modern ones, seem to come out looking like that) to his actual sordid history. The great surpise of the film was that it wasn't really a Western at all, but an attempt to create an artistic psychological drama. The first motion picture directed by Arthur Penn (of *Bonnie and Clyde* and *Alice's Restaurant* fame) and based on a television script by Gore Vidal, it was much more sophisticated than the average Western. (I had not seen it before so consequently it was quite a surprise. Today it is regarded as a kind of underground classic.) Still, it did sufficiently fictionalize the story, and Paul Newman, hard as he tried to play Billy as a brutal, if misunderstood, psychopath, came off sympathetically. (One of the girls kept sighing, "Don't you just love Paul Newman," all through it.) The first reel (which is all the class saw) showed how young William Bonney set out to avenge the murder of his employer (a kindly "father image" of a man) by coaxing two men into a gun duel. In the film, he miraculously beats both men to the draw and as the reel ends he is being pursued by a posse with the audience clearly cheering him on.

From the motion picture **The Left-Handed Gun.** Copyright © 1958 by Warner Bros. Pictures, Inc.

Following the film I read the class some contemporary descriptions of the real William Bonney as, among other things, "an effeminate, weasel-eyed back-shooter." Since the kids had seen his photograph, I asked them to reconcile his screen image with reality. Why has he been glamorized so often? Do we get any satisfaction in making our villains sympathetic or heroic? Why choose a hand-some actor like Paul Newman to play such a role?

The class reacted, but not nearly as vocally as they did after the first feature. They obviously liked this film better. They more easily identified with Paul Newman than John Wayne (indicative of our times?). And, they were impressed with the film's "action."

I questioned what they meant by "action." "Shooting," "Fighting," "Hard riding' were stock responses.

"Violence?" I queried. There was a pause. I asked again if they valued violence on the screen and if they did, what are the implications for today's world of war, assassinations, and riots. The discussion ended here. I like to think that their silence was a sign of introspection.

The third film was *Ride the High Country,* a little known, relatively recent (1962) movie starring two former Western hero prototypes, Randolph Scott and Joel McCrea. This one I had seen before on television, and I found it a fascinating portrayal of the spiritual and ethical code of the Western movie lawman. Two old men, former marshals, team together to guard a shipment of gold from a mining camp and escort it to a bank. Their time is passed. The automobile has begun to replace the horse; their eyesight is failing; their legs cramp from riding. Their plight is difficult for the audience to take—especially when it considers who the two actors are (McCrea had portrayed The Virginian and Buffalo Bill; Scott had been both Wyatt Earp and Bat Masterson).

Realizing he has outlived his times, Scott decides to steal the gold as back payment for all of his unrewarded deeds. McCrea, ethical and true to the end, tries to stop him. By the last reel, however, confronted by a chance to defend two young lovers in distress from a quartet of the meanest brothers in screen history, Scott and McCrea team up, as in the old days, and fight for the true code of the Western lawman. In the last scene, McCrea dies, facing west, as his partner vows to go straight, return the gold, and uphold the tradition. It is a Western's Western.[2]

Although I only showed the last reel in class, I was able to show the other two thirds the day before, after school, by coaxing another teacher to take his class to the library. Most of the kids, therefore, did see the whole film.

The discussion here centered on the idea of law and order. Western lawmen have traditionally been known as upholders of justice and are sympathetically portrayed. These two were the best of all time. How can we reconcile our admiration for them *and* Billy the Kid? Why don't we admire today's police the same way? Weren't lawmen the cops of their time? Were they really that noble?

Class response was mixed. Several wanted to know why no such figures were around in Giants in the Earth. Others found the film corny and pretentious. I asked them if they would have thought so a month or two ago if they had seen it in the movies. Again response was mixed, but some said no. At that point one student remarked that this whole unit was "bugging" him and that on Saturday night he had walked out on Jim Brown (who is rapidly becoming the Black John Wayne) in *100 Rifles* because it "annoyed" him.

The last film in the unit was designed to set the class up for the symbolic

---

[2] I must add that cinematically this is a brilliant film. Made by the one director who really seems to understand both Western folklore and history, Sam Peckinpah (whose **Wild Bunch** I'll deal with separately), it has so many qualities it deserves study as an entity in itself.

destruction of the Western hero—to see if we really could live without him. I
showed *Lonely Are the Brave*. Since I have described this excellent film in Chap.
1 and indicated the emotional effect it has on kids, I will not summarize it again.
However, here I showed it in three parts, a reel a day, and I had the students
write brief essays predicting what would happen in the next reel. Except for one
who had seen it before, no student was prepared for the shock of a dying cowboy
and his horse on a rainsoaked highway under a truck full of toilet fixtures.

"THE HERO IS DEAD.
THE HERO IS DEAD.
LONG LIVE THE HERO."

The kids were upset by the ending. "Movies just shouldn't end that way."
"That man should have gotten away."

I tried to tell them, half-heartedly, that Western heroes, including this one,
were phony. What is there to be so upset about? Maybe he got what all movie
cowboys really deserve? (I'm not sure that *I* believe this either.)

Some agreed with my statements when the shock of the film wore off. Others
did not. The unit was now finished.

The final essay was based on the paraphrase of John Ford: "The country needs
heroes. When the legend becomes a fact . . . show the legend. America's heroes
are Western heroes." The students were to agree, disagree, or whatever, in reference to everything they had learned during the past month. Here are some of
their comments.

"I agree . . . , but we need real heroes, not cowboy fakers who kill Indians and are
racists." (Girl)

"Giants in the Earth was real; it had no heroes. I don't need them myself, but most people
won't like this book. To them movies will always be real." (Girl)

"Where was Shane when Per Hansa needed him? On second thought, Shane wouldn't
have been much help. All he could do was shoot." (Boy)

"Black cowboys have been left out too long. Western movies are racist, and I won't waste
my money." (Boy)

"I really think Black Americans need heroes, but true heroes. We can't lower ourselves to
the level of cowboy pictures. Because if we do, we are just as bad." (Boy)

"I always liked action movies. Now I'm not sure what action is." (Girl)

"Why can't we just watch and enjoy?" (Girl)

"I agree with Eldridge Cleaver. We'd better grow up fast. Something is wrong." (Girl)

"Most people believe in cowboys. I don't." (Girl)

"How can we ever see a true picture of the West if they keep making everybody look so
good. Paul Newman should not play a cowboy." (Girl)

"I think Westerns gave us heroes who dare to do things we are afraid to do. That's why
we like them so much." (Boy)

"One thing for sure, if we showed the real Westerners in movies, nobody'd go." (Boy)

"Maybe we are a sick society." (Girl)

The unit was my first real attempt to have kids look at film as an influential
aspect of our environment as both reflection and creator of social attitudes. It
was a beautiful experience for me. The kids' conclusions are some indication, I
hope, of what it meant to them.

POSTSCRIPT

Looking back on the past experiences described in the foregoing, I realize there is a great deal of additional potential in such a unit. Western films have had tremendous influence in American culture in shaping myth and legend. Another approach to concluding the unit might be to have students return to the reality of the West with which the study began. A very realistic Western film could be used at this point to underscore the impact of the myth. Naturally, the problem is that there just haven't been too many realistic Westerns. Some films may "look" authentic, indeed all of the John Ford films have such a realistic atmosphere, but then characters are stereotyped. An example of this kind of film is Ford's *My Darling Clementine,* based on the famous gunfight at OK Corral in Tombstone, Arizona with Wyatt Earp, his brothers, and Doc Holiday on one side against the notorious Clanton gang. The exteriors of the film are marvelous (a half-built church; a dirty, cheesy looking town; Henry Fonda as Earp wearing a handlebar mustache). But the script is pure Hollywood, with Holiday (Victor Mature), a tubercular alcoholic, attempting to remove a bullet from the chest of his ex-girlfriend (Linda Darnell), but losing his medical touch. All of the other film versions of this incident (*Frontier Marshal, Gunfight at OK Corral,* etc.) at least mention the fact that Doc Holiday was a retired dentist, something *My Darling Clementine* omits.

From the motion picture **Hud**. Courtesy of Films Inc.—Paramount Pictures.

There is one film, however, in the Western genre that does present reality. This is Martin Ritt's *Hud,* with Paul Newman. *Hud* is about the modern West, a West of desolate boredom (where big times include rodeos, cheap beer, and an affair in the back seat of a car). Yet the lead character, Hud Bannon (Newman), is a Western individualist in the traditional sense, and he is loathsome. A teacher can do a great deal with this film in presenting Western reality. Indeed there are two fine pieces a class can read after seeing *Hud*. One is Pauline Kael's review of the film in her book I Lost It at the Movies, which points out the realism of *Hud's* West. The other is an article by Larry McMurtry, author of the book Horsemen Pass By on which *Hud* is based, called "Cowboys, Movies, Myths, and Cadillacs: Realism in the Western." This article, by a man raised in the West who has written works avoiding mythology, ends up defending Western movies as entertainment because they are unreal. Screening *Hud* with these two readings would make an excellent conclusion to the unit. Originally I had intended to use it, but the film was not available for the date I needed it. (Always plan your program far in advance.)

I hope I have made my point about using films as social and historical documents. The rest of Part II will concentrate on further suggestions for such use.

STUDENTS' BIBLIOGRAPHY

DURHAM, Philip, and Jones, Everett. The Negro Cowboys. New York: Dodd, 1965, pp. 220-230.

*ROLVAAG, Obe E. Giants in the Earth (novel). New York: Harper and Row, 1927, pp. 424-465.

TEACHERS' BIBLIOGRAPHY

*BILLINGTON, Ray A. America's Frontier Heritage. New York: Holt, Rinehart and Winston, 1967. Standard historical reference source.

*BOGDANOVICH, Peter. John Ford. Berkeley: University of California Press, 1968. A good analysis of the style of one of America's great "auteur" directors. It includes an excellent filmography.

FENIN, George N., and Everson, William K. The Western: From Silents to Cinerama. New York: Orion Press, 1962. A detailed study of the Western movie and an invaluable reference source. Still, it has a tendency to romanticize its subject more than necessary.

GRUBER, Frank. Zane Grey: A Biography. New York: World Publishing, 1970. Biography of the Baltimore dentist whose Western stories became subjects for many films. Grey, like so many of the makers of the Western myth, was a romantic Easterner.

HORAN, James D., and Sann, Paul. Pictorial History of the Wild West. New York: Crown, 1954. Excellent photographs.

KAEL, Pauline. I Lost It at the Movies. Boston: Little, Brown and Co., 1965. See chapter on *Hud,* pp. 79-94.

——. Going Steady. Boston: Little, Brown and Co., 1970. See the reprint of her *New Yorker Magazine* review of *The Stalking Moon* on violence in the Western, pp. 248-253.

*KITSES, Jim. Horizons West: Studies of Authorship Within the Western. Bloomington: Indiana University Press, 1970.

*KOPIT, Arthur, L. Indians (play). New York: Hill and Wang, 1969. This symbolic play on the destruction of the Indian with Buffalo Bill as the ineffectual White "liberal" might be valuable reading as a class project in a unit like this.

*McMURTRY, Larry. "Cowboys, Movies, Myths, and Cadillacs: Realism in the Western" in Man and the Movies, Robinson, William R., Ed. Baton Rouge: Louisiana State University Press, 1967, pp. 46-52.

MYERS, John M., Ed. The Westerners: A Round-Up of Reminiscences. Englewood Cliffs, N.J.: Prentice-Hall, 1969. A good anthology of the writings of real Westerners.

ROSA, Joseph G. The Gunfighter: Man or Myth. Oklahoma City: University of Oklahoma Press, 1969. A readable piece of history thoroughly debunking the fast-draw myth. Students will want to read this too.

*SMITH, Henry N. Virgin Land: The American West as Symbol and Myth. New York: Vintage Books, 1957. The standard historical treatment of 19th century popular writing about the West ("Ned Buntline" novels, etc.). It uses literature much as I hope to use film.

*STILL, Bayrd, Ed. The West: A Contemporary Account of the American Westward Expansion. New York: Capricorn Books, 1961. Useful anthology for quotations of actual historical participants.

*WARSHOW, Robert. "The Westerner" reprinted from *Partisan Review* (1954) in Talbot, Daniel, Ed., Film: An Anthology, 2nd ed. Berkeley: University of California Press, 1966. Warshow's article was one of the first serious appraisals of Westerns as an American art form.

*WEBB, Walter P. The Great Plains. New York: Grosset and Dunlap, 1957. Classic of Western history and very much anti-myth.

WHITE, Edward. The Eastern Establishment and the Western Experience: The West of Frederic Remington, Theodore Roosevelt, and Owen Wister. New Haven: Yale University Press, 1968. An analysis of three Eastern gentlemen who were greatly responsible for romanticizing the West in reaction to Eastern urbanization and industrialization.

FILMOGRAPHY

Corral. 12 minutes. Black and white. National Film Board of Canada Production, 1954. Purchase or rental from Contemporary-McGraw-Hill Films.

The Western Hero. 28 minutes. Black and white. CBS TV *20th Century* series, 1965. Check local libraries for loan.

She Wore a Yellow Ribbon. 103 minutes. Color. Directed by John Ford, 1947. Rental from Audio-Brandon Films.

The Left-Handed Gun. 102 minutes. Black and white. Directed by Arthur Penn, 1957. Rental from Audio-Brandon Films.

Ride the High Country. 94 minutes. Color (cinemascope print available). Directed by Sam Peckinpah, 1962. Rental from Films Inc.

Lonely Are the Brave. See citation in Chap. 1.

Other Possibilities[3]

The Indian

Arrowhead. 105 minutes. Color. Directed by Charles Marquis Warren, 1953. One of the meanest anti-Indian Westerns ever made, with Jack Palance as a fero-

---

[3] These films can be used to further develop the unit.

cious Apache Chief and Charleton Heston as the White scout who defeats him. Rental from Films Inc.

Broken Arrow. 93 minutes. Color. Directed by Delmer Daves, 1952. A pro-Indian movie based on a well-known book about the noble Apache chief Cochise. Extremely well made and with genuine sympathy for the plight of the Indian. However, the good Indians are portrayed by White actors, Jeff Chandler and Debra Paget, and they sound like New England aristocrats. Only Jay Silverheels (remember Tonto?) as the evil Geronimo represents his people with a speaking part. A teacher could use this to contrast with something like *Arrowhead,* but he must point out how both films stereotype the Indian. Rental from Films Inc.

Cheyenne Autumn. 156 minutes. Color. Directed by John Ford, 1964. Ford, whose earlier films killed off more Indians than the entire Seventh Cavalry, really tried to make amends with this version of Mari Sandoz's novel. The film is well done and highly relevant for today's young people. But those Indians—Ricardo Montalban, Gilbert Roland, Sal Mineo—are worthy of more discussion than all the liberalism of the script. Why don't we have any Indian actors? Rental from Audio-Brandon Films.

Hombre. 111 minutes. Color (cinemascope print available). Directed by Martin Ritt, 1967. Paul Newman as a White Indian in a tough, "new-style" film where the Indian is sympathetically portrayed without the platitudes of *Broken Arrow.* Good dialogue and performances as well as excellent use of old Western photographs in the credits. Still at the end, "Indian" Newman saves the Whites by sacrificing his life. Worthy of discussion for its uniqueness *and* its ultimate capitulation to Western conventions. Rental from Films Inc.

Tell Them Willie Boy Was Here. 98 minutes. Color. Directed by Abraham Polansky, 1969. Excellent study of anti-Indian prejudice in the West based on a true incident. The film uses the pursuit of Willie Boy, an Indian, to expose the values of White society. Its major flaw (standard for films about Indians) is the casting of Katherine Ross as a young squaw. Rental from Universal 16.

They Died With Their Boots On. 140 minutes. Black and white. Directed by Raoul Walsh, 1941. No unit on the Indians and the cavalry could be complete without mentioning this extravagant epic on George Armstrong Custer. Errol Flynn plays Custer in what must be Hollywood's greatest whitewash job of all time. Use the film as direct contrast to the actual facts of the massacre and analyze why it is so thoroughly dishonest. Rental from Films Inc.

The Outlaw

Jesse James. 108 minutes. Black and white. Directed by Henry King, 1939. Or, *The True Story of Jesse James.* 93 minutes. Color. Directed by Nicholas Ray, 1957. Both films gloss over the career of one of the most notorious villains of Western history. Take your pick, Tyrone Power (1939) or Robert Wagner (1957) as poor, misunderstood Jesse. Rental of 1939 version from Museum of Modern Art; 1957 version from Films Inc.

Butch Cassidy and the Sundance Kid. 115 minutes. Color. Directed by George

Roy Hill, 1969. Popular, funny movie that updates the outlaw myth and gives its characters human frailties that are quite endearing. An excellent example of today's "hip" version of the outlaw myth. Rental from Films Inc.

The Gunfighter

Shane. 117 minutes. Color. Directed by George Stevens, 1953. A famous film that now seems badly dated. (My students seeing it on television hated it.) The gunfighter legend is given a quietly glamorous, even moralistic treatment. Pioneer families like the ones portrayed here never knew a *Shane.* This could be used effectively to contrast with <u>Giants in the Earth</u>. Rental from Films Inc.

The Gunfighter. 85 minutes. Black and white. Directed by Henry King, 1950. The best film of the genre. A quiet, underplayed treatment of the aging gunfighter trying to reform, but haunted by his past. Its theme has been copied often. Rental from Films Inc.

Warlock. 122 minutes. Color (cinemascope version available). Directed by Edward Dmytryk, 1959. An interesting film about a town that hires several gunfighters (Henry Fonda and Anthony Quinn) to clean it up. When their job is finished, they become the new exploiters of the town. It is unique in that the gunfighters are not portrayed heroically. Rental from Films Inc.

The Plainsman. 113 minutes. Black and white. Directed by Cecil B. DeMille, 1936. The granddaddy of the mythological Western, with Gary Cooper and Jean Arthur as "Wild Bill" Hickock and Calamity Jane. A good activity for a class seeing this would be to have them compare the screen images to those of the real Hickock and Calamity Jane. Rental from Universal 16.

The Lawman

My Darling Clementine. 100 minutes. Black and white. Directed by John Ford, 1946. Wyatt Earp, Doc Holiday, and the lawman myth in a pseudorealistic style. Rental from Museum of Modern Art or Audio-Brandon Films.

Gunfight at OK Corral. 110 minutes. Color. Directed by John Sturges, 1957. More of the Earp-Holiday legend, but played in gaudy style by Burt Lancaster and Kirk Douglas. Typical action Western. Rental from Films Inc

High Noon. 85 minutes. Black and white. Directed by Fred Zinneman, 1952. The best of the genre, it actually portrays the lawman as a human being. He is afraid. Contrary to myths created by Westerns that copy its style, Gary Cooper's famous showdown with the Miller gang is not a fast-draw contest. The film might best be studied in context with the times that produced it— the McCarthyist early 1950s. Writer Carl Foreman had a kind of protest in mind in his script. Rental from Audio-Brandon Films.

"Realistic" Westerns

Hud. 112 minutes. Black and white (cinemascope print available). Directed by Martin Ritt, 1963. Rental from Films Inc.

The Real West. 58 minutes. Black and white. NBC *Project 20* Series (narrated by Gary Cooper), 1959. This should be used to develop the extension of the myth, not as a source of history. Purchase or rental from Contemporary-McGraw-Hill Films.

Will Penny. 100 minutes. Color. Directed by Tom Gries, 1966. A rarity in screen
    Westerns, a believable hero. Will Penny is aging, illiterate, and lonely. Short
    on dialogue, the film "feels" like the West of the 1880s. Beautifully photo-
    graphed. Rental from Films Inc.
The Last Hunt. 108 minutes. Color. Directed by Richard Brooks, 1955. This
    screen version of Milton Lott's brutal novel of the frontier buffalo hunters
    retains much of the realism of the book. It is most interesting in its
    description of the actual killing of buffalo. Rental from Films Inc.
Cowboy. 92 minutes. Color. Directed by Delmer Daves, 1958. An Easterner's
    memoir (Frank Harris) of the West he visited, filmed with quiet dignity and
    without stereotyped heroics. With Jack Lemmon and Glenn Ford. Rental
    from Audio-Brandon Films.

This list could go on endlessly. A suggestion to teachers who want to try this
unit, but are severely limited by lack of rental fund, would be to rent *any*
Western film they can get their hands on. The same effect could be achieved by
renting a grade "D" western with Rod Cameron or Buster Crabbe from a local
film distributor. Some local camera shops operate film exchanges specializing in
these, and they rent as cheaply as $3.00 per film. Universal 16 has plenty of
"cheapie" Westerns at low rental rates. With titles like *The Raiders, Wells Fargo,
Star in the Dust,* and *The Cimarron Kid,* how could you go wrong? The myth is
as plain as day in any of them.

One final note. Obviously there are good Western films, which, realistic or not,
have many valuable things to say. (Indeed even the bad ones have valuable things
to say.) The four features I used in my unit were all quality films and could be
studied quite separately from this type of framework. Still if one wants to teach
about the myth, the sources are plentiful.

Four Faces of War–
A Classroom Unit on American Cinematic Interpretations of War

In June 1968, after some reported reluctance, Warner Brothers released John Wayne's *The Green Berets*, the first honest-to-goodness film propagandizing for a specific war since 1945. Following its opening, the few critics who covered it unanimously condemned it as absurd, oversimplified, and ridiculous.[1] Renata Adler, then daily movie critic for the *New York Times*, found the film totally unbearable. After chastising its falseness and jingoism in her daily column, she wrote a follow-up story ten days later entitled "The Absolute End to the Romance of War." In it she further attacked the clichés of the film and concluded that *The Green Berets* would mark the end of American cinematic glorification of war. In her conclusion to the article she said:

"And that is what is pivotal about *The Green Berets*: whether people will pay admission to it. If so, the fantasy-making machine of war will be losing its grip and everyone will begin to condescend to films. If not, it will also have marked a turning point. Films can devote themselves to the immense and serious problem of finding an imaginative substitute for war . . . . Violence and war simply do not have it any more, except in the nostalgic black and whites. The war fantasy substitute problem is arising on every domestic barricade. For the movies, though, as terminally represented in *The Green Berets*, I think the war is over."[2]

Some time has now elapsed since Miss Adler wrote her critique. *The Green Berets* has turned out to be a big financial success, indicating people did pay admission to see it—in droves.[3] Since *The Green Berets*, films on the subject of war, either anti-war like *Catch 22* or glorifying war like *Where Eagles Dare*, have been huge money-makers. War films have traditionally been popular in this country, and there doesn't seem to be any forthcoming lull in this popularity. Miss Adler to the contrary, the "war" she speaks of is indeed still on.

---

[1] In my research, I did locate one semi-favorable notice in the journal **Films in Review**. The critic praised the second unit battle scenes and the film's conclusion showing a little Vietnamese boy grieving over the death of an American soldier. John Wayne, noticing his grief, places the soldier's green beret on the boy's head. The critic called the scene "quite moving." **Films in Review**, vol. 19, August-September 1968, pp. 453-454.

[2] Reprinted in Adler, Renata, A Year in the Dark. New York: Random House, 1970, p. 190.

[3] This film has only been available in 16-mm distribution a short time, and, according to one of its distributors, it is in tremendous demand for nontheatrical showings.

Students examining the social impact of films need to analyze the nature of the war movie genre. America has been grinding out films about war since the earliest days of silents. Why have our film-makers been so fascinated with the subject? Why do such films have so much enduring popularity? Obviously our country as a war culture—four major armed conflicts in the first 70 years of the twentieth century—has much to do with it. For better or worse, American society has been (and still is) militaristically oriented, and films as reflectors of the culture merely underscore this. Yet there is no one type of war film. *Catch 22* is a war movie, so is *The Green Berets,* and likewise *The Guns of Navarone.* Outside of the depiction of combat (equally bloody in all three films), they have little in common with each other. But all three have been extremely popular. How can we explain this? Do these films appeal to the same audience, or to three different audiences? Which is more representative of American attitudes toward war? Is there a single American attitude toward war?

The unit I am about to propose gives students a chance to analyze the complex nature of the war movie. By screening some of the various types within the genre and examining the attitudes they communicate, students can hopefully take a look at the American character in a new perspective.

For the purpose of the unit, I have arbitrarily divided the war film into four distinct categories: War Films as Propaganda for War, War Films as Nostalgia, War Films as Adventure, and Anti-War Films as Propaganda Against War.

Since I have created these categories, some additional explanation is in order. War Films as Propaganda for War are those that have been made with the direct social purpose of persuading the public of the necessity or morality (or both) of a specific war. These films have either been made when war was imminent or during wartime. The greatest outflow of such movies came, of course, during the World War II years.

The category of War Films as Nostalgia includes movies that were made in post-war periods, reflecting on the heroism, valor, perseverence (and sometimes even fun) of past wars. Such films continue to be made today, looking back on World War II. They often take a pseudohistorical approach, usually demonstrating the achievements of "our side" and the ineptitude of the "enemy." (Recent examples include *The Longest Day* and *The Battle of the Bulge.*)

The War Films as Adventure grouping includes the movies traditionally emphasizing the heroics and excitement of the overwhelming mission into enemy territory in which a few of "our" men at great personal risk and tremendous odds valiantly defeat the enemy. Though fewer of these films have been made than those of other categories, they tend to be the biggest successes at the box office (*The Guns of Navarone* and *The Dirty Dozen* for example).

Anti-War Films, which are also a form of propaganda, make up the fourth category. These are films, which in some way (either through brutally realistic portrayal of battle scenes, or a humanistic understanding of the "enemy", or a realization of fault with our own side) depict the futility of warfare. Such films have also enjoyed some financial popularity, and of the four categories, probably the greatest critical acclaim.

The job of the teacher in a unit like this one is to examine all of the alternatives in the cinematic literature (I have surveyed much of it here for that purpose) and then select some key examples of each phase for classroom scrutiny. It is most important that some of these films be studied in the context of the times that produced them; hence, the ideal place for such a unit would be in the history class. Films propagandizing for war fulfilled a social necessity during World War II, and many of the same critics who praised a film like *Bataan* in 1943 for its strong stance for a united military effort, had equally praised the eloquent anti-war film *All Quiet on the Western Front* during the 1930s for its pacifist attitudes. Each film in this case represents a particular social mood at a specific time.

Of course, this has not always been true. In 1968, the bitterly anti-war *How I Won the War* was released around the same time as *The Green Berets*. And the "action-filled" *Where Eagles Dare* followed in about six months. Consequently, students also need to examine the overlapping popularity of films in all the categories and the reasons for it. (It has often been alleged that anti-war movies have done poorly at the box office, but certainly *Catch 22* and the anti-establishment comedy M*A*S*H have begun to prove that wrong. Yet these have not eclipsed the popularity of nostalgic war movies such as *Patton* or adventure films such as *Kelly's Heroes.*)

The four categories, of course, are merely suggestions. A class could limit this study to one of them. For example, students could examine the portrayal of the enemy in propaganda films dealing with World War I, World War II, and Vietnam. Or, a class could compare such portrayals in pro-and anti-war films.

The point is that war movies have had an enduring popularity among Americans despite basic thematic differences. A study of the content of the various types within the genre can provide some interesting insights into the national attitude (or attitudes) toward war, both historically and now.

A SURVEY OF THE CINEMATIC LITERATURE

War Films as Propaganda for War

In times of national emergency, particularly wartime, it is expected that a country's mass media devote themselves to the goal of exemplifying unity. The movies' first genuine effort at pro-war propaganda came with the outbreak of World War I. During the early years of the struggle, before official American entry, the British popularized their cause here by denouncing their German enemy as "the savage Hun." Posters and publications came into this country depicting the barbarism of this treacherous enemy. Fanned by the national outrage of incidents like the sinking of the *Lusitania* and the *Arabic,* this propaganda is alleged to have had a tremendous effect on the American people. With United States entry into the war in 1917, the American screen began its earliest attempt to persuade people of the nobility of the war. Following the British example of depicting a savage enemy, the war propaganda films were loaded with visual images of the ferocious "Hun." One typical example of this kind of film was entitled *Why America Will Win,* made by the Fox Company in 1918. Supposedly the biography of John J. Pershing, the film concentrates on the general's personal conflict with the enemy. (In one scene, Pershing's wife is terrorized by German agents in a burning house.) In the end the film predicts an Allied victory as

Pershing tells the Kaiser "what's what." While Berlin is leveled by the invading American forces, the film ends with Kaiser Wilhelm being struck by lightning.[4]

Any study of this type of war film should begin with those made during America's involvement in World War I (1917-1918). Unfortunately, very few of these films are in existence today. The one major World War I propaganda film that is available for study is the best known and most successful of the group, D. W. Griffith's *Hearts of the World.* (Griffith's other two anti-German films of this period, *The Great Love* and *The Greatest Thing in Life,* are not available for study. I'm not even sure there are any prints in existence.)

Hearts of the World was made in England with the well-wishes of the American and British governments. Its story, about two lovers separated by the German occupation of a French village, is simple and one-dimensional. The film's real power is its depiction of the Prussian-Hun stereotype. Griffith's Germans are caricatures right out of those British posters. They are murderers, cowards, and defilers of women. They are somewhat like the Blacks in Griffith's earlier success *Birth of a Nation,* since they are total stereotypes without any recognizable human qualities. Students screening this film will probably find the characterization gross and funny. But it is interesting to note that in 1918, with a few dissenting voices,[5] *Hearts of the World* was a huge critical and financial success.[6]

World War II, naturally, provided the largest quantity of pro-war propaganda films. Most of these were of very high quality, and some still hold up quite well cinematically by today's standards. These films all share a tremendous historical importance, which students should be aware of. The teacher needs to point out the deep isolationist sentiment that existed internationally after World War I, particularly in this country. The rise of European and Asiatic aggressors did not sufficiently shake most Americans from their apathetic attitudes. Consequently movies were mobilized, and often with semi-official government sanction they began to bring the message of an impending war to the masses. When war broke out, the motion picture industry consistently upheld the righteousness of the American cause, and this trend continued until the last year of the war, when a few war films with slightly different attitudes were made.

One of the first and probably the most persuasive of the pro-war films of this period was Louis de Rochemont's *The Ramparts We Watch,* made by the *March of Time* Series in 1940. This full-length documentary of the lack of stability in the world caused by German and Japanese aggression is an excellent starting point for a class studying such films.

There were, of course, many commercial feature films produced prior to America's entry into the war conveying a similar preparedness message. Alfred Hitchcock's *Foreign Correspondent* dramatized the destruction of a vicious Nazi spy ring, and in its last brilliant scene, during the bombing of Britain, American

---

[4] Nothing remains of this film today. My information on it comes from an obscure clipping in the Museum of Modern Art's motion picture file.

[5] In Pennsylvania, with its large German-American population, the State Board of Motion Picture Censors ordered that a two-minute scene be cut depicting . . . "a drunken orgy in a palatial German dugout and several unimportant close-ups. All other scenes of Hun brutality will be allowed to remain in the film." **Philadelphia Record,** May 4, 1918.

[6] For a vivid description of the production of the film and its success, see the memoir of actress Lillian Gish, The Movies, Mr. Griffith and Me. Englewood Cliffs, New Jersey: Prentice-Hall Inc., 1969, pp. 185-203.

reporter Joel McCrea broadcasts to the United States about the blackouts caused by air raids—"Keep those lights burning America."

From the motion picture **Hearts of the World.** Courtesy of Museum of Modern Art.

Other films like *Confessions of a Nazi Spy* (with Edward G. Robinson infiltrating a German espionage operation) in 1939 and *Man Hunt* (with Walter Pidgeon as a big-game hunter determined to assassinate Hitler) in 1941 kept the propaganda fires burning until official American entry into the war.

The English, already in the war and with little need to persuade themselves of the necessity of it, exported to America some devastating portraits of their struggle. The documentary *Target for Tonight* (1941) and Noel Coward's brilliant *In Which We Serve* demonstrated on American screens the necessity of the struggle. The United States entry into the war produced a flood of movies about the justice of the American cause and the zealous optimism that despite early defeats, victory would come.[7] Among the best of this series and most representative were: *Wake Island* (1942), *Bataan* (1943), *Sahara* (1944), and *Lifeboat* (early 1944). Any one or all four can serve a teacher seeking an exemplary pro-war propaganda film.

Wake Island was the first American commercial movie to depict an actual battle—the futile but valiant defense of Wake Island by a handful of tough Marines. The fighting is harshly portrayed, demonstrating the brilliant valor of the American fighting men. Brian Donlevy, in one of his most famous roles as the gritty Major Caton, when asked to surrender after two weeks of torturous battle, replies defiantly, "Tell'em to come and get us."

The brave men die as the film ends in the spirit of the Alamo. Imagine the impact of Donlevy's words or the brutal ending on American audiences in 1942. The defeat at Wake Island was a reality, and now the film, with its fictional characters, had dramatized that reality, bringing with it an impact no newspaper headlines could convey.

A very similar film (and cinematically a better one) was *Bataan.* Based on the Japanese victory in the Philippines in 1942 and the heroic stand of a few American military men (all the services are represented) against unbelievable odds, the film again emphasizes the "remember the Alamo" spirit. The fictional servicemen are a microcosm of America. (Their names run the gamut of nationalities: "Dane," "Feingold," "Ramirez," "Matowski," "Malloy," "Lassiter," and a heroic Black man named "Wesley Epps"), and as they die one by one (each more bravely than the other), they symbolize the total involvement of Americans in the war. The last scene has Robert Taylor (Sergeant Bill Dane), the sole survivor, emerging in the morning mist, calling to the Japanese "Come on out in the open and fight!"

Sahara, a British-American film with Humphrey Bogart released in 1944, continued the theme of a few valiant men against a whole army of the enemy. This time the heroes are an American tank crew separated from their unit, a handful of British regulars, and a Lybian Black in the service of the Allies. Together they defeat the Germans by effectively pretending to have water in their desert fox hole, while the thirsty Nazis surrender to them in desperation. In the meantime, the Allies' philosophy is demonstrated in conversations with an evil German and a weak Italian, both prisoners of the small force. In this film, the Allies win, unlike *Bataan* and *Wake Island* (as they had already been victorious in North Africa by the time *Sahara* was released), signifying there will be more victories where these came from. Audiences in 1944 must have been astounded that the Germans had won anything after watching Bogart and his men win in *Sahara.* Students may be similarly amazed.

Alfred Hitchcock's *Lifeboat,* based on a story by John Steinbeck and released in early 1944, is a propaganda film of a somewhat different nature. A British freighter has been blown up by a torpedo from a Nazi U-boat, which has also been destroyed. The few survivors (a sophisticated authoress—Tallulah Bankhead, a rich businessman, a British seaman, two American seamen—one a Brooklyn tough, the

---

[7] The late James Agee, one of America's earliest artistically minded movie critics, reviewed most of these films in the early 1940s. His reviews can be an excellent source in helping teachers select films of this era for classes. See Agee, James, Agee on Film, vol. I. New York: Grosset and Dunlap, 1969., **passim.**

other a "conscious" proletarian, a young nurse, and a Black steward) find shelter in a lifeboat. Soon they take on an unwelcome passenger, a German (Walter Slezak), who turns out to have been the captain of the submarine that put them there. Gradually the Nazi, who began as a prisoner, becomes the master of the others. He plots their course, convincing them that captivity is better than starvation. The others become listless from lack of food and apathetic. They are content to follow his dictates (even the young, angry socialist sailor, John Hodiak, gives up, becoming romantically involved with the wealthy Miss Bankhead, as if to symbolize his decadence).

From the motion picture **Lifeboat.** Courtesy of Films Inc.—20th Century Fox.

The Nazi is as strong as the others are weak. He rows the boat triumphantly as they marvel at his stamina (not knowing, as the audience does, of his hidden compass, water, and energy pills). In one scene he even has them singing German songs. Eventually they find him out and viciously beat him and throw him overboard (all but the Black man, who prays instead. Hollywood in 1944 still liked its Blacks to be as moral as possible). Following some brief discussion that they were stronger than their enemy after all, they are rescued.

Lifeboat caused quite a furor in its day, being accused by noted film critics like Bosley Crowther of the *New York Times* of depicting the enemy as stronger than we were. Crowther's criticism of the film implied that it was subversive.[8] Actually the propaganda in *Lifeboat* is a kind of warning to the audiences of the times that only through strength and unity can we defeat an enemy like the

---

[8] Bosley Crowther, "Adrift in 'Lifeboat' ", **The New York Times,** January 23, 1944.

Nazis. It certainly presents the enemy as a more ferocious adversary than any of the other films of its era.

Lifeboat can work extremely well in a classroom if the students keep in mind that the Nazi's evil is visible to the audience long before it is known to the people in the boat. Imagine the impact on such audiences in 1944. The film's message is that we have to fight this enemy with everything we've got.

As World War II drew to a close, the war film gradually became less propaganda-oriented and more complex. John Huston's documentary short for the War Department *The Battle of San Pietro* (1944) depicted the heavy toll of battle by showing the masses of American casualties and the sad existence of homeless Italian refugees. Two commercial features made just prior to the end of the war demonstrated this changing attitude. Instead of propagandizing the cause, Lewis Milestone's (who made *All Quiet on the Western Front*) *A Walk in the Sun* (1945), and, even more so, William Wellman's *Story of GI Joe* (which had the nerve to show an American "hero" go through a nervous breakdown), demonstrated the effects of war on men and the futility of combat. Both films seem to represent America's weariness with war, and both are almost anti-war in their philosophies.

Students examining the films propagandizing war have rich material to choose from in the World War II era. Since that time, this type of film has been, with one exception, non-existent. There were no major films made to justify and explain America's entry into Korea in 1950.[9] And this is unusual since during the anti-Communist purges of the early 1950s, many Hollywood films were made to describe the "red menace."[10]

The only pro-war propaganda film produced in this country since 1945 has been John Wayne's *The Green Berets* (based on Robin Moore's best-selling novel). There is a snobbishness among critics about this film. Many refused to review it. Those who did, as I've indicated, panned it brutally and haven't mentioned it since (as if they wished it would disappear). The Museum of Modern Art, which has a fairly accurate motion picture file on most films released (clippings, program notes from distributors, etc.) has listings for such cinematic efforts as *The Green Slime* and *The Green Cockatoo*, but no folder for *The Green Berets.* Yet the fact is this film has had (and if 16-mm demand for it is an accurate measure, still has) great appeal for the so-called "silent majority" of Americans.

Personally, I detest the film as much as any of the critics do, but I think it belongs in a classroom for studies of this kind. As the lone example of a defense of a war since World War II, it is an anachronism among today's films. In structure and style, it resembles many of those World War II epics (the individual bravery of the foot soldier, the distinguished Black man, the American compassion for women and children, the enemy as decadent and cowardly—there is one scene of Vietcong officers in full uniform drinking wine—the explicit patriotic appeal) and is even technically superior to some of them. Director Wayne has taken the old formula from *Bataan, Sahara,* and others and dusted it off for Vietnam. No study of the war propaganda film could be complete without it.

---

[9] There were a few "B" pictures made about the Korean campaign during the war, but none really glorified the American effort in the tradition of **Wake Island**. The best known of these was the potboiler on American POW's resisting brain washing in **The Bamboo Prison**, released after the war in 1954.

[10] See Chap. 15.

From the motion picture **The Green Berets.** Copyright © 1968 by Warner Bros.—Seven Arts, Inc.

War Films as Nostalgia

The nostalgic war movie is much like its pro-war propaganda counterpart, except that it has no immediacy. The propaganda films had a specific purpose— to generate unity and patriotism. The nostalgic films have no such goal. They are reflective, romanticized reminiscences of the glory of past victories. As I stated earlier, the films of this category often take on a kind of historical guise—reenactment of a particular campaign or battle. These films tend to glorify war, no matter how brutally they portray the fighting, since their object is always to win sympathy for "our" side as it struggles for victory. The enemy in such epics is the same one-dimensional stereotype prominent in the war-time films, except now he becomes a perennial whipping boy for successive post-war generations. Thus the Jap and the Nazi are still the enemy in war films today, even though World War II has been over for almost three decades.

Nostalgic war movies underscore the glorification of war and need to be examined by students for their impact on audiences.

During the post-World War I period of the 1920s and 1930s, this type of war film was not prominent. Partly because of the success of anti-war movies like *The Big Parade* and *All Quiet on the Western Front* and partly because of domestic social conditions caused by the Depression and isolationist sentiment from disillusionment with war, the audiences of this time were content to have their military instincts satisfied at a distance by the medieval person of *Robin Hood* or the noble legionnaires in *Lives of a Bengal Lancer*. With the exception of an occasional Wallace Beery programmer about the peace-time services, Hollywood's output in this category was rather low.

The only two "important" films with any enduring popularity which reminisced about World War I were *The Fighting 69th* (1940, with James Cagney and Pat O'Brien about the molding of a rough and ready regiment) and Howard Hawks' famous screen biography *Sergeant York* with Gary Cooper as the First World War's most decorated hero (1941). The latter film is still interesting in its portrayal of poor rural folk, and the acting holds up quite well. It is also interesting to watch how Alvin York (Cooper), at first an avowed pacifist, is persuaded by his commanding officer of the justice of the Allied cause. Coming out when it did, in 1941, *Sergeant York* may have had specific relevance for the impending Second World War, even though its subject was the First.

After World War II, Hollywood began to pour out a series of nostalgic war epics demonstrating the power and guts of the American fighting men. The vast number of war films released from 1946 to 1954 in this category is too numerous to mention. There are a few, however, that exemplify the genre.

The Sands of Iwo Jima (1949) starred John Wayne as a tough top sergeant who molds a group of green Marine recruits into a company so tough that it "licks the Japs" at Iwo Jima. The battle scenes in this film are realistic and the acting, particularly Wayne as the tough but lonely sergeant, is uniformly good. But *The Sands of Iwo Jima* is a glorification of a great military victory. In the last scene, as an anticlimax, Wayne is shot in the back by a sniping "Jap." This scene raises audience anger as did Robert Taylor's last fighting speech in *Bataan*. But that was in 1943. *The Sands of Iwo Jima* arouses its audience against an enemy emerging from the dust of Hiroshima and Nagasaki. Students screening it should be aware that it is a post-war film and should question its impact in an era of peace.

The Hollywood reenactment of the Battle of the Bulge *Battleground* was very popular when it was released in 1949. Although directed by William Wellman (who made the realistic *Story of GI Joe*), the film is loaded with superficial characters designed to be "tough but lovable." There is no horror in its battle scenes, which are designed for action's sake. The Germans are the usual one-dimensional villains who naturally get what they deserve in the end. *Battleground* is a perfect example of the nostalgic war movie: exciting, slick, and superficial.

Probably the best of this type of film made in the post-war period was Lewis Milestone's *The Halls of Montezuma*. Despite its heroic title and its stock GI characterizations, the film is well acted and does have something to say about the horrible impact of war on the men forced to fight it. Richard Widmark as a battle-weary officer is particularly effective. Still the enemy is the same blood thirsty Jap left over from *Wake Island, Bataan,* and more recently *The Sands of Iwo Jima.*

The post-war nostalgic movie is evident in Hollywood's output during the late 40s, the 50s, and the 1960s. One of the biggest, most expensive films of this category was *The Longest Day,* which is now available for classroom study. Based on Cornelius Ryan's best seller about the Allied invasion of Normandy on June 6, 1944 (D-Day), the film is an episodic study of the Allied triumph. Intelligently directed, it does show the German high command's counterplanning (in German, with English subtitles), and most of these scenes are quite effective. The film fits the nostalgic category because of its characterizations and casting. Brave officers lonely, "horny" GIs—some scared to death of battle until the actual heat of it where they perform heroically, a philosophical British flyer fearing his next mission will be his last (Richard Burton)—in short, all of the stock stereotypes found in similar nostalgic war films. But this time they are played by major screen personalities. Instead of war movie standards like Richard Jaeckel and Skip Homier as the lonely GIs, *The Longest Day* has Paul Anka and Sal Mineo. The valiant officers are John Wayne, Robert Mitchum, Robert Ryan, Henry Fonda, Peter Lawford, and most other "big" Hollywood names you could think of. The film becomes a veritable "who's who" and whatever realism and history it has to offer deteriorates into a recognition game ("Isn't that Red Buttons up in that tree? Or is it Rod Steiger?").

The nostalgic war film is far from finished as the recent popularity of the film biography *Patton* indicates. This is a strange film. It is brilliantly acted by George C. Scott as the "uncommon" general. The character of General George Patton has always been a controversial one: was he a great hero and military genius, or was he a psychopath in uniform? The film indicates he was all of these things. (He is shown slapping a shell-shocked soldier mercilessly, and he brilliantly leads his men on a magnificent rescue mission during the Battle of the Bulge), but in the end, the audience cannot help admiring the man they have spent the last three hours with. (I wonder whether it identifies with the general, or the actor who plays him.) In the meantime, World War II comes back on the cinemascope screen with all the realism of *Battleground* and *The Longest Day.*

Students can view any of these cliché-ridden films to exemplify this category. Questions should be raised concerning the lasting popularity of such films. In what ways are they similar to the pro-war propaganda films? In what ways do they differ? Why is it that many of the propaganda films included heroic Blacks, while the nostalgic films have no such roles? What attitudes do they project to audiences about war? Do they glorify war?

War Films as Adventure

In recent years some war films have taken on a slightly different tone. Removed from the deadly impact of real war, Hollywood film-makers have begun to relegate the "action" of World War II to romantic high adventure (much in the tradition of films of past wars such as the Civil War or the Indian battles in the West). These films are not realistic, nor are they nostalgic, since few war veterans could reminisce about the daring exploits that are standard heroics in such adventures. Thus, this category of war movies is escapist, and consequently it has been the most successful at the box office.

Screening one of these in the classroom, students should compare the heroic exploits to the action involving soldiers in the previous two categories. They should also concentrate on why something as horrifying as the recent Second World War could be handled on the screen as high adventure.

One of the earliest films of this genre was *Destination Gobi*, released in 1953. Based on a successful magazine serial about a group of Navy weathermen sent to the Gobi Desert in Mongolia for crucial weather information, the film is standard adventure fare. The sailors have to placate some desert tribesmen by furnishing them with saddles, and in turn, the tribesmen aid them in escaping from the

Japanese. The exotic locale and the removal of the incidents from the standard battlefield sequences common to war films make *Destination Gobi* an adventure story during World War II, rather than strictly a war movie.

The most successful films of this category have been the recent expensive productions such as *The Bridge on the River Kwai* and the *Guns of Navarone*. *River Kwai* was supposed to be an anti-war film, and I know some critics have seen it that way. But the fact is that with the exception of the mass killings at the end (when nobody is sure who is shooting whom, and Jack Hawkins observing it shouts "Madness"), the film is very much an adventure story. The characterization of the American prisoner who escapes (William Holden) and who leads the rescue party to return to the jungle prison is pure adventure. And, the publicity for the film during its initial release, and in subsequent revivals, has been to hail it as "the greatest, most exciting adventure ever filmed."

The Guns of Navarone, of course, has no anti-war pretensions. Its story of a group of commandos assigned to destroy some mythical German guns on a mythical Greek island is pure escapism. The exploits of the commandos are designed to keep the excitement high (including the unbelievable scaling of a papier mâché mountain that would frighten Sir Edmund Hillary). The Nazis are the enemy and are played in good stereotyped Prussian style. Naturally *The Guns of Navarone* was a huge success. (It set some kind of rating record when it was shown on television recently.)

Another film in this category, which has enjoyed fantastic success, is Robert Aldrich's *The Dirty Dozen.* This unbelievably violent film about a group of criminals trained by the army to perform an impossible commando mission behind German lines is one of the most skillfully made examples of war adventure films. The direction is top flight, as is most of the acting, but the film's popularity is undoubtedly based on its relentless action (or violence). Shootings, daring escapes, explosions, more shootings—*The Dirty Dozen* is the bloodiest example of this category.

As I've indicated, war adventure films are more and more in vogue for reasons worthy of lengthy classroom analysis. Undoubtedly most students have seen at least one of the films I've just mentioned. The heroics and action in them should be compared to similar sequences in films of the other two categories. The recent success of director Brian Hutton's *Where Eagles Dare* (in which Richard Burton and Clint Eastwood apparently destroy the entire Third Reich) or his more recent *Kelly's Heroes* is certainly indicative that war as adventure is a popular form of entertainment in this country. The question is, why?

Anti-War Films as Propaganda Against War

For an industry as militaristically inclined as Hollywood, it seems rather surprising that there are so many American anti-war films. By definition, an anti-war film is a film that condemns war as wasteful and futile. Often such films are extremely violent, using an overkill tactic to bring home the point that war is brutal. Anti-war films tend to concentrate on characterizations. Sometimes they are self-critical, pointing out flaws in our own military machine. Or, they present the enemy sympathetically as a human being equally caught up in the brutality and degradation of war.

From the motion picture **Where Eagles Dare.** Courtesy of Films Inc.—MGM

There has generally been an assumption among intellectuals and critics that such films are better than those in the other categories because they portray the horror of war more realistically. To a certain extent this is true, though several of the more recent examples of this genre are either overly self-conscious ("This movie is *really* anti-war—look at the arms and heads fly") or painfully over-simplified (the generals in *Paths of Glory* are so obviously evil that they are stereotyped villains devoid of human qualities). An interesting preliminary reading for students examining this category is by a pacifist critic Colin Young in his essay "Nobody Dies: Shades of Patriotism in the Hollywood War and 'Anti-war' Film."[11]

The earliest anti-war films are still among the most effective. King Vidor's silent classic *The Big Parade* (1925) says nothing humane about the nature of the enemy in World War I, but genuinely conveys the horror of modern warfare and its effects on men. Although the acting is now dated, the drama of men in combat is still very effective.

Lewis Milestone's classic film *All Quiet on the Western Front* (1930), based on German author Erich Maria Remarque's novel, is still the greatest of all war movies. The lives of the young German soldiers during World War I are sympathetically and humanely portrayed. These Germans are a far cry from D. W. Griffith's "Huns" in *Hearts of the World.* The film still retains its power, and war has never looked more horrible. Teachers should point out that participating in the film convinced its star Lew Ayres to become a confirmed pacifist (something that hurt his career during World War II).

---

[11]Printed in Hughes, Robert, Ed., Film, Book 2: Films of Peace and War. New York: Grove Press, 1962, pp. 87-110. This book is now available in paperback and would make an excellent supplementary reading for the entire unit.

Since World War II, a number of American anti-war films have been made that tried to recapture the tradition of *The Big Parade* and *All Quiet on the Western Front*. Stanley Kubrick's *Paths of Glory*, based on Humphrey Cobb's novel of the 1930s about the French Army's execution policy during World War I, is skillfully made. Its battle scenes are equal to those in *All Quiet on the Western Front*. Yet despite its technical excellence, *Paths of Glory* telegraphs all of its punches. The generals are self-seeking villains covering up for their own errors by ordering the execution of a few soldiers to serve as examples against regimental cowardice. Kirk Douglas as the defense lawyer for the accused men is the total compassionate hero. Thus, with all of its visual power, *Paths of Glory* becomes a standard story of good guys vs. bad guys, except this time they are part of the same army. Students should compare this confrontation to some of those with the enemy in the films of the other categories.

World War II anti-war films suffer from similar flaws. Carl Foreman's *The Victors* is an episodic screen essay on the evils of war. It follows a company of soldiers through the invasion of Europe during World War II, watching them become progressively degraded by participation in war. Some of its scenes are very effective (especially the execution of a soldier in the snow on Christmas morning, with Frank Sinatra's record of "Have Yourself a Merry Little Christmas" blaring over the public address system), while others are merely pretentious. (In the last scene an American in post-war Berlin meets a drunken Russian on an empty street. The two men knife each other, allegedly symbolizing the continuation of war.)

Cornel Wilde's anti-war film *Beach Red* is similarly self-conscious. Focusing on an American Marine regiment on a Pacific island, the film presents the points of view of both the Americans and their Japanese enemies. This is quite admirable, since it is one of the few American war films that presents the Japanese as human beings. Still, *Beach Red* is top-heavy with flashbacks of the peaceful homelife, and Cornel Wilde, who is not as good an actor as he is a director, is always soliloquizing about the waste of war. This film is without subtlety, and its anti-war theme is, therefore, too feeble to have much effect.

Catch 22, based on Joseph Heller's bitterly satirical novel, is also self-conscious, but deliberately so. It is directly designed for a specific audience—the pacifistically oriented young, who have worshipped Heller's book. *Catch 22* is an anti-war movie for people who are already anti-war. It can have no real appeal for the lovers of *Where Eagles Dare* or *The Longest Day*. As such, it may be useful in the classroom as an example of a growing philosophy. But as propaganda against war, it will win few new converts.

I can recommend two films that have anti-war sentiments, but convey them more subtly, and, I believe, effectively.

The Enemy Below is one of the most sensitive treatments of combat I have ever seen. The captain of an American destroyer, a former merchant seaman, has been cast in the role of killer. He doesn't like his job, but he performs it efficiently, commanding his ship in its duty of destroying enemy submarines. The captain of a German sub, disgusted with the Nazi politics of his country, is similarly tired of war, though he, too, is an expert at his craft. The two ships take turns, stalking one another, and end up destroying each other, as the two officers' mutual respect grows. In the end they meet as they work to rescue the members of their crews.

The Enemy Below doesn't broadcast its anti-war philosophy. Through excellent special effects, the film realistically portrays the destroyer-submarine conflict. The captains (Robert Mitchum and Curt Jurgens) beautifully underplay their roles, and the dialogue is simple and believable.

No one could ever accuse the director of *The Dirty Dozen* of being anti-war, but Robert Aldrich made one film that examined the relationships between officers and men more introspectively than any other in this category. *Attack* deals with a group of American soldiers in France around the time of the German offensive in the Battle of the Bulge. Two lieutenants in the outfit (Jack Palance and William Smithers) are decent, effective leaders, but their superior officer, Captain Erskine Cooney (Eddie Albert), is a childish psychopathic coward. Complicating matters is the colonel in charge of the entire company (Lee Marvin) who has civilian political ambitions and is thus keeping Cooney in his post because the captain's father is a man of great influence.

The plot of *Attack* revolves around the conflicts of the officers over the captain's cowardice. Later, one of the lieutenants is forced to shoot the captain (who is about to force his men to surrender to the Germans at gunpoint) in defense of his men. In the last scene the ambitious colonel, who suspects what has happened, is willing to overlook everything if the lieutenant will sign a requisition stating the captain died a hero. The lieutenant refuses, preparing to turn himself in.

This film takes a brutal look at the manipulation of power within our own military. Its characters are all very believable, including the crazed captain whose unhappy background motivates his actions.

The Enemy Below and *Attack* are the best kind of anti-war films, since they steer clear of the over-kill clichés of that genre. They would be the best examples for classroom scrutiny in comparison with films in the other three categories.

CONCLUSION

In this survey I have tried to point out the vast body of screen literature available for study on the American interpretations of war. The four types of war films represent, I believe, a significant facet of our national personality. Students of history and the social sciences need to analyze the tremendous impact of war on our society. The war film is an important reflection of that impact.

FILMOGRAPHY

War Films as Propaganda for War

Hearts of the World. 180 minutes. Silent. Black and white. Directed by
      D. W. Griffith, 1918. Rental from Audio-Brandon Films.
The Ramparts We Watch. 60 minutes. Black and white. Directed by Louis de
      Rochemont (*March of Time* series), 1940. Rental from Audio-Brandon
      Films.
Foreign Correspondent. 119 minutes. Black and white. Directed by Alfred
      Hitchcock, 1940. Check local film exchanges for rental.
Confessions of a Nazi Spy. 102 minutes. Black and white. Directed by Anatole
      Litvak, 1939. Rental from Audio-Brandon Films.

Man Hunt. 105 minutes. Black and white. Directed by Fritz Lang, 1941. Rental from Films Inc.

Target for Tonight. 48 minutes. Black and white. Directed by Henry Watt (British), 1941. Check local film exchanges for rental and libraries for free loan.

In Which We Serve. 113 minutes. Black and white. Directed by Noel Coward and David Lean (British, screenplay by Noel Coward), 1942. Rental from Walter Reade 16.

Wake Island. 78 minutes. Black and white. Directed by John Farrow, 1942. Rental from Universal 16.

Bataan. 114 minutes. Black and white. Directed by Tay Garnett, 1943. Rental from Films Inc.

Sahara. 97 minutes. Black and white. Directed by Zoltan Korda, 1944. Rental from Audio-Brandon Films.

Lifeboat. 97 minutes. Black and white. Directed by Alfred Hitchcock, 1944. Rental from Audio-Brandon Films.

The Green Berets. 141 minutes. Color. Directed by John Wayne and Ray Kellog, 1968.

Some World War II exceptions (films made during the war but not basically propaganda):

The Battle of San Pietro. 30 minutes. Black and white. Directed (and narrated) by John Huston, 1944. Rental from Museum of Modern Art.

A Walk in the Sun. 117 minutes. Black and white. Directed by Lewis Milestone, 1945. Rental from Modern Film Booking Bureau.

The Story of GI Joe. 100 minutes. Black and white. Directed by William Wellman, 1945. Rental from Mogulls' Film Exchange or Willoughby-Peerless Film Exchange.

Alternative Pro-War Propaganda Films

Why We Fight. A series of documentaries produced for the U. S. War Department by Frank Capra designed to explain the world's events to the American soldier. These films were intelligently made, using explicit narration, newsreel clips, and animation to illustrate the nature of the war. The films in the series run in length from 42 minutes to 80 minutes and include titles like *Prelude to War* (1943), *The Nazis Strike* (1943), *The Battle of Britain* (1944), and so on. The series represents the very best, most intelligent propaganda produced in this country. Most of the films are available for rental from the Museum of Modern Art.

Casablanca. 102 minutes. Black and white. Directed by Michael Curtiz, 1942. This famous romantic film with Humphrey Bogart and Ingrid Bergman is loaded with patriotic sentiment as the hero realizes his duty in joining the French resistance against the Nazis. *Casablanca* is a classic film, and its propaganda content deserves study. Rental from Audio-Brandon Films, Contemporary-McGraw-Hill-Films, or Twyman Films.

All Through the Night. 107 minutes. Black and white. Directed by Vincent Sherman, 1942. A typical home-front propaganda movie with "lovable"

New York gangsters led by Humphrey Bogart (with Phil Silvers and Jackie Gleason) tracking down a Nazi spy ring. Check local film exchanges for rental.

Guadalcanal Diary. 93 minutes. Black and white. Directed by Lewis Seiler, 1943. A standard re-creation of a brutal early World War II battle in which the American fighting man demonstrates great courage against fantastic odds. In the tradition of others of the genre (starring Lloyd Nolan and William Bendix, who appeared in most of them). Rental from Films Inc.

Air Force. 124 minutes. Black and white. Directed by Howard Hawks, 1943. A big Hollywood production, with many battle scenes and a semi-documentary approach. A good example of the constant optimism of the movie industry in war time. Rental from Willoughby-Peerless Film Exchange.

The Bamboo Prison. 80 minutes. Black and white. Directed by Lewis Seiler, 1954. This is the nearest thing to a film propagandizing the Korean War, released after its conclusion. It is actually a grade "B" movie, made on a low budget about a GI subverting a brainwashing scheme in a North Korean prison. Rental from Audio-Brandon Films.

War Films as Nostalgia

The Fighting 69th. 90 minutes. Black and white. Directed by William Keighley, 1940. Rental from United Artists 16.

Sergeant York. 134 minutes. Black and white. Directed by Howard Hawks, 1941. Rental from Films Inc.

The Sands of Iwo Jima. 109 minutes. Black and white. Directed by Allan Dwan, 1949. Rental from Films Inc.

Battleground. 118 minutes. Black and white. Directed by William Wellman, 1949. Rental from Films Inc.

The Halls of Montezuma. 113 minutes. Color. Directed by Lewis Milestone, 1950. Rental from Films Inc.

The Longest Day. 180 minutes. Black and white (cinemascope print available). Directed by Andrew Marton, Ken Annakin, and Bernhard Wicki, 1962. Rental from Films Inc.

Patton. 175 minutes. Color (cinemascope print available). Directed by Franklin J. Schaffner, 1970. Rental from Films Inc.

Alternative Nostalgic War Films

What Price Glory? 116 minutes. Silent. Black and white. Directed by Raoul Walsh, 1926. Based on the famous play about the comradeship among Marines during the First World War, this film was supposed to have been anti-war. Despite showing some of the horrors of battle, it actually celebrates the military way of life. The sound version of this film made by John Ford in 1952 is currently not available in 16 mm. Rental of the silent version from Museum of Modern Art.

The Frogmen. 96 minutes. Black and white. Directed by Lloyd Bacon, 1951. A heroically oriented film about underwater demolition experts battling evil Japs. Rental from Films Inc.

Go for Broke. 92 minutes. Black and white. Directed by Robert Pirosh, 1951. A standard GI epic in the tradition of *Battleground* (with Van Johnson), except this time the one-dimensional soldiers are Japanese-Americans in Europe fighting the Nazis. Meant as a tribute to the Nisei soldiers, who were heroic in battle, the film never discusses any of the social issues involving Japanese-Americans. The Oriental actors merely play the stock William Bendix, Richard Jaeckel stereotype GIs. Rental from Films Inc.

The Flying Leathernecks. 102 minutes. Color. Directed by Nicholas Ray, 1951. John Wayne and Robert Ryan as tough Marine fighter pilots against the Japs. Typical of the crop of these films in the early 1950s. Rental from Audio-Brandon Films.

To Hell and Back. 106 minutes. Color. Directed by Jesse Hibbs, 1955. War hero Audie Murphy's story (starring Murphy) details his heroics while surrounding him with stock military types and the evil German enemy. Rental from Universal 16.

In Harm's Way. 165 minutes. Black and white (cinemascope print available). Directed by Otto Preminger, 1965. A genuine throwback to the *Sands of Iwo Jima,* this totally nostalgic view of World War II with John Wayne and Kirk Douglas would have been an efficient propaganda film, if it hadn't been made in 1965. This one has to be seen to be believed. Terrible, but typical. Rental from Films Inc.

The Battle of the Bulge. 140 minutes. Color. Directed by Ken Annakin, 1965. A semi-documentary attempt to recreate the famous battle, this film is not as cliché-ridden as *Battleground,* but is still very typical of this genre. Rental from Twyman Films or Swank Films.

War as Adventure Films

Destination Gobi. 89 minutes. Color. Directed by Robert Wise, 1953. Rental from Films Inc.

The Bridge on the River Kwai. 161 minutes. Color. Directed by David Lean (British), 1957. Rental from Audio-Brandon Films, Contemporary-McGraw-Hill Films, Twyman Films, or Swank Films.

The Guns of Navarone. 155 minutes. Color. Directed by J. Lee Thompson, 1961. Rental from Audio-Brandon Films, Twyman Films, or Swank Films.

The Dirty Dozen. 140 minutes. Color. Directed by Robert Aldrich, 1967. Rental from Films Inc.

Where Eagles Dare. 158 minutes. Color (cinemascope print available). Directed by Brian Hutton, 1969. Rental from Films Inc.

Kelly's Heroes. 146 minutes. Color. Directed by Brian Hutton, 1970. Rental from Films Inc.

Alternative War as Adventure Films

Operation Crossbow. 116 minutes. Color (cinemascope print available). Directed by Michael Anderson, 1965. A standard heroically daring mission with three Allied agents sent behind German lines to destroy underground missiles. Rental from Films Inc.

Von Ryan's Express. 117 minutes. Color (cinemascope print available). Directed
by Mark Robson, 1965. Based on the best-selling novel, this film is about
an American Air Force colonel who leads a massive escape from a Nazi
prison in Italy. He steals a train and most of the film traces the pursuit by
the Nazis. Frank Sinatra is Frank Sinatra as the brave colonel. Rental from
Films Inc.

Anti-War Films as Propaganda Against War

The Big Parade. 130 minutes. Silent. Black and white. Directed by King Vidor,
1925. Rental from Films Inc.
All Quiet on the Western Front. 105 minutes. Black and white. Directed by Lewis
Milestone, 1930. Rental from Universal 16.
Paths of Glory. 86 minutes. Black and white. Directed by Stanley Kubrick, 1957.
Rental from United Artists 16.
The Victors. 175 minutes. Black and white. Directed by Carl Foreman, 1963.
Rental from Audio-Brandon Films, Twyman Films, or Swank Films.
Beach Red. 103 minutes. Color. Directed by Cornel Wilde, 1967. Rental from
United Artists 16.
The Enemy Below. 98 minutes. Color (cinemascope print available). Directed by
Dick Powell, 1957. Rental from Films Inc.
Attack. 107 minutes. Black and white. Directed by Robert Aldrich, 1956. Rental
from United Artists 16.
Catch 22. 120 minutes. Color. Directed by Mike Nichols, 1970. Not yet available
in nontheatrical release. Watch for it.

Alternative Anti-War Films

The Grand Illusion. 111 minutes. Black and white. Directed by Jean Renoir
(French), 1937. English subtitles. The classic drama of understanding
between French prisoners and their German jailer during World War I is
still an eloquent plea against the insanity of war. Rental from Janus Films.
Decision Before Dawn. 119 minutes. Black and white. Directed by Anatole
Litvak, 1951. A brilliant film about a German prisoner who decides to
work for the Allies against the Nazis. Oscar Werner's portrayal of the
German helps to destroy many of the post-war "nostalgia" films. Rental
from Films Inc.
None but the Brave. 105 minutes. Color. Directed by Frank Sinatra, 1966. An
awkward film, with its heart in the right place, about the coexistence of
American and Japanese platoons on a deserted island. It has some interesting moments, and the Japanese actors are fine; but it eventually deteriorates into a standard war movie. Rental from Warner Brothers 16.
The Americanization of Emily. 115 minutes. Black and white. Directed by
Arthur Hiller, 1964. Three quarters of this comedy-drama about a man
who'll do anything to keep out of combat is both funny and significant.
Somehow the ending deteriorates the effect by turning this beautiful
coward into a hero. Despite the copout, this is an interesting film for
students. Rental from Films Inc.

How I Won the War. 111 minutes. Color. Directed by Richard Lester (British), 1968. I have not seen this film, which never received much of a run in this country, but I have been informed that is a well-made satire on the futility of war. I also understand it is quite violent. Rental from United Artists 16.

Oh! What a Lovely War. 139 minutes. Color (cinemascope print available). Directed by Richard Attenborough (British), 1969. This excellent musical satire on World War I is a fairly effective condemnation of war. Its major value for the classroom, however, is in its vivid historical recreation through song and dialogue of the era of the First World War. Rental from Films Inc.

In the Year of the Pig. 101 minutes. Black and white. Directed by Emilio de Antonio, 1969. An intelligent, pointed documentary about American involvement in Vietnam. It is thoroughly anti-war, but it stops short of being pure polemic. Rental from Contemporary-McGraw-Hill Films.

How Dark Is a Dark Continent?–
Myths about Tropical Africa Created by Motion Pictures

In 1931 a distinguished film critic wrote of W. S. Van Dyke's *Trader Horn,* "Here is romance for you, real romance . . . of menacing jungles, roaring lions, rivers swarming with crocodiles and shrieking black savages ruled by a white goddess with beautiful golden hair. . . ."

The first full-length American film made in Africa had been released. It promised thrills, fast action, brutality, and suspense. The "dark continent" had been conquered by the Hollywood movie crew. Now it could all be shown—Africa at her "savage" best. As the critic above indicated, nothing fell short of expectation. Edgar Rice Burroughs would have been proud.

As a child I missed the *Trader Horn* generation by at least 15 years, and I never saw any of the earliest *Tarzan* epics (silent or sound) until quite recently. Yet I grew up, as did most of us, with the picture in my mind of Africa as some far off, hot jungle teeming with ferocious animals and inhabited by savage black warriors. Growing up in the TV age, I remember staring daily at the 12-inch screen that featured *Ramar of the Jungle* and the old Hollywood serials *Adventures of Clyde Beatty* and *Tim Tyler's Luck.*

My taste in movies was on a somewhat higher level, since Tarzan films seemed to me childish, and so I was always treated to the really "big" African epics. *King Solomon's Mines* and *Mogambo* were two of my favorites. These, after all, were the authentic "stuff," actually made in Africa. The jungles, the lions, the black savages—all were real.

Of course it wasn't all mystery and adventure. I realized that those poor "Africans" needed clothing, food, and medical care. I remember seeing a documentary on the great work of Dr. Albert Schweitzer and his hospitals, and greatly admiring the bravery of the missionaries who risked their lives to help those poor deprived black souls. I couldn't imagine why those savages would want to turn and kill such kind people. But they did. The Mau Mau came out of the jungle and destroyed his White friends. I know; I saw him do it in *Simba, Safari,* and *Something of Value.*

Being a child of the media, I absorbed what I saw and believed it. And I concluded (as I believe many of us have) that Africa spawned a savage people, a lower form of life. How could the American descendants of such people be expected to turn out much better?

Today I teach African and Afro-American history. Each semester I begin my course with a word association game with my students. I say "Africa" and point to one of them to respond. "Jungle," "Savage," "Spear," "Dark continent," "Tarzan," "Lions," and so on, just as I'd have answered five years ago. Admittedly, Black high school students have attained some degree of sophistication about this from the "movement," and from a few I hear "Black," "Cultured," "Motherland," "Civilized," etc. However, most of their responses are stereotyped. I played the same game with White kids last spring, and the concepts were even more mono-lithic.

My teaching, following this diagnostic exercise to sound out their ideas on Africa, is thus oriented to the explosion of the myth and to the presentation of reality. However, our media still bombard us with so much myth, that reality is hard to get at and believe. Recently a very popular film among the kids I teach was *Dark of the Sun* with Jim Brown. Allegedly about the crisis in the Congo, this film made no attempt to deal with political issues, concentrating instead on the rescue of Whites from savage rebels. The same old story but with Jim Brown's help yet!

The following teaching unit is a proposal; an idea. I have yet to test it and I put it in writing in the hope that others will try it, modify it, and put together some method that teachers can use to unwash the brains of our society about an immensely complex continent and people. If the movies have been the villains I have suggested, then it is the movies that must be seen again, analyzed, and exposed.

This unit is specifically designed for high school seniors in an Afro-American history class. It can apply, however, to students from ninth grade and up, and can easily be incorporated into units on anthropology, world cultures, and world geography. It should take about 25 class periods, including blocked time to show six feature films.

REALITY

Africa is a multiethnic continent of tremendous geographic variation. It is not a "jungle."

Method: The teacher must now concentrate on presenting the true facts about Africa. Geographic, ethnic, and linguistic diversity must be stressed. A multimedia approach would be ideal.

1. *Films:* There are a few valuable documentaries on Africa accurately de-picting life in various cultures. Most of these, however, are also tainted with West-ern value judgements and racist innuendos. Definitely *not* recommended is a film called *Africa Addio* made by the makers of *Mondo Cane*. It is an attempt to prove savagery by fast cuts and fancy editing. Also not recommended are films issued by various missionary organizations or industries, like Firestone Rubber, for obvious reasons. The best of those available are:

(a) *African Village Life*—A three-part film by Julian Bryan of rural life in contemporary Mali. It notes in detail the cultural complexities of a non-Western society.

(b) *Family of Ghana*—A good short film on village life in a modern West African nation. Especially interesting, since the family involved are sea-coast dwellers and fishermen, which is definitely not the stereotype.

(c) ABC TV's *Africa*—A monumental three-hour color television program, it is available in total or broken down by subject from Contemporary-McGraw-Hill Films. I especially recommend the sections on urban Africa and recent political developments.

(d) *In Search of a Past*—A part of CBS TV's *Of Black America* Series, this vivid film shows three teenage Afro-Americans visiting West Africa, the land of their cultural heritage.

(e) *Omawale: The Child Returns Home*—This film documents the trip of Black writer John A. Williams (author of Cissie and The Man Who Cried "I Am") to West Africa. While not as technically well done as *In Search of a Past,* it provides a valuable look at a man consciously seeking his cultural heritage.

(f) *Tanzania: The Quiet Revolution*—An extremely interesting look at the struggle of an emerging nation in coping with economic, social (particularly racial), and international problems. It is one of the best films on Africa today.

(g) *Africa: The Hidden Frontiers*—This film is similar to theme to *Tanzania,* but its focus is on Kenya, where the racial problems (including the Asiatic minority) have been far more difficult to solve.

2. *Books:* The three books listed here are at or above high school reading level. There are more simply written works for younger students on this subject. I especially recommend the Zenith Press paperback series on Africa, which includes Basil Davidson's The Sources of African History.

(a) Curtin, Philip. African History. New York: MacMillan, 1964. A pamphlet in the Service Center for Teachers Series of the American Historical Association, this deals with the status of African studies today. Although this may be somewhat difficult to read for a few students, it is factual, concise, and easy to obtain.

(b) Singleton, F. Seth, and Shingler, John. Africa in Perspective. New York: Hayden, 1967. According to critics, this is the best available in depth study of Africa and its people. Available in paperback.

(c) Vlahos, Olivia. African Beginnings. New York: Viking Press, 1967. An excellent text on African history written especially for high school students. Available in paperback.

3. *Guest Speakers:* In most big cities and university towns there are a number of African students, and my experience has indicated that many of them would gladly lecture to your classes. Check out the foreign students' office at a nearby college for contacts. Another possibility is former Peace Corpsmen who served in Africa. They are likely to have slides and souvenirs to share with the class.

4. *Museums:* In Philadelphia, for instance the University of Pennsylvania Museum has a fascinating display of West and Central African art. In New York, the Rockefeller Collection of "primitive" art (I wish we could get rid of that word!) has an extensive African collection. I don't know about other areas of the country, but a trip of this kind would give the reality you are striving for a new dimension.

5. *Student-Made Slide-Tape Presentation:* In this type of unit, the more direct student involvement in the actual planning and teaching, the better. One

way of doing this (which has worked in the past for me) is to have the students prepare relevant slides taken from pictorial histories or museums (if permissible) involving the cultural heritage of Africa. The slides from books should be taken with a good macrolens camera for accurate pictures. Check to see if your school district has one. Funds for film can qualify for purchase of "classroom supplies." When the slides are processed, the students should then seek out various recordings of African music and tape them, matching the sounds with the picture of the culture. They could then present this slide-tape in a carousel projector (something you should insist your school system purchase), and arrange and narrate it themselves. Two good pictorial histories of Africa are:

(a) Williams, John. Africa: Her History, Lands, and People Told with Pictures. New York: Cooper Square Press, 1965. Available in paperback.
(b) Davidson, Basil. African Kingdoms. New York: Time-Life Books, 1966.

Some recommended recordings of various types of African music are: *African Music,* Ethnic Folkways Records; *Africa, South of the Sahara, African Coast Rhythms,* and *Folk Music of West Africa,* Riverside Records; and *Missa Luba,* Phillips Records.

MYTH

Once the groundwork on the real Africa has been covered (the amount of time and detail on this should be up to the teacher), the real core of the unit must begin. The framework here is the commercial motion picture as conveyor of myth. The films I have selected are among the "best" of the genre, all of them actually filmed in Africa. My proposal is that the students view them and analyze their points of view in light of their impact on the public in shaping concepts of Africa.

Method: A list of considerations for analysis should be made before each film. Students can do this themselves. Some things to consider might be:

What is the geographic region portrayed?
Is it representative of the geography of Africa?
How are the Black people portrayed?
How are they treated by the Whites?
What is the basis for the film's appeal?
Does it succeed as entertainment? Why?
How does the musical score relate to the action?
What concept of Africa does the film leave with the viewer?

The films have been divided according to the different phases of the myth which they represent.

1. *"The Great White Hunter" Theme:*

(a) *Trader Horn*—The "original" film made in Africa. So old (1930) it creaks, but its footage has appeared in hundreds of made-in-Hollywood jungle epics, including most of the Tarzan films. (The first of the Johnny Weissmuller series was directed by *Trader Horn's* W. S. Van Dyke.) It is loaded with the kind of selective photography designed to make things look savage and ferocious.

(b) *King Solomon's Mines*—Based on the H. R. Haggard novel, which Victorian England devoured generations before, this beautifully made color film takes a party of Whites through East and Central Africa in search of a lost explorer and fabulous wealth. Much more sophisticated than *Trader Horn,* it nevertheless gives a very selective look at Africa as the eternal "dark continent."

From the motion picture **The Naked Prey.** Courtesy of Films Inc.—Paramount Pictures.

2. *"The Savage Environment" Theme:*

(a) *The Naked Prey*—An extraordinarily well-made film (1965) by Cornel Wilde, which uses the "Most Dangerous Game" theme by placing a tribe of very hostile "savages" stalking an unarmed White man in a battle of wits and skill. Guess who wins? Yet the suspense of the film is unrelenting and because of this, the audience can't help identifying with the White man. This shows the myth at its strongest because of the power of the film.

3. *"The Imperialism" Theme ("White Man's Burden"):*

(a) *Four Feathers*—This saga of an Englishman's attempt to live down a cowardly reputation was filmed in the Sudan. It includes lots of the old "Sun never sets. . . Queen and Country" stuff and everyone cheers as the evil Black infidels are defeated by Kitchener's dragoons in the end. This film was also remade in the Sudan in 1956 as *Storm Over the Nile.*

(b) *Something of Value*—Richard Brooks' adaptation of the famous

Robert Ruark novel on Mau Mau in Kenya. Although there is some attempt to show sympathy for the Blacks, the film, like the novel, condemns Mau Mau as savagery and the Black hero, Sidney Poitier, (who else?) dies for his sins. (It is important to note that Mau Mau was a cultural revolution as well as political and was aimed more at fellow Kikuyu tribesmen than at Whites. See the Bibliography.)

(c) *The Nun's Story*—It may raise a few eyebrows that I have included Fred Zinneman's masterful film about the pains of learning the religious life. It is indeed an excellent film, and it is not basically about Africa. However, this is what makes its impact even more significant. The entire middle third of the film takes place in the Belgian Congo where the young nun works in a hospital. Although she always doubts herself as a spiritual force, and at the end of the film she even renounces her vows to work against Hitler, her one great contribution to the faith is the conversion of a "savage" Black man who had previously worshipped his "devil gods." Here in the midst of this tender and compassionate motion picture is the most blatantly racist disregard for a non-Western culture. This personifies the myth on the highest level. It is truly a barometer of America's regard for African culture.

Conclusions: Why have we created these myths? Is it ignorance, conspiracy, ethnocentrism, or some combination of all?

Method: Leave this to your students. Their thoughts here may represent a whole new evaluation of our culture.

TEACHERS' BIBLIOGRAPHY

*BOHANNAN, Paul. Africa and Africans. Garden City, N. Y.: Doubleday, 1964. A very good introduction to Africa which sets out to destroy previous myths about the continent.

CURTIN, Philip. The Image of Africa: British Ideas and Action, 1780-1850.. Madison: University of Wisconsin Press, 1964. An excellent analysis of British ethnocentrism and its conditioning of a concept of Africa as a "hellish" place.

*DAVIDSON, Basil. The African Past: Chronicles from Anitiquity to Modern Times. New York: Atlantic Monthly Press, 1964. A source book of first-hand accounts of travelers and explorers.

FENTON, Robert W. The Big Swingers. Englewood Cliffs, N. J.: Prentice-Hall, 1967. An amusing biography of Edgar Rice Burroughs, creator of Tarzan, who had never been to Africa.

*JORDAN, Winthrop. White Over Black. New York: Penguin Books, 1969. The National Book Award winner, this traces the historical development of American attitudes toward Blacks. Early chapters deal with Africa.

ROBINSON, Ronald, and Gallagher, John. Africa and the Victorian. New York: St. Martin's Press, 1961. Similar to Curtin's book, but containing many insights into the Victorian mind on race and sex. It is useful also for its dealing with the popular literature on Africa of the times.

*ROSBERG, Carl G., Jr., and Nottingham, John. The Myth of Mau Mau: Nationalism in Kenya. New York: Praeger, 1966. Use this recent work with *Something of Value*. It methodically destroys many of the film's judgements of Mau Mau. It is based on the best sources available. Especially useful for analyzing *Something of Value*.

FILMOGRAPHY

Realistic Documentaries

African Village Life. Part I: 28 minutes; part II: 25 minutes; part III: 20 minutes. Color. Presented by Julian Bryan, 1967. Purchase or rental from International Film Foundation.

Family of Ghana. 27 minutes. Black and white. National Film Board of Canada Production, 1965. Purchase or rental from Contemporary-McGraw-Hill Films.

Africa. 180 minutes total (many segments available separately). Color. ABC TV Production (narrated by Gregory Peck), 1968. Purchase or rental from Contemporary-McGraw-Hill Films.

In Search of a Past. 55 minutes. Color. CBS TV's *Of Black America* Series, 1968. Purchase or rental from Bailey-Film Associates.

Omawale: The Child Returns. 30 minutes. Black and white. NET Production, 1965. Purchase or rental from NET Film Service.

Tanzania: The Quiet Revolution. 60 minutes. Black and white. NET Production, 1966. Purchase or rental from NET Film Service.

Africa: The Hidden Frontiers. 60 minutes. Black and white. NET Production, 1966. Rental from NET Film Service.

Other Possibilities

South Africa is so different both geographically and socially from the rest of tropical Africa, it should be taught as a separate entity. Its race relations based on an autocratic White minority's domination over the huge Black majority have been dealt with in a few intelligent films.

Come Back, Africa. 84 minutes. Black and white. Directed by Lionel Rogosin, 1959. A brutal documentary depicting the horror faced by Blacks in contemporary Johannesburg. This film was made in secret for fear that the South African police would destroy the prints. Rental from Contemporary-McGraw-Hill Films.

Cry the Beloved Country. 105 minutes. Black and white. Directed by Zoltan Korda (British), 1951. This film version of Alan Paton's novel about an old rural Black minister seeking his condemned son in the big city provides a sympathetic look at Blacks in South Africa. Starring Canada Lee in his last role and young Sidney Poitier in one of his earliest. Rental from Audio-Brandon Films.

South African Essay. Part I: 60 minutes; part II: 60 minutes. Black and white. NET Production, 1966. A comprehensive review of South African affairs. Purchase or rental from NET Film Service.

The Myth in Feature Films

Trader Horn. 120 minutes. Black and white. Directed by W. S. Van Dyke, 1930. Rental from Films Inc.

King Solomon's Mines. 102 minutes. Color. Directed by Compton Bennett and Andrew Marton, 1950. Rental from Films Inc.

The Naked Prey. 94 minutes. Color. Directed by Cornel Wilde, 1966. Rental from Films Inc.

Four Feathers. 115 minutes. Color. Directed by Zoltan Korda (British), 1939. Rental from Mogull's Film Exchange; also check local rental sources.

Storm Over the Nile (remake of *Four Feathers*). 113 minutes. Color. Directed by Zoltan Korda (British), 1956. Check local rental sources.

Something of Value. 113 minutes. Black and white. Directed by Richard Brooks, 1957. Rental from Films Inc.

The Nun's Story. 150 minutes. Color. Directed by Fred Zinneman, 1959. Rental from Audio-Brandon Films.

Alternatives

Tarzan, the Ape Man. 99 minutes. Black and white. Directed by W. S. Van Dyke, 1932. The "original" talking version of the series with Johnny Weissmuller. It uses many "jungle" footage from *Trader Horn*. Rental from Films Inc.

Mogambo. 115 minutes. Color. Directed by John Ford, 1953. Clark Gable, Ava Gardner, and Grace Kelly in exotic safari background. A press agent's dream. The Blacks are all "boys" and the authentic African backgrounds are merely a vehicle for Gable's heroics. It illustrates a typical Hollywood look at the "dark continent." Rental from Films Inc.

Africa—Texas Style. 106 minutes. Color. Directed by Andrew Marton, 1967. A movie for children (and the pilot for TV's *Cowboy in Africa* Series) with the "great White hunter" as an American cowboy with an Indian companion. It is "family" movies like this that provide most misconceptions about Africa, because they are basically entertaining. Rental from Films Inc.

Hatari. 159 minutes. Color. Directed by Howard Hawks, 1962. A long, plotless movie about an international group of animal capturers and their comic encounters. All the Blacks are "natives" or "boys." John Wayne stars with lots of precocious animals. The African background is only an exotic setting, despite the film's Swahili title. Rental from Films Inc.

Stanley and Livingston. 101 minutes. Black and white. Directed by Henry King, 1939. A typical piece of Hollywood "history" with Spencer Tracy as the brave American reporter Stanley in search of the story of a lifetime. The African stock footage is awkwardly used and the treatment of Africa literally as a "dark continent" with strained seriousness is actually funny today. Have students read about the real Henry M. Stanley (a brilliant opportunist) and then discuss his screen counterpart. Rental from Films Inc.

Safari. 91 minutes. Color. Directed by Edward H. Griffith, 1956. Victor Mature as the great White hunter vs. ferocious Mau Mau's. Filmed in Kenya, *Safari* has the standard misinterpretation of the Mau Mau movement and could be used instead of *Something of Value*. Rental from Audio-Brandon Films.

Dark of the Sun. 100 minutes. Color (cinemascope print available). Directed by

Jack Cardiff, 1968. It is impossible to watch this film, which is supposed to be about some mercenaries (White and Black) rescuing White citizens during the recent Congo civil war, without concluding that the Congolese are a bunch of savages. The film pushes the myth to its most violent extreme. Rental from Films Inc.

Some Films about Africa which Cannot Be Typed

The African Queen. 105 minutes. Color. Directed by John Huston, 1951. The Bogart-Hepburn classic merely uses the African setting as the vehicle for their grand adventure, but the early part of James Agee's script takes some interesting potshots at Western missionaries. Rental from Swank Films.

Khartoum. 128 minutes. Color (cinemascope print available). Directed by Basil Dearden (British), 1965. An intelligent, generally accurate re-creation of the famous Sudanese battle, with Charlton Heston as General Gordon and Sir Laurence Olivier as the Mahdi. This is a far cry from the jingoism of *Four Feathers*. Rental from United Artists 16.

Zulu. 138 minutes. Color. Directed by Cy Endfield (British), 1964. The true story of the struggle of an English outpost at Roarke's Drift, Natal, against thousands of Zulu warriors. The film is all from the British point of view, but it is accurate in its depiction of Zulu military tactics. It is much more complex than most films of its genre. Rental from Audio-Brandon Films.

Everything But a Man–
The Black Man in the Movies

Seeing the brilliant but ambivalent film *Patton* (discussed separately in Chap. 11), I was particularly upset by the portrayal of the famous general's Black sergeant-orderly. It was bad enough to see a bootlicking, "yes-suh" type role in a recent film, but what hurt most was that the actor playing it wasn't Eddie "Rochester" Anderson or Willie Best—it was James Edwards (who just over 20 years ago in *Home of the Brave* established himself as the first young, attractive Black actor since Paul Robeson). I was even more saddened because Edwards passed away recently and *Patton* was his last picture. What a tragedy that an actor so gifted had to end his career as a military "Stepin Fetchit," especially in this age of the "new" cinematic image of Blacks.

The motion picture Black stereotype is generally well known. In the earliest silent films, White actors in burnt cork, reminiscent of the old minstrel shows, impersonated Blacks as lazy, stupid, irresponsible "darkies." Occasionally Blacks were given parts in such films, if they played the roles expected of them. One of the most popular comedy series in the early days of movies was *Rastus,* produced around 1910, with an all-Black cast in stereotyped parts. With D. W. Griffith's cinematic masterpiece *The Birth of a Nation,* the Black man was not only shown to have docile characteristics, but primitive, violent emotions as well, which required close and careful regulation by Whites. In the talkies, Blacks were generally cast in such roles as domestics, stable boys, chauffeurs, or as in the all-talking, all-colored features like *Hallelujah,* fanatical preachers or lazy crap-shooters. In the immediate post-World War II period, the image began to change somewhat with "social" dramas chastising our racial intolerance, and films such as *Lost Boundaries* and *Home of the Brave* became increasingly popular. Actors like Canada Lee (who made few films because of his determination not to play a "darky"), James Edwards, and young Sidney Poitier began to usher in a newer, more human portrayal of the Black man. Today, the motion picture industry would have us believe that Blacks are now thoroughly humanized in films, indicated by the box-office popularity of Poitier, Jim Brown, and Calvin Lockhart. The "new Negro" has emerged on the screen. He is young, tough, heroic, and even virile (interestingly, the most prominent stereotypical characteristic attributed to Blacks in society is the last one to reach the screen). Stepin Fetchit is supposed to be out of style. And yet James Edwards polishes George C. Scott's boots.

If popular mythology and its causes are valid subjects for classroom scrutiny, students have to examine the changing or not so changing nature of the Black stereotype on film, questioning the reasons for it and the impact that it has on Black and White audiences. This can be done historically, with the teacher presenting appropriate films in chronological order, having the class note to what extent the portrayal has changed. Special attention should be paid to the screen images of Blacks today. Have they really changed that much since *Rastus* and *Birth of a Nation*? What is the impact of a Sidney Poitier on America's race relations in general? And, are White kids seeing mostly stereotyped impressions of Blacks in the mass media?

"A stereotype is an oversimplified generalization that emphasizes only selected traits of another group. It tends to evoke a generalized reaction to any member of that group."[1]

Once the definition of stereotypes has been established, the class can discuss the roots and origins of the Black stereotype image from slavery. One thing must be made clear before any films are shown: motion pictures did not create the images of Blacks; they simply reflect and reinforce popular attitudes and expectations. Consequently, seeing the films provides a reasonably accurate index of American attitudes on race throughout the twentieth century.

To introduce this unit, one film is absolutely invaluable. Indeed, for many teachers with limited rental budgets, this film can serve as the entire unit if handled correctly. In the summer of 1968, Xerox Corporation and CBS Television presented a series called *Of Black America*. Although the films in this series were of variable quality, the introductory episode *Black History: Lost, Stolen, or Strayed* was exceptional by any standard. Narrated with great style by Bill Cosby, this film is the most valuable composite portrait of the Black man in motion pictures I have ever seen. Although its title suggests a retelling of Black history, the film deals with that subject only superficially, noting a few of the important contributions of Black inventors and explorers. Its real content is a collection of old film clips, ranging from the 1903 version of *Uncle Tom's Cabin* and selections from Griffith's *Birth of a Nation*, to Stepin Fetchit, Hattie McDaniel, and television's *Amos and Andy*. It even includes a scene from Stanley Kramer's *Guess Who's Coming to Dinner* to illustrate the "new image."

Class discussion should be based on these episodes. Where did the stereotype come from? Why did so many films capitalize on it? What effect do such portrayals have on the audiences who see them? (There is one scene, from a very popular Depression film *The Littlest Rebel*, showing Shirley Temple with a group of Black slave children. They have made her a doll for a birthday present. Narrator Bill Cosby sarcastically comments, "They loved their little mistress. And she loved them." She thanks them for the doll and then returns to her birthday party, promising to save them all some cake. They cheer. Cosby comes back on the screen, concluding the first reel, "This is a lot of fun, isn't it?")

Black History: Lost, Stolen, or Strayed presents such a wide range of cinematic history of the stereotype that a teacher with limited time could have his class

---

[1] Marden, Charles F., and Meyer, Gladys. Minorities in American Society, 3rd ed. New York: Van Nostrand Reinhold, 1968, p. 33

spend a week discussing the film and then adequately conclude the unit. However, this kind of film study is so revealing that I recommend a further examination of the impact of screen literature.

Two of the silent versions of *Uncle Tom's Cabin* are available for 16-mm rental. The first, made by movie pioneer Edwin S. Porter in 1903, is brief and stagey. It features an all-White cast with grossly exaggerated action; but it was quite popular as one of the earliest American movies. The other available version of Harriet Beecher Stowe's classic (it was made six times) is the 1926 edition, starring a Black actor named James B. Lowe (who succeeded another Black man Charles Gilpin, who had quit in protest against the exaggerated role). The class could view one of these and compare the characterizations with Mrs. Stowe's abolitionist novel. Actually, the films *are* fairly accurate interpretations of the characters in the novel, which is a commentary on how old the stereotypes are.

D. W. Griffith's famous *The Birth of a Nation* (1915) probably did more to hurt the image of Blacks than any film or other mass medium before or since. *Birth of a Nation* is, of course, a cinematic masterpiece—a landmark in film technique, symbolism, and spectacle. *Black History: Lost, Stolen, or Strayed* has a couple of scenes from it (the Black reconstruction legislatures of the South behaving like animals, and the White hero's discovery that Blacks are fearful of ghosts; hence the creation of the Ku Klux Klan's white-sheeted riders), but for its images to be appreciated, students should see it in its entirety. I will deal with the history-making impact of this film in Chap. 16, since it is far more than a presentation of negative Black stereotypes. However, classes seeing it during this unit should read part of Lewis Jacobs' classic essay on D. W. Griffith from his book The Rise of the American Film.[2] This outlines the plot of the film and explains many of its technical innovations, which students today might take for granted. Another valuable reading for the class would be film critic James Agee's famous defense of the film and his belief that Griffith was not anti-Black.[3]

The film, itself, is loaded with stereotyped images of Blacks. In the early pre-Civil War scenes, the slaves are shown as happy and contented. Master Cameron, demonstrating their contentment to a Northern visitor, shows them shuffling happily. (This looks particularly funny today, since most of the slaves were White actors in blackface.) Later during reconstruction, the villainous mulatto Silas Lynch plots the destruction of the White South, using his Northern White allies and the ex-slaves as dupes. Lynch is particularly despicable because he lusts after Elsie Stoneman (Lillian Gish), the film's heroine. Near the end, he almost succeeds at forcing her to marry him, until the Klan saves the day.

Lynch embodies the stereotype in its most "dangerous" form. He is the sexual figure Whites have traditionally feared most historically. Even more sexually ferocious is the character of Gus, a no-account (full-blooded Black) ex-slave, who attempts to rape the gentle Flora Cameron (sister of the hero). Rather than submit to the vile Black, Flora threatens to jump over a cliff if he takes

---

[2] Reprinted in Talbot, Daniel, Ed., Film: An Anthology, 2nd ed. Berkeley: University of California Press, 1966, pp. 309-324.

[3] Agee, James. Agee on Film. New York: Grosset and Dunlap, 1969. Keep in mind, Griffith and Agee were both Southerners, and the stereotypes were part of their environment. Available in paperback.

another step towards her. He does, and in the film's most dramatic moment, she takes the fatal jump.[4]

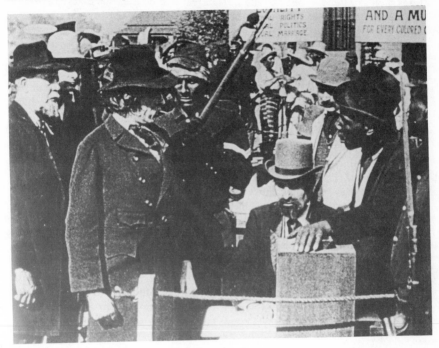

From the motion picture **Birth of a Nation.** Courtesy of Museum of Modern Art.

There are other scenes showing Blacks in their expected images. For instance, the "good" loyal ex-slaves are dominated by a huge mammy who in the end proves herself stronger than any Black man as she battles to save her White superiors.

The Birth of a Nation is a fantastic classroom resource. It demonstrates the national mood towards Blacks in 1915 (when "Jim Crow" and lynch law were in their prime). Its stereotypes are representative of what most Whites felt about Blacks in that era. And, it illustrates the impact of the motion picture medium, since for many Americans it was the first movie they had ever seen. Its popularity gave extended life to anti-Black feelings already existing, and the modern Ku Klux Klan emerged in the decade following its release.

Students will be fascinated with the film, both for its cinematic skill and its prejudices. It deserves detailed classroom study.

D. W. Griffith's concept of the Black man did not dominate future motion pictures. Griffith himself softened his feelings somewhat in a World War I propaganda film *The Greatest Thing in Life* by showing a White soldier kissing

---

[4] An excellent source for a follow-up study of the sexually ferocious stereotypes of Lynch and Gus is the explanation of the origin of the southern "rape complex" in Cash, Wilbur J., <u>The Mind of the South</u>. New York: Knopf, 1960. Students should be encouraged to read this. Available in paperback.

his dying Black comrade in honor of his bravery. (I should note that this was the beginning of a trend in war propaganda films. At the start of World War II, pictures such as *Lifeboat, Sahara,* and *Bataan* featured courageous Blacks fighting for the American cause. Even John Wayne's pro-Vietnam *Green Berets* has the obligatory brave Black soldier. This would make for interesting discussion concerning the practicality of changing the image in war time.)

In the late silents and throughout the first three decades of talkies, Blacks were relegated to brief roles as harmless, likable creatures, cleaning, cooking, and carrying suitcases. The teacher could show any popular film of the 1930s or 1940s, for instance, and there would be a small role for a Black man or woman in some domestic occupation. Some samples of these include dancer Bill Robinson in most of the Shirley Temple films; Stepin Fetchit in John Ford's *Judge Priest* (1935), with Will Rogers; Hattie McDaniel as the maid in dozens of Depression comedies, or, along with Butterfly McQueen and countless other Black actors as the loyal slaves in *Gone with the Wind;* Mantan Moreland as Charlie Chan's eye-rolling chauffeur; Willie Best, "Snowflake"; Eddie "Rochester" Anderson; and countless others. Occasionally there were "bigger" parts, like Sparks the preacher (Leigh Whipper) in *The Oxbow Incident* (serving as a kind of conscience for the White lynch mob—a role that would be repeated in later films where a single Black serves as an example of goodness for the misguided Whites), or Rex Ingram as the exotic genie in *The Thief of Baghdad.* But in absolutely no case were Blacks portrayed with any depth. They were without complex emotions (always "happy"); they rarely had last names (and references to them as "boys" and "girls" were common); and, with the exception of *Birth of a Nation,* they never even had any vices. They weren't human. They were just there, like set decorations.

I don't know whether it would be worth class time to screen films with "featured" appearances of Black actors. None of the roles had real impact on the plots of any of these films. The parts were small and always insignificant. Does it pay to sit through a soap opera such as *Mildred Pierce* just to catch five minutes of Butterfly McQueen as a nitwit maid? Yet millions of people who saw that film and who identified with the trials and tribulations of Joan Crawford, also saw, however fleetingly, that bumbling Black maid. Students should be made aware of the "incidental" impact of so many of those bit parts.

Black History: Lost, Stolen, or Strayed has a few clips of such roles and maybe they are enough. Still, I wish some film distributor would put together a reel of nothing but Black stereotyped parts for studies like this. There were so many, and their message was so clear—"Black is inferior."

There is one type of old film that a class can look at for a more detailed presentation of Hollywood's view of Blacks. The all-talking, all-singing, all-dancing (all-shuffling), all-colored spectacles were quite popular in their times. These were not the small, low-budget Black films made exclusively for segregated theaters. *Hallelujah* (1929), *The Green Pastures* (1936), and *Cabin in the Sky* (1943) were the products of major studios and important (White) directors. They were written by Whites and produced by them, but their characters were Black. All three have a similar theme, folk religion, and are loaded with thunderous spirituals and joyful music. And the characters in them embody all of the "darky" traits prominent in movies since *Uncle Tom's Cabin.* These films are available in

16 mm, and at least one should be screened in its entirety by a class. One important thing to consider when viewing them is their popularity among Black audiences. An interesting essay by Harold Cruse in his book <u>Rebellion or Revolution</u> deals with the unrealistic interpretation of Black life in Marc Connoley's *The Green Pastures,* but praises the talents of its Black cast.[5] This would make a useful class reading.

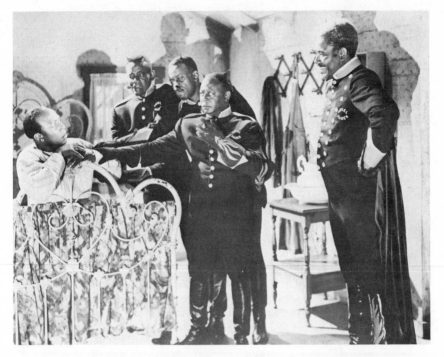

From the motion picture **Cabin in the Sky.** Courtesy of Films Inc.—MGM.

Later, more popular examples of the White-created Black film were the adaptations of the stage musicals *Carmen Jones* and *Porgy and Bess.* These more recent films were skillfully made and beautifully sung. Yet they are neither dramatically nor musically indigenous to Black people. Black author Harold Cruse in his voluminous study <u>The Crisis of the Negro Intellectual</u> comments that *Porgy and Bess* is so riddled with stereotypes and so degrading, that no Black should ever again accept one of its roles. He submits that since it is a White conception of the subject, it should legitimately be performed only by White actors wearing blackface.[6] This too could serve as an enlightening class reading.

With the exception of the portrayals in World War II propaganda films, and,

---

[5] Cruse, Harold. <u>Rebellion or Revolution</u>. New York: William Morrow, 1968, pp. 41-47. The review was written for the Communist **Daily Worker** in 1951 and concerns a revival of the play. However, the commentary is equally applicable to the film. Available in paperback.

[6] Cruse, Harold. <u>Crisis of the Negro Intellectual</u>. New York: William Morrow, 1967, pp. 103-107. Available in paperback.

possibly the early Paul Robeson films such as O'Neill's Emperor Jones (which I cannot comment on since his films have disappeared from all circulation, probably because of his leftist politics), American movie stereotypes of Blacks did not change. Then in the late 1940s a series of social dramas critical of America's handling of its race problem were made. Students should screen one or more of these, although they are now seriously dated. This genre includes *Lost Boundaries, Pinky, Home of the Brave,* and *Intruder in the Dust* (which according to many critics is the best film ever made about Blacks).

Lost Boundaries and *Pinky* essentially deal with the same theme: the mulatto living in the White world suffering from a deep inner conflict between whether to continue "passing" or to accept one's Blackness. Both were enlightened stories for their times, though White actors Mel Ferrer and Jeanne Crain, respectively, played the leads. Viewing them today is painful. Their patronizing sentimentality and oversimplification of issues is laughable. (I watched *Pinky* on television for about an hour before it became unendurable.) Yet White audiences were quite taken with them when they were released. They were looked upon as significant changes in the attitudes of film-makers.

Home of the Brave holds up a lot better. Based originally on a play where the central character was a Jew, this film about a young Black soldier inadvertently assigned to a White regiment during World War II still has quite a bit of power. The Black suffers from the racist chastising of some of his peers and eventually suffers a mental breakdown. Brilliantly acted by James Edwards, the character is both sympathetic and believable. But although he is more human than most of his screen counterparts, he is still the lone Black in the White world. Consequently, the audience sees him only reacting to Whites, rarely, if ever, in control of his own destiny. The characterization is still, therefore, one-dimensional, with the scorned Black serving as a lesson in White intolerance. He only exists in the framework of the morality play. He is a spirit, not really a man.

Intruder in the Dust, as I've indicated, is hailed as the best film about Blacks of the period, and perhaps of all time. The film version of William Faulkner's noted novel does, indeed, provide a new, more realistic human image of a Black man. Lucas Beauchamp (played with quiet authority by Juano Hernandez) is accused of murdering a White man, yet he never shuffles or pleads for mercy. He is dignified and forever proud, and this is an image unlike any previously on the screen. In the title essay of his book Shadow and Act, Black author Ralph Ellison gives a composite review of all four films and concludes that only in *Intruder in the Dust,* both as a film and a novel, is there any real human treatment of a Black character. He claims it is one of the few films that Black audiences would respond to favorably.[7] This would make an excellent class reading even if none of the films in the genre is shown.

Personally, I have reservations about *Intruder in the Dust.* Despite Mr. Ellison's praise and that of many respected critics, I don't think the character of Lucas Beauchamp is very human either. Faulkner's novel and the film have indeed created a proud Black man in defiance of previous stereotypes, but they have forced him to serve again as the conscience for the White community. Chick, the White teenager who has long been indebted to Lucas for saving his life, must find

---

[7] Ellison, Ralph. Shadow and Act. New York: Random House, 1964, pp. 273-281. Available in paperback.

evidence to prove that the old Black man is innocent. The story establishes that the murdered White man was a despicable character and that Lucas would have had plenty of reason for killing him. But the "good" Whites in the novel and the film must prove Lucas innocent, which in fact he is. The first question I would raise to a class that has just screened this film is why *must* Lucas be innocent. Wouldn't it have been more realistic if he had killed the man? Certainly in rural Southern communities in Faulkner's Mississippi, Blacks have been driven to the point of physical violence toward Whites. Wouldn't it have been more effective if those "good" Whites had to grapple with the institutions that may have made such a crime justifiable? *Intruder in the Dust* skirts this issue. The Black man is innocent, and the Whites who saved him are better men for having discovered this. How much more effective would it have been if they had to understand his crime?

From the motion picture **Intruder in the Dust.** Courtesy of Films Inc.—MGM.

During the 1950s, the Black man's image on the screen slowly began to change, although Willie Best and Stepin Fetchit were still playing stock roles during this period. A young, good-looking Black actor had emerged from featured parts in films like *No Way Out* (a brutal condemnation of racism, with Richard Widmark as a psychopath "nigger hater") and the *Blackboard Jungle.* Sidney Poitier ushered in a whole new era for the Black screen image (and, as some critics claim, a whole new stereotype).

Most of Poitier's films are available for classroom showings, and I recommend that at least two of them be screened to illustrate the changing nature of the stereotype. Probably the best of the early Sidney Poitier films is Stanley Kramer's *The Defiant Ones*. Two men escape from a Southern chain gang hopelessly chained together. One is a small-time White crook (Tony Curtis in what has to be the performance of a lifetime), who is fiercely anti-Black. The other is a Black man, more intelligent and decent than his White "comrade," but realistically bitter and tough. Symbolically tied together by the chain, these two men are forced to work as one to secure their escape. Their relationship, if never friendly, becomes one of respect and tolerance for each other. And the film powerfully builds this up. It is the end of the picture that raises questions, and doubts, for many of those who see it today. Curtis and Poitier have made their escape to a train. All they need to do is jump on it and it will transport them away from the pursuing posse. Poitier jumps on and extends his hand to the running Curtis. The two hands touch, but the White man hasn't the strength to follow through. He falls onto the track as the train speeds away from him. At this point, Poitier, as if pulled by the chain that once bound them, falls too. Thus in the end both men await recapture, but as brothers.

From the motion picture **The Defiant Ones.** Courtesy of United Artists.

Up to that last scene *The Defiant Ones* is one of the greatest Hollywood films. When I saw it in 1958, as a teenager, it genuinely moved me. But seeing it today, there is something unnerving about that ending. When it was shown on television recently, I assigned all of my classes to watch it. What I suspected was absolutely right. Today's Black kids simply won't swallow that ending. "Why did Poitier fall off that train? He was free."

The White liberalism of 1958 could not see fit to reverse things and have

Curtis fall off after Poitier. The ending as it stands implies Blacks need Whites, and there is nothing mutual about that. Teachers using this film should be prepared to deal with alternatives to that conclusion.

The Defiant Ones established Sidney Poitier as a bonafide Hollywood star. (He received an Oscar nomination for his portrayal.) Since that time, he has built a personal image that no other Black actor has come close to. He is a screen hero, in both the traditional sense and in a unique way as well. (As Bill Cosby says in *Black History: Lost, Stolen, or Strayed*, Sidney is "always helping little old ladies across the street . . . whether they want to go or not.") His later films, *A Patch of Blue, Lilies of the Field, To Sir With Love, In the Heat of the Night*, and *Guess Who's Coming to Dinner* all illustrate this, and at least one should be screened in the classroom. A required reading with any of these films should be an article from the *New York Times* written at the height of Poitier's popularity prior to the release early the next year of *Guess Who's Coming to Dinner*. The article, "Why Does White America Love Sidney Poitier So?" by Clifford Mason, cites the actor's heroic image as an important breakthrough compared to the old stereotypes, but points out that none of the roles identifies him as a human being.[8] Unlike most White heroes, Poitier does not get the girl. This article was the first of several to accuse him of being a sexless Black "eunuch," a figment of the White liberal's imagination. This criticism, of course, continues today, exemplified in a critique of Poitier's *They Call Me Mr. Tibbs*. Although in this one he has a wife and family, and is shown in bed with her, he is living in a totally White world. As critic Vincent Canby says, "his blackness is now invisible."[9]

A class screening any of Poitier's more recent films (since *Lilies of the Field*) can determine for itself whether such criticism is warranted. One thing is clear. Although the Black image on the screen has changed over the decades, it still has not been sufficiently humanized. There are exceptions to this, of course. *Nothing but a Man* (which I have mentioned so often) and *The Cool World* are realistic. Then too, there are so many other Black actors in films today. How do their roles compare to the old stereotypes and the Poitier image? Are Jim Brown (in *100 Rifles* making love to Raquel Welch), Ossie Davis (as a tough runaway slave in *The Scalphunters*), or Calvin Lockhart (the "super" Black teacher in *Halls of Anger*) an improvement over the old image? In what ways?

This kind of academic analysis has endless possibilities. In the filmography, I have listed as many films as I could. However, as I conclude this survey of 40 years of cinematic literature, that image of the late James Edwards with a whisk broom in his hands brushing off George C. Scott's coat continues to haunt me. One thing is apparent—motion pictures are a White medium, and the attitudes they reflect are White attitudes.

BIBLIOGRAPHY

ADLER, Renata. <u>A Year in the Dark</u>. New York: Random House, 1970. The former *New York Times* film critic's collection of past reviews. This

---

[8] Mason, Clifford, "Why Does White America Love Sidney Poitier So?", **New York Times,** September 10, 1967, section II, p. 21.

[9] Canby, Vincent, "Milestones Can Be Millstones," **New York Times,** July 19, 1970, section II, p. 5. This also should be reprinted as a class reading.

includes a thoughtful essay on Sidney Poitier's role in *Guess Who's Coming to Dinner,* pp. 63-68.

*AGEE, James. Agee on Film. New York: Grosset and Dunlap, 1969.

CANBY, Vincent. "Milestones Can Be Millstones," *New York Times,* July 19, 1970, section II, p. 5.

*CASH, Wilbur. The Mind of the South. New York: Knopf, 1960.

*CRUSE, Harold. The Crisis of the Negro Intellectual. New York: William Morrow, 1967.

—. Rebellion or Revolution. New York: William Morrow, 1968.

*ELLISON, Ralph. Shadow and Act. New York: Random House, 1964.

*JACOBS, Lewis. "D. W. Griffith," reprinted in Daniel, Talbot, Ed., Film: An Anthology, 2nd ed. Berkeley: University of California Press, 1966.

MASON, Clifford, "Why Does White America Love Sidney Poitier So?" *New York Times,* September 10, 1967, section II, p. 21.

NOBLE, Peter. The Negro in Films. Port Washington, N. Y.: Kennikat, 1969; and New York: Arno Press. An excellent, comprehensive study on the subject up to 1948.

WEBB, Constance. Richard Wright: A Biography. New York: Putnam, 1968. This contains an interesting explanation of the filming of the noted Black author's novel Native Son in Argentina in 1950. It appears there are no longer any public prints of this film. See pp. 292-304.

Additional Possibility

DELORIA, Vine, Jr. We Talk, You Listen. New York: Macmillan, 1970. Deloria's noted Indian manifesto includes a thought-provoking chapter on Indian stereotypes in the mass media. This presents some useful parallels in discussing the Black image. See pp. 33-44.

FILMOGRAPHY

Introduction

Black History: Lost, Stolen, or Strayed. 58 minutes. Color. CBS TV's *Of Black America* Series (narrated by Bill Cosby), 1968. Purchase or rental from Bailey-Film Associates.

Silent Films

Uncle Tom's Cabin. Available as part of the Edwin S. Porter "package." Directed by Edwin S. Porter, 1903. Rental from Museum of Modern Art. This can only be acquired on a 55-minute reel that includes four other Porter films.

Uncle Tom's Cabin. 93 minutes. Black and white. Directed by Harry Pollard, 1926. This version has a sound track with narration by Raymond Massey. Rental from Audio-Brandon Films.

The Birth of a Nation. 195 minutes. Black and white. Directed by D. W. Griffith (from the novel The Clansman by Thomas Dixon), 1915. There is also a 130-minute version available. Rental from Museum of Modern Art.

Featured "Stereotypes" of the 30s, 40s, and 50s

Many of the films with the most blatant examples of the stereotypes I have not been able to find in 16-mm distribution. The following are merely a few suggested titles.

So Red the Rose. 83 minutes. Black and white. Directed by King Vidor, 1936. The ol' plantation and the Civil War, with "evil" slaves led by Black actor Clarence Muse in revolt. Their rebellion is crushed when their White mistress, Margaret Sullavan, tearfully pleads with them. Rental from Universal 16.

The Littlest Rebel. 80 minutes. Black and white. Directed by David Butler, 1936. Little Shirley Temple teaches her slaves, including Bill Robinson and Willie Best, courage in the face of the Yankee invaders. Rental from Films Inc.

Ghost Breakers. 85 minutes. Black and white. Directed by George Marshall, 1940. Standard Bob Hope comedy, with Willie Best, for laughs, caught in a haunted house. This was a standard gag scene for many Black film actors. Rental from Universal 16.

Virginia. 109 minutes. Black and white. Directed by Edmund H. Griffith, 1941. Modern times force the break-up of the ol' plantation. Loaded with nostalgia and "darky" stereotypes. Rental from Universal 16.

The Charlie Chan Series. 1931-1949. This series of films about the Chinese detective (himself a stereotype) had many episodes involving Chan's Black chauffeur, Mantan Moreland, who was noted for his ability to roll his eyes to show fear. Many of these are available, and I recommend their use. They represent America's stereotyping of minorities at its most explicit level. Check local film exchanges for rental.

The Oxbow Incident. 76 minutes. Black and white. Directed by William Wellman, 1943. A well-known, excellent film about mob "justice," it includes an interesting Black character—Sparks, an itinerant preacher. Played by Leigh Whipper, Sparks by speaking against the mob and praying for the souls of the accused men serves as a kind of conscience for Whites. This is a new kind of stereotype, which would be repeated often in later films. Rental from Films Inc. and Audio-Brandon Films.

Bend of the River. 91 minutes. Color. Directed by Anthony Mann, 1952. A popular James Stewart Western, featuring Stepin Fetchit in what was probably his last standard role. Rental from Universal 16.

War Propaganda Films with Black Actors

Lifeboat. 97 minutes. Black and white. Directed by Alfred Hitchcock, 1944. Canada Lee, as one of the survivors, in this famous film. Lee is somewhat removed from the negative stereotype. Rental from Films Inc.

Bataan. 93 minutes. Black and white. Directed by Tay Garnett, 1943. The doomed soldiers of this famous battle have among them a distinguished, heroic Black comrade, Kenneth Spencer. This film was made at the beginning of World War II, and its propaganda was extremely effective. Rental from Films Inc.

Sahara. 97 minutes. Black and white. Directed by Zoltan Korda, 1943. A classic
war film, with Humphrey Bogart, about a group of men (including a Black
Libyan soldier played by Rex Ingram) trapped by Germans in North Africa.
Their courage persists, and the Black is among the most heroic. Actor
Ingram later played Uncle Remus in Disney's *Song of the South.* Rental
from Audio-Brandon Films.

The Green Berets. 141 minutes. Color. Directed by John Wayne and Ray Kellogg,
1968. Wayne's cliché-ridden propaganda film for the Vietnam War features
a brave Black man, Raymond St. Jacques. St. Jacques later admitted that
he was ashamed of the movie. Rental from Audio-Brandon Films.

All-Black Features

Hallelujah. 107 minutes. Black and white. Directed by King Vidor, 1929. Rental
from Films Inc.

The Green Pastures. 110 minutes. Black and white. Directed by Marc Connelly
and William Keighly, 1936. Rental from Films Inc. and United Artists 16.

Cabin in the Sky. 100 minutes. Black and white. Directed by Vincent Minnelli,
1943. Rental from Films Inc.

Carmen Jones. 107 minutes. Color (cinemascope print available). Directed by
Otto Preminger, 1955. Rental from Films Inc.

Porgy and Bess. 138 minutes. Color. Directed by Otto Preminger, 1959. Rental
from Samuel Goldwyn 16.

Social Dramas Concerning Blacks

This grouping excludes the Sidney Poitier Films. Notice how few there are
without him.

Lost Boundaries. 99 minutes. Black and white. Directed by Alfred L. Werker, 1949.
Rental from Warner Brothers 16.

Pinky. 102 minutes. Black and white. Directed by Elia Kazan, 1949. Rental from
Films Inc.

Home of the Brave. 85 minutes. Black and white. Directed by Mark Robson, 1949.
Rental from Audio-Brandon Films and Twyman Films.

Intruder in the Dust. 87 minutes. Black and white. Directed by Clarence Brown,
1949. Rental from Films Inc.

Island in the Sun. 119 minutes. Color. Directed by Robert Rossen, 1957. Terrible
film about a couple of interracial romances in Jamaica. It's hard to believe
this stuff was once considered daring. With Harry Belafonte and Dorothy
Dandridge as the exotic objects of White appetites. Rental from Films Inc.

Odds Against Tomorrow. 95 minutes. Black and white. Directed by Robert Wise,
1959. A robbery melodrama involving the animosity between two of the
gang members: a fierce bigot (Robert Ryan) and a Black (Harry Belafonte).
The film has a pretentious air, but Belafonte's role has quite a bit of depth.
Still, because he is Black, he is somehow made more noble than the rest of
the thieves. Rental from United Artists 16.

Imitation of Life. 124 minutes. Color. Directed by Douglas Sirk, 1959. A remake of the 1934 film about a family, its loyal maid, and her mulatto daughter who passes for White. This film brings back all of the female stereotypes in the portrayal of that maid. The original version is not available in 16 mm. This one is only recommended to show how recently (1959) Blacks have been dramatized this way. Rental from Universal 16.

Sergeant Rutledge. 118 minutes. Color. Directed by John Ford, 1960. This film about the Black Tenth Cavalry of the old West sounds as if it would be terrific. Unfortunately its Black actors have very little to do or say except to look good in uniform. Woody Strode, in the title role, plays a trooper on trial for killing a White girl. Most of the movie involves the White hero's proving him innocent. Check local film exchanges for rental.

Shadows. 81 minutes. Black and white. Directed by John Cassavetes, 1960. I have not seen Cassavetes' improvisational film about an interracial romance, but I have been informed that it deals with its subject honestly. Rental from Audio-Brandon Films.

Gone Are the Days (Purlie Victorious). 97 minutes. Black and white. Directed by Nicholas Webster, 1963. The film version of Ossie Davis' hilarious satire Purlie Victorious. In this film the stereotypes serve an excellent satirical purpose. Rental from Audio-Brandon Films.

The Cool World. See citation in Chap. 3.

Nothing But a Man. Still the best film around about Blacks. Absolutely no stereotypes. See citation in Chap. 1.

One Potato, Two Potato. See citation in Chap. 5.

The Story of a Three Day Pass. 87 minutes. Black and white. Directed by Melvin Van Peebles (French), 1967. English subtitles. This film, although produced in French, is the first commercial feature ever directed by a Black man, Melvin Van Peebles. Its story of a Black GI's brief romance with a Parisian girl leaves much to be desired, but the characterization is honest, and Van Peebles has made an important breakthrough. Rental from Audio-Brandon Films.

The Comedians. 160 minutes. Color (cinemascope print available). Directed by Peter Glenville, 1967. This film version of Graham Green's best seller about modern Haiti is badly hurt by a murky Elizabeth Taylor-Richard Burton romance. But the Black supporting actors are great, and their roles are complex and dignified. With James Earl Jones, Raymond St. Jacques, and Roscoe Lee Brown. Rental from Films Inc.

The Scalphunters. 102 minutes. Color. Directed by Sidney Pollack, 1968. A Western that treats the race issue humorously as a rugged frontiersman (Burt Lancaster) and a brilliant runaway slave (Ossie Davis) team up to fight a band of renegade outlaws. Unrealistic, but funny, and the Black character is really "alive." Rental from United Artists 16.

Joanna. 107 minutes. Color (cinemascope print available). Directed by Michael Sarne, 1968. A pretentious film about a "mod" London "chick," who falls in love with a Black man. It is interesting only since its portrayal of the lover by Calvin Lockhart is in the typical matinée idol vein (kind of a Black Paul Newman). Rental from Films Inc.

Slaves. 110 minutes. Color. Directed by Herbert Biberman, 1969. This film was supposed to be the first honest look at American slavery. Although the

Blacks are the "good guys," *Slaves* is merely a one-dimensional piece of sentimentality. It's like a film version of a William Lloyd Garrison speech. Everybody, Black and White, is stereotyped. View this to see how little movies have changed, despite its more pro-Black approach. Rental from Walter Reade 16.

Up Tight. 104 minutes. Color. Directed by Jules Dassin, 1968. The movies' first portrayal of Black power. This film is only partially successful. It is really a remake of the Irish classic *The Informer,* and the parallels of the two rebellions aren't exact enough to justify this interpretation. Still its characters are vividly depicted and performed. Rental from Films Inc.

Halls of Anger. 100 minutes. Color. Directed by Paul Bogart, 1970. Here is a film with lots of Black actors, all competent (especially Calvin Lockhart in the lead). They are young and angry and quite in keeping with the film's plot about a Black high school about to be integrated by some Whites. However, though the characterizations are adequate, the story line is so exaggerated and badly directed that the Blacks emerge looking like vicious savages. (There is one scene of some Black students brutally beating a White girl without the slightest provocation. This is rude sensationalism at best.) Rental from United Artists 16.

Cotton Comes to Harlem. 90 minutes. Color. Directed by Ossie Davis, 1970. A riotous "Black" comedy based on Chester Himes' novel about two tough Black cops. The film is refreshing for its soul brother point of view and it is loaded with "inside" jokes. *Cotton* represents a great step forward in the portrayal of Blacks as human beings. Rental from United Artists 16.

The Sidney Poitier "Stereotype"

Listed here are the actor's better-known films in chronological order, according to what is available in 16 mm. It is important to note that most of the racial dramas of the past two decades featured Poitier. Few other Black actors had his opportunities. Class discussion on these films should go beyond their content and deal with the tokenism of Hollywood in this respect. It should also question whether or not the new stereotype accusations are true.

No Way Out. 106 minutes. Black and white. Directed by Joseph L. Mankiewicz, 1950. Poitier as a Black doctor who is tormented by a racist (Richard Widmark). In the end, loyal to his profession, he must save the racist's life. Rental from Films Inc.

The Blackboard Jungle. 101 minutes. Black and white. Directed by Richard Brooks, 1955. This is still a powerful film about a teacher in a tough slum school. Gregory Miller, a Black student, tough and bitter, in the end helps the teacher win over the class. One of Poitier's best acting jobs. Rental from Films Inc.

Edge of the City. 85 minutes. Black and white. Directed by Martin Ritt, 1956. A White wanderer (John Cassavetes) learns about humanity from his Black coworker (Sidney Poitier). The Black man is murdered by a racist and his White friend avenges it by beating up the killer. He thus learns the "meaning of life." This is a tough melodrama, but the Black man's role is that of conscience to the Whites. He is that spirit-like character of the war propaganda films and the *Oxbow Incident.* Rental from Films Inc.

The Defiant Ones. 97 minutes. Black and white. Directed by Stanley Kramer, 1958. Rental from United Artists 16.

All the Young Men. 87 minutes. Black and white. Directed by Hal Bartlett, 1960. A Korean War film about a Black sergeant and a tough veteran member of the outfit competing for the men's affection. Later when the White is wounded, a blood transfusion really binds the men together. Pretentious. Rental from Twyman Films or Swank Films.

Paris Blues. 98 minutes. Black and white. Directed by Martin Ritt, 1961. Paul Newman and Sidney Poitier as two American jazz musicians in Paris who meet two female tourists (Joanne Woodward and Diahann Carroll). Though the film has little plot, the romance between Poitier and Miss Carroll is nicely developed, and except for *A Raisin in the Sun,* it marks the actor's first screen attachment to a woman. Rental from United Artists 16.

A Raisin in the Sun. See citation in Chap. 5.

Pressure Point. 89 minutes. Black and white. Directed by Hubert Cornfield, 1962. Good psychological study of an American Nazi (Bobby Darin) in the care of a Black psychiatrist. Rental from United Artists 16.

Lilies of the Field. 97 minutes. Black and white. Directed by Ralph Nelson, 1963. Poitier's Oscar-winning performance as a wandering handyman who helps some refugee nuns build a chapel in the Arizona desert. This film is very entertaining, but it marks the beginning of the actor's evolution into "I serve" parts. Rental from Audio-Brandon Films.

The Long Ships. 125 minutes. Color. Directed by Jack Cardiff, 1964. A run-of-the-mill adventure about some Vikings lost in an African empire. Poitier plays a villainous sultan, and although he has since denounced the role as a mistake, critic Clifford Mason in his *New York Times* article implies it is a milestone for a Black actor. Check local film exchanges for rental.

The Bedford Incident. 102 minutes. Black and white. Directed by James B. Harris, 1965. Poitier plays a reporter on board an atomic submarine commanded by a fanatical captain bent on starting an atomic war. Critic Mason argues that the Poitier role as critic of the captain is too weakly written. I see it as the stereotyped "conscience" of the ship, the "holier than thou" spirit that Blacks must assume among sinful Whites. Rental from Audio-Brandon Films.

Duel at Diablo. 103 minutes. Color. Directed by Ralph Nelson, 1966. A far-fetched Western that has the dubious distinction of making Poitier the first gun-toting Black cowboy in screen history. (Actually actor Frank Silvera had been playing such parts for years, but as a White man or a Mexican.) Otherwise his role is merely sidekick to hero James Garner. Rental from United Artists 16.

To Sir with Love. 105 minutes. Color. Directed by James Clavell, 1967. Sentimental story of a Black teacher in a White British slum school. There are some suggestions of a possible romance with a White teacher, but they are brushed aside. This film was very successful. Rental from Columbia Cinematheque.

In the Heat of the Night. 109 minutes. Color. Directed by Norman Jewison, 1967. This film won the Academy Award, as did actor Rod Steiger for his portrayal of a tough, but sympathetic Southern police chief. Poitier plays a Northern cop on leave, who singlehandedly solves a notorious crime.

Mr. Mason's article is particularly critical of the one-dimensional nature of the role. Rental from United Artists 16.

Guess Who's Coming to Dinner. 108 minutes. Color. Directed by Stanley Kramer, 1968. The story of parents' (Spencer Tracy and Katherine Hepburn) reaction to their daughter's betrothal to a Black man. Their future son-in-law is a superhuman figure. (Nobel prize-winning surgeon, missionary, decorated by the U. N., etc.) This film is highly controversial despite its light treatment of the subject (it is supposed to be a comedy), since many Blacks are upset by Poitier's role. They claim the whole thing is racist, since a man of his stature shouldn't have to humble himself to ask for the hand of a silly White teenager (Katherine Houghton). Screen this film in light of today's widening polarity between the races and see how you react. Rental from Columbia Cinematheque.

From the motion picture **To Sir with Love.** Courtesy of Columbia Pictures.

The Great Depression on Film–
A Classroom Unit Using Movies as Historical Sources

The thirties are suddenly in vogue. Fashion designers have reached back into the Depression era for inspirations, opulent restaurants have opened with names like "Spats," attempting to recapture the flavor of those times; *Dinner at Eight* and *Room Service* have had successful revivals on Broadway; a best-selling book is based on people's reminiscences about the thirties (Hard Times: An Oral History of the Depression); and two of the highest grossing movies in recent years have attempted to recreate that era (*Bonnie and Clyde* and *They Shoot Horses, Don't They?*). Capitalizing on this renewed interest in the period, some enterprising film distributor circulated prints of *Forty-Second Street* and *The Gold Diggers of 1933* in first-run theaters, advertising: "What did people do to beat the sadness of the Depression? They went to the movies . . . to see things like . . . ."

This resurgence of interest in one of the worst decades of American history puzzles me somewhat. Most of it is based on pure nostalgia, concentrating on objects of the past rather than experiences. If the musicals of Busby Berkeley and pictures such as *King Kong* are camp today, it should also be kept in mind that in their times these movies were enjoyed and even taken seriously (in the escapist sense) by people living during what one writer has called "The Anxious Years."[1]

As a history teacher, I am constantly searching for useful new materials to give students an opportunity to experience history (or parts of it) rather than just read about it secondhand. There are a few films available that are popular among some educators documenting with narration and film clips the "history" of the Depression. Films such as *Project 20's Life in the Thirties* or the *Biography* Series' episode on Franklin Roosevelt's New Deal are adequate visual aids, but they don't go far enough in communicating the experiences of a bygone era.

The renewed interest in the thirties by the mass media has given me hope that history students can go beyond standard text-oriented materials. The unit I am about to propose involves a thorough integration of the study of the contemporary motion pictures and literature (with the emphasis on the former)

---

[1] Filler, Louis, Ed., The Anxious Years: America in the 1930's. New York: Putnam, 1964.

of the Depression decade in the classroom to create a "feel" for the life style of the past.

The cinematic literature in this area is rich enough, despite the disappearance of many of the early sound films of the time, for a vivid historical portrait of life during the Great Depression.

The first step in recreating the era for students is the assignment of some vivid literary portraits of the times. Frederick Lewis Allen's journalistic and highly readable Since Yesterday would be an ideal choice for an introductory survey. There are other books that could serve equally well here (including Studs Terkel's best seller Hard Times), and I will list some alternatives in the bibliography.

Fiction too is rich on the thirties, a decade that marked an unprecedented outpouring of novels on political (particularly on the left) and social themes. A Depression reading list including novels such as James T. Farrell's Studs Lonigan trilogy, Faulkner's Sanctuary, Thomas Wolfe's You Can't Go Home Again, Jack Conroy's The Disinherited, Horace McCoy's They Shoot Horses Don't They? (on which the recent film is based), and Richard Wright's Native Son would be highly appropriate.

There are some excellent literary anthologies that might be even more useful, since they encompass entire trends by providing samples from the works of major writers of the period. The American Writer and The Great Depression (Harvey Swados, Ed.) and The Anxious Years: America in the 1930's (Louis Filler, Ed.) are two of the best available.

These readings can serve the purpose of setting the stage (or screen) for the cinematic study to follow.

A classroom analysis of the Great Depression on film must necessarily be divided into two stages. The first stage of the study involves films that directly portray the hardships and aspirations of the people of the thirties struggling to survive. These films are the social portraits of their times, the introspective, often sad, descriptions of the conditions of poverty.

The second stage of this study, and perhaps the most difficult to deal with, makes use of the vast body of Hollywood products that were designed to entertain audiences and provide forms of escape from the rigors of reality. One might argue that movies have always done this regardless of the times, and, of course, this is true. However, there are certain films made during the 1930s that are particularly indigenous to that era. Such films are what we today would label as dated or old-fashioned. And this is exactly my point. Students should examine these dated, escapist films (like the Busby Berkeley musicals, *My Man Godfrey,* and *Lives of a Bengal Lancer*) to determine what entertained audiences during the Depression and to what extent these entertainment values still exist today.

Naturally there were many films made during that decade which fit neither category. *The Good Earth* (1937) is a film that still charms and excites audiences. So do *The Wizard of Oz* (1938, witness all of its television exposure), *Gone With the Wind, Captains Courageous,* and *A Tale of Two Cities.* This is equally true of the riotous comedies of the Marx Brothers and W. C. Fields, proving that real humor transcends any age. Fritz Lang's *Fury,* despite its release date (1936), is still one of the most vivid screen portraits of mob violence ever filmed. It could be shown to a class right now and retain much of its angry message. Such films have a great enduring quality and don't become dated in the traditional sense.

Therefore, I have eliminated most of them (*The Grapes of Wrath* is an exception) from this study, since they are more than mere reflections of the Depression.

MOVIES AS CONTEMPORARY SOCIAL PORTRAITS OF THE DEPRESSION

One of the best historical film sources available to educators is Louis de Rochemont's classic newsreel series *The March of Time.* From 1935 until the late 1940s, under the sponsorship of Time-Life Inc., this series, with its characteristic narration, summarized (and occasionally editorialized about) the events of the times. The series' episodes during the 1930s are particularly vivid, documenting many of the problems of the Depression, and the New Deal government policies that coped with them. Any of the episodes on domestic issues from 1935-1939 would serve as an excellent, factual introduction to this part of the unit. *The March of Time* shorts have an advantage over even the best recent documentaries on the thirties, since they show the student exactly what people saw during that decade. Most of the series is available through the Museum of Modern Art.

Once a historical outline of the period has been established through preliminary readings and *The March of Time,* the class can begin to look at various cinematic presentations of the conditions of the thirties. The ideal film to begin this study with is King Vidor's *Our Daily Bread.* Made in 1934 and considered explosively socialistic in its time (it was a box-office failure despite its director's reputation for winners),[2] *Our Daily Bread* effectively dramatizes the hopes and aspirations of that tragic era. John and Mary Simms (Tom Keene and Karen Morley) are typical victims of the Depression. Both are jobless and their savings have dwindled to nothing. Seeking to escape their dilemma, they move to the country, hoping the land will provide them with a livelihood. The film concentrates on the couple's experiences with the land. Although a relative gives them a place to farm, neither knows anything about agriculture. This, together with the severe erosion caused by dust bowls, makes their problem as bad in the country as it was in the city. Yet they persevere, and through cooperation with several migrant families, they succeed in irrigating the land and making it work for them.[3]

The last few minutes of *Our Daily Bread* signify the hopes of the Depression generation. Threatened with a drought, the people work together to divert the water from a nearby creek onto their land for irrigation. The last scenes are virtually without dialogue, portraying the day and night struggle of the people digging ditches to release the water. Pickaxes swing in unison. Nostalgic background music is only occasionally interrupted by the encouraging cheers of the women and children. The water rolls down the hill, filling the ditches and then, happily soaking into the crops. In the last scene, the people are busily harvesting the crop as a chorus triumphantly chants in the background.

Much of the power remains in *Our Daily Bread,* and its sympathetic treatment of the poor is still moving. But it is the film's conclusion that should make the

---

[2] Baxter, John. Hollywood in the Thirties. Cranbury, N. J.: A. S. Barnes, 1968, pp. 113-114.

[3] It was the idea of cooperative farming that made the film controversial in 1934. Ibid.

most interesting point to students. The message communicated is that no matter what else fails, if man perseveres and cooperates with his fellow man, the land will be the savior.

An excellent follow-up to *Our Daily Bread*, and one which challenges its assumptions, is Pare Lorentz's documentary for the United States Film Service (a New Deal institution) *The Plow that Broke the Plains* (1936). This powerful short film is more than just a vivid portrait of the horrible conditions of American farmland during the dust bowls of the thirties. It is an ecological warning against man's waste and abuse of his natural resources, and despite its age, could be shown at any environmental teach-in today. Beginning with the history of the Great Plains, using an animated map to outline the area, the film documents the fantastic wealth of the region's wheat fields following World War I. With poetic narration and stirring music it demonstrates the power of land. (In one scene, shots of combat tanks are alternated with those of tractors so that often they are indistinguishable from each other as the narrator announces, "Wheat to win the war.")

Later, however, came the droughts of the thirties, coupled with the Depression. A farmer is shown walking across a barren, dry wasteland. The camera focuses on the faces of hungry children (one shot of a baby playing with an idle plow is particularly effective) and farmers abandoning their land and homes for the caravans of cars on the highways going West. The film ends as the camera pans across the empty desolate land. The last shot is that of a dead tree on what appears to be a great desert.

The Plow that Broke the Plains is devastating. An audience watching it in 1936 must have been terribly depressed, since the film's message is that man's failure to prepare for the dry spells and his abuse of the soil caused the problem. The rural poverty portrayed on the screen was reality in 1936. There was no sign of hope or a hallelujah chorus to end this film.[4]

Students should discuss *The Plow that Broke the Plains* by comparing it to *Our Daily Bread*. While the latter film expressed that hope rested with the land, the documentary implied that unless something is done on a grand scale to save that land, all hope would be lost.[5] The narrator emphasizes at one point that 50,000 people per month were leaving the land in 1936, contrary to the optimism of *Our Daily Bread*.

Pare Lorentz followed up his successful documentary with a similar film about the Mississippi. *The River* (1937) follows the same general format of *The Plow*, showing the vast wealth along the river delta (cotton in the South, lumber in the North) and the prosperity of the nation from it. Then that theme shifts to the present, i.e., 1937, showing the horrible floods of that year destroying farmland, homes, and entire cities. Using similar stirring narration (which is so poetic it is

---

[4] Initially, **The Plow** had difficulty getting bookings in commercial theaters, since it was produced by the government. Later with critical accolades behind it, it did receive some commercial distribution. Snyder, Robert L., *Pare Lorentz and the Documentary Film*. Norman: University of Oklahoma Press, 1968, pp. 21-49, **passim**.

[5] Many Great Plains legislators took offense with **The Plow** feeling it reflected on their states' inability to protect the land. As late as 1939, Congressman (now Senator) Karl Mundt of South Dakota requested the government withdraw the film from circulation for its misrepresentation of his state. See **U. S. Congressional Record**, House Proceedings, February 16, 1939, pp. 2130-2131. This is available with much of the critical evaluation (most of which was praise) of the film in the Museum of Modern Art's folio on **The Plow that Broke the Plains**. This also includes a government-issued study guide for the film prepared in 1938.

reprinted in Louis Filler's anthology <u>The Anxious Years</u>) and music, *The River* documents how human waste of natural resources has compounded the tragedy of the Depression, making it an environmental problem as well as an economic one. The film ends on a hopeful note as it documents the success of the New Deal's institution of the Tennessee Valley Authority to deal with flood control, conservation, and electric power. But basically *The River*, like its predecessor, is both a portrait of the Depression in rural America and an indictment against human waste.

Probably the best-known screen portrait of the Depression in rural America is John Ford's film of Steinbeck's <u>The Grapes of Wrath</u>, which needs no summary or description. This famous film, released in 1940, is almost as timely and relevant today as it was in its own time. The struggle of the Joad family, forced to leave their barren Oklahoma farm and head for California, is the eternal struggle of the honest poor. Yet the story is also an excellent portrait of the Depression years. The film emerges as a dramatized version of *The Plow that Broke the Plains,* examining the plight of the rural American hardest hit by the economic disaster of the times. Some of the references to the benefits of a cooperative ideology and a scene in which some local roughnecks want to wreck a New Deal "model" campsite for migrant farmers, which they feel is "Red"-inspired, are philosophically "nineteen-thirtyish" (as is Steinbeck's novel to an even greater extent). *The Grapes of Wrath* is so much a part of this era, that no unit analyzing its history could possibly do without it.

From the motion picture **Grapes of Wrath**. Courtesy of Films Inc.—20th Century Fox.

It is interesting to note that so many films of the thirties concentrated on the effects of the Depression on agriculture and rural life, and so little on the urban scene. The big city most often served as the locale for the saga of the gangster (whose motives and behavior on screen were only indirectly related to the Depression) or the scene of those escapist comedies about millionaires. I will deal

From the motion picture **Dead End.** Courtesy of Films Inc.—20th Century Fox.

with both types of films in the second stage of this study, since they were more reflections of the era than portrayals of it.

The only major film still available that has anything effective to say about the Depression in the city is William Wyler's *Dead End* (1937). Based on Sidney Kingsley's noted play (but considerably altered for the screen by Lillian Hellman), this film dramatizes in almost soap-opera fashion the problems of the times through several characters. Among them are "Baby Face" Martin (Humphrey Bogart), a notorious gangster; Dave (Joel McCrea), an idealistic architect without a job; Torina (Sylvia Sidney), Dave's girl friend; and a street gang of kids (the original "Dead End" kids). The gangster has returned home to see his mother and old girl friend (both of whom disappoint him, since his mother throws him out and his girl has become a prostitute). The kids look up to him though and begin to emulate his behavior. Later in desperation, the idealistic Dave kills the gangster and with the reward money hopes to destroy all the tenements and slums that are "dead ends" for kids forced to grow up in them. He hopes to prevent the kids in the gang from growing up like "Baby Face" Martin.

Dead End is dated. Much of the dialogue (except for Bogart's and the kids') is corny and unbelievable. The stagey indoor sets detract from any attempts the film makes at reality. Yet it is an excellent statement of the fears and dreams of the urban generation of the thirties. The idealism of Dave is a kind of summation of the idealism of the times. *Dead End,* despite its cinematic awkwardness, is the urban equivalent of *Our Daily Bread* and *The Grapes of Wrath*, and it helps to demonstrate the ideas of the thirties. Students might benefit even more by reading Sidney Kingsley's play first, since the idealistic character of Dave does not exist in it. This philosophical spokesman of the times is a vehicle in the screenplay. Students should discuss the effectiveness of the character in the film.

There is one other feature film that could fit the category of social portrait— Preston Sturges' satirical comedy *Sullivan's Travels*. This film was made in 1942 when America (with the economic impetus of World War II) was supposedly coming out of the Depression. Yet in 1941, there were still more than five million unemployed. Thus, in spite of its slight chronological removal from the thirties, the message of *Sullivan's Travels* is strictly Depression. A successful director of musical-comedy movies, John L. Sullivan (Joel McCrea) decides he wants to make a serious film about poverty in the country. When his producers tell him he knows nothing about the subject, he decides to tour the country, masquerading as a hobo. The bulk of the film involves his adventures on the road, some of which are very funny, others quite touching. Later he returns to Hollywood (having fallen in love with an unemployed actress who had joined his masquerade), ready to embark on his project. Feeling compelled to do something more for the poor people he now knows, he decides to return to a shanty town and anonymously distribute 100 dollar bills. In the process of his good works, he is beaten, robbed, and left in a railroad car, which carries him away. A series of contrivances follow in which our hero finds himself imprisoned in a chain gang, suffering from amnesia. However, in good Hollywood fashion (satirically), everything works itself out. And in the end, he decides to abandon his serious film and devote his talents to making the world laugh, which it needs so badly. *Sullivan's Travels* is dedicated "to the memory of all who have made us laugh."

This film, despite its dated clichés and the acting of Veronica Lake (no wonder she's considered "camp"), is an ideal transitional piece in a unit like this. Thematically it portrays, through comedy, some of the persistent problems of the Depression still unsolved by 1942. Thus it is a legitimate, if not outstanding, companion piece to *The Grapes of Wrath* and *Dead End*. However, in the film itself, the protagonist has claimed that the poor need entertainment and laughter as well as economic and social aid to help relieve the burden of their existence. It is a fact that commercially all of the Depression films I have mentioned up to *Sullivan's Travels* were financially unsuccessful. The really popular films of the thirties (as they have been in other eras including today) were the escapist comedies, musicals, and adventure epics. Students who have analyzed these social portrayals of the times now need to examine some of the films that were most popular among people in the thirties and why.

MOVIES AS SOCIAL REFLECTIONS OF THE DEPRESSION

During 1932, one of the most dismal of the Depression years, Paramount Pictures released one of its most popular films of the decade. *If I Had a Million* starred virtually every major actor the studio had under contract (Gary Cooper, George Raft, W. C. Fields, Charles Laughton, Frances Dee, Charlie Ruggles . . .) and was directed by six of its most noted directors (James Cruze, H. Bruce Humberstone, Stephen Roberts, William A. Seiter, Ernst Lubitsch, and Norman Taurog). The plot revolves around a dying millionaire who decides to leave a million dollars apiece to eight people whose names he picks at random from the phone book (much to the disappointment of his greedy relatives). The people selected (a forger, a "rowdy marine," a condemned murderer, a hen-pecked husband, a bar maid. . .) are treated as separate episodes, focusing on their reactions and the effects of the newly acquired wealth on their lives. As the 1932 publicity for the film put it: "To some it brings only tragedy; to some, frustrations; to some, long-sought romance; and to some, exuberant happiness."

If I Had a Million is the kind of film I was talking about earlier which could be labeled as "dated" to the thirties. The idea of common people receiving a million dollars from an anonymous donor had tremendous escapist appeal to audiences who were preoccupied with huge financial problems. And, since the ultimate moral in most of the episodes was that the money was no substitute for love, or family loyalty, or honor, the film was quaintly reassuring that the best things in life, indeed, were free.

Naturally the "money isn't everything" theme is an old Hollywood cliché used in films before and since *If I Had a Million*. A popular television series of the mid-fifties, *The Millionaire,* was loosely based on the movie itself. Apparently, there will always be an audience for this kind of stuff. Yet, when one studies *If I Had a Million* in the context of 1932, it becomes apparent that this film was made specifically to appeal to the dreams and fantasies of a people trapped by economic insecurity. To publicize the movie, Paramount launched a mobilized advertising campaign using a contest as a major attraction. The contest, "Be a Millionaire for a Day," consisted of people writing 300-word essays on the theme, "What I'd do if I had a million." The essays would be submitted at the theaters showing the film. Local winners from each city or town would be chosen and then their essays were to be compared nationally. The grand prize was to be 24 hours of "unbridled luxury," featuring a trip to New York, a suite at the Waldorf, a chauffeur, maid and butler, and everything else a "typical" millionaire had.

The contest and the film generated so much interest that a Utica, New York bank used baby pictures of the stars in its ads with a caption about how every child should have his own bank account so that he can begin preparing to become a millionaire. The bank also gave two free tickets to see *If I Had a Million* to each new depositor.[6] Since this was a time when banks were failing across the country as withdrawals far exceeded deposits (prior to President Roosevelt's famous reform "bank holiday" in 1933), the use of the film to publicize a bank is particularly interesting.

If I Had a Million is a unique kind of historical source. Designed as pure entertainment for its times, it has become over the years an index of the ideology of the past. A class studying the history of the thirties could screen it and discuss the impact it might have had on audiences in 1932. A teacher could use it as an introduction for further research on the social history of the pre-New Deal Depression era. Students could, as I have done, examine the advertising of the film and relate this to the economic and social situation of 1932. Or, they could study other films on the "millionaire" theme produced during this period. There were many. The point is that the motion pictures of this period, particularly those that were made for pure entertainment, provide valuable insights for students into the social history of the thirties.

Other films lend themselves equally well to this kind of study. The witty and idealistic comedies of director Frank Capra such as *It Happened One Night* (the famous 1933 romance about a runaway millionairess and a jobless reporter, who inadvertently become traveling companions) or *Mr. Deeds Goes to Town* (a 1936 comedy about a greeting card poet who inherits 20 million dollars and tries to give it away to the needy, only to be looked upon as crazy and forced to prove his sanity). These famous films were made to provide happiness and entertainment to the audiences of their time, and they should be studied in light of the era that produced them.

Many dramas produced during the Depression succeeded as entertainment because of their bigger-than-life qualities. Capra's famous *Lost Horizon* (1937) is an example of this. Similarly, the lavish Busby Berkeley musicals, the Errol Flynn epics, and the endless succession of horror films helped audiences temporarily shut out the misery and insecurity of the Depression. This is even true to some extent of the series of violent gangster films of the era (most notably *Little Caesar* and *Public Enemy*), which provided rugged identification figures—tough guys who flaunted themselves against society (i.e., poverty, authority, responsibility), and who, despite the brutal ends to which they all succumbed, represented individualism and guts to audiences in need of some vicarious escape.

In the filmography, I have divided many of these cinematic examples according to genres. The teacher can then select one or two to experiment with this type of study in his class. Motion pictures were the cheapest and most popular form of entertainment during the Depression. Studying them can provide fascinating reflections of a past life style, which no book could hope to capture.

---

[6] This information is available in the Paramount Pictures press book of 1932 on microfilm in the New York Library of the Performing Arts. Most of it can also be found in any newspaper ad for the film in 1932.

STUDENTS' BIBLIOGRAPHY

Historical Works

*ALLEN, Frederick L. Since Yesterday. New York: Bantam Books, 1961.
*BENDINER, Robert. Just around the Corner: A Highly Selective History of the Thirties. New York: Harper and Row, 1967. A well-written, popular account of the Depression that should appeal to students.
*GALBRAITH, John K. The Great Crash, 1929. Boston, Mass.: Houghton Mifflin, 1955.
*KEMPTON, Murray. Part of Our Time: Some Monuments and Ruins of the Thirties. New York: Delta Books, 1955. An interesting work which maintains that many of the "hard times" of the thirties are exaggerated.
*LEUCHTENBURG, William E. Franklin D. Roosevelt and the New Deal. New York: Harper and Row, 1963.
*SHANNON, David, Ed. The Great Depression. Englewood Cliffs, N. J.: Prentice-Hall, 1960. A good historical anthology.
*TERKEL, Studs. Hard Times: An Oral History of the Great Depression in America. New York: Pantheon Books, 1970.

Literary Anthologies

*FILLER, Louis, Ed. The Anxious Years: America in the 1930's. New York: Putnam, 1964.
*SWADOS, Harvey, Ed. The American Writer and the Great Depression. Indianapolis, Ind.: Bobbs-Merrill, 1966.

TEACHERS' BIBLIOGRAPHY

*BAXTER, John. Hollywood in the Thirties. New York: A. S. Barnes, 1968. Despite its title and a few interesting behind-the-scenes stories, this book is incomprehensive. The author, an Englishman, is more in awe of his subject matter than descriptive of it. This book is sadly typical of much film scholarship.
*BONE, Robert A. The Negro Novel in America, rev. ed. New Haven, Conn.: Yale University Press, 1965. This noted analysis of Black writing includes a detailed section on the literature of the thirties.
CROWTHER, Bosley. The Great Films: Fifty Golden Years of Motion Pictures. New York: Putnam, 1967. The former New York Times critic has some revealing things to say about such Depression films as Public Enemy, It Happened One Night, and King Kong.
ROTHA, Paul, and Griffith, Richard. The Film till Now: A Survey of World Cinema, 3rd ed. New York: Twayne Publishers, 1960. A badly written but detailed study including a section on the films of the thirties.
*SARRIS, Andrew. The American Cinema: Directors and Directions: 1929-1968. New York: E. P. Dutton, 1969.

SNYDER, Robert L. Pare Lorentz and the Documentary Film. Norman: University of Oklahoma Press, 1968. A scholarly work on the career of one of the thirties' most significant film-makers.

FILMOGRAPHY

Recent Films Depicting Life in the Thirties

Documentaries

Life in the Thirties. 52 minutes. Black and white. NBC TV *Project 20* Series, 1960. Purchase or rental from Contemporary-McGraw-Hill Films.
Franklin Delano Roosevelt. Part I (1933-1940): 26 minutes. Black and white. *Biography* Series, 1962. Purchase or rental from Contemporary-McGraw-Hill Films.
The Roosevelt Years Series. 8 episodes, approximately 20 minutes each in length. Black and white. ABC TV Production. Purchase of individual episodes or entire series from Films Inc.

Feature Films

Bonnie and Clyde. 111 minutes. Color. Directed by Arthur Penn, 1967. Rental from Warner Brothers 16.
They Shoot Horses Don't They? 120 minutes. Color. Directed by Sidney Pollack, 1969. Rental from Films Inc.
Wild River. 105 minutes. Color (cinemascope print available). Directed by Elia Kazan, 1960. A slow-moving but interesting film about the efforts of a TVA Federal agent to persuade the rural residents of the valley of the benefits of New Deal progress. Rental from Films Inc.

Contemporary Social Portraits of the Depression

The March of Time Series. Produced by Louis de Rochemont for Time-Life Inc. Numerous episodes on the social and political atmosphere of the Depression era, 1935-1940. Rental from Museum of Modern Art, which has most episodes in the series.
Our Daily Bread. 74 minutes. Black and white. Directed by King Vidor, 1934. Rental from Janus Films or Museum of Modern Art.
The Plow that Broke the Plains. 21 minutes. Black and white. Written and directed by Pare Lorentz, 1936. Rental from Museum of Modern Art. Also check local film libraries for free loan.
The River. 30 minutes. Black and white. Written and directed by Pare Lorentz, 1937. Rental from Museum of Modern Art. Also check local film libraries for free loan.
The Grapes of Wrath. 127 minutes. Black and white. Directed by John Ford, 1940. Rental from Films Inc. or Museum of Modern Art.
Dead End. 93 minutes. Black and white. Directed by William Wyler, 1937. Rental from Samuel Goldwyn 16.

Sullivan's Travels. 91 minutes. Black and white. Directed by Preston Sturges, 1942. Rental from Museum of Modern Art or Universal 16.

Other Possibilities

Valley Town. 25 minutes. Black and white. Directed by Willar Van Dyke, 1940. Similar in style and structure to the Pare Lorentz films, this documentary depicts the Depression in a small industrial city where semi-skilled workers are being replaced by machines. Rental from Museum of Modern Art. Also check local film libraries for free loan.

Street Scene. 80 minutes. Black and white. Directed by King Vidor (based on a play by Elmer Rice), 1931. An early Depression melodrama about big city slum life, this movie really looks its age. Still it is a useful companion to a film like *Dead End*. Rental from Mogull's Film Exchange.

Angels with Dirty Faces. 97 minutes. Black and white. Directed by Michael Curtiz, 1938. This film, using the "Dead End" kids, looks like an uninspired sequel to *Dead End*, with the youths looking up to gangster James Cagney. Although ineptly handled, it is more of a social drama than a gangster film. Rental from Willoughby-Peerless Film Exchange or United Artists 16.

Tobacco Road. 84 minutes. Black and white. Directed by John Ford, 1941. This film version of Erskine Caldwell's famous Depression novel (and later play) is a vivid depiction of poverty in the rural South. Rental from Warner Brothers 16.

Social Reflections of the Depression

Comedies

If I Had a Million. 88 minutes. Black and white. Directed by James Cruze, H. Bruce Humberstone, Stephen Roberts, William A. Seiter, Ernst Lubitsch, and Norman Taurog, 1932. Rental from Universal 16.

It Happened One Night. 105 minutes. Black and white. Directed by Frank Capra, 1933. Rental from Columbia Cinematheque or Institutional Cinema Service.

Mr. Deeds Goes to Town. 115 minutes. Black and white. Directed by Frank Capra, 1936. Rental from Audio-Brandon Films or Twyman Films.

Easy Living. 66 minutes. Black and white. Directed by Mitchell Leisen, 1937. A typical comedy of the era about a poor girl who suddenly finds a mink coat. A series of assorted adventures follow causing her to fall in love with a millionaire. Later this film served as the inspiration for a Cary Grant-Doris Day comedy. Rental from Universal 16 or Twyman Films.

Hallelujah, I'm a Bum. 75 minutes. Black and white. Directed by Lewis Milestone, 1932. A musical comedy with Al Jolson as a hobo's hobo, the mayor of Central Park. A very typical, money-isn't-everything movie of the period. Rental from Audio-Brandon Films or Twyman Films. (Also listed under the title *Hearts of New York*.)

Kid Millions. 90 minutes. Black and white. Directed by Roy Del Ruth, 1934. A musical comedy in which Eddie Cantor inherits a million dollars. Rental from Films Inc.

My Man Godfrey. 95 minutes. Black and white. Directed by Gregory La Cava,

1936. Butler William Powell teaches his millionaire employers, including their lovely daughter, about the true meaning of life. Later remade unsuccessfully in the late fifties. (Small wonder why.) Rental from Universal 16.

Little Miss Marker. 80 minutes. Black and white. Directed by Alexander Hall, 1934. The typical film of the popular child star Shirley Temple, this time as an angelic waif who charms a group of New York gangsters. Audiences in the thirties ate this kind of stuff up, and although the movie has been remade since, I wonder if it has any appeal for today's filmgoer. Rental from Universal 16.

Musicals

The influence of Busby Berkeley, choreographer and director, shines through most of the escapist musicals of the period. These films had little plot beyond boy meets girl for backstage romance, but the production numbers were lavish by any standard. The following is a list of some of these typical Depression products.

Musicals of the 30's. The Museum of Modern Art has put together a package of two reels of excerpts from many of the most popular musicals of the decade. It includes the most lavish scenes from the *Gold Diggers* films, *Forty-Second Street, Flying Down to Rio,* and others. I recommend this package as opposed to any single film of the genre for teachers seeking to give students a sample of the entertainment of the era. Both reels together are 78 minutes, but a teacher could easily use one. Rental from Museum of Modern Art.

Footlight Parade. 104 minutes. Black and white. Directed by Lloyd Bacon, 1933. Rental from Audio-Brandon Films or Contemporary-McGraw-Hill Films; also check local film sources.

Gold Diggers of 1933. 98 minutes. Black and white. Directed by Mervyn LeRoy, 1933. Rental same as above.

Forty-Second Street. 90 minutes. Black and white. Directed by Lloyd Bacon, 1933. Rental same as above.

Fashions of 1934. 78 minutes. Black and white. Directed by William Dieterle, 1934. Rental same as above.

Gold Diggers of 1935. 98 minutes. Black and white. Directed by Busby Berkeley, 1935. Rental same as above.

In Caliente. 84 minutes. Black and white. Directed by Lloyd Bacon, 1935. Rental same as above.

Gold Diggers of 1937. 101 minutes. Black and white. Directed by Lloyd Bacon, 1936. Rental same as above.

Varsity Show. 80 minutes. Black and white. Directed by William Keighley, 1937. Rental same as above.

Garden of the Moon. 94 minutes. Black and white. Directed by Busby Berkeley, 1938. Rental same as above.

Melodramas (A Few Samples)

Lost Horizon. 130 minutes. Black and white. Directed by Frank Capra, 1937. Rental from Audio-Brandon Films or Twyman Films.

Dinner at Eight. 113 minutes. Black and white. Directed by George Cukor, 1933. Based on the Edna Ferber-George S. Kaufman play, this film about a group of wealthy people feeling the effects of the Depression is still moving. The cast—John Barrymore, Jean Harlow, Marie Dressler, Wallace Beery, and Billie Burke—is a thirties who's who. Rental from Films Inc.

Red Dust. 83 minutes. Black and white. Directed by Victor Fleming, 1932. Considered one of the sexiest films of its time, this Jean Harlow-Clark Gable epic about romance on a Malayan rubber plantation was very popular in 1932. It was later altered considerably and remade as *Mogambo* (also with Clark Gable) in 1953. Rental from Films Inc.

Morning Glory. 70 minutes. Directed by Lowell Sherman, 1933. Young Katherine Hepburn won an Oscar for her performance as the struggling understudy who becomes the star of the show. Students will probably laugh at the dialogue, but it was one of the most popular films of its time. Rental from Films Inc.

San Francisco. 115 minutes. Black and white. Directed by W. S. Van Dyke, 1936. This film about a ruthless gambler (Clark Gable), a singer (Jeanette MacDonald), and a priest (Spencer Tracy) set in San Francisco just before the earthquake of 1906 is still exciting. But the characterizations are standard examples of what was typical in escapist melodrama of the thirties. The earthquake scenes are among the best special effects ever filmed. Rental from Films Inc.

Horror Films

Most of these films aren't as dated as those of the other genres, since they continue to frighten television audiences today. I will cite a few only to exemplify the kind of fantasizing illusions so typical of films in this period.

King Kong. 100 minutes. Black and white. Directed by Merian C. Cooper and Ernest Schoedsack, 1933. This great film still fascinates me every time I see it. In its time it was extremely popular, the only movie ever to play simultaneously at New York's Radio City Music Hall and the Roxy. Rental from Films Inc.

Dracula. 85 minutes. Black and white. Directed by Tod Browning, 1931. This was not the first film version of Bram Stoker's classic vampire tale (the German *Nosferatu* of 1922 is far superior) and the acting is particularly hammy. But it ushered in a whole series of similar shockers during the thirties, most of which were superior to it. Rental from Universal 16.

Frankenstein. 71 minutes. Black and white. Directed by James Whale, 1931. Boris Karloff's portrayal of the monster is well known, but this film is as wooden and creaky as *Dracula.* Audiences loved it, however. Rental from Universal 16 (as are most of the other horror "classics" of this period such as *The Wolf Man, The Mummy, The Invisible Man,* etc.).

Spectacle and Adventure

Cleopatra. 95 minutes. Black and white. Directed by Cecil B. DeMille, 1934. Costume films should not become easily dated because they allegedly portray history. But this pompous spectacle, typical of Cecil B. DeMille's output in this decade, is hammy and downright funny. Students watching it will be baffled over its once serious appeal, and since the purpose of such a study is to explain this, *Cleopatra* is a good example of Depression cinema for a classroom. Rental from Universal 16.

Lives of a Bengal Lancer. 109 minutes. Black and white. Directed by Henry Hathaway, 1935. And *Gunga Din.* 117 minutes. Black and white. Directed by George Stevens, 1939. Both films are typical examples of the heart-tugging imperialistic adventures. Both films are loaded with the "White man's burden" ideology and blood-thirsty action. Though imaginatively directed, they are historical proof of America's Anglo-Saxon ethnocentrism and racist disdain for other cultures. There are those who would challenge me here, justifying the cinematic qualities of such films, but I question the society that takes pleasure in this stuff. Thank goodness this type of film is no longer in vogue. Rental of *Lives of a Bengal Lancer* from Museum of Modern Art or Universal 16; *Gunga Din* from Films Inc. or Janus Films.

Captain Blood. 98 minutes. Black and white. Directed by Michael Curtiz, 1935. The first of the Errol Flynn swashbucklers (which continued into the 1950s), full of sword fights, fast action, and romance (with Olivia de Havilland). Still entertaining, films of this type have passed from the scene, though Flynn was a box-office champion in the thirties. Rental from Films Inc.

Conquest. 111 minutes. Black and white. Directed by Clarence Brown, 1937. Charles Boyer as Napoleon and Greta Garbo as a Polish countess with whom he has an affair. This lavish production, which cost two million dollars (very expensive in 1937), is a rival to any of the similarly costly epics of Cecil B. DeMille. Rental from Films Inc.

Gangster Films

Little Caesar. 80 minutes. Black and white. Directed by Mervyn LeRoy, 1931. Rental from Audio-Brandon Films, Willoughby-Peerless Film Exchange, or United Artists 16.

Public Enemy. 74 minutes. Black and white. Directed by William Wellman, 1931. Rental from Audio-Brandon Films, Willoughby-Peerless Film Exchange, or United Artists 16.

Note: Most of the other films of this genre, except for *Scarface* (1932, which is not available in 16 mm), are variations of the two listed above. Most local film rental sources handle these, and any one could serve as an example of the gangster appeal in the thirties.

Movies and McCarthyism–
A Unit of Study Using
Motion Pictures as Historical Sources

In late 1947, appearing as a witness before the House Un-American Activities Committee, Jack L. Warner, head of one of the largest and most influential movie studios in Hollywood, was asked to give the names of known Communists in the movie industry. He replied by listing several names of prominent writers, directors, and actors, while at the same time, extolling his own patriotism. Near the conclusion of his testimony, much to his embarrassment, a member of the committee recalled that in 1943, Mr. Warner had personally produced what was probably the most pro-Russian film ever made, *Mission to Moscow,* which helped to propagandize the coming detente between this country and the Soviet Union as common enemies of Nazi Germany. Warner, in response, again stated his great loyalty to the United States, even claiming he favored setting up a system whereby anyone not liking our country should be shipped to Russia. It was at this point that a young member of the committee, named Richard Nixon, asked Mr. Warner how many anti-Communist films his studio had made. He replied (rather meekly) that it was preparing one.[1]

Apparently Mr. Warner's preparation was a long one, since his studio didn't contribute its share to the anti-Communist purge until 1951. But when it did, it released what would be one of the most effective Red-baiting propaganda movies– *I Was a Communist for the FBI.* This film was made in an era that some Americans said was "a resurgence of patriotism" and what others called "a period of rigid conformity and intellectual repression." It was the era of America's second great Red scare; a time when terms such as "iron curtain" and "cold war" became part of the American vocabulary; the period of our history that molded the foreign policy that confounds us today; and the high point in the political career of one of the most controversial figures in American history–Senator Joseph McCarthy.

As a history teacher I become more and more perplexed about the relevancy of my subject. So often the study of American history becomes a stagnant, meaningless exercise in textbook discipline. Students "learn" the material for a test, "study" it, spit it back to the teacher, and forget it. They may recall some of its anecdotes

---

[1] This entire incident and indeed all of the Hollywood hearings are brilliantly described in Walter Goodman's history of the House Un-American Activities Committee, The Committee. New York: Farrar, Straus and Giroux, 1968, pp. 190-225. Available in paperback.

in the future, but merely as trivia, and rarely is history used to explain a cause and effect relationship between past and present. I'm not always sure this is possible, but I do feel that units in contemporary (twentieth century) history can be made more meaningful by studying the wide variety of sources in the increasing number of mass media. What I am about to propose is an exemplary study of a most controversial period of our modern history—the anti-Communist sentiments in the United States from the post-World War II period until the decline of Senator Joseph McCarthy in 1954—by having students examine motion pictures related to it.

From the motion picture **Point of Order.** Courtesy of Walter Reade, Inc.

With the popularity of Abraham Polansky's film *Tell Them Willie Boy Was Here*, our youth has become increasingly aware of the McCarthyist era, since director Polansky had been blacklisted by the movie industry for the past 22 years. (Polansky's last "signed" film was *Force of Evil* made in 1948.) Many young people know just enough about this period to be motivated to study it further. They know of the Polansky affair; they may be aware of the American film-makers in exile like Joseph Losey and Jules Dassin; they hear prominent newscasters warning us that with the repressive statements of certain "high public officials" we may be returning to the McCarthy era; they hear their peers protest a foreign policy shaped by an era of a bogus Red Menace. It is the teacher's job to tie all of this together with a sense of history.

This unit is geared to senior high school or college students in US or contemporary history classes. It can also serve as a part of a sociology curriculum examining the social mores of a historical era. To introduce the material, some traditional methods will probably be necessary. Certainly the class should use a basic reading to provide the background and reference information for the study. I have never seen a high school American history text that covers this period adequately, and therefore I recommend a class set of the paperback edition of

Eric Goldman's The Crucial Decade: and After: America 1945-1960 (Vintage Books, 1960), with emphasis on chapters 1-10. This book is very well written and easy enough to read for most high school students. It is also, despite the noted liberalism of its author, written with a great deal of understanding for the motives of the "Red hunters," if not total objectivity.

There are some documentary films available dealing with this era. Two 30-minute films on Senator McCarthy can be obtained from Contemporary-McGraw-Hill Films (New York), though neither is useful for much more than a visual aid. One of them is from the *Twentieth Century* TV Series, narrated by Walter Cronkite; the other is part of the *Biography* Series (which in its desire for total objectivity never even deals with McCarthy as a controversial figure).

The most well-known documentary on McCarthy is Emilio de Antonio's edited version of the TV kinescopes of the Army-McCarthy hearings of the 1954, *Point of Order.* Although fascinating to watch, this film has very little narration and it presumes the viewer already knows everything about McCarthy and the spirit of the times. Consequently, students find this confusing, unless they see it with sufficient historical background. After all, it deals with the decline of an era and would be most useful at the conclusion of the unit.

There is one excellent film on McCarthy's rise to power, and it can serve as a perfect supplement to the Goldman book. Interestingly enough, this too is made by de Antonio, who perhaps realized the need for some introduction to *Point of Order.* It is called *Charge and Countercharge* and when rented, it comes with a 13-page teacher's guide by Professor James P. Shenton of Columbia University.

Once the students have surveyed the basic facts of the era, an in-depth study of the propaganda can begin. The teacher might assign a list of books that were written during the period or by participants who wrote later in retrospect.

BOOKS OF THE RIGHT

PHILBRICK, Herbert A. I Led Three Lives. New York: Grosset and Dunlap, 1952. Perhaps the most famous of the anti-Communist writings, this book served as the basis for a popular TV series for many years. Indeed, it is still aired in syndication by certain local TV stations. This memoir of a counterspy is exciting reading, although it deals with Communist activities in this country during World War II, not the 1950s, which the television program portrayed.

*CHAMBERS, Whittaker. Witness. New York: Random House, 1952. The Alger Hiss exposé.

NIXON, Richard. Six Crises. New York: Doubleday, 1962. Nixon, of course, advanced his political career greatly in this period as a "crusading" member of the House Un-American Activities Committee.

REAGAN, Ronald, and Hubler, Richard, G. Where's the Rest of Me? New York: Hawthorn, 1965. Reagan's autobiography, which explains his own moral reassessment of himself during the Hollywood hearings of the late 1940s.

*HOOVER, J. Edgar. Masters of Deceit. New York: Holt, Rinehart and Winston, 1958. The standard work on the effects of the Communist conspiracy in America.

BOOKS OF THE LEFT

HISS, Alger. In the Court of Public Opinion. New York: Knopf, 1957.
TRUMBO, Dalton. The Year of the Toad. New York: Crossroads, 1949. The protest of one of the most famous and talented Hollywood writers to be blacklisted.
BESSIE, Alvah. Inquisition in Eden. New York: MacMillan, 1965. Another victim of the blacklist's protest.
*MILLER, Arthur. The Crucible (play). New York: Bantam Books, 1959. The dramatist's great symbolic condemnation of the whole era through a historical parallel to the Salem Witch Trials.

The films of the period, of course, should provide the most vivid historical portrait. The student by now should have learned about the results of the House Un-American Activities Committee's investigation of Hollywood, and the self-imposed purge of the industry's leftist influences.

It might seem logical at this point to take a look at some of the more well-known films written and directed by the accused Communists of the industry. Indeed many admitted they had belonged to or sympathized with the movement at one time or another. And those who refused to testify at the hearings and were indicted for contempt of Congress were even jailed for a short time.[2] Yet a study of the films of these men might be futile in the classroom, since one might search vainly for direct pro-Russian or even anti-American ideology in films like *Back to Bataan, Sahara, Since You Went Away, Kitty Foyle, The Naked City, Forever Amber,* or any of their others. The only really pro-Russian films made were during World War II with the blessings of the Roosevelt administration and the major studio bosses (including Jack L. Warner).[3] After all, Russia had suddenly become a valuable ally.

It would be more beneficial for the students to examine some of the films in reaction to the Communist fear. Their content was clear—to show America successfully warding off a foreign enemy.

THE ANTI-COMMUNIST FILMS

I Was a Communist for the FBI (Warner Brothers). Taken from the popular *Saturday Evening Post* articles by Agent Matt Cvetic (as told to Pete Martin) who infiltrated a Communist espionage ring. The film, in documentary style, is a painful oversimplification of the issues, with the Communists portrayed as one-dimensional, gangster types. Yet in its time it was highly

---

[2] Ten men (writers and directors) were cited for contempt and were immediately blacklisted by their industry. At least three of them are now reestablished in motion pictures and have been for some time: Edward Dmytryk, Dalton Trumbo, and Ring Lardner, Jr. Another, Herbert Biberman, "came back" recently with the film **Slaves.** However, although only ten were actually indicted for their affiliations, many other "name" personalities were put off limits. These included Carl Foreman, Michael Wilson, Clifford Odets, Robert Rossen, Abraham Polansky, Joseph Losey, Jules Dassin, and many others. A complete study of the entire affair can be found in Jones, Dorothy B., "Communism and the Movies: A Study of Film Content" which is part of Report on Blacklisting, John Cogley, Ed. New York: Fund for the Republic, 1956, pp. 196-304.

[3] Ibid.

regarded as indicated by 3½ stars in the *New York Daily News*. It is often run on television and is available from several small 16-mm distributors.

Big Jim McLain (Warner Brothers). "Big John (Wayne) as 'Big Jim' smokes out Reds in Hawaii," was how this film was publicized. A bad film by any standard, the heroics and simplified plot were typical of Hollywood's output on the subject. Wayne's own thoroughly anti-Communist philosophy is closely related to what is portrayed in this film, however. And his beliefs still have considerable political influence.

My Son John (Paramount). An attempt to provide anti-Communist propaganda on a big scale, as evidenced by its noted director (Leo McCarey) and cast (Helen Hayes and Robert Walker, Senior). Allegedly about how a family deals with the problem of a nonconformist son who becomes a Communist, threatening to destroy all the family stands for. Terrible, but typical.

Pick-Up on South Street (20th Century Fox). A heavily contrived, exciting movie about a pickpocket (American criminal type) who unwittingly steals the purse of a Communist agent and gets caught in a conflict between his criminal instincts and his patriotism. Guess which wins out? Silly as the film seems, it must have had some impact on its times. *The New York Daily News* gave it 3 stars and called it a "brutally realistic drama," and, like others of its genre, it is representative propaganda.

Night People (20th Century Fox). A cold-war espionage film, with big budget (filmed in color, cinemascope, and on location in Berlin), and big cast (including Gregory Peck). Its plot deals with the rescue of a young American from the clutches of the "Reds" in East Berlin, with the usual heroics and not-to-be-believed villainous types. This film is particularly interesting because it has been reviewed in a composite essay by critic Pauline Kael in her book I Lost It at the Movies. This essay contrasts it (as being typical right-wing propaganda) to Herbert Biberman's equally inept leftist film (made in protest against the McCarthyists) *Salt of the Earth*. The essay should be reproduced for the students.

Trial. This is without doubt the best of the anti-Communist pictures. Taken from a best-selling novel, it portrays American Communists as realistically dedicated (and dangerous) people, who exploit a novice lawyer and a young Mexican migrant for the good of their cause. It should be shown with one of the more inept films of the period for contrast.

Of course, the sources listed here are merely suggestions. There are other books and films students can examine. It depends on one's emphasis. Yet, I am convinced that incorporating such materials into the teaching of history makes history live. The anti-Communist writings and films of the 1950s are historical sources and should be analyzed as such. The movie industry especially, which reacted to the accusations against it by fearfully conforming and purging itself of a large portion of its creative talents, is worthy of study. Part of its reaction came in films like those cited, which were designed to atone for any signs of lack of patriotism. One writer described the era this way:

"It was insane, looney, ghastly . . . . Hollywood has always been a hotbed of conformity . . . . By their very nature, these institutions (of the mass media) yield to external pressure; it is in fact their substitute for inspiration. The difference between art of even the lowest order and mass entertainment is that one is created by internal pressure and the other by external pressure."[4]

TEACHERS' BIBLIOGRAPHY

Note: Much of the research on the subject matter of the films was done with the use of the TV Feature Film Source Book, available through the Broadcast Information Bureau, Inc., New York. Also useful was the Yearbook of Motion Pictures, 1950-54 and 1956.

COGLEY, John, Ed. Report on Blacklisting, 2 vols. New York: Fund for the Republic, 1956. See the section by Dorothy B. Jones in vol. I.
*GOODMAN, Walter. The Committee.New York: Farrar, Straus and Giroux, 1968. History of the House Un-American Activities Committee.
*KAEL, Pauline. I Lost It At the Movies. Boston: Little, Brown and Co., 1965.
*ROVERE, Richard H. Senator Joe McCarthy. New York: Harcourt Brace Jovanovich, 1959.
*SARRIS, Andrew. The American Cinema: Directors and Directions: 1929-1968. New York: E. P. Dutton, 1968.
SCHUMACH, Murray. The Face on the Cutting Room Floor. New York: William Morrow, 1964. History of film censorship with a good section on the blacklist era.

FILMOGRAPHY

Historical Surveys

Senator Joseph McCarthy. 27 minutes. Black and white. *Biography* Series, 1963. Purchase or rental from Contemporary-McGraw-Hill Films.
Senator Joe McCarthy. 26 minutes. Black and white. CBS TV's *Twentieth Century* Series, 1961. Purchase or rental from Contemporary-McGraw-Hill Films.
Point of Order. 90 minutes. Black and white. Directed by Emilio de Antonio, 1964. Rental from Walter Reade 16 Films.
Charge and Countercharge. 43 minutes. Black and white. Directed by Emilio de Antonio, 1969. Rental from Appleton-Century-Crofts Films.
McCarthy vs. Welch. 25 minutes. Black and white. Wolper Productions, Inc. (narrated by Edmond O'Brien), 1967. Purchase from Films Inc.

"Leftist" Films

Mission to Moscow. 123 minutes. Black and white. Directed by Michael Curtiz, 1943. Rental from Contemporary-McGraw-Hill Films. See James Agee's humorously perceptive review of this film in Agee on Film.
Salt of the Earth. 94 minutes. Black and white. Directed by Herbert Biberman, 1954. Rental from Audio-Brandon Films.

---

[4] Rovere, Richard. Senator Joe McCarthy. New York: Harcourt Brace Jovanovich, 1959. Available in paperback.

Anti-Communist Films

I Was a Communist for the FBI. 83 minutes. Black and white. Directed by Gordon Douglas, 1951. Check local film sources for rental.

Big Jim McLain. 90 minutes. Black and white. Directed by Edward Ludwig, 1952. Rental from Warner Brothers 16.

My Son John. 122 minutes. Black and white. Directed by Leo McCarey, 1952. Check local film sources for rental.

Pick-Up on South Street. 80 minutes. Black and white. Directed by Samuel Fuller, 1953. Rental from Willoughby-Peerless Film Exchange.

Night People. 93 minutes. Color (cinemascope print available). Directed by Nunnally Johnson, 1954. Rental from Films Inc.

Trial. 107 minutes. Black and white. Directed by Mark Robson, 1955. Rental from Films Inc.

Movies and History–
Some Further Observations and Suggestions

Curriculum guides for history teachers tie them to dated, antiseptic texts and standard audio-visual aids. The usual "recommended" films (at the back of each text chapter) for United States, World, non-Western, and Negro history are yesterday's television documentaries (which few kids ever watched when they were aired) and "special" productions ranging from rice farming in Burma to the "authentic" story of colonial Williamsburg. Nowhere are commercial motion pictures given any recognition except (absurdly) as illustrations of historical eras. (I have seen *Ivanhoe* with Robert Taylor referred to as a good portrait of medieval life. The novel isn't even a good portrait of that.)

Curriculum writers for boards of education aren't the only ones to blame for this "recommended" abuse of film. Motion picture distributors, trying to push their products, have at times badly misled unsophisticated, well-meaning educators. At one recent teachers' conference, I saw advertisements recommending Samuel Bronston's absurd epic *55 Days at Peking* as a device for teaching about American Far Eastern policy. This film, loosely based on some events during the Boxer Rebellion in China (which was an understandable nationalist uprising by Chinese tired of seeing their country exploited by foreigners), is simply a Western with Chinese as attacking Indians (actually Spaniards since the film was made in Spain). *55 Days at Peking* may be an interesting symptom of Hollywood's traditional imperialistic output, but it is definitely not a portrayal of American history.

In some of the previous chapters, I have suggested a number of possible uses for films as historical sources. Now I would like to consider some additional possibilities in this direction in order to guide teachers away from the standard curricular audio-visual aids approach and caution them against misleading advertising by film distributors.

This chapter is divided into four parts, each presenting another possible way of teaching history with film. The first part deals with motion pictures as historically representative of the times that produced them. This is a follow-up to previous chapters on the same theme. Part two suggests the study of films that *made* history. This involves an examination of a few films that had a definite social impact on their times. (Naturally, there are not too many of these.) The third section is devoted to those films that do in some way accurately portray the past (through careful attention to scenic design, costuming, dialogue, accurate re-creation of events, etc.). And part four is my own very subjective and critical survey of the relatively few classroom documentaries that can be useful as audio-visual aids. (I include this last section for those who really believe that films used in this way have much effect in a classroom. Actually, this approach is the weakest use of the medium, and as a history teacher myself, I shun it as often as possible.)

FILMS AS HISTORY—AN ADDITIONAL EXAMPLE

In Chap. 14, I tried to indicate that movies, because of their contemporary commercial appeal, often provide reflections of the ideas and attitudes of the era that produced them. Recent films such as *Easy Rider, Medium Cool, Joe,* or *Woodstock* may be studied by some future generation interested in the history of the sixties and seventies. Certainly these films, which are commercially attractive to a large audience, indicate something about the life-style of our own era.

A good classroom unit in understanding film as a historical medium would be to have students do a comparative study of two films of two different generations on a similar theme. The student could analyze the content of the films, contrasting, where possible, the characterizations, social messages, and plot contrivances in light of the atmosphere of the society that produced them.

There have been two motion pictures produced with the title *The Charge of the Light Brigade.* The first of these was a lavish American production made in 1936 starring Errol Flynn (then a young box-office champion) and Olivia de Havilland. The second film with that title was a British-made, even more lavish production (wide screen, technirama process, which, of course, was not yet invented in 1936), released in 1968.

At first glance, someone who has not seen either film, or who has seen the original but not the latter, would naturally conclude that one is a remake (or revision) of the other. Remakes of old films are not uncommon, and usually they are less successful than the originals on which they are based (*Mutiny on the Bounty, Cimmaron, Stage-Coach,* etc.). Yet if one examines both versions of *The Charge of the Light Brigade,* one discovers that they are not the same at all. They are two totally different stories, with different characters, situations, and philosophies. The first is a film about the 1930s while the second is about the 1960s—even though the locale of both films is the Crimean War of the late 1850s.

The 1936 *Charge* completely eliminates all of the actual historical background of the event depicted in Tennyson's poem. Errol Flynn portrays a dashing cavalryman on duty in India, combatting hostile rebels against British rule, including a dastardly villain—the Emperor of Suristan (sounds like a laxative), Surat Kahn. In good imperialistic style, Flynn warns the British colonial officials not to trust the "savage." In the meantime, poor Errol has problems of his own, since his fiancée has fallen in love with his diplomat brother. Nevertheless, he keeps his watchful eye on the evil Kahn and, sure enough, the cowardly villain (now in cahoots with the Russians, natural enemies of England) attacks an undermanned garrison. Allowing Flynn and his fiancée to escape (it seems our hero once saved the Kahn's life and so as repayment . . .), the villain has everyone in the outpost murdered, including the women and children. Flynn returns with reinforcements only to find the bodies of the dead. He and his regiment vow to avenge the massacre and destroy the savage Surat Kahn.

Through a series of historical coincidences (brilliantly arranged by the Warner Brothers scriptwriters), England goes to war with Russia to protect Turkey.

From the motion picture **Charge of the Light Brigade** (1936). Courtesy of United Artists.

Flynn's regiment is shipped to the Crimean front, only to discover that fighting with the Russians at Balaclava is the villainous Surat Kahn. The plot really begins to thicken as Flynn realizes the chance for vengeance. Given an order telling the light brigade of cavalry to hold its position and not attack the Russians, our hero, realizing his enemy is on the other side of the valley, forges a new order, much to the joy of his equally vengeful men. And thus the light brigade makes its historic suicidal charge. On the screen flash the exciting stanzas of Tennyson's poem: "Half a league, half a league, half a league onward, etc."

The charge is a brilliant example of Hollywood warfare, with Flynn wounded several times still crashing past the Russian artillery to get his man. Just as he dies, he hurls his lance into the stomach of old, evil Surat. The "savage" drops and

100 more British lances are thrust into him, striking a blow for Anglo-Saxon purity around the world!

If I have made this old film sound sillier than it actually is, I apologize. It's all quite exciting and very typical of similar escapist films of the thirties (*Gunga Din, Lives of a Bengal Lancer, The Last Outpost,* etc.). But what amazes me is how seriously the film was taken in its time. Even though it didn't pay the slightest attention to the historical facts of the incident (even Tennyson's poem had mentioned someone had blundered to order such a ridiculous charge), one critic hailed its "trustworthy research." A 1936 educators' group, The Photoplay Appreciation Movement, hired a Harvard scholar to write a classroom study guide, using the film. This guide explains away the anti-historical contrivances by claiming that no audience could accept a dramatization of a military blunder, thus the charge had to be a logical decision so that the audience could identify with the story.[1] The guide later pays some attention to the actual facts of the situation, but hails the film as an even better portrait of the British rule in India.

This version of *The Charge of the Light Brigade* is a historical source for students. It provides clues about how Americans felt about non-Western cultures in the 1930s. It justifies an act of military insanity by labeling it as heroic. It embodies past attitudes towards entertainment and escapism. The film was a big financial success and won quite a bit of critical acclaim. If students seeing it today laugh at its simplistic philosophy and comic-book dialogue, it indicates that attitudes may have changed. Errol Flynn's kind of heroics are now history.

The 1968 version of *The Charge of the Light Brigade,* directed by Tony Richardson, does strive for historical accuracy. Based on Cecil Woodham-Smith's well researched work The Reason Why, the film uses the actual characters of British history (the vain Lord Cardigan, the pompous and narrow-minded Lord Lucan, and the ineffectual, slightly senile Secretary of War, Lord Raglan), and every scene is etched to capture the true look of the 1850s. The director skillfully alternates his scenes, showing the contrast between the foppish incompetent officers and the hardened, abused common soldiers. The young dashing officer, a Captain Nolan (David Hemmings), is similar to the Flynn type, but in the end the irrational desire of this heroic fellow ultimately leads to the blunder that destroys the light brigade.

In addition to being historically accurate, this film belongs as much to the 1960s as the earlier version belonged to its age. This *Charge of the Light Brigade* is anti-war. By portraying the officers as callous pigs and headstrong fools and by showing the mistreatment of the rank and file troops, the film hits hard at the military. There is one scene that is directly geared for today's audiences. Lord Raglan (John Gielgud), a foolish, senile man (at one point he calls the Russian enemy "the French," getting his wars confused), tries to explain the necessity of war with Russia over Turkey. If Turkey should fall to the Russians, he argues, "the Balkans will be next, and then the Mediterranean. . . the rest of Europe will fall like a stack of cards until England herself will be in danger." This, of course, is the "domino theory" often used to justify American involvement in Vietnam.

---

[1] A Guide to the Study of the Photoplay Based on Tennyson's Poem "The Charge of the Light Brigade." Photoplay Studies Series, vol. II, November 1936. I found this copy in the file under the film's title at the Museum of Modern Art. I don't know how many other copies remain.

This film is not escapist. Its realism and anti-war propaganda are designed to pain the viewer. Yet despite all of its relevance, this version of *The Charge of the Light Brigade* was a box-office loser.

I suggest that history students screen and analyze the two films as portraits of the ages that produced them. They should discuss the attitudes toward war, heroism, the military, historical accuracy, and escapist entertainment implicit in both of them. They should also discuss the reasons for the success of the first version and the failure of the second, especially since the recent version is such a good film on every level. Could it be that no anti-war philosophy can be believable coming from a film entitled *The Charge of the Light Brigade*? Or, is it that today's attitudes towards heroism and escapism are not so different from those of the thirties?

These are questions for students to cope with. They are far removed from the usual kind of historical study, but they are questions about the nature of history and our relationship to it.

Filmography

The Charge of the Light Brigade. 114 minutes. Black and white. Directed by Michael Curtiz, 1936. Rental from Films Inc. or United Artists 16.

The Charge of the Light Brigade. 130 minutes. Color (cinemascope print available). Directed by Tony Richardson (British), 1968. Rental from United Artists 16.

From the motion picture **Charge of the Light Brigade** (1968). Courtesy of United Artists.

FILMS THAT MADE HISTORY

Motion pictures are a relatively new medium. Consequently it would be difficult for a teacher to conduct a course on "Films that Changed the World." With literature, this is possible—Common Sense, Uncle Tom's Cabin, The Influence of Sea Power on History, Mein Kampf all had tremendous impact on their times. The relative newness of film, coupled with the attitudes towards it as a mere source of entertainment, has limited the cinematic output of great social or political works. Still film has been used, both consciously and unconsciously, as a propaganda medium, and I have already dealt with that to some extent. Historically speaking, there are at least two films that students can analyze as history makers, movies that actually shaped (or helped to shape) social and political events. The two films that can fit such a definition are D. W. Griffith's *The Birth of a Nation* and Leni Riefensthal's *Triumph of the Will (Triumph des Willens)*.

I have already summarized the plot of Griffith's monumental work in Chap. 13. Students can view the film in a totally different context, however. The history of the Wilsonian phase of the so-called "Progressive Era" is very much intertwined with *The Birth of a Nation*. The film was released at the height of "Jim Crow" racism in Southern and "border" states, and it reflects the attitudes of the majority of White Americans of that time, including, to a certain extent, the President of the United States Woodrow Wilson.[2] Indeed, Wilson, several ranking members of Congress, and the Chief Justice of the Supreme Court screened the film at the request of the author Thomas Dixon, on whose racist novel The Clansman the film was based. Dixon had been a former history student of Wilson's at Johns Hopkins. Following the screening, the President and his companions generally praised the film and Wilson is alleged to have congratulated Dixon for presenting "history written in lightning."[3]

Later the infant NAACP attemped to have the film edited to remove some of the vicious anti-Black propaganda, but met with relatively little success.[4]

Students should examine this film for its impact on its times, possibly doing additional research on it in microfilms of the newspapers and magazines of 1915. They should address themselves to the following issues:

1. To what extent did *Birth of a Nation*'s glorification of the post-Civil War Ku Klux Klan influence the rebirth of that body soon after the film was released?

2. What was the impact of this artistically rendered film on its audience, many of whom had never seen a motion picture before in their lives?

3. How indicative are the attitudes of the film towards Blacks in relationship to popular feelings in 1915?

4. What was there about the American history books of that era that made *Birth of a Nation* seem so historically respectable?

---

[2] Wilson's anti-Black attitudes and policies have been documented by most historians of the period. For a detailed summary of the President's feelings about Blacks, see Wolgemuth, Kathleen, "Woodrow Wilson's Appointment Policy and the Negro," **Journal of Southern History**, vol. 24, November 1958, pp. 457-471.

[3] A detailed account of this incident and the subsequent battle of the newly formed NAACP to have **Birth of a Nation** withdrawn or cut is provided in an excellent historical essay: Thomas R. Cripps, "The Reaction of the Negro to the Motion Picture **Birth of a Nation**," **The Historian** (Journal of the National History Honor Society), vol. 25, May 1963, pp. 344-362. I would like to see this reprinted for a wider circulation.

[4] Ibid.

Viewing this film, which had such tremendous social impact on its times, can be a fantastic classroom experience. The potential for further research and analytical class discussion is unquestionable.

From the motion picture **Birth of a Nation.** Courtesy of Museum of Modern Art.

Leni Riefensthal's famous Nazi propaganda film *Triumph of the Will* is allegedly a filmed record of the Nuremberg Party Convention of 1934. Anyone seeing the first few minutes, however, will realize that this is no simple documentary of a political rally. Using every sophisticated cinematic technique of the times, Miss Riefensthal created a celluloid pageant and spectacle rivaling D. W. Griffith's *Intolerance.* Actually the entire convention was deliberately staged as a pageant for the specific purpose of being filmed in this manner.[5]

The film is fascinating even today, particularly the early scenes. A plane descends from an almost endless body of clouds over a peaceful looking Gothic city. The shadow of the plane resembles a cross and as it lands with tumultuous music in the background, it is as if Christ has returned to earth. Out of the plane emerges Adolf Hitler facing a mammoth crowd. The camera dwells deliberately on the faces of young, blonde Aryan men crying in unison "Heil Hitler."

The rest of the film demonstrates the symbolic pageantry of Nazism: night parades lit by torches, Wagnerian music, endless marching. The political nature of the convention itself is almost swept aside, providing only brief phrases from

[5] For an interesting description of the technical filming of **Triumph of the Will,** see Seigfried Kracauer, From Caligari to Hitler, A Psychological History of the German Film. Princeton, N. J.: Princeton University Press, 1947. Available in paperback.

most of the speeches. Most of the scenes saturate the viewer with marching, loud music, and more marching, photographed from every camera angle imaginable.

The film is a remarkable piece of propaganda, and classes studying the history of this period should be required to see it. They should examine its content, attempting to decipher its symbols and metaphors. They should, through research and discussion, become aware of the great impact *Triumph of the Will* had in Germany in the mid-thirties.

One of the finest pieces of film scholarship I have ever read, David Stewart Hull's Film in the Third Reich, describes it this way:

"The purpose of the film was twofold: To show Germans the solidarity of the Party, particularly following the Rohm affair; and to introduce the leaders, many of whom spoke a few words, to this pretelevision society. Another, more subtle, purpose was to impress foreign audiences, and at the same time to scare the hell out of them. The film succeeded on all counts."[6]

Students may not be as taken with *Triumph of the Will* as with *Birth of a Nation.* The full two-hour version becomes strenuous viewing by the last reel. There is literally too much marching. But if one considers the historical militaristic background of Germany and her shameful condition after World War I, it is not hard to imagine the nostalgic impact of all the pomp, and ceremony, and even the marching.

The history-making films are still too few to warrant a course in "Films that Changed the World," but the examples of *The Birth of a Nation* and *Triumph of the Will* demonstrate the potential power of the medium. They belong in the history class.

Filmography

The Birth of a Nation. 195 minutes (also a 130-minute version available). Silent. Directed by D. W. Griffith, 1915. Rental from Museum of Modern Art.
Triumph of the Will (Triumph des Willens). 120 minutes. Black and white. Directed by Leni Riefensthal (German), 1934. Rental from Museum of Modern Art (without English subtitles), Contemporary-McGraw-Hill Films (with English subtitles), or Audio-Brandon Films (with English subtitles). The Museum of Modern Art does have an abbreviated, 40-minute version with subtitles at a very low rental rate. This version should be sufficient for high school classes.

FEATURE FILMS THAT ACCURATELY PORTRAY HISTORY

As I have indicated, there are very few dramatic feature films that pay careful attention to historical detail. Epics such as *Spartacus* and *El Cid* may be highly entertaining films, but they are not accurate portrayals of the past. Historian Frederick Jackson Turner once wrote that writers of history interpret the past in light of the present; therefore, even carefully researched history is far from objective. But historical films, like most historical novels, are made with the direct

---

[6]Hull, David Stewart. Film in the Third Reich, A Study of the German Cinema, 1933-1948. Berkeley: University of California Press, 1969, p. 75.

purpose of appealing to today's audience. The Middle Ages were brutal, super-
stitious times beset with crime and disease. The colorful romanticism of *Ivanhoe*
and *El Cid* are figments of the imaginations of novelists and film directors.

It is understandable why movies have not been preoccupied with researching
historical details. The past is not colorful and romantic, and showing a deglamor-
ized Middle Ages or Renaissance is bad business commercially. For these reasons
the following list of films is very brief. The titles included are those which in
some way present the events of the past realistically. Using films of this type to
teach history is not as effective as viewing the actual films made during a historical
period, or in the case of pre-twentieth century history, reading the contemporary
literature and examining the art. However, at least the following motion pictures
pay some intelligent respect to history by providing a feeling for the reality of
the past.

Filmography

The Organizer. 126 minutes. Black and white. Directed by Mario Monicelli
(Italian), 1964. English subtitles (there is an English dubbed print available
on request). To me, this is the greatest historical film of them all. Telling
the story of a meek, idealistic scholar (Marcello Mastroianni), who becomes
a labor leader in Turin during the 1880s, the film totally captures the look
and spirit of the age. The horrible conditions of the factories which were
badly lit and ventilated, the unsafe machinery (a man loses a hand in a press),
the squalor and poverty of an industrial town are all captured by vivid
cinematography resembling the actual photographs of the 1880s. The entire struggle of the workers is portrayed, including the ultimate capitulation
of their strike. I cannot recommend this great film highly enough. It is
superior to any book in describing the working conditions and early struggles of labor to organize in the late nineteenth century. Its Italian locale is
merely an example of the universal situation of workers of those times. No
teacher of the history of labor should neglect this masterpiece—a true rarity
among commercial films. Rental from Walter Reade 16.
Potemkin. 86 minutes. Black and white. Silent. Directed by Sergei M. Eisenstein
(Russian), 1925. Eisenstein's famous film about the short-lived anti-Czarist
rebellion of 1905 during which the sailors of the battleship Potemkin
mutinied, is a nostalgic reflection of the past, typical of the feelings in
Bolshevik Russia in 1925. Yet despite its lack of objectivity, the attention
to historical details and events is brilliant. It looks like a newsreel of the
1905 rebellion. Rental from Museum of Modern Art or Audio-Brandon
Films.
Ivan the Terrible. Part I: 96 minutes; part II: 90 minutes. Black and white. Directed by Sergei M. Eisenstein (Russian), 1944 and 1946. English subtitles.
I have not seen either of these epics by the Russian master, but I have been
told by people who should know that both films are brilliant recreations of
historical details. This is all the more significant considering that they were
made in war time with much interference from the Stalinist government.
Rental from Audio-Brandon Films.
The Seventh Seal. 96 minutes. Black and white. Directed by Ingmar Bergman

(Swedish), 1956. English subtitles. This noted, brilliant fantasy about a
knight returned from the Crusades playing a game of chess with Death to
hold off the toil of the black plague is the best film ever made about medieval life. It portrays the fears and superstitions of that age and actually
penetrates the medieval mind. I am surprised that the film is rarely used in the
classroom, particularly courses in the history of the Middle Ages. Rental
from Janus Films.

From the motion picture **The Organizer.** Courtesy of Walter Reade, Inc.

Fellini Satyricon. 120 minutes. Color. Directed by Federico Fellini (Italian), 1970.
English subtitles. One of the most amazing, unusual, repulsive, brilliant films
I have ever seen. The greatest director of our time has taken the work of
Roman author Petronias and created a sickening, fragmented portrait of the
ancient world as it probably was. Any teacher planning to use this must see
it first, since much of it is in questionable taste unless viewed in the context
of history. No wonder Rome fell. Rental from United Artists 16.

The Gospel According to St. Matthew. 137 minutes. Black and white. Directed by
Pier Paolo Pasolini (Italian), 1964. English subtitles. I don't know if any
biblical film can ever be historically accurate, but this simple, believable
rendering of the St. Matthew text, without earth-shaking miracles and pompous speeches, creates a realistic experience. Rental from Audio-Brandon
Films.

A Night to Remember. 123 minutes. Black and white. Directed by Roy Baker
(British), 1959. This film based on the rather trivial historical incident of
the sinking of the Titanic (from the book by Walter Lord, a master of his-

torical trivia) is nonetheless impressive for its accurate detailing of the event. Rental from Walter Reade 16.

America, America. 168 minutes. Black and white. Directed by Elia Kazan, 1964. This is one of the few American films I have seen that pays attention to historical detail. The story of the struggle of a young Greek who attempts to make his way to America at the turn of the century is an excellent, realistic screen portrait of immigration. Despite a few plot contrivances, a teacher could use *America, America* effectively in a unit on immigration. Rental from Warner Brothers 16.

Oh! What a Lovely War. I have already mentioned this film as an excellent anti-war statement. It is an equally excellent portrayal of history containing the songs, look, and spirit of the World War I era. See citation in Chap. 11.

Open City. 105 minutes. Black and white. Directed by Roberto Rossellini (Italian), 1945. English subtitles. This amazing film about the Italian anti-Nazi resistance was filmed both on the spot and immediately after the German occupation of Rome. It is history. Rental from Audio-Brandon Films or Contemporary-McGraw-Hill Films.

HISTORICAL DOCUMENTARIES AS CLASSROOM SUPPLEMENTS

Many so-called "educational" films are produced for classroom consumption. A good portion of these are historical, and most, as I've indicated, are merely watered down visual aids, much like film strips. The following is a list of what I consider the best films of this type.

Feature-Length Documentaries

I have already cited three useful films in this area in Chap. 2: *Rise and Fall of the Third Reich, The Twisted Cross,* and *Blood on the Balcony.*

To Die in Madrid. 90 minutes. Black and white. Directed by Frederic Rossif (Spanish), 1965. English narration by John Gielgud, Irene Worth, William Hutt, and George Gonneau. A skillful presentation of film clips from the Spanish Civil War (1937-38), with intelligent narration. This film sympathizes with the anti-Franco forces, but its lack of objectivity doesn't detract much from its factual presentation. Rental from Audio-Brandon Films.

The Finest Hours. 114 minutes. Color. Directed by Peter Baylis (British), 1964. Narrated by Orson Welles. This is a reasonably good portrait of the life of Sir Winston Churchill, including some lovely color filming of his native countryside and newsreel clips of his political career. Rental from Audio-Brandon Films or Twyman Films.

The Guns of August. 90 minutes. Black and white. Produced by Jean Aurel, 1963. this documentary on the early days of World War I comes from the exciting Barbara Tuchman book on which it is based, but it does include some good film clips of the times. Rental from Universal 16.

Over There, 1914-1918. 90 minutes. Black and white. Produced by Jean Aurel, 1963. An interesting compilation of film clips on the First World War. Rental from Contemporary-McGraw-Hill Films.

Four Days in November. 100 minutes. Color. Directed by Mel Stuart, 1964. A moving documentary on the assassination and funeral of President John F. Kennedy. Rental from United Artists 16.

Historical Series

The following films were made as series for television or direct classroom use. They are listed in this manner since the quality of the series tends to be uniform.

The Saga of Western Man. Color. ABC Television. John Secondari, producer. Through intelligent narration, excellent historical props, and first-class production values, these films are very useful classroom supplements. They are available for purchase or rental from Contemporary-McGraw-Hill Films. The available titles are:

> *I, Leonardo Da Vinci.* 54 minutes.
> *1492.* 54 minutes.
> *Cortez and the Legend.* Narrated by Kirk Douglas. 52 minutes.
> *The Pilgrim Adventure.* 54 minutes.
> *1776.* 54 minutes.
> *Custer: The American Surge Westward.* 33 minutes.
> *1898.* 54 minutes. Especially recommended for its comprehension of the social complexities of the period in America.
> *Robert Scott and the Search for the South Pole.* 55 minutes.
> *1964.* 54 minutes.
> *The Road to Gettysburg.* 54 minutes.

The Project 20 Series. Black and white. NBC Television. This series of historical documentaries is inconsistent. A few of the episodes are very good; others (like *The Great War* and *The Real West*) are gross oversimplifications of history. Cited here are those that I have seen used effectively. Purchase or rental from Contemporary-McGraw-Hill Films.

> *End of the Trail: The American Plains Indian.* Narrated by Walter Brennan. 53 minutes.
> *The Island Called Ellis* (immigration). 53 minutes. Color.
> *Life in the Thirties.* 52 minutes.
> *Not So Long Ago.* 1945-1950, narrated by Bob Hope. 54 minutes.

The Twentieth Century Series. Black and white. CBS News. Narrated by Walter Cronkite. Many of the episodes of this popular documentary series accurately portray recent history, making excellent use of old film clips. Listed below are the best. Purchase or rental from Contemporary-McGraw-Hill Films.

> *The Women Get the Vote.* 27 minutes.
> *The Movies Learn to Talk.* 26 minutes.
> *Aftermath of World War I.* 27 minutes.
> *War in Spain—Prelude to World War II.* 30 minutes.
> *The Week that Shook the World* (August 23-September 1, 1939; Hitler's aggression). 25 minutes.
> *Trial at Nuremberg.* 26 minutes.

The Fall of China. 27 minutes.
Revolt in Hungary. 27 minutes.
Minister of Hate (Joseph Goebbels). 27 minutes.

The New York Times Black History Series. Together with its affiliate, The Arno Press, the *Times* is in the process of producing films for classrooms on Afro-American history. The four films currently in circulation so far are of excellent quality. They are very well researched and skillfully narrated. All are in color. This series is far superior to any other currently available and is the only one in this field that I can recommend. Purchase only from *The New York Times* Library Services and Information Division.

The Hurdler (Dr. Charles Drew). 16 minutes.
Slavery and Slave Resistance. 26 minutes.
Black Men and Iron Horses (Contributions to the railroads). 18 minutes.
The Lady in the Lincoln Memorial (Marian Anderson vs."Jim Crow").
18 minutes.

Western Civilization: Majesty and Madness. A new series of expensively made classroom films for high school and college by Learning Corporation of America (a subsidiary of Columbia Pictures). These films come highly recommended from historians, and all evidence is of detailed research and careful production. Color. All films 25 minutes in length. Purchase only from Learning Corporation of America.

The Crusades: Saints and Sinners
Charlemagne: Holy Barbarism
Medieval England: The Peasants Revolt
The French Revolution: The Bastille
The French Revolution: The Terror
Galileo: The Challenge of Reason
Napoleon: The Making of a Dictator
Napoleon: The End of a Dictator
The Changing World of Charles Dickens

Individual Short Films

The Ancient Africans. 27 minutes. Color. Directed by Julien Bryan, 1970. This is probably the best of Bryan's uniformly excellent series of documentaries. A vivid survey of Africa's past portrayed with expert cinematic skill, including Phillip Stapp's imaginative animation. In many respects, this film is as good an introduction to African history as most texts used for that purpose. Purchase from International Film Foundation.

The Ancient Egyptian. 27 minutes. Color. Directed by Julien Bryan, 1963. A beautifully filmed historical and archeological portrait of Egypt. The film has relatively little narration and would be a useful motivator for further study in this area. Purchase or rental from International Film Foundation.

The Ancient Peruvian. 27 minutes. Color. Directed by Julien Bryan, 1967. Similar to the Egyptian film, this details life in the Inca empire. Purchase or rental from International Film Foundation.

City of Gold. 23 minutes. Black and white. National Film Board of Canada Production, 1958. This is the best still-photographed documentary I have ever seen. It provides a vivid portrait of the great Klondike gold strike of the 1890s, focusing on rowdy Dawson City. Purchase or rental from Contemporary-McGraw-Hill Films.

Profiles in Courage: Frederick Douglass. 48 minutes. Black and white. NBC TV and Robert Saudek Productions, 1964. A dramatized biography of the great Black abolitionist, well played by Robert Hooks. This was one of the best films of the *Profiles in Courage* Series and the only one I have seen available to the public. Purchase from I. Q. Films.

The Inheritance. 60 minutes. Black and white. Directed by Harold Mayer for the Amalgamated Clothing Workers of America (narrated by Robert Ryan), 1964. This is a pictorially excellent documentary on both the Americanization of immigrants and the struggle of labor to organize. Rental from Contemporary-McGraw-Hill Films.

Some of the Boys. 33 minutes. Black and white. 1965. I have rarely seen this beautiful documentary on the Civil War, based on the actual letters of soldiers and stunning Matthew Brady photographs, cited in other film guides. It is truly excellent. Purchase or rental from Henk Newenhouse. (Address: 1017 Longacre Road, Northbrook, Ill. 60062.)

The True Story of the Civil War. 33 minutes. Black and white. 1956. An Academy Award winning short, this film makes excellent use of Matthew Brady pictures to document the major battles of the war between the states. Purchase or rental from Contemporary-McGraw-Hill Films.

Note: The absence of documentary films on African and Asian history is not my fault. Film-makers need to address themselves more to non-Western subjects.

America the Violent–

The Motion Picture as a Reflection of a National Tendency

"Violence is as American as cherry pie!" A few years ago Black militant H. Rap Brown made national headlines with this now famous truism about our society. Since Brown's well-known "rap," this country has undergone a thorough self-analysis resulting from a rash of political assassinations and civil disorders. A typical Lyndon Johnson commission was created in 1968 to investigate the causes of violent trends in our society. A team of competent social scientists recently submitted an 800-plus-page report to that commission comprised of a detailed historical analysis of America's violent tradition. It is truly prophetic that this report in essence concluded that violence, indeed, was "as American as cherry pie."[1]

Our country has become preoccupied with this violent streak. Numerous studies have been published recently accusing the mass media, particularly movies and television, of glamorizing and glorifying violence. In one of the most popular of these studies, the author concludes, after surveying the products of the media, that almost half of the motion pictures shown on television in 1969 were "clearly violent."[2] He further infers that such films have a negative influence on children who are saturated by them.

The results of such studies and the publicity they attract has led the television industry to adopt a code of "toning down" the violence in many of its network programs. It appears that some of the media may be on the verge of a new attitude in this area.

Since a conscious campaign has begun against violence (at least in terms of current rhetoric), it seems to me that an analysis of the subject belongs in the classroom. I propose, as I have done so often in this book, that students examine various motion pictures that may be guilty of glorifying violence in our society. The purpose of this classroom study is primarily to motivate students to do detailed, sociological research in this area in order to separate fact from rhetoric.

There is one point that I should again make clear about the nature of the film

---

[1] For details of the study, see The History of Violence in America: A Report to the National Commission on the Causes and Prevention of Violence, Hugh Davis Graham and Robert Ted Gurr, Eds. New York: Frederick A. Praeger, 1969.

[2] Arnold, Arnold. Violence and Your Child. Chicago: Henry Regnery Co., 1969, p. 196. This author is a nationally syndicated columnist who has written on child behavior for laymen for a long time.

medium. Films do not alone create and cannot be responsible for any national attitudes. They do, however, by reflecting the nature of the society that creates them, nurture and reinforce such attitudes; hence movies are only as violent as America is in general. The question, therefore, that students examining films in this area should address themselves to is: How violent is America?

The job of the teacher in this unit is to program a series of films that treat violent themes. Each film should represent a different genre and a different way of handling violence. After viewing a few of these and discussing them, the students can begin to engage in a specific research program to determine what influence such films may have.

An ideal introduction for this motivational unit is NET's informative documentary *This Question of Violence*. The film presents, in much the same way as the Report to the National Commission on Violence, the historically violent tradition in America, emphasizing the hostile "frontier heritage" involving the expansion of the country at the expense of the Indian. It aslo features numerous conversations with psychologists about the causes of individual aggression found among Blacks and others who have been "culturally deprived." The mass media are shown as symptoms of the violent atmosphere in society, not as the causes of it.

This film is a useful introduction (much as a general textbook would be) in that it is just detailed enough to stimulate questions and a desire for further study. After students discuss it, the teacher should present the first of a repertory of films emphasizing our violent streak.

The first film I recommend to be shown is a very funny short entitled *The Headcracker Suite*. This is a product of National Football League Films which takes brief, slow-motion scenes from several rough football games and matches them against the music of *The Nutcracker Suite*. It is howlingly funny when the music reaches a crescendo as a player is tackled and stomped on in slow motion. However, soon the viewer begins to realize that the humor is due to the camera's focus on the players' pain. Football is a nationally popular game played under highly violent conditions. Our pleasure in it provides interesting food for thought.[3]

Following this, the class should take a look as some standard commercial "action" movies that portray violence in a matter-of-fact way. Fighting, shooting, and killing are merely part of the narratives of such films, and indeed are the keys to the movies' entertainment value. I have dealt with some of these specifically here and listed alternatives in the filmography.

The Western film is based on "action" for its style. In a typical recent Western like *Nevada Smith* with Steve McQueen, the plot revolves around the revenge the hero must take on the three men who murdered his parents. (This is a fairly standard plot of the genre.) One by one McQueen tracks down the killers. He finds the first in a saloon and kills him after a lengthy (and exciting) knife fight. Later he tracks the second one to a Louisiana chain gang. Getting himself imprisoned, he wins the man's confidence, escapes with him and then, again after a struggle (which gives the hero the justification of self-defense), kills him. The picture runs at least another half-hour until McQueen catches up with the third

---

[3] I must note that **Headcracker Suite** is not currently available for classrooms though NFL Films might possibly contract with a distributor to make prints for this purpose. In the meantime, any short football film can serve the same function, and many are available from local libraries and distributors.

villain, whose gang he joins to avoid suspicion. After helping rob a stagecoach and gun down the driver and guard, our hero confronts his man only to realize, in good moral Hollywood fashion, that vengeance is not the answer. Thus he lets the man go as the film ends. This was very righteous of him, considering he has killed or helped kill at least four others along the way, including the innocent stage driver and guard.

Nevada Smith is an "action" Western. The violence and killing are taken for granted, and the film is quite representative of its type. Similarly popular are films about gangsters (such as the recent hit *Point Blank* with Lee Marvin as a gunman out to "get" his old mob); detectives (*Harper,* with Paul Newman, included killings, muggings, and brutal fights at a rigorous clip); war adventures (the popular *Dirty Dozen* in which the heroes blow up an underground "pleasure palace" for Nazis and their women, sending at least a 1000 people to kingdom-come); and those James Bond type spy films where bodies fly through the air like mosquitoes. The teacher could use any of these to demonstrate the matter-of-fact attitude many popular types of movies have toward violence.

From the motion picture **Bonnie and Clyde.** Copyright © 1967 by Warner Bros.— Seven Arts, Inc.

Interestingly enough, films such as those I have just mentioned never created much of a public furor. They have all been, or soon will be, shown on television virtually intact. Critics evaluated such films as good or bad based on their acting, story line, or direction. Students beginning their research might examine some of the more popular reviews to notice this general acceptance.

The standard, matter-of-fact action film is not even the one under attack by most social critics. The films that have generated the most heat about violence have been those in which extreme bloodletting follows each death. These "over-kill" movies include the series of Italian-made Clint Eastwood Westerns (*A Fistful of Dollars, The Good, the Bad, and the Ugly,* etc.)[4] and the Roger Corman gangster films (*The St. Valentine's Day Massacre* and *Bloody Mamma*). Such films are extremely brutal, but the number of killings and muggings in them do not exceed those in *Nevada Smith*, which was an action picture. Students should examine one of these "overkill" films and discuss whether they are more harmful to viewers than standard "action" movies.

There is another type of violent film that has begun to appear recently. This film is more brutal and bloodier than any of those previously mentioned, the reason being that it is supposedly "anti-violence." Such films are made with the purpose of shocking their audience against bloodshed by providing an extremely grotesque view of fighting and killing. One of the earliest examples of this type of film is Canadian animator Norman McLaren's *Neighbors*. Two men who live next door to each other are shown sitting peacefully in their yards. Suddenly (the human figures are animated as cartoons through a process called pixillation), a flower appears directly between their two properties. After failing to determine peacefully to whom it belongs, the men start to fight brutally (emphasized by the pixillated effect) until they literally destroy each other. (At one point in their battle, they are made to resemble savages.) The moral "Love thy neighbor" appears on the screen as the film ends. McLaren had intended his film as a protest against the stupidity of war and violence. To do so he created this simplistic, obviously grotesque metaphor. He has used violence to condemn violence. The question for students now is, Does this work? Do viewers come away from the film with the message that violence is wasteful and futile? Would *Neighbors* explain this to children? Or does the film make violence appear funny and remove it from reality?

This conscious saturation of violent behavior on the screen for moral purposes has been the subject in some highly controversial films, most particularly, Sam Peckinpah's *The Wild Bunch*. No film in the last few years has stimulated quite as much pro and con debate as this one.

The Wild Bunch is a Western, set at the twilight of the frontier around 1910. The "bunch" is a gang of aging badmen who find themselves foiled in their attempts at a last "big haul" time and again by the tight security of the railroads and banks. At the beginning of the film, they enter a small border town to rob a bank. This kind of scene has been used to introduce numerous Westerns, yet here it is different. As the gang rides slowly through the town, disguised as soldiers, the camera alternately focuses on a group of children torturing a scorpion by pushing it with sticks through an anthill. The scene is set for man's violent nature to explode and it does. The bunch is trapped by a railroad agent and an army of bounty hunters. Shots ring out in all directions as a temperance parade of old men, women, and children march right into the center of the street when the fighting begins. Bodies explode, as blood covers the screen in slow motion. The chaotic horror is positively

---

[4] Curiously, **A Fistful of Dollars,** about a nameless cowboy who comes into a town and singlehandedly and brutally destroys a gang of cutthroats, is based on a Japanese Samurai movie **Yojimbo,** which in turn adapted its theme from American Westerns. Critics praised **Yojimbo,** which is just as bloody and "exciting," while condemning **A Fistful of Dollars** as unnecessarily violent.

nauseating to watch and when the shooting subsides, the remains of the town resemble an atomic holocaust.

The rest of the film is even bloodier. The few remaining members of the bunch, vicious killers all, but obviously no worse than the grimy bounty hunters pursuing them, go to Mexico, where they become involved with a local general in the revolution there. After a doing a job for this general, they return to find that one of their gang, a young Mexican, is to be tortured for insulting their employer. The four remaining members of the bunch decide to do something "decent." In typical Western fashion, they confront the general to return their comrade. He replies by cutting the man's throat (the viewer actually sees this semi-decapitation). Enraged, the "heroes" draw their guns, and everybody in sight gets blasted. This scene runs almost eight minutes and it consists of more shooting, killing, and bloodletting (most of which is in slow motion) than the screen has ever portrayed.

Some critics have condemned the film as disgusting and indecent. Others have praised it for its realistic explosion of the Western movie myth. (Imagine if the people in *Nevada Smith* had bled like that.)

From the motion picture **The Wild Bunch**. Copyright © 1969 by Warner Bros.—Seven Arts, Inc.

The Wild Bunch becomes required screening in a unit like this. The director's intentions are obvious. He wants people to examine both the violent tradition of this country and the way things would look in Westerns (or other "action" movies) if the brutality were treated realistically. The question is, Does the method work? Can film-makers condemn violence by flaunting it at audiences?

Thus far I have suggested that students examine a few of the motion pictures we produce which handle violent themes. The teacher can supplement the films by providing some written, critical evaluations of the effects of violence on the screen and the ways (if any) it can be acceptably portrayed. There are three interesting essays by film critics that could be used here. British essayist Phillip French, in his article "Violence in Cinema" reprinted in the anthology Sight and Sound and Society, analyzes several of the popular films of the late 1950s and early 1960s and their violent overtones. He is obviously seeking some guidelines justifying some violence in films, but condemns most of it. However, he really doesn't have any basic criterion for such guidelines.[5]

Similarly, critic Judith Crist, in her book of compiled reviews of the 1960s The Private Eye, The Cowboy and the Very Naked Girl, abhors the sickening violence of *A Fistful of Dollars* and *St. Valentine's Day Massacre,* but finds justification for *The Dirty Dozen* and *Bonnie and Clyde.* She too would like to differentiate between good film violence and bad.[6]

Noted movie critic Pauline Kael, in an article in *New Yorker,* attempts the same thing, bitterly condemning the meaningless violence of *The Adventurers* while defending the seriousness of purpose of *The Wild Bunch* (though she admits that it was not successful in achieving its anti-violent ends).[7]

Students should read one or all of these essays to illustrate that thus far there are no sensible criteria for evaluating violent films. The psychologists and social scientists testifying before the National Commission on Violence would like to eliminate all violence from the screen. To most of them, *The Wild Bunch* is no more "moral" than *A Fistfull of Dollars* or *Nevada Smith.*

Once the students have seen some of the films and discussed the significant issues, they should be sufficently motivated to do some detailed research. Some of the questions they will invariably address themselves to are:

1. Why is violence in some form the basic content of so many films?
2. What effects do violent films, of all types, have on those who see them—particularly children?
3. Is there any relationship between screen violence and actual crime? To what extent?
4. Are some violent films more "moral" than others?
5. Is it possible that violent movies are healthy in that they provide a vicarious release for personal hostilities?
6. Can the mass media find any entertaining substitute for the excitement of violence?
7. Can the American public tolerate nonviolent movies?

Naturally the students will be digging into many of the sources used by the social scientists who prepared the report for the National Commission. They will begin to discover that films are merely a symptom of the trends of society. And

---

[5] White, David M., and Averson, Richard, Eds. Sight and Sound and Society. Boston: Beacon Press, 1968, pp. 320-334.

[6] Crist, Judith. The Private Eye, The Cowboy and the Very Naked Girl. New York: Holt, Rinehart and Winston, 1968, pp. 250-253. Available in paperback.

[7] Kael, Pauline, "Scavengers with Computers," New Yorker, March 21, 1970, pp. 161-162, 165.

they will realize that for the movies to change, the hostile attitudes in this country must disappear. In the meantime, anyone for cherry pie?

FILMOGRAPHY

Listed here are some examples of films that can be shown to analyze screen violence. If a teacher is limited in funds, he can merely assign his class a movie on television or even a cartoon (those cat and mouse things involve more fighting and maiming than any average war picture).

Introductory Film

This Question of Violence. 59 minutes. Black and white. NET Production, 1968. Purchase or rental from NET Film Service.

Standard Action Films

Violence is simply taken for granted with no unnecessary bloodshed.

Headcracker Suite. 5 minutes. Color. Currently not available in 16-mm distribution. For other football films, check local libraries or team promotional departments for free loan.

Nevada Smith. 135 minutes. Color (cinemascope print available). Directed by Henry Hathaway, 1966. Rental from Films Inc.

The Professionals. 117 minutes. Color. Directed by Richard Brooks, 1966. An all-star (Burt Lancaster, Lee Marvin, Robert Ryan, Jack Palance, Woody Strode), empty-headed Western about four "experts" in various phases of violence, who are hired to rescue a rich man's wife from a Mexican bandit. This film is very similar in locale and situation to *The Wild Bunch.* The major difference is that *The Professionals* is an "action" movie, where all of the killings (and there are many) look painless. Screening these two films together would offer a good contrast in the ways films treat violence. Rental from Columbia Cinematheque.

Point Blank. 92 minutes. Color (cinemascope print available). Directed by John Boorman, 1967. An extremely brutal gangster film that won some high critical acclaim when it was released. Rental from Films Inc.

Robin and the Seven Hoods. 123 minutes. Color. Directed by Gordon Douglas, 1964. Frank Sinatra and "friends" in a musical-comedy gangster spoof, which is more violent than most of the genre it's supposed to be spoofing. The film includes a song by Sammy Davis about "the fun of reaching for a gun." A teacher could use this to show how widely violence is accepted as entertainment. Rental from Twyman Films or Swank Films.

Harper. 121 minutes. Color. Directed by Jack Smight, 1966. Paul Newman as a tough detective in a film meant to be reminiscent of the Humphrey Bogart tough private eye type. Lots of brutal fights and a few killings. Critics hailed it as "great fun." Rental from Twyman Films or Swank Films.

The Dirty Dozen. Typical war (i.e., killing) as adventure movie. See citation in Chap. 11.

Our Man Flint. 107 minutes. Color (cinemascope print available). Directed by Daniel Mann, 1966. The James Bond films are good examples of violence used as audience escapism. Unfortunately they are not available in 16 mm (probably because they are still quite popular in theaters). The "Flint" films are close enough, however. All of the "fun" of the explosions and flying bodies so typical of this type of film is included. Rental from Films Inc.

Murderer's Row. 108 minutes. Color. Directed by Henry Levin, 1967. More Bond sex-violence, this time with Dean Martin as superagent Matt Helm. This disgusting film is typical of the genre at its worst (best?). Rental from Twyman Films or Swank Films.

Violent Films

Some critics have accused these of glorifying brutality.

A Fistful of Dollars. 96 minutes. Color. Directed by Sergio Leone, 1966. A brutal, Italian-made Western in which everybody bleeds. Rental from United Artists 16. (The Japanese film on which it is based is equally violent, though it was never accused of this. *Yojimbo* is available in 16 mm. 110 minutes. Black and white. Directed by Akira Kurosawa, 1961. Rental from Audio-Brandon Films or Janus Films.)

The St. Valentine's Day Massacre. 100 minutes. Color (cinemascope print available). Directed by Roger Corman, 1967. One of the bloodiest gangster films ever made, *The St. Valentine's Day Massacre* was unanimously condemned as "too much." Interestingly, it is no more violent than any of the James Bond type films. Rental from Films Inc.

Anti-Violence Violent Films (?)

Neighbors. 10 minutes. Color. Directed by Norman McLaren, 1952. Purchase or rental from Contemporary-McGraw-Hill Films.

The Wild Bunch. 145 minutes. Color. Directed by Sam Peckinpah, 1969. Rental from Warner Brothers 16.

The Long Day's Dying. 93 minutes. Color (cinemascope only). Directed by Peter Collinson (British), 1968. A recent British anti-war film that makes its point by violently killing everyone in sight. Rental from Films Inc.

Soldier Blue. 112 minutes. Color. Directed by Ralph Nelson, 1970. Despite this film's inane romantic subplot (concerning a White squaw, who's been cast out by her tribe, in love with a young cavalryman), it's hard to argue with its overbearing violence. Documenting two actual events when the U. S. Cavalry mindlessly massacred Indians, including women and children, the portrayal of violence is part of historical fact. I wonder how mass audiences react to all of its slaughter. Rental from Films Inc.

PART III

A Practical Guide to Teaching with Films

PRIMARY COMMITMENT

The first time I really became enthused about teaching with films was after observing a group of so-called hard-core delinquent boys engaged in a rap session on whether Marlon Brando should have "finked" on his pals in *On the Waterfront*. These kids were not exactly what you could call serious students. Each one had a lengthy police record, though they ranged in age from 15 to 19, but the day I saw them you'd never know it. Their teacher was a small, soft-spoken man, who except for being seated among them, could have passed for an observer. The "class" discussion lasted until the bell rang without a lull. When they left, their teacher showed me samples of things they had written about *On the Waterfront*. The papers weren't grammatically pretty and the spelling was atrocious, but they had plenty in them, and, as I was to discover, it was the first written assignment most of them had done in years.

Maybe a book like this, with all of its "information" to persuade teachers of the educational value of films, is no substitute for the first-hand experience of actually seeing it work. I have tried so often in these pages to indicate that movies, in addition to their literary and social content, are fantastic intellectual equalizers. The academically "slowest" kid is on the same plane with the teacher when they sit down to share the experience of *On the Waterfront*, or *The Cool World*, or *The Pawnbroker*. He can relate to the medium and he can progress because of it.

In order for teachers to begin planning their own celluloid curricula, they first have to *believe*, as I do, in the educational legitimacy of the film medium. This is something that can't be faked. When the class sees its first film, it must understand that the experience is equivalent to reading a book and will be treated the same way in the course of study. If the teacher shows a film and then lets it die by moving on to what the textbook says, he has sabotaged the experience and the kids will simply think of films as "teacher's day off."

Perhaps, because I'm fearful of such continued abuse of the medium, I have had to emphasize again the relevancy of films to kids. I wish all teachers could observe classroom situations like the one I saw to "turn them on."

Once the sincere commitment I speak of exists, the planning of a cinematic course of study can really begin.

GETTING STARTED

Any teacher interested in preparing a film-oriented curriculum has to ask himself a few basic questions:

What do I show?
What equipment do I need to show it with?
How do I arrange the time to show it?
What will it cost?
What will it cost?
What will it cost?

Naturally the last question (questions) conditions the answers to all of the others and presents the stickiest problem. Many teachers I've spoken to have zealously desired to use films more frequently, but their biggest drawback is money. Indeed, as I approach the coming school semester, I am at the very end of a grant I received two years ago and scrambling for funds appears to be my biggest problem, too. The purpose of this guide is to provide answers to the preceding questions. Starting with the most difficult problem of costs is, therefore, essential.

HOW TO FUND A CELLULOID CURRICULUM

I don't know. I have no answers. I worry about the same problem every year.

After quite a bit of experience in film teaching, I have learned one fundamental thing—movies for the classroom cost money. The average rental for one showing to a group of 50 students or less for a short film (under one hour) is $15. The average cost of a black and white feature film for the same size audience is $50. Recent color features run in rental price range from $50 to $250 under the same conditions. There are wide variations here, however. Some feature films can be rented as cheaply as $15. (One catalog lists *Home of the Brave* at $15, *High Noon* at $20, and *On the Waterfront* at $25.) Still one's choice of films should not merely be conditioned by rental costs, and some opportunity must be available for a teacher to obtain the best features for his units regardless of the price.

There are no panaceas for the problem of funding. Film distributors are in business to make a profit, and although many of them are more than patient about waiting for their bills to be paid, they simply can't give us their products for nothing. Therefore, the best I can do with this crucial problem is list a number of suggestions that aided me in the past few years.

Potential Sources of Funds and Alternatives

School or Department Audio-Visual Budgets

Every school, even the most destitute (like mine), sets aside some annual amount of money for the purchase or rental of various audio-visual aids. Each teacher is entitled to some slice of this budget (no matter how small), and it would not be inappropriate to request that one's share be allocated to rent a feature film. If these funds are skimpy, two or three interested teachers could pool their allotments, combining classes to show the film.

Many schools, according to the leading 16-mm distributors, already have special budgets set aside for film rentals. I realize that often these funds are used to rent films for large assembly showings and, as I've indicated, this is one of the least effective uses of the medium, since the auditorium situation has little transfer value for the classroom. And the films shown under such conditions are usually the arbitrary choices of administrators. An enterprising teacher or team of teachers could propose an alternative way to use this budget. Instead of paying large rental fees for auditorium screenings, why not divert the money to payment for several features at lower rates to be used in individual classrooms. Most film distributors base their charges on the size of the audience for a single showing. Thus it is usually more expensive to rent a feature for an assembly program containing a disinterested group of 500 students, than to rent two or even three films (depending on the base rate) for individual classes of 50 students or less to whom the films relate as regular subject matter.

The point is that most schools are somewhat flexible in how they spend their audio-visual aids funds. An enterprising film teacher should try to persuade his administration to divert some of this money toward celluloid curricula.

Outside Grants

My first source of funds for a year of teaching with films came from a useful incentive program of the Philadelphia Board of Education. The Board made available a small number of special teacher grants for innovative programs for classroom experimentation. I proposed a course of study using films as literary sources and requested $600 to fund it. I was awarded a grant of $350, which is just about what I needed for the course. (Please *note*: Always request more. Think big.)

The Philadelphia system still maintains its grant program though there are always far more applicants than recipients. Individual school boards across the country must have similar programs, and considering the financial troubles in Philadelphia, these grants certainly can't be any tougher to get. If your school system has no such program, suggest one. Explain, in good pedagogical language, how such grants will provide innovative incentives for teachers to meet the onslaught of demands for curriculum relevancy by students, parents, and educational philosophers. Such innovative grant programs do give teachers the chance to experiment with new material and alter dated curricula. Certainly some money should be earmarked for that purpose.

I have been extremely lucky. For the past two years my school has been the recipient of a large private grant from a group of Black businessmen, and part of the money has been given to me to rent and purchase films. As that money runs out, I too must try to seek new sources by applying the methods I'm suggesting here.

As of this writing, there is no general fund removed from local school districts that film-oriented teachers can draw upon. The American Film Institute in Washington, D. C. does provide some grant money to novice film-makers, but so far, little of its funds have been allocated for school teachers. Still, it is possible that by the time this book is published, the Institute's practice will have changed in this area. A letter containing the outline of a film teaching program in application for a grant certainly wouldn't hurt. The address of the American Film Institute is 1815 H Street, N. W., Washington, D. C. 20006.

Free Film Sources

If all attempts at obtaining a film rental budget fail (and I imagine in many cases they will), there are still alternatives left. First of all, most major school districts have their own film libraries. Unfortunately, many of these are loaded with obsolete, juvenile films that are useless today. Indeed the reason I saw *How to Catch a Cold* so often is because my school district owned it. A teacher should survey all of the films available in such a library. There probably won't be any commercial features, but perhaps it has some of the better short documentaries (similar to some of the ones I've listed). Again, an enterprising teacher can submit some written suggestions (call them "recommendations," it sounds more powerful) about obtaining more recent films and, possibly some features. Still, I wouldn't want to depend on this kind of source too heavily.

Several big-city free library systems do have film loan services. My experience with such libraries indicates they are generally more up to date and contain better films than school system sources. New York, Philadelphia, Pittsburgh, and Chicago all have excellent catalogs of the very best in short films, and are adding more features all the time. The major problem they present is that they can only lend a film for a 24-hour period. Reservations for free loan of the most popular titles sometimes tie them up for months. Therefore, the teacher hoping to use this source effectively has to book his films far in advance for the exact days he intends to show them. Under such circumstances, September is not too early to book a film for a day in mid-June.

A number of film rental distributors send teachers brochures listing free films available for the classroom. However, such films are industrial or travel propaganda made to sell products or company images. Unless a class is directly engaged in such a propaganda study, these films are useless. And, many of them are poorly made. The same is true with much of the free loan stuff from the Federal and various state governments.

There is one additional excellent free source of films. If your city is lucky enough to have a Canadian Consulate office, you will find that as part of its policy of maintaining good inter-American relations it probably has a film library containing many of the better shorts from the National Film Board of Canada. (The consulate's libraries have most of the well known films of animator Norman McLaren, including *Neighbors*.) If there is no office in your area, or if the local consulate has no film library, information on borrowing films can be obtained from the Canadian Embassy in Washington, D. C. This is a free source definitely worth looking into.

Take Them to the Movies

Even an extensive use of the free film sources won't supply the teacher with very many features. If rental money isn't available, the next best solution is to take the class to a theater and see a meaningful film to relate to the course of study. I have begun to do this, even with a rental budget. When several of my students were debating on whether screen violence influences crime, I went with them to see Sam Peckinpah's *The Wild Bunch*. The masterful *Lawrence of Arabia* won't be available in 16 mm for a long time, and it is definitely important enough for classroom study. Hence, the only way to see it is in a movie theater.

There is one problem about accompanying students to a theater that bothers me. It costs them money. I feel very guilty about requesting that kids shell out two or three dollars at a clip to see a film I'm going to concentrate on in the classroom. It shouldn't be their financial responsibility, regardless of their individual economic levels. I know of one "Art" theater that books excellent revivals which has a student discount admission rate. If I bring a group of 20 or more, that rate will even be lower. A teacher should contact local theater owners concerning this. On a typical Monday or Tuesday night, few neighborhood theaters get many patrons. Bringing a group of students to the theater provides badly needed business on one of those nights, and a discount rate could provide an incentive to do it more often. It may even be possible to work out an arrangement with a theater owner to book a specific film for one of these occasions. If he knows he'll have a guaranteed audience, he just might comply.

Still, no teacher should depend heavily on this source, since no student should have to share in the financing of an educational program.

Assign Movies on Television

If you're really desperate to create some kind of celluloid curriculum and have exhausted all other possible sources, there's always television. Networks are buying up movies faster than ever (although there may soon be a lull in this because of the Motion Picture Association's rating system). These films are relatively new, and if one can stand the constant commercial interruptions, not too badly cut. Films like *Dr. Strangelove, The Manchurian Candidate, A Hard Day's Night,* and *Alfie* can still be appreciated on the small screen, and a teacher can certainly assign them.

Of course the problems with any television assignments immediately come to mind. Not everybody can be home at a particular time to watch it. Kids work, TV sets break, younger brothers and sisters take program precedence, and so on. The biggest problem with assigning movies on television, however, is scheduling. It is difficult to find out more than a week in advance when the film you want your class to see will be shown. How can you plan ahead under such circumstances? In order for a celluloid curriculum to work, the teacher has to be able to relate the films directly to the subject matter, and that takes advanced planning. The only suggestion I can offer concerning movies on television is to write to the network in August or September, requesting a weekly schedule of its film programming for the year. And then, of course, you're limited to whatever the network shows. This means perhaps as few as one or none of its films will be suitable. Still if you've got nothing else. . . .

The funding problem is the most difficult for teachers to overcome. The suggestions I've listed may be meager, but they can represent some hope to the teacher with no financial resources. I realize also that there are many school systems that have no problems in this area. In such systems it's merely a matter of persuading administrators to allocate some money for film teaching. Therefore, assuming that some monetary backing is at the teacher's disposal, I will move on to a few of the other important questions about teaching with films.

DECIDING WHAT TO SHOW

I would be willing to bet that if a teacher went to his principal and said that he was planning to show his literature class *Pride and Prejudice, Hamlet, The Yearling, A Tale of Two Cities,* and *The Prince and the Pauper,* he could have all of the money he would need for rentals and equipment. But if that teacher announced (just citing one of the units in this book, for example) that he was going to use *The Pawnbroker, Medium Cool, Blow-Up,* and *The Hustler,* mere access to the principal's office might be closed to him for a long time.

There is undoubtedly a set of narrow, almost puritanical standards that too many educational administrators hold towards films. A film version of an "acceptable" novel is fine. A popular, commercially successful movie is not supposed to be suitable. In my first year of film teaching, one of my "superiors" saw my list of choices for the semester. He was surprised and skeptical over my inclusion of *A Thousand Clowns.* "Why, that's a comedy," he commented.

The first step in planning a course around cinematic content materials is that the individual teacher, not the administration, must determine what films he will use. The teacher should have some idea what appeals to the kind of students he works with. His criteria for selecting films must be similar to those used in choosing class readings. Like books, the film should have some basic relationship to the students' own experiences, to give them something with which to identify. And, again as with books, the films should help raise the philosophical and intellectual level of the class. The one problem of books which films eliminate, however, is that of reading level. Regardless how poorly a kid reads, he can, if properly motivated, adequately interpret the content of a film.

In order for a teacher to know the best films he can use with his classes, he should see them. I doubt if a teacher would assign his students a book he hasn't read, and he must use that same standard with films. Now, no doubt, many readers are saying to themselves that it would take years to catch up on all of the notable movies they've missed. Indeed, this is a problem, though there are some solutions.

I am not yet 30 years old. Although I've always been attracted to movies, as have most of my generation, it is only recently that I've accepted them as a valid educational source. My own involvement in this area comes from a desire to learn as much as possible about the subject. Once the teacher is convinced of the great potential of a celluloid curriculum, he will be motivated (you know, the way students are supposed to be . . .) to survey its sources. Reading this book provides some of the necessary background; certainly it gives some information about a lot of possibilities for the classroom. And there are other books that survey film sources in even more detail. (A list of these appears in the bibliography.)

One of the best ways to keep abreast of which films might be useful is to read critical reviews. There are certainly enough of these in publication. Any daily newspaper reviews movies that open in town. National magazines like *Time, Newsweek, Life, Redbook, Esquire, Playboy, New Yorker, Saturday Review, New Republic,* and *Holiday* all review films regularly. *Parents' Magazine* contains an entire section on current motion pictures, though its "holier-than-thou" rating system isn't much help. Specialized publications of the film world provide intelligent, up-to-date reviews and an interested teacher should examine journals like the

British *Sight and Sound, Films in Review,* University of California's *Film Quarterly,* and the newly revamped *Show Magazine.* The excellent publication for teachers *Media and Methods* provides evaluation of films for the expressed purpose of commenting on their classroom adaptability.

The first rule for anyone interested in professional reviews is not to expect much agreement among them. It's almost a game among critics to see who can interpret the most, or the least, from a current movie. Consequently if Judith Crist or Rex Reed find a film "delightful," John Simon or Stanley Kauffman will probably hate it. And vice versa. Critics are journalists and often their first commitment is to write entertainingly. Their opinions, are simply *their* opinions. The teacher should read as many as possible, not so much for their evaluations, but to get some idea of the content of the great number of films in release. My own favorite is the daily critic for the *New York Times* Vincent Canby. This is probably because I agree with him most often. Pauline Kael of the *New Yorker* has the best literary style. Stanley Kauffman of *The New Republic* is the most pretentious (he once wrote a lengthy review of *Fellini Satyricon,* exalting the genius of the director in depth, only, almost apologetically, in the end concluding that there wasn't much to the film). Andrew Sarris of *The Village Voice* is the most exasperating. And Judith Crist of Television's *Today Show* and *New York Magazine* is usually closest to the layman's opinion. I read them all, and interested teachers should too.

Even if critical reviews can provide some information on current films, how is the teacher supposed to know about past movies, which are the ones now available for classrooms anyway? I can only answer this based on my own methods. First of all, the better film critics have found it lucrative to publish their past reviews in book form. Pauline Kael's three books (I Lost It at the Movies, Kiss Kiss Bang Bang, and Going Steady), which I've cited throughout these pages, provide an excellent index of major domestic and foreign films since the late fifties. Judith Crist, Stanley Kauffman, John Simon, Dwight MacDonald (the former supercritic of *Esquire*—he hates everything), and Bosley Crowther (the retired *New York Times* "god" of opinion) have all published their composite reviews and these too can help provide some necessary background. The most useful collection of reviews in helping me adjust to this field was the late James Agee's (one of our first serious film critics) Agee on Film, vol. I, consisting of most of his writings on the movies of the forties.

The best way to keep abreast of past films, and the cheapest, is television. I know all the "purist" arguments about how commercial interruptions and cuts ruin great films, and to a certain extent they're true. But as a teacher desperately trying to survey motion pictures as educational sources, many of which were made before I was born, it's better than nothing. I think that I have seen more movies on television than in theaters. Network movies, late shows (late, late shows), afternoon "matinées," can provide a rich background in film literature. Useful guides for television films are the paperback indexes listing hundreds of titles and brief synopses. There are currently two such guides available: Leonard Matlin, Ed., TV Movies and Steven Scheuer, Ed., Movies on TV. Once the teacher has surveyed the screen literature, he will be capable of making significant choices for the classroom. As I've tried to indicate in the filmographies in this book, the sources are abundant.

"BLOWING-UP THE CLASSROOM"—RECENT CINEMATIC "FREEDOM"
AND THE MOTION PICTURE PRODUCTION CODE

One of the biggest problems confronting film teachers today, particularly in high schools, is the controversy over the new "permissiveness" in portraying sex on the screen. In 1965, the release of *The Pawnbroker* caused quite a furor as the Catholic Legion of Decency gave it a "condemned" rating because of the explicit scene in which a prostitute flaunted her bare breasts. The Motion Picture Association of America, which is the film industry's self-regulatory censoring agency, similarly denied the film a seal of approval, although after producer Ely Landau appealed its decision, demonstrating the scene's artistic necessity, the seal was granted.[1] In 1966, Michaelangelo Antonioni's *Blow-Up* was released without the coveted seal.[2]

Hoping to solve the problem of the controversy of the seal, The Motion Picture Association created a self-regulatory coding system for films released after November 1968. That system evaluates movies according to their sexual content, treatment of violence, drugs, and profane language on the screen. The current rating structure of films in release is as follows: "G"—films for general audiences, with no age restrictions; "G. P."—films with "mature content, parental discretion advised, but no age restrictions (this category was formerly labelled "M"); "R"—restricted, no admittance to those under age 17 without accompaniment of parent or adult guardian; "X"—no admittance to any persons under 17 years of age.

Naturally the films in the "R" and "X" categories deal heavily in explicit sex, nudity, and profane language. I'm not sure what specific criteria are used to determine an "X" from an "R." One official of the Motion Picture Association told me each film is evaluated individually.

I'm not about to argue the merits or demerits of the rating system. My major concern is showing relevant films in the classroom. The problem presented by the codes for me is that it makes my selections increasingly risky. For example, I have already recommended *The Pawnbroker* and *Blow-Up*. Neither film is as sexually explicit as some of the stuff on screens today like *Beyond the Valley of the Dolls* for example. Nor does either film contain its nude scenes for the purpose of sheer sensationalism. The bare breasts of the prostitute in *The Pawnbroker* serve as an emotional trigger to Saul Nazerman's horrible memory of the Nazi torture of his naked wife. The brief snatches of nudity in *Blow-Up* are used to demonstrate the photographer's preoccupation with self-satisfying sex in contrast to his apathy towards any moral commitment. Both films, I hope I've proven, are excellent classroom sources, though because of their controversial nature, the teacher using them is put on the spot.

Today's rated films pose an even greater problem. The Oscar-winning *Midnight Cowboy* was rated "X." How can a teacher justify using it with a group of teenagers if "officially" theaters are not supposed to admit them to see it at all. (Theaters can't be enforcing the ratings very thoroughly since most of my stu-

---

[1] For an interesting description of this case as well as others like it, see Alexander Walker, <u>Sex in the Movies</u>. Baltimore: Penguin Books, 1969. This book does not include information on the current MPAA rating code, however,

[2] Until the current rating system, which now handles such situations with the "X" category, the seal was never actually a requirement to release a film. However, disapproval of the MPAA generally limited the number of theaters a film could be booked in. **Blow-Up,** however, did not lose money as a result of this condemnation. **ibid.** p. 186; pp. 261-262.

dents had not only seen *Midnight Cowboy*, but much "X-ier" films such as *Vixens* and *Myra Breckenridge*.) *Medium Cool* was originally given an "X" rating, though after an appeal by its producers, the MPAA changed it to an "R."

From the motion picture **Midnight Cowboy**. Courtesy of United Artists.

What is a teacher to do? Clearly no teacher wants to show his classes hard-core pornography. Many of the "X" rated films are merely exploitive and trashy. But *Midnight Cowboy* isn't. I've only seen one other "X" film, and that was *Putney Swope*. Despite all of its crudeness, this film too might have potential classroom value use someday. (Its satire on race relations is hilarious.) Many recent excellent films currently becoming available in 16 mm have "R" ratings, and I've recommended some (*If . . ., The Wild Bunch, Medium Cool, Last Summer, Goodbye Columbus*).

Like most of the problems cited in this portion of the book, I have no specific solution. Many parents who abide by the code aren't going to like the idea of such films being used in school. Administrators are sure to frown on it. And, in some cases, the kids themselves may object.

I have again been reasonably lucky in my own experience. Both principals I've worked under have trusted my discretion in selecting films and in handling any controversies. And there have been some. As a novice in this field, a few years ago when I showed *Dr. Strangelove*, a young lady in my class walked out when Col. Jack D. Ripper (Sterling Hayden) announced that fluoridation of water made him impotent. Later the student told me that her religion forbade her from listening to any public discussion about sex.

Since that time I have tried to be as considerate of students' personal feelings as possible, and before I show a film whose content may be even slightly offensive, I try to survey class opinion. Recently, prior to showing the film *Privilege*, I discovered that a girl in my class was a Pentecostal lay-preacher. I told her privately that the film's anti-religious nature might offend her, and gave her the option not to see or be responsible for it. She chose to "take a look" at it first before deciding. Much to my surprise, she stayed for the entire film, and then in subsequent class discussions proceeded to intelligently tear its sacrilegious theme to pieces.

If there is any rule to follow when selecting controversial films for the classroom, it must be to consider your students first. A teacher should know his class before he tries anything of a disputable nature. Hence, if he's going to show *Blow-Up* or *Midnight Cowboy*, he shouldn't start the term with it. The teacher creates the context for his films and he does that with a knowledge of the maturity of his class. His tasteful handling of the situation will lessen any misunderstanding about his purpose.

I realize my next bit of advice will sound like a terrible "cop out," but it might be a good idea to clear things with the administration first. If you've prepared your class for the content of the film and can demonstrate the validity of it in terms of curriculum, any "reasonably" intelligent principal or department head should understand. If the administration is hardheaded about it, maybe you should have a less controversial alternative in mind (until the revolution, that is).

These are sad realities. The only hope I can offer to teachers who are confronted by pristine standards for selecting films is to consider what has happened to classroom literature in the past few years. When I was in high school, Catcher in the Rye was off limits. Today it's becoming a literary standard, as are Manchild in the Promised Land and Catch-22. Maybe the same acceptance for "modern" films is not far off.

EQUIPMENT

Once the teacher has acquired some money and has decided on a repertory of films (or compromised on one), most of his problems should clear up. Note that I said "should" clear up, since every year I notice one overriding dilemma that film teachers face. They are terrified of movie projectors. Most teachers, in my experience, simply cannot operate a standard 16-mm projector. The library of excellent quality films which my school purchased with a special grant not long ago is currently in danger of depletion because of teacher abuse of equipment. Contrary to popular mythology, motion picture projectors, even those awful self-threaders, do not eat celluloid. A film that is split down the middle or with mangled sprockets is the result of a human error in threading the machine. Although many states require a teacher to take a course in the technical handling of audio-visual aids, such courses seem to have little transfer value to performance on the job.

I can speak this way because I used to think I was the only film teacher when I started my curriculum a few years ago who could not operate a projector. For the entire first semester of working with a celluloid curriculum, I never had to touch a machine. A student of mine overheard me tell a fellow teacher that I couldn't run a projector and volunteered to show me. When I saw him demonstrate how skillfully he could handle it, I made him my permanent assistant. He handled everything. If a film split, he fixed it. If bulbs burned out, he replaced them. He even set up the screen. I was spoiled, since my young associate never let me down. And then a terrible thing happened. . . he graduated. There I was at the start of the next semester with a whole series of films on order and no one to operate that projector. I put a notice in the school bulletin, advertising for help. The kids who applied simply couldn't get the job right, and yet I couldn't show them any better. I asked other teachers, but most of them claimed that it had been years since their audio-visual training, and they'd forgotten. In desperation I had only one choice—I had to learn to do it myself.

After several days of trial and error, I had mastered the art. I was really surprised how easy it was. (My school has the standard Graflex 16, model 915 projector which is one of the simplest to operate.) I am probably one of the most mechanically awkward people in the world. Yet I learned to run that projector, and it is a cardinal rule in this field that the teacher has to be the master of his equipment. If a bulb burns out, it must be replaced quickly because most films have been borrowed for showing for a limited time. If the projector malfunctions, fixing it the next day, or even within the next few hours, might be too late to screen that movie. Therefore, it is an absolute rule that teachers run their own machines.

I'm not enough of a technician to recommend one projector over another. I've had great success with the Graflex 16 because of its operative ease, but most new projectors (Bell and Howell, RCA, etc.) are equally simple. Self-threading projectors, in my experience, tend to break down too easily, and if a teacher makes a mistake in operating the automatic threader, the likelihood is that the film will tear.

One interesting alternative to the standard 16-mm machine is the Technicolor 1000 super 8-mm projector. This very sensitive machine uses cartridges of film that merely need to be locked in place correctly. A simple flip of a switch and the film, in a sense, shows itself. You don't even have to rewind it. Many 16-mm film distributors have begun to "blow-down" prints into these "super 8" cartridges. Contemporary-McGraw-Hill Films, for example, has made many of its best shorts available in this form (*The Hat, The Hangman, The Hand, Time Piece, Two Men and a Wardrobe*, etc.). Certainly the great advantage of these cartridges is that it is almost impossible to tear the film. Considering the size of the machine, the sound quality and picture are generally excellent (although, some people with more technical eyes than mine have pointed out that a room needs to be much darker for full appreciation than with 16 mm). Since many companies are beginning to market films in this format, it might be a good idea to check into it further. The projectors are not as expensive as many 16-mm machines, and they may represent a wave of the future.

Another "futuristic" sample of motion picture "hardware" is the new television cassette recorder, particularly AVCO Corporation's Cartrivision. This system of adding a special adapter to a television set is quite remarkable. It can be used as a self-controlled video-tape recorder, or it can play prepackaged films in cassette form. Embassy Pictures and United Artists are currently reproducing feature films for this format, and once the system becomes generally available, such films are supposed to rent for as little as $3 per showing. Naturally, the problem is that they are limited to the size of the television screen. This may hamper their appreciability for serious cinema students. Still, this entire system of movies as television cassettes is an interesting development and may, in the long run, solve many of the funding problems teachers now have. It will be interesting to see how this system develops as schools become more aware of it.[3]

TIMING—THE FILM VS. THE SCHEDULE

The teacher's lesson plan for the 2nd period (9:00 a.m.—9:45 a.m.) reads as follows:

9:00—Thread projector.
9:03—Class enters.
9:05—Introduce film *Circle of the Sun* (30 minutes).
9:08—Show film.
9:38—Survey class reactions.
9:43—Assignment.
9:45—Dismissed.

The actual class session deviated from it "slightly" (he told his department head):

8:48—Pick up projector in supply closet. It isn't there.
9:05—Projector located in faculty men's room. Last teacher to use it yesterday had no key for supply closet, so . . . .
9:08—Apologize to class for lateness.
9:09—Thread projector.
9:15—Start film.
9:16—Stop film and tighten loop around sound drum.
9:20—Principal makes public address system announcement. Two illegally parked cars blocking delivery entrance. Also, condolences to basketball team for "tough" 108-37 loss.
9:27—Resume film.
9:29—Projection lamp burns out, no picture. Stop machine.
9:30—Dispatch call for help to Instructional Materials Center. Desperately need bulb.
9:35—Student returns with bulb. Wrong one, filmstrip projector bulb sent by mistake.
9:36—Class discussion, unauthorized.
9:38—Teacher runs to IMC, grabs correct bulb, runs back to room. Alienates librarian he neglected to bid good morning to.
9:41—Returns to room. Class "discussion" at a roar.
9:42—Replace bulb. Teacher burns hand on the overheated bulb.
9:44½—Resume film.
9:45—Bell rings. Period over. Teacher buries head in arms and cries.

Perhaps the greatest single enemy a film teacher has to confront is the schedule. Teachers and administrators have been brainwashed into believing that a

---

school day must function divided into 45-minute entities. The fact is that there is no educational justification whatsoever that a student learns best under such conditions. The standard schedule is a convenience, nothing more. For teachers interested in using films, it can be a deadly trap. The incident I have just described is true, and I'm reasonably sure that many readers are right now identifying with that poor teacher (me). The average 45-minute classroom period (in my school it is now actually less) just isn't enough time to show even the shortest films. Barring incidents like the ones I've described, by the time kids get seated, roll is taken, shades are lowered, projector is threaded, etc., the period still slips away before most films can be completed. And these are shorts. How can a teacher show feature films under such conditions?

The best solution to this administrative hangup is to create a flexible scheduling pattern. Many schools (not in my district) have modular schedules where teachers needing extended class time for lengthy projects, including feature films, can keep a class longer, borrowing time from a colleague. He, in turn, has the same option, when he chooses to use it.

Another possibility, again already practiced by some schools, is to lengthen English and Social Studies classes to two regular periods one day and eliminate them the next. This way students attend the required five periods, but do so in three or four days. Teachers using films under such conditions have time to show them.

As I've already explained in the memoir chapters, my school has none of this. The best arrangement I could make (and one I am suggesting) was to get one class of students scheduled to English, Social Studies, and Math in the same room for consecutive periods. This way the teachers can arrange to borrow time from each other.

Still the only way I have consistently been able to use feature films with the rest of my classes is by showing them divided into three or four episodes. I am aware of the "purist" argument against splitting a film, and I basically agree with it. But confronted with no other alternatives (as I believe many teachers are), it can work. For example, *The Loneliness of the Long Distance Runner* is 103 minutes long. It comes in a package of three reels of roughly equal length (actually the last reel is a bit shorter than the other two). I have shown it to my classes over a three-day span. Because of the film's reliance on flashbacks and its surprise ending, splitting it up can be facilitated by providing the classes with an assignment after each of the first two reels predicting the forthcoming events. This helps to sustain the continuity of the film. Interestingly, in my school where attendance is a big problem, when I split up a film I find that the size of my classes remains constant during the expanded showing. I have even "hooked" a few potential truants into coming to school regularly by stringing films out in this manner.

Occasionally, features don't physically lend themselves to this practice. One film I showed was divided into three very uneven reels. The first had almost 60 minutes of film on it. The other two, considerably less. I had to solve this by "marking my place" after 40 minutes into the large reel with a piece of tape. I then unwound to that point the following day and threaded the projector from there to show the rest of the reel. This whole procedure can be very time consuming, but it will work.

The only other alternatives a teacher has for showing full-length feature films are to bring kids into school early or keep them late. I've tried both methods and neither is very good. Schools like mine start so early it's no longer possible to request coming in ahead of time. I realize a great many institutions run after-school film programs (which are not part of the classroom activities), but this isn't very effective either. Kids and teachers have after-school jobs and responsibilities, and it's impossible to require attendance at a time so inconvenient for so many.

Obviously the best solution to the schedule problem is to create some kind of modular system. Perhaps if enough teachers can demonstrate the fallacy of the standard schedule and the needs for flexibility, the crucial time problem restricting a celluloid curriculum can be eliminated.

BOOKING THE FILM—THE TEACHER AND THE 16-MM DISTRIBUTOR

Once the teacher has acquired some money, surveyed the motion picture field for good classroom sources, learned how to operate his equipment, and worked out a reasonable screening schedule, he is ready to do business with film distributors. The following suggestions (again based on my experiences) can facilitate the procedure of ordering films:

1. Send for catalogs from *all* of the film distributors you can. These catalogs provide valuable film rental information, including price and borrower's responsibility, as well as data on the films themselves (length, age, synopses, critical evaluation, etc.). A list of distributors' addresses appears at the end of this chapter. Catalogs are usually free.

2. When reading the catalogs, remember no distributor makes his products sound bad. Because film renting is a business, it is perfectly legitimate to accentuate the positive. Therefore, the teacher, by learning about the motion picture sources ahead of time, cannot be misled by catalog advertising. (For instance, I know of one distributor that lists Otto Preminger's political potboiler *Advise and Consent* under films with "religious meaning." Now I would say that's stretching things a bit. Considering the sensationalistic nature of Preminger's products, even *The Cardinal* doesn't have much religious meaning.) Most catalog advertisements don't misrepresent films, however. They merely publicize them.

3. Use the catalogs to compare prices. Although several film agencies handle titles exclusively, there are companies who handle many of the same movies. Thus if one is asking $50 for *Mr. Roberts* (a film appearing in many catalogs), and another releases it for $37.50, you know whom to rent it from.

4. Whenever possible, book your films by phone. This has the convenience of letting you know immediately whether the film is available on the date you need it. You'll have to follow up the conversation with a confirming letter, but calling is still a valuable time saver. Several of the distributors will let you call collect. It will say this in the catalog.

5. Always book films as early as possible, since so many titles are in great demand. If you delay in ordering the film you want, it may be booked when you need it. I always try to book films for the entire school year in September by estimating the length of each unit I teach.

6. High school teachers should always inquire about rental rates directly.

Some companies will provide a discount for a high school showing to a class of 50 or less students at a rate below the listed catalog price. (This is not true of Films Inc., Audio-Brandon, or Contemporary-McGraw-Hill, whose rates are already relatively low.)

7. Be sure to specify the nature of the print that you want. Many color films are also available in black and white at a slightly lower cost (though it isn't worth the saving). Also, several recent films are available in cinemascope, which requires an anamorphic lens attachment to a projector. If you have the equipment and want this print (usually at no extra cost), then specifically request it.

8. If you find it necessary to cancel a film, do so in writing as soon as possible. Many companies indicate that you cannot cancel after a certain date (from two weeks to five days before the film is scheduled for showing), and it is possible you could get stuck with the film anyway.

9. Return prints immediately after you've shown them. Most distributors require that the special delivery, insured, return postage be paid by the borrower so consider that as part of your rental budget. But get those films back on time. Films delayed can subvert another teacher's program (I've been affected by someone else's tardiness several times).

A CLOSER LOOK AT THE FILM DISTRIBUTOR

Many of the major film rental agencies have certain unique qualities worth noting. Some specialize in certain types of films; others provide study guides and useful classroom materials with rentals. Here is a rundown (in no specific order) of some of the special features of major distributors.

Films Inc. One of the largest agencies for 16-mm rentals. It exclusively handles most of the major American films of Metro-Goldwyn-Mayer, Twentieth Century Fox, Paramount (recent features), and National General. In addition Films Inc. has "classics" from Warner Brothers and RKO. It also publishes several valuable guides for its films available on request.

Audio-Brandon Films. A recent merger has combined two of the largest national film distributors. Its catalog features the best in foreign films, particularly Italian, containing most of Fellini's masterpieces.

Contemporary-McGraw-Hill Films. Another relatively recent merger is responsible for producing one of the largest of film rental libraries. The distributor of the best in short subjects (for rent or sale), including exclusive handling of the National Film Board of Canada products, it also has an excellent selection of features (particularly films from France). Contemporary-McGraw-Hill publishes a number of study guides for many of its documentaries.

Museum of Modern Art. The Museum's concern for artistic film study is world renowned. Its catalog features the best in cinematic history of the international film industry. It is also an excellent source for high-quality experimental films.

Walter Reade 16 (formerly **Continental 16**). The exclusive handler of the best in international cinema, the Walter Reade catalog has some especially good films from Britain. Also the distributor for Sterling Educational Films.

Janus Films. A very specialized distributor, with a small but excellent catalog of international films. Many of the most notable features of Ingmar Bergman are its specialty.

Warner Brothers 16. Warners is relatively new in the 16-mm business, but it is the exclusive distributor of a number of excellent recent American films.

Universal 16 (formerly **United World Films**). With one of the largest catalogs of American films, Universal handles all of its own products, as well as many of the "classic" titles from Paramount Studios. It is now in the process of producing study guides for several of its films.

United Artists 16. The exclusive distributor of all films released by United Artists, including some of the best American films ever made.

Columbia Cinematheque (formerly **Royal 16**). A small, but generally excellent library, including exclusive distribution of *Dr. Strangelove* and *A Man for all Seasons.* High schools should inquire about its rental rates.

Samuel Goldwyn 16 mm. This is a brand new distributing house which is in the process of acquiring the old Samuel Goldwyn films of the thirties and forties. It already lists titles like *The Best Years of Our Lives, Dead End,* and *Pride of the Yankees.* These titles and all the other Goldwyn productions will be exclusively handled by this distributor.

NET Film Service. National Educational Television produces some of the finest programming on the air. Virtually all of its filmed documentaries are available from its offices at Indiana University. I have cited many of its titles throughout the book, and I'm pleased to note that NET charges the lowest rental rates (and purchase rates) of all film distributors. A fantastic source, and a bargain.

Zipporah Films (formerly **OSTI Films**). Frederick Wiseman handles exclusive distribution of his own brilliant documentaries. Rental rates are high because of the small size of the operation, but all of Wiseman's films are worth the price.

There are a great many other national film distributors, as well as local camera exchanges that handle 16-mm rentals. The following section lists several of them with their addresses.

MAJOR 16-MM FILM RENTAL LIBRARIES

American Radio and Television Commercials Festival. 6 West 57th St., New York, N. Y. 10019. Tel.: (212)593-1900.

Anti-Defamation League of B'Nai Brith. 225 South 15th St., Philadelphia, Penna. 19102. Tel.: (215) PE 5-4267.

Appleton-Century-Crofts Films. 267 West 25th St., New York, N. Y. 10001. Tel.: (212) 675-5330.

Audio-Brandon Films. 34 MacQuesten Parkway So., Mount Vernon, N. Y. 10550. Tel.: (914) 664-5051. *Branches:* 2138 East 7th St., Chicago, Ill. 60649. Tel.: (312) MU 4-2531. 406 Clement St., San Francisco, Calif. 94118. Tel.: (415) SK 2-4800.

AVCO Embassy Pictures Corp. 1301 Avenue of the Americas, New York, N. Y. 10019. Tel.: (212) 956-5500.

Bailey Film Associates. 6509 De Longpre Ave., Hollywood, Calif. 90028. Tel.: (213) 466-4331.

Capital Film Exchange. 309 North 13th St., Philadelphia, Penna. 19107. Tel.: (215) LO 7-2698

Carousel Films. 1501 Broadway, Suite 1503, New York, N.Y. 10036. Tel.: (212) 279-6734

Charlou Productions, Inc. 165 West 46th St., New York, N. Y. 10036. Tel.: (212) 247-3337.

Churchill Films. 662 North Robertson Blvd., Los Angeles, Calif. 90069. Tel.: (213) 657-5110.

Columbia Cinematheque. 711 Fifth Ave., New York, N. Y. 10022. Tel.: (212) 751-7529

Columbia University Center for Mass Communications. 440 West 110th St., New York, N. Y. 10025. Tel.: (212) UN 5-2000

Contemporary-McGraw-Hill Films. 230 West 42nd St., New York, N. Y. Tel.: (212) 971-3333. *Eastern Office:* Princeton Road, Highstown, N. J. 08520. Tel.: (609) 448-1700. *Midwest Office:* 828 Custer Ave., Evanston, Ill. 60202. Tel.: (312) 869-5010. *Western Office:* 1714 Stockton St., San Francisco, Calif. 94133. Tel.: (415) 362-3115.

The Film Center. 915 Twelfth Street, N. W., Washington, D. C. 20005. Tel.: (202) 393-1205.

Films Inc.–9 offices, regionally. 1) 227 Pharr Road, N. E., Atlanta, Ga. 30305. Tel.: (404) 237-0341. (Georgia, Alabama, Florida, Mississippi, North and South Carolina, and Tennessee.) 2) 161 Massachusetts Ave., Boston, Mass. 02115. Tel.: (617) 937-1110. (Massachusetts, Connecticut, Maine, New Hampshire, Rhode Island, and Vermont.) 3) 1414 Dragon St., Dallas, Tex. 75207. Tel.: (214) 741-4071. (Texas, Arkansas, Louisiana, New Mexico, and Oklahoma.) 4) 5625 Hollywood Blvd., Hollywood, Calif. 90028. Tel:. (213) 466-5481. (California, Arizona, Colorado, Nevada, Utah, and Wyoming.) 5) 3501 Queens Blvd., Long Island City, N. Y. Tel.: (212) 937-1110. (New York, New Jersey, Delaware, Maryland, Pennsylvania, Virginia, and Washington, D. C.) 6) 2129 N. E. Broadway, Portland, Oreg. 97232. Tel.: (503) 282-5558. (Oregon, Idaho, Montana, and Washington.) 7) 44 East South Temple, Salt Lake City, Utah. Tel.: (801) 328-8191. (Utah and Idaho.) 8) 3034 Canon St. (Kerr Film Exchange), San Diego, Calif. Tel.: (714) 224-2406. (San Diego Metropolitan Area) 9) 4420 Oakton St., Skokie, Ill. 60076. Tel.: (312) 676-1088 (Skokie), (312) 583-3330 (Chicago). (Illinois, Indiana, Iowa, Kansas, Kentucky, Michigan, Minnesota, Missouri, Nebraska, North and South Dakota, West Virginia, and Ohio.)

Film Makers Cooperative. 175 Lexington Ave., New York, N.Y. 10016. Tel.: (212) 889-3820.

Grove Press Films/Cinema 16. 80 University Place, New York, N. Y. 10003. Tel.: (212) 989-6400.

Hurlock Cine World Film Library. 230 West 41st St., New York, N. Y. 10036. Tel.: (212) 868-0748.

Institutional Cinema Service. 29 East 10th St., New York, N. Y. 10003. Tel.: (212) 673-3990.

International Film Bureau. 332 South Michigan Ave., Chicago, Ill. 60604. Tel.: (312) 427-4545.

International Film Foundation. 475 Fifth Ave., New York, N. Y. 10017. Tel.: (212) 685-4998.

Janus Films. 745 Fifth Ave., New York, N. Y. 10022. Tel.: (212) 753-7100

Learning Corporation of America (Columbia Pictures). 711 Fifth Ave., New York, N. Y. 10022. Tel.: (212) PL 1-4400.

Mass Media Ministries. 2116 North Charles St., Baltimore, Md. 21218. Tel.: (301) 727-3270.

Modern Sound Pictures. 1410 Howard St., Omaha, Neb. 68102. Tel.: (402) 341-8476.

Mogull's Film Exchange. 235 West 46th St., New York, N. Y. 10036. Tel.: (212) PL 7-1414.

Museum of Modern Art, Department of Film Circulating Programs. 11 West 53rd St., New York, N. Y. 10022. Tel.: (212) 245-8900.

NET Film Service. Audio Visual Center, Indiana University, Bloomington, Ind. 47401. Tel.: (812) 337-2103.

National Film Board of Canada. 680 Fifth Ave., Suite 819, New York, N. Y. 10019. Tel.: (212) 586-2400

New York Times—Arno Press. Film Division, 229 West 43rd St., New York, N. Y. 10036. Tel.: (212) 556-1651

Pyramid Films. P. O. Box 1048, Santa Monica, Calif. 90406.

Roa's Films. 1696 North Astor St., Milwaukee, Wisc. 53202. Tel.: (414) 271-0861.

Rogosin Films, Inc. 144 Bleecker St., New York, N. Y. 10012.

Samuel Goldwyn 16 mm. 1041 North Formosa Ave., Hollywood, Calif. 90046 Tel.: (231) 851-7234.

Swank Motion Pictures. 201 South Jefferson Ave., St. Louis, Mo. 63166. Tel.: (314) 531-5100.

Teaching Film Custodians, Inc. 25 West 43rd St., New York, N. Y. 10036. Tel.: (212) OX 5-1640. Film excerpts for lease only.

Trans-World Films. 332 South Michigan Ave., Chicago, Ill. 60604. Tel.: (312) 922-1530.

Twelfth and Oxford Sts. Film-Makers Corp. 1550 North 7th St., Philadelphia, Penna. Tel.: (215) PO 3-2585.

Twyman Films. 329 Salem Ave., Dayton, Ohio 45401. Tel.: (513) 222-4014.

United Artists 16. 729 Seventh Ave., New York, N. Y. 10019. Tel.: (212) 245-6000.

University of California, Extension Media Center. 2223 Fulton St., Berkeley, Calif. 94720. Tel.: (415) 845-6000.

Universal 16. 221 Park Ave. So., New York, N. Y. 10003. Tel.: (212) 777-6600.

Walter Reade 16. 241 East 34th St., New York, N. Y. 10016. Tel.: (212) 683-6300.

Warner Brothers 16. 666 Fifth Ave., New York, N. Y. 10019. Tel.: (212) 246-1000.

Willoughby-Peerless Film Exchange. 115 West 31st St., New York, N. Y. 10017. Tel.: (212) 564-1600, ext. 236.

Zipporah Films. 54 Lewis Wharf, Boston, Mass. 02110. Tel.: (617) 742-6680.

PART IV

And So On...

Additional Filmography
and Bibliography

FILMOGRAPHY

During the course of this book I have mentioned a few hundred film titles and supplied information concerning their availability in 16 mm for the classroom. All films cited up to now have been directly related to the individual teaching units in each chapter. In this sense they were strictly my films, listed and discussed in a very personal context. Therefore, since this book is primarily a teachers' guide, I have decided to amend all previous filmographies with this lengthy concluding chapter on "everything else" of any value to the teacher whom I've (hopefully) helped convert to the notion of a celluloid curriculum. The titles listed here are those which, in my opinion, can work as well in the classroom as all the films previously mentioned. For these the teacher should create his own format, although I'll make some suggestions along the way. Naturally this list could be longer, and I'm sure that I have left out many favorites. The major criteria for my selections have been cinematic and content relevancy for kids (this should always be the first priority) and availability in 16 mm for classrooms. I have listed a few films that are not yet accessible, but are good bets for the near future. Here then, in alphabetical order, are other films to turn kids on with.

A Nous la Liberté. 87 minutes. Black and white. Directed by Rene Clair (French), 1931. English subtitles. Rene Clair's classic satire on man and the machine still retains much of its gentle, comic flavor. In many ways it is a Depression film (with the hero's realization that the poor man's life is the best), but the scenes in the factory are satirically funny. This film should also be of interest to film history students, since it was a pioneer in techniques of sound, particularly its musical score. Rental from Contemporary-McGraw-Hill Films.
Alice's Restaurant. 111 minutes. Color. Directed by Arthur Penn, 1969. Arthur Penn's lyrical ode to our nonconformist youth. The multiplotted scenario vacillates between comedy and heavy drama, but the film succeeds in portraying the "hip" world without patronizing it. An unknown actress named Pat Quinn is excellent as the famous Alice Brock, and though Arlo Guthrie isn't much of an actor, his draft induction scene is hilarious. Rental from United Artists 16.

The American Film. 37 minutes. Color, and black and white. Produced for the White House Festival of the Arts (narrated by Charlton Heston), 1966. This is an excellent film about the creativity of the motion picture director. Using clips from the works of five significant American directors (Fred Zinneman, *High Noon;* William Wyler, *Friendly Persuasion;* Alfred Hitchcock, *North by North West*; Elia Kazan, *On the Waterfront*; George Stevens, *Shane*), the film thoroughly describes their individual creativity. A must for courses in film-making or aesthetic film study. Five-year lease (at a reasonable rate) from Teaching Film Custodians.

American Time Capsule. 3 minutes. Color. Directed by Charles Braverman, 1968. This original little film composed of rapidly flashing still pictures of American history made a tremendous impression when shown on the Smothers Brothers' television program. It is now available for classrooms, with a number of uses. Students can discuss the director's interpretation of U. S. history, since despite the rapidity of the images, a definite philosophy permeates the film. It is also an interesting look at the impact of TV commercials on how quickly we absorb the multitude of images. I once used it half jokingly as a review of a year's work in history. Much to my surprise, the students missed very little of the content. Purchase or rental from Pyramid Films.

And Now Miguel. 63 minutes. Black and white. Written and directed by Joseph Krumgold, 1955. And, *And Now Miguel*. 95 minutes. Color. Directed by Robert Radnitz, 1965. Apparently there are two film versions of the famous children's novel (winner of the Newberry Award of Children's Literature), although I have only seen the second. Interestingly, author Joseph Krumgold made his film first and then based the novel on the screenplay. The second version is in turn based on the novel. Since there are so few intelligently made films for children, both versions are extremely useful in the elementary school. Students could do a kind of evolutionary transmedia study, starting with the Krumgold film, then the novel, and then the more recent film, noting all of the changes the story undergoes. Or just show one of the films and discuss the simple, beautiful story of a little Mexican-American boy who is impatient to grow up. Rental of the 1955 version from Contemporary-McGraw-Hill Films; the 1965 version from Universal 16 or Twyman Films.

The Angel Levine. 114 minutes. Color. Directed by Jan Kadar, 1970. I have never been a fan of those fantasies about angels (or ghosts) who have to perform tasks on earth in order to enter heaven. However, *The Angel Levine* (based on a Bernard Malamud short story) is extremely well done, with Harry Belafonte as the Black-Jewish angel and Zero Mostel as the object of his mission. Rental from United Artists 16.

Archaeology. 14 minutes. Black and white. Directed by Andrzej Brzozowski (Polish), 1967. Some archaeologists begin excavating an area of land. They divide it into four sections and methodically start to dig. Gradually they discover more and more "artifacts" of the society they're searching for. Finally, through their findings, the audience discovers they've been digging at Auschwitz, the notorious Nazi concentration camp. The whole thing is done without dialogue or music. Only the sounds of digging are heard, and it's very effective. Purchase or rental from Contemporary-McGraw-Hill Films.

Bad Day at Black Rock. 81 minutes. Color (cinemascope print available). Directed by John Sturges, 1954. This well-known "modern Western" about a one-armed veteran's visit to a small desert town where he is supposed to deliver a medal won by a now dead Japanese-American is loaded with suspense. The film is also an interesting statement on mob conformity and collective guilt. Spencer Tracy is memorable as the one-armed hero. Rental from Films Inc.

Belle de Jour. 100 minutes. Color. Directed by Luis Bunel (French), 1968. English subtitles or English language dubbed version. Alphabetical order dictates that I list Luis Bunel's obscure but beautiful film about a bored housewife who becomes an afternoon prostitute, closely after *And Now Miguel. Belle de Jour* is certainly not for children, but since it is neither lewd nor especially erotic despite its theme, it does qualify for fascinating classroom discussion for high school seniors and college students. The director concentrates on the psychological motives by probing the housewife's dreams, often deliberately mystifying the viewer about where reality and illusion separate. *Belle* was shown recently at a film festival at the Philadelphia Museum of Art, and several of my students saw it. Though none was sure of its meaning, all of them were anxious to discuss the psychology behind the images. Rental from Hurlock Cineworld.

The Best Years of Our Lives. 172 minutes. Black and white. Directed by William Wyler, 1946. William Wyler's classic portrait of the civilian readjustments made by three men returning from World War II is still powerful. The three stories are skillfully woven together from the start as the men meet on the flight home, and what could easily have become soap opera emerges as a brilliant commentary on the ways war changes people's lives. The acting is still quite believable, particularly the armless Harold Russell, who is today known for his work in helping rehabilitate similarly disabled veterans. Most students are simply not aware of this film, and the classroom is the ideal place for its revival. Rental from Samuel Goldwyn 16 mm.

The Bicycle Thief. 87 minutes. Black and white. Directed by Vittorio De Sica (Italian), 1949. English subtitles. Probably the most famous of the so-called "neorealist" films, *The Bicycle Thief* impresses me most as a bittersweet portrait of post-war Italy. The plight of a man and his young son in search of a stolen bicycle (which the man needs to keep his job) is still quite touching. Rental from Audio-Brandon Films.

The Big Carnival (Original title: **Ace in a Hole**). 112 minutes. Black and white. Directed by Billy Wilder, 1951. This cynical drama about an unscrupulous newspaper man (Kirk Douglas) who capitalizes on the plight of a man trapped by a mountain cave-in for a "great story," is both thought-provoking and tragic. The film was a failure when it was originally released in 1951, probably because of the depressing theme (in the end the trapped man dies), but for today's audiences it has much to say about professional ethics and the potential irresponsibility of the news media. I highly recommend it. Rental from Films Inc.

A Big Hand for the Little Lady. 95 minutes. Color. Directed by Fielder Cook, 1966. This is one of those entertaining adaptations from the "Golden Age" of television (as were *Marty, Twelve Angry Men,* and *Days of Wine and Roses*). Set in the West, *Big Hand for the Little Lady* is a very funny suspense comedy with a clever twist at the end. The cast is solidly professional (Henry Fonda, Joanne Woodward, Jason Robards, Paul Ford, and Burgess Meredith), and the dialogue is sharply written. Rental from Twyman Films, Swank Films, or Willoughby-Peerless Film Exchange.

Black Orpheus. 103 minutes. Color. Directed by Marcel Camus (French), 1960. Portuguese dialogue, English subtitles. The first time I saw this film based on the Greek legend of Orpheus and Eurydice, I was overwhelmed by the Brazilian scenery (Rio at carnival time) and the fantastic "bossa nova" music of Antonio Carlos Jobim. Seeing it again recently, I was amazed how closely the portrayal of the Brazilian Blacks resembles the stereotyped American "folk operas" like *Porgy and Bess* and *Cabin in the Sky*. The film is valuable in the limits of the stereotype study or as an aesthetically beautiful exercise in film-making (for its editing, color, and music). Otherwise, it has been severly overrated. Rental from Janus Films.

The Blue Angel. 112 minutes. Black and white. Directed by Josef Von Sternberg (German), 1929. English subtitles. Von Sternberg's classic film about the psychological undoing of a respected professor who becomes a love slave to a beautiful cabaret singer (Marlene Dietrich) is an interesting contemporary view of pre-Nazi Germany. Otherwise, its primary value is as a piece of cinematic history with its pioneering use of sound. *The Blue Angel* was remade as an American film in 1957, and although faithful to the original script, it was a mawkish exercise. Rental of the original from Janus Films or The Museum of Modern Art (in German, without subtitles).

Body and Soul. 104 minutes. Black and white. Directed by Robert Rossen (screenplay by Abraham Polansky), 1947. By far the best boxing drama of them all. John Garfield was an actor who died too young, and his portrayal of an unscrupulous fighter is in keeping with the style of many of today's successful anti-heroes (Paul Newman, George C. Scott, Robert Forster, etc.). Also, the role of Ben, the Black sparring partner and former champ (Canada Lee), is a long way from the demeaning stereotype. Rental from Willoughby-Peerless Film Exchange.

The Bridge. 102 minutes. Black and white. Directed by Bernard Wicki (German), 1959. English subtitles or English language dubbed version. This is one of the saddest films I have ever seen. As World War II draws to a close, a small group of German teenaged boys are drafted to guard a small bridge. The youths anxiously tend to their duty only to be destroyed in the forthcoming Allied onslaught. *The Bridge* is a brutal comment on the futility of war, and with the exception of *All Quiet on the Western Front,* it dwarfs all American anti-war films. Rental from Audio-Brandon Films, Swank Films, or Hurlock Cineworld.

The Cabinet of Dr. Caligari. .77 minutes. Black and white. Directed by Robert Wiene (German), 1920. Silent. *The* classic silent screen exercise in pop art and psychological horror is still visually fascinating. Students could screen it as a piece of cinema history or they could apply it to Siegfried Kracauer's thesis that it symbolized the sickness of the German national character which led to Nazism. (<u>From Caligari to Hitler</u>. Princeton, N. J.: Princeton

University Press, 1947.) Rental from Museum of Modern Art (an edited, 55-minute version is also available) or Audio-Brandon Films.

Casanova '70. 113 minutes. Color. Directed by Mario Monicelli (Italian), 1965. English subtitles. This is one of the funniest films about sex ever produced. A handsome military officer (Marcello Mastroianni) cannot have a sexual relationship unless some danger is involved. Because of his "problem," episodes of the film focus on the unusual nature of his affairs (seducing a female lion tamer in the cage with her pets, straddling a window ledge to wait for a lover's husband to step into the next room, and so on . . .). Behind all of the humor of this outrageously funny movie is a thought-provoking commentary on contemporary male sexual behavior. Rental from Audio-Brandon films.

Cat Ballou. 96 minutes. Color. Directed by Elliot Silverstein, 1965. This fast and funny Western spoof was a big commercial success when new, mostly because of Lee Marvin's Oscar-winning portrayal of an old drunken gunfighter. The film really has little satirical commentary and comparing it to a standard Western won't be of much value. It's just a good example of entertaining movie-making and may be useful in a lesson on "how it's done." Rental from Twyman Films or Swank Films.

A Child's Eyes. 10 minutes. Color. Directed by Richard Snodgrass, 1967. A beautiful short film focusing on the reactions of small children through their voices and crayon art work to the assassination of John F. Kennedy. This film is a sadly realistic commentary on growing up in our chaotic times. Purchase or rental from Contemporary-McGraw-Hill Films.

Children of Paradise (Les Enfants du Paradis). 188 minutes. Black and white. Directed by Marcel Carne (French), 1945. English subtitles. This classic French drama about the theater and a romance between a pantomimist and a wealthy woman didn't make a great impression on me when I saw it. The version I saw was cut to about two hours and that was slow moving. However, I know mine is a minority opinion in this case, since the film is generally recognized as a masterpiece of screen literature. In his book The Great Films (New York: Putnam, 1967), former *New York Times* critic Bosley Crowther describes the rigid conditions under which it was made during the Nazi occupation of France (pp. 169-172). Perhaps this film would be best used in a class in French language and literature, since so much of its meaning is indigenously French. Rental of the full, uncut version from Contemporary-McGraw-Hill Films.

Clay (Origin of the Species). 8 minutes. Black and white. Directed by Eliot Noyes, Jr., 1958. A cleverly animated film demonstrating shapes of various life forms made of clay devouring each other. Each form gradually becomes more complex, and it's all supposed to symbolize evolution. A jazz background provides an appropriate accompaniment. Purchase or rental from Contemporary-McGraw-Hill Films.

The Coming of Sound. 70 minutes. Black and white. A special "package" of clips of early sound films (1927-1929) from the Museum of Modern Art, including George Bernard Shaw's filmed interview, Disney's *Steamboat Willie*, a clip from *The Jazz Singer*, etc. This "package" is a must for anyone studying the history of film. Rental from Museum of Modern Art.

Contemporary Reflections on Babbitt and The Grapes of Wrath. 58 minutes. Color. CBS TV News Production, 1968. This is an interesting documentary on the relevancy of two classic pieces of American literature. The first half of the film features actor Pat Hingle delivering a conservative, business-oriented speech to a group of mid-Western executives. It is the same speech George Babbitt delivered during his political campaign in Sinclair Lewis's cynical novel. The second half concentrates on a migrant Appalachian family on the road to Cincinnati, as narrator Richard Boone reads appropriate passeges from Steinbeck's Grapes of Wrath. The film may seem a little too pretentious for some, but it can be a useful supplement in American literature courses. Purchase or rental from Bailey-Film Associates.

The Critic. 4 minutes. Color. Animated. Directed by Ernest Pintoff (commentary by Mel Brooks), 1963. This very funny little film provides the common man's reaction to modern art. The narrative consists of "critical" statements such as "What the hell's this?" and it provides a humorous attack on false values and anti-intellectualism. Purchase or rental from Audio-Brandon Films.

Crossfire. 86 minutes. Black and white. Directed by Edward Dmytryk (screenplay by Richard Brooks), 1947. Post-World War II "social" dramas (particularly those I have already discussed about Blacks) were once considered significant introspective commentaries on American life. Today they all appear rather overrated and preachy. *Crossfire,* one of the first American films to document the perils of anti-Semitism, is similarly faded. The characterizations are superficial and only Robert Ryan's performance as a Jew-hating soldier has any impact today. Still a film like this can be useful as a barometer of past tastes and old-style liberalism. Rental from Museum of Modern Art and Audio-Brandon Films.

The Diary of Anne Frank. 180 minutes. Black and white (cinemascope print available). Directed by George Stevens, 1959. The motion picture version of the well-known book and play has never been one of my favorites. The direction is heavy-handed, and much of the acting (including old Ed Wynn as Mr. Dussell and Millie Perkins as Anne) is really poor. I include it here since it is better than no film version at all (barely), and I know many teachers will use it no matter what I say. Rental from Films Inc.

Downhill Racer. 102 minutes. Color. Directed by Michael Ritchie, 1969. A rare film about sports and sportsmanship, which is thoroughly believable. Robert Redford portrays a champion skier on the American Olympic Team whose personal ambitions take precedence over the goals of his team. This is a really fascinating portrait of what may be the prototype American athlete. Rental from Films Inc.

Dream of the Wild Horses. 9 minutes. Color. Directed by Denys Colomb de Daunant (French), 1962. This visually beautiful slow-motion film of horses running through water and fire has recently been copied by a television commercial. Actually its mood (heightened by electronic background music) is dreamlike and poetic. I especially recommend it for art classes studying the beauty of animal form. Purchase or rental from Contemporary-McGraw-Hill Films.

The East Is Red. 130 minutes. Color. A production of The People's Republic of

China, 1965. English subtitles. This is the only Chinese-made film I know of available in the United States. Overly long and repetitious (the Chinese obviously aren't aware of the techniques of *Triumph of the Will*), the film is, nevertheless, a significant exercise in propaganda. For serious students of history and contemporary foreign affairs, *The East Is Red* is a "must." Rental from Contemporary-McGraw-Hill Films.

8½. 135 minutes. Black and white. Directed by Federico Fellini (Italian), 1963. English subtitles. Fellini's autobiographical fun and games about a past 40 director's "breakdown" is funny and psychologically fascinating. I'm not sure I can recommend any specific use for it other than pure cinematic study, but it is so beautifully made and well acted (particularly Marcello Mastroianni) that it is bound to be "discovered" for the classroom. Rental from Audio-Brandon Films.

The Entertainer. 97 minutes. Black and white. Directed by Tony Richardson (British), 1960. John Osborne's character study play about an obnoxious third-rate vaudevillian is a powerful film only because of Laurence Olivier's portrayal. Olivier's Archie Rice is one of the great characterizations on film, and students will find themselves despising him, without disregarding his basic humanity. Archie is more that a caricature of a dirty old man; he is a sad human being fearful of facing old age and the lack of communication within his own family. The film captures the atmosphere of the cheap music halls and lower-middle class neighborhoods of England, and it provides the screen with a brilliant character study. Rental from Walter Reade 16.

The Exiles. 72 minutes. Black and white. Directed by Kent Mackenzie, 1959-61. A haunting documentary about three reservation Indians who migrate to Los Angeles to find work. Kent Mackenzie's film is the best of its genre. The entire story is told from the point of view of the three Indians as they demonstrate the frustration of being outsiders in a White, urban world. I highly recommend it for classes studying contemporary Indian problems. It can be used, along with *Circle of the Sun,* very effectively here. It is also an example of the best in documentary film-making. Rental from Contemporary-McGraw-Hill Films.

Fires on the Plain. 105 minutes. Black and white. Directed by Kon Ichikawa (Japanese), 1959. English subtitles. There is no doubt that this is one of the most sickening films ever made (*New York Times* critic Bosley Crowther found it "horrible" and "repulsive"). Its subject is cannibalism among some Japanese army survivors on Leyte, in the Philippines, and although it is a symbolic morality play, the whole thing is very difficult to sit through. Critic Pauline Kael in her book I Lost It at the Movies (Boston: Little, Brown and Co., 1965) hails it as a masterpiece, however, and her review provides a reasonable justification for the film (pp. 225-228). *Fires on the Plain* might be useful in advanced college film courses or in classes studying moral philosophy. Rental from Audio Brandon Films.

Five Easy Pieces. 108 minutes. Color. Directed by Bob Rafelson, 1970. This unusual film about a former concert pianist who drifts through life aimlessly is an interesting commentary on uncommitted man. Jack Nicholson's portrayal of this anti-hero is a landmark in screen acting. Soon to be available for rental from Columbia Cinematheque.

Flavio. 12 minutes. Black and white. Directed and written by Gordon Parks, 1964. Black photographer Gordon Parks went to Brazil to film this compassionate document of ghetto life in Rio de Janeiro's notorious favellas (slums). Parks captures the tragedy of everyday life there by focusing on a ten-year-old boy, Flavio, who describes his way of life. The boy is strong-willed and mature, helping to support his parents and nine sisters and brothers even though he is physically very sick. A tragic commentary on human suffering resulting from poverty. Purchase or rental from Contemporary-McGraw-Hill Films.

Forbidden Games. 90 minutes. Black and white. Directed by Rene Clement (French), 1952. English subtitles. A classic French anti-war film about two children growing up in an atmosphere of war. An orphaned little girl and her boy playmate watch the constant ritual of funerals in their village. Soon they begin to play a game burying dead animals and marking their graves with ornaments that they steal from a nearby church. The film comes to a tragic conclusion as the playmates are separated, after the adults (ironically) force them to end their games. *Forbidden Games* is more than an anti-war film; it is a brilliant statement about the effects violence has on children. (This film could be used very well in a unit with *A Child's Eyes* and Donald Richie's *War Games,* which I will discuss shortly). Rental from Janus Films or Audio-Brandon Films.

Force of Evil. 78 minutes. Black and white. Directed by Abraham Polansky, 1948. This realistic drama about numbers racketeers is interesting because it was the last "signed" film of director Abraham Polansky prior to his blacklisting by the movie industry. Many film societies have hailed the director and this sample of his work as great. The thing that impresses me about it most is how well the acting of John Garfield holds up. His style is very timely. Rental from Willoughby-Peerless Film Exchange.

The Fortune Cookie. 125 minutes. Black and white. Directed by Billy Wilder, 1966. This extremely funny satire on accident frauds is painfully truthful much of the time. A conniving lawyer persuades his meek brother-in-law Jack Lemmon to fake an injury for a profitable lawsuit. Although Lemmon eventually loses his nerve and exposes the scheme, the planning and conniving along the way make for razor-edged satire. Walter Matthau won an Academy Award as "Whiplash Willie," the unscrupulous lawyer. Rental from United Artists 16.

Four Families. 61 minutes. Black and white. National Film Board of Canada Production, 1961. An excellent film for students of anthropology, sociology, and world cultures. The prominent anthropologist Margaret Mead narrates the child-rearing procedures and family structures in four cultures: Japan, France, India, and Canada. This kind of comparative study is enhanced by some expert documentary film technique. Purchase or rental from Contemporary-McGraw-Hill Films.

The 400 Blows. 98 minutes. Black and white. Directed by Francois Truffaut (French), 1959. English subtitles. A great film about an alienated 12-year-old who becomes a juvenile delinquent. The simple plot shows the motivation for his behavior (a broken home life), his apprehension and imprisonment in a reform school, and his brief escape. The filming is compassionate and the famous last scene when the frame freezes like a snapshot as the boy is about to be recaptured emphasizes the tragedy. Rental from Janus Films.

From Here to Eternity. 118 minutes. Black and white. Directed by Fred Zinneman, 1953. This film version of James Jones' racy novel about the peacetime army just prior to Pearl Harbor was considered sexually explicit in its day. By today's standards, much of its romantic action is quite tame, but the acting is still great, particularly Frank Sinatra as a rebellious private who is beaten to death by a vicious sergeant (Ernest Borgnine). The film, like the book, is a valuable portrait of the old Depression army prior to World War II, when society's misfits joined up for the regular diet and a place to sleep. Rental from Audio-Brandon Films, Contemporary-McGraw-Hill Films, Twyman Films, or Swank Films.

Fury. 94 minutes. Black and white. Directed by Fritz Lang, 1936. Fritz Lang's classic film on mob violence and lynch law may look its age, but the acting and dialogue still ring true. Considering the times, when Hollywood films were meant to provide fun and escapism, *Fury* is all the more significant. For some interesting commentary by director Fritz Lang on how he made it and what the studio (MGM) forced him to cut out, see Peter Bogdanovich's Fritz Lang in America (New York: Frederick A. Praeger, 1969). Rental from Films Inc. There are also two brief clips from *Fury* (the lynching sequence, 17 minutes and the trial sequence, 14 minutes) available for lease from Teaching Film Custodians.

The General. 90 minutes. Black and white. Directed by Buster Keaton and Clyde Bruckman, 1926. Silent. The great Keaton's most memorable film about the little hero's efforts to capture a train for the Union Army during the Civil War is still one of the most exciting comedies ever made. Rental from Audio-Brandon Films (as are most of Keaton's major comedies).

Georgy Girl. 100 minutes. Black and white. Directed by Silvio Narizzano (British), 1966. Lynn Redgrave became an overnight sensation for her portrayal of a heavy-set, good-hearted post-adolescent whose misadventures are both comic and sad. When her girlfriend deserts her irresponsible husband and baby, Georgy ends up taking care of both. In the meantime she is pursued by a rich but lecherous old man (James Mason), whom she eventually "sells out" to and marries to provide a home for the baby. Students, by the way, will not buy that ending. Rental from Columbia Cinematheque.

The Goddess. 105 minutes. Black and white. Directed by John Cromwell (screenplay by Paddy Chayefsky), 1958. For some reason, this film has never received the acclaim it so richly deserves. Paralleling the career of many of Hollywood's screen "goddesses," particularly Marilyn Monroe (who was alive at the time), it tells the story of the sad, lonely life of a girl without much talent who is catapulted to stardom. This is *not* a soap opera like *Harlow.* Its dialogue is realistic and the lead is superbly acted by Kim Stanley. Seeing it again recently I was even more impressed, particularly by its sadly prophetic ending. *The Goddess* is an excellent portrait of our society's relationship with its "stars." Rental from Audio-Brandon Films.

The Gold Rush. 81 minutes. Black and white. Directed by Charlie Chaplin, 1925. Silent. One of the few Chaplin features available in 16 mm, and still a brilliant comedy. No student of cinema history should miss it. Rental from Audio-Brandon Films or Swank Films.

The Golden Fish. 20 minutes. Color. Directed by Edmond Sechan (French), 1959. A beautiful short film about a little boy's love for his two pets, a canary and a gold fish, and the cat that almost does away with both. The film is simple, but the climactic scene in which the cat actually puts the fish back in its bowl is astounding. This film would be very useful in a unit on film for elementary school classes. Purchase or rental from Audio-Brandon Films or Swank Films.

Goodby Columbus. 105 minutes. Color. Directed by Larry Peerce, 1969. Philip Roth's raunchy novella is a savagely funny attack on middle-class values, and the film is even better. The story of a bright but aimless young man who falls for a nouveau riche girl from the suburbs is loaded with explicit sexuality (it was rated "R") and nudity. Also, the film has been accused of being anti-Semitic, since it portrays the girl's wealthy Jewish family as broad, ostentatious stereotypes (though the writer and director are both Jewish). Actually the sex and the stereotypes make an important statement about the generation gap and false materialism. Indeed the stereotypes are used in a self-critical, self-humorous fashion, much as Dick Gregory treats Blacks in his comedy routine. I therefore recommend the film, with caution. The teacher should see it first and determine for himself whether it has any value. Rental from Films Inc.

The Graduate. 120 minutes. Color. Directed by Mike Nichols, 1967. Perhaps the best American film of the sixties. *The Graduate* belongs in the classroom because it relates so well to the hang-ups of contemporary youth. Dustin Hoffman's Benjamin is the Holden Caulfield of cinema. Rental from AVCO-Embassy Pictures.

Greed. 114 minutes. Black and white. Directed by Erich Von Stroheim, 1923. Silent. Few silent films have impressed me as much as this one. Based on Frank Norris' rugged novel McTeague, *Greed* is a vivid portrait of men possessed by materialism. The most exciting scenes, at the climax, were actually filmed in the sweltering heat of Death Valley. This film can be used in a transmedia study with the novel, emphasizing the ability of the silent screen to tell a story, or as a vivid piece of cinematic history (there are dozens of stories of how perfectionist Von Stroheim nearly bankrupted his studio trying to finish the film). Rental from Films Inc. or Audio-Brandon Films.

A Hard Day's Night. 90 minutes. Black and white. Directed by Richard Lester (British), 1964. The first and best of the Beatles' films, directed in zonked-out television commercial style by Richard Lester. Much of the cinematic action has been overrated, but the film still presents a humorous look at one of the most interesting cultural phenomenons of the century, the Beatles. Rental from United Artists 16.

Harvest of Shame. 58 minutes. Black and white. CBS TV News Production (narrated by Edward R. Murrow), 1961. A brilliant early example of television muckraking is provided by the exposé of the conditions of migrant labor in the late fifties. It is interesting to note how little these conditions have changed in the ten years since this film created a rather loud stir among Federal officials. *Harvest of Shame* could effectively complement a unit on labor, along with the *The Organizer, The Inheritance,* and *Huelga* (which I will deal with in this listing). Purchase or rental from Contemporary-McGraw-Hill Films.

The Haunting. 112 minutes. Black and white. Directed by Robert Wise, 1963. A splendid scary movie based on Shirley Jackson's novel The Haunting of Hill House. The film is impressive because of its ability to shock without using any special gimmicks. The intense camera work and the skillfully hysterical acting of Julie Harris and Claire Bloom make the whole thing quite believable. Film-making students might be particularly interested in director Robert Wise's style. Rental from Films Inc.

He Who Must Die. 116 minutes. Black and white. Directed by Jules Dassin (French), 1958. English language dubbed version. Based on a novel by Nikos Kazantzakis (author of Zorba the Greek), this film is a kind of modern Passion Play, as a shepherd portraying Christ in a local reenactment of the Passion actually begins to take his role seriously. The point of the film is that if Christ returned to earth, he would be crucified again, and the shepherd who compassionately wants the town to welcome some foreign refugees is persecuted in return. An interesting film for religious and philosophical study. Rental from United Artists 16.

Hospital. 83 minutes. Black and white. Directed by Frederick Wiseman, 1969. Another excellent Wiseman documentary, skillfully edited with participants speaking for themselves. This time the scene is a large New York public hospital, and all of the problems of overcrowding, shabby conditions, and understaffing are shown. Yet *Hospital* is less of an exposé of bad conditions (as *Titicut Follies* was), and more of a sad portrait of the poor who are forced to use the inadequate facilities. This film could be used very well in health classes, particularly those that train students for volunteer hospital work. It is also, as are all of Wiseman's films, a thought-provoking sociological comment. Purchase or rental from Zipporah Films.

Huelga. 50 minutes. Color. Directed by Skeets McGrew, 1965. This film has already won several awards for its honest and sympathetic documentation of the struggle of California's Mexican-American grape pickers. Their long strike in a number of the California fields, organized by Caesar Chavez, was symbolic of the struggle of all farm workers for a decent, livable wage. *Huelga* is the perfect companion piece to *Harvest of Shame,* since it demonstrates a potential solution to the problems of farm laborers through union organization. Purchase or rental from Contemporary-McGraw-Hill Films.

Intolerance. 191 minutes. Black and white. Directed by D. W. Griffith, 1916. Silent. Many critics hail this film as cinematically superior to Griffith's earlier work *Birth of a Nation.* Actually, its complex format of intercutting four stories of four time periods simultaneously (the present, Louis the XIV's France, ancient Babylon, and the crucifixion) is confusing and cumbersome. The acting too seems more heavy handed than in *Birth of a Nation,* and the overlapping theme of man's injustice to man comes across as pure corn. Yet for sheer motion picture spectacle, *Intolerance* was truly a technical pioneer (particularly in the Babylonian sequences). The film is useful to students of film history and historians in general as a portrait of another side of the personality of the most influential film-maker who ever lived. Rental from Museum of Modern Art (a 127-minute print is also available) or Audio-Brandon Films.

Invasion of the Body Snatchers. 80 minutes. Black and white. Directed by Don Siegel, 1956. Excellent example of the science fiction horror genre. Based on a popular short novel, the story of an outerspace invasion of vegetable-like seed pods that reproduce duplicate human beings is believably presented thanks to good, low-keyed direction and acting. The whole thing is really quite chilling, and films of this type should be analyzed for the reasons why they are so scary. Rental from Audio-Brandon Films.

The Iron Horse. 165 minutes. Black and white. Directed by John Ford, 1924. Silent. This classic Western is of interest primarily to students of film history for its mobile camera effects and realistic location shooting. The scenes of railroad construction and the Indian battles are spectacular even by today's standards. Interestingly, I have seen at least one history book that uses a still photo from the film to illustrate the "authentic" building of the transcontinental railroad. Rental from Films Inc. or Museum of Modern Art.

Jesse Owens Returns to Berlin. 51 minutes. Black and white. Produced by Bud Greenspan, 1968. A moving film about a genuine American hero. Black athlete Jesse Owens returns to Berlin 30 years after his crowning Olympic victory, destroying Hitler's racist mythology. The film includes some clips from Leni Riefensthal's *Olympia.* Narrated by Jesse Owens. Purchase or rental from Contemporary-McGraw-Hill Films.

Joe. 107 minutes. Color. Directed by John Avildsen, 1970. An amazing film about our times, *Joe* is a horrifyingly real view of the "silent majority." The portrayal of a "typical" lower-middle class American construction worker ("hard hat"), whose prejudices reflect his own insecurity, is very believable, even if the plot, which revolves around Joe's admiring relationship with a wealthy man who has murdered a "hippie," often borders on the absurd (particularly the violent conclusion). Peter Boyle plays the title role so well you actually believe that he lives down the street. A film like this is destined for the classroom, despite its excesses, since it is an unprecedented commentary on the polarization in our society. Rental from Warner Bros. 16.

Jules and Jim. 104 minutes. Black and white (cinemascope print available). Directed by Francois Truffaut (French), 1961. English subtitles. One of the strangest but most beautiful films I have ever seen. The story of the love affair of two men (Jules, a German, and Jim, a Frenchman) for a beautiful, mystical woman (Kathe) spans 30 years of European history, beginning in the pre-World War I era and concluding just prior to World War II. During this time the mysterious Kathe haunts the two men, alternately loving each. In the end she kills herself and Jim (who has broken away from her) by driving a car over a bridge as Jules watches. I'm not sure I know what it all symbolizes; I only know that whenever I see it I am more fascinated by it. The filming is superb, particularly the attention to historical detail. *Jules and Jim* is a true representation of cinema as an art form. Rental from Janus Films.

Juliet of the Spirits. 137 minutes. Color. Directed by Federico Fellini (Italian), 1965. English subtitles. Fellini's film about a fortyish married woman fearful that her husband is unfaithful emerges as a kind of erotic Alice-in-Wonderland. The woman (Giulietta Masina) engages in constant fantasies that symbolize her deep insecurities. These fantasies are splendidly filmed and provide viewers with an endless topic for discussion. Rental from Audio-Brandon Films.

Kes. 110 minutes. Color. Directed by Ken Loach (British), 1970. This realistic film is allegedly about a lower class Yorkshire teenager's affection for his trained kestrel falcon. However, *Kes* is not an animal movie. Using the boy-bird relationship to underscore the basic good nature of the youth, the film is more of a portrait of life in a working-class mining community. The scenes in the high school are a vivid condemnation of a brutalizing educational system. This film could ideally be paired with *Loneliness of the Long-Distance Runner,* since both examine similar institutions of British working-class society. The major drawback with *Kes* is the uncompromising use of the Yorkshire dialect, which often strains American ears. But it is still very much worth seeing. Rental from United Artists 16.

King Rat. 134 minutes. Black and white. Directed by Bryan Forbes (British), 1965. Perhaps the definitive English language film on prisoners of war (I'm counting *Bridge on the River Kwai*), *King Rat* is a brutal study of survival and the decline of the human spirit. An American POW (George Segal) in a Japanese camp becomes an almost criminal power as he controls the black market and gradually forces the other members of the camp (most of whom are upper-class British officers) to be dependent on him. Many of the scenes are sickening (especially when the officers have unknowingly purchased rat meat from the American and eaten it), but these are in keeping with its somber theme. The film's conclusion actually justifies the American's actions, since he has learned to survive, and this should make for some interesting class discussion. Rental from Audio-Brandon Films, Twyman Films, or Swank Films.

The Kitchen. 74 minutes. Black and white. Directed by James Hill (British), 1961. This filmed version of Arnold Wesker's play is an interesting study of human emotions. The kitchen of a large luxury restaurant is the entire locale as the film concentrates on the working-class attitudes of the employees whose job is to please the upper-class clientele of the restaurant. The kitchen itself is almost hellishly hectic as the workers constantly conflict with each other to prepare for the patrons. I suppose they are meant to symbolize the universal working class, since playwright Wesker is a Marxist. Anyway, the film is one of a kind, and it is interesting. Rental from Audio-Brandon Films.

Kwaidan. 160 minutes. Color. Directed by Masaki Kibayashi (Japanese), 1965. A beautiful, exciting film consisting of four Japanese ghost stories. The stories are reminiscent of the best of Poe and they are filmed with great care. *Kwaidan* would be useful in a literary unit on the short story on film (it has no decent American counterpart) or in a study on the nature of the horror story, horror film. Rental from Walter Reade 16.

La Strada. 107 minutes. Black and white. Directed by Federico Fellini (Italian), 1956. English subtitles or English dubbed version available. This great film about a brutal strongman, his shy little mistress, and a cynical clown in a traveling circus is so famous it needs no summary. It is a brilliant example of cinematic poetry, and one that students will want to discuss at length. Rental from Audio-Brandon Films.

The Last Hurrah. 121 minutes. Black and white. Directed by John Ford, 1958.
Films about politics are never realistic enough for me, and John Ford's
nostalgic treatment of Frank O'Conner's novel is no exception. The story is
allegedly based on the career of Boston Mayor Jim Curley, who was something of a tyrant. Spencer Tracy as his fictional counterpart is just too
lovable. Still, the film is entertaining and loaded with sentimental Irish
characters. Perhaps some enterprising teacher would like to have a unit on
the Irish stereotype on film. He could start with *The Last Hurrah*. Rental
From Audio-Brandon Films, Contemporary-McGraw-Hill Films, Twyman
Films, or Swank Films.

Last Summer. 97 minutes. Color. Directed by Frank Perry, 1969. Frank Perry's
greatest talent as a director is his ability to handle young performers. He
was very successful with the youthful stars of *David and Lisa* (Keir Dullea
and Janet Margolin), and he has done a remarkable job with the four young
leads of *Last Summer* (Catherine Burns, Barbara Hershey, Richard Thomas,
and Bruce Davison). I say this because I believe that *Last Summer* has been
grossly overpraised. The story of a subtlely vicious girl who manipulates
two teenaged boys to destroy innocent things (first a sea gull, then a kindly
Puerto Rican man, whom they brutally insult, and finally a shy girl, whom
they rape) is full of ludicrous symbolism. Still the film was very popular
and teachers may want to use it as a commentary on today's youth (which
it isn't). Rental from Hurlock Cineworld.

Last Year at Marienbad. 93 minutes. Black and white. Directed by Alain Resnais
(French), 1961. English subtitles. Here's a film that would be loads of fun
in a classroom. The obscure story of three nameless people ("A," "M," and
"X") at the resort hotel may merely be about some marital infidelity, but
it is presented so skillfully that students will be on edge trying to put all the
pieces together. *Last Year at Marienbad* is like a brilliant, vague poem, and
it requires a good deal of intellectualizing on the part of the viewer. One
thing for sure, students will be fascinated by it. Rental from Audio-Brandon
Films.

The Little Kidnappers. 95 minutes. Black and white. Directed by Philip Leacock
(British), 1953. Though not as socially significant as *Forbidden Games*
(which it in some ways resembles), this fine British film is an excellent
portrait of children's behavior. Two orphaned boys living with their embittered uncle in Nova Scotia long for a pet to fondle with affection. Their
uncle forbids it, but the boys find a baby in the woods, which they feed
and care for as their pet. Though the film later bogs down in sentimentality
as the old uncle is softened because the boys are accused of kidnapping, it
is for the most part an intelligent study of children. Rental from Janus
Films.

Lonely Boy. 28 minutes. Black and white. Directed by Wolf Koenig and Roman
Kroiter, 1962. This well-known National Film Board of Canada documentary is a great portrait of a modern singing idol. Following a road tour with
entertainer Paul Anka, the film concentrates on his behind-the-scenes life.
His agents predict he'll be the greatest of stars. Crowds of young girls
storm him wherever he goes. Yet, soon it becomes obvious that Paul Anka
the "star" has little relationship with the person. Anka's signature song,

"I'm such a lonely boy . . ." becomes an appropriate title for his life as a star. This film could be used effectively with the previously mentioned *Privilege* and *The Goddess*. Purchase or rental from Contemporary-McGraw-Hill Films.

The Magnificent Seven (Seven Samurai). 141 minutes. Black and white. Directed by Akira Kurosawa (Japanese), 1954. English subtitles. This famous film about how seven tough Samurai warriors save a fear-stricken village from bandits is a good example of Japanese heroic literature. It is also well acted and directed. The American version, a Western with Yul Brynner and Steve McQueen, retains much of the flavor, illustrating the relationship between the myths of the Japanese Samurai and the American Western gunfighter. Rental of the Japanese film from Audio-Brandon Films. *The Magnificent Seven* (U. S.). 127 minutes. Color (cinemascope print available). Directed by John Sturges, 1960. Rental from United Artists 16.

A Man and a Woman. 102 minutes. Color. Directed by Claude Lelouch (French), 1966. English subtitles or English language dubbed version available. This former Academy Award winner is a good example of how cinematography and technique can substitute for story. Beautifully filmed in color and some black and white sequences, flashily edited, and backed up by a lovely musical score, the overly sentimental love story of a widow and a race car driver is almost believable. Most of my students saw it on television recently (which ruined it for me) and still found it visually beautiful. The film might be especially useful in a film-making class. Rental from Hurlock Cineworld.

Man in the White Suit. 86 minutes. Black and white. Directed by Alexander Mackendrick (British), 1952. Excellent satire about a scientist who invents a suit of clothes that will not wrinkle, tear, wear out, or even get dirty. The action revolves around all of the economic and social repercussions of the invention, and it is all very funny. Alec Guiness plays the scientist who almost bankrupts the Western world. A film like this has great classroom potential. Rental from Contemporary-McGraw-Hill Films.

Man of Aran. 77 minutes. Black and white. Directed by Robert Flaherty, 1934. The greatest of all documentary film-makers was the late Robert Flaherty. Despite the age of his films, they still capture the essential spirit of life of the cultures they photograph. *Man of Aran* is a beautiful portrait of the people of the Aran Islands (off the coast of Ireland) and how they live by confronting the forces of nature: the land and sea. Lease or rental from Contemporary-McGraw-Hill Films.

The Manchurian Candidate. 126 minutes. Black and white. Directed by John Frankenheimer, 1962. One of the most believable pieces of science fiction ever filmed. A group of American prisoners in Korea are "brainwashed," and one of them is actually conditioned to become a political assassin. The plot is quite complicated, since the killer's politically ambitious mother is involved with the Communists, as is her right-wing senator husband. The film is a fascinating commentary on the contemporary world, both politically and psychologically. Rental from United Artists 16.

Martin Luther King: The Man and the March. 83 minutes. Color. Public Broadcast Laboratory, 1968. In the weeks prior to Dr. King's assassination, the Public Broadcast Laboratory (PBL) began filming a documentary on King as a leader. The film was to have included his participation in the Memphis garbage workers' strike, and the cameras had actually recorded the events until minutes before his tragic death. The result is this incomplete motion picture, which records the last days of the great Nobel Prize winner's life. A candid, warm portrait of King the man, it is also, of course, historically significant. Purchase or rental from NET Film Service.

Me and the Colonel. 109 minutes. Black and white. Directed by Peter Glenville, 1959. This film version of the play Jacobowsky and the Colonel is a little too sentimental for me, though I can see its validity in the classroom. A Jewish refugee and an anti-Semitic Polish colonel are forced to flee the Nazis together. Gradually they build a respectful relationship toward each other. Danny Kaye and Curt Jurgens star. Rental from Audio-Brandon Films or Contemporary-McGraw-Hill Films.

The Men. 85 minutes. Black and white. Directed by Fred Zinneman, 1950. This portrait of the rehabilitation of paraplegic World War II veterans is still a powerful movie. Marlon Brando in his first screen role is excellent as a man courageously trying to learn to live without ever being able to walk again. Rental from Audio-Brandon Films, Twyman Films, or Willoughby-Peerless Film Exchange.

Metropolis. 133 minutes. Black and white. Directed by Fritz Lang (German), 1926. Silent. Fritz Lang's classic futuristic fantasy is a cross between Buck Rogers and George Orwell. The film is an interesting look at how the future was interpreted in Germany in the twenties. Of special interest for students of film history. Rental from Museum of Modern Art (a 94-minute version is also available).

Mickey One. 93 minutes. Black and white. Directed by Arthur Penn, 1965. Critics hotly debate whether this film is a masterpiece or junk. I happen to like it, and I think students will be interested in it. A second-rate night club comic fears that mobsters are after him and runs away. He hides and changes his name, but still fears they are closing in on him. The film is engrossing because the viewer is never sure whether the protagonist's fears are real or hallucinations. Warren Beatty is excellent as the frightened man, and director Arthur Penn appears to have been warming up for his great *Bonnie and Clyde* with this haunting little movie. Rental from Audio-Brandon Films, Twyman Films, or Swank Films.

Midnight Cowboy. 127 minutes. Color. Directed by John Schlesinger, 1969. It will have to come sooner or later. This beautiful film about the friendship of a male stud and a consumptive derelict is destined for classroom study. Students will want to discuss the tragic background of Joe Buck (described in dream-like black and white flashbacks), the pathetic existence of Ratso Rizzo, and the strange relationship between the two men. *Midnight Cowboy* has a Motion Picture Production Code rating of "X." It is loaded with obscene language, explicit sex (including homosexuality), and nudity. Yet it is never vulgar. The sex and the language are an integral part of the existence of the characters and they make it realistic. *Midnight Cowboy* is too good a film to be left out of the classroom repertory, "X" rating or not. Rental from United Artists 16.

The Misfits. 124 minutes. Black and white. Directed by John Huston, 1961. A critical and commercial failure when it was released, this film, scripted by Arthur Miller, is really quite powerful. Its story concerns a group of modern cowboys who hunt wild mustangs for a living. Yet these men, who pride themselves as the best individualists, are actually capturing the horses to be used for dog food. A woman joins them (Marilyn Monroe), who begins to see through their false values. Obviously Miller had some symbolic message about false values in mind, and at least some of it comes through. This was the last film for two of its stars, Clark Gable and Marilyn Monroe. Both were in top form. Rental from United Artists 16.

Moana. 85 minutes. Black and white. Directed by Robert Flaherty, 1926. Silent. Flaherty's second major documentary is a brilliant filming of Samoan culture. As old as this film is, its cinematic truthfulness still makes it splendid anthropology. According to the Museum of Modern Art's synopsis, it was in reviewing this film that critic John Grierson first coined the word "documentary." Rental from Museum of Modern Art or Contemporary-McGraw-Hill Films.

The Mouse that Roared. 83 minutes. Color. Directed by Jack Arnold (British), 1959. I guess by now it must seem that satire is the only kind of comedy I like. Certainly this satire on world affairs qualifies as one of the funniest films. The Duchy of Grand Fenwick, whose army uses bows and arrows, decides to declare war on the United States, surrender, and become eligible for foreign aid. A series of mix-ups result, and Grand Fenwick becomes the most powerful nation in the world. Peter Sellers is great in three roles (including the Grand Duchess). This film would be ideal in a unit on satirical literature or in a serious study of foreign affairs. Rental from Audio-Brandon Films, Twyman Films, or Swank Films.

Mutiny on the Bounty. 132 minutes. Black and white. Directed by Frank Lloyd, 1935. And *Mutiny on the Bounty*. 179 minutes. Color (cinemascope print only). Directed by Lewis Milestone (and others), 1962. I am now about to make some enemies in the field of film study. The original version of the Nordoff and Hall classic is traditionally considered a great film. Charles Laughton's evil Captain Bligh and Clark Gable's saintly Fletcher Christian are the most revered villain and hero in screen annals. The general opinion has also condemned the 1962 remake as a tragic mistake, and the argument against remaking a classic stands firm. I disagree. The 1935 version of *Mutiny on the Bounty* is a good old film. It represents adventure escapism at its best. The 1962 film, while loaded with cinematic mistakes (parts of it were shot a year or more after the film was allegedly completed), is a valiant attempt to give the old story some depth. Marlon Brando's Christian, an English "fop" whose conscience gradually forces him, reluctantly, to destroy his naval career by leading the mutiny, is a complex human being. So is Trevor Howard's Bligh. And the crew, in this film, is composed of hotheads and roughnecks (led by Richard Harris). This is much closer to the reality of the Bounty situation than in the first film. The real survivors settled on Pitcairn Island, and according to authors Nordoff and Hall in the third volume of the Bounty Trilogy, proceeded to feud until they virtually annihilated each other. I realize this film is loaded with flaws and that Brando's temperament held up production for months. But seeing both versions recently, I'm far more impressed with the latter for its ambition and depth. The original *Bounty* is simply the old black vs. white heroics, and I don't believe young audiences care much for that any more. Both versions are available for rental from Films Inc.

From the motion picture **Mutiny on the Bounty** (1935). Courtesy of Films Inc.—MGM.

Nanook of the North. 60 minutes. Black and white. Directed by Robert Flaherty, 1922. The great Flaherty's first documentary about the rugged struggle of an Eskimo to survive in the Arctic wastelands. The camera work is still fascinating and the viewer can "feel" the Eskimo life style. Interestingly, the hero, Nanook, who demonstrates his great knack for survival in the film, starved to death a year later. Rental from Museum of Modern Art or Contemporary-McGraw-Hill Films.

A Night at the Opera. 93 minutes. Black and white. Directed by Sam Wood, 1935. Marx Brothers comedy is slapstick and broad, definitely not satire. Yet, today it is as funny as ever, exemplified in this, which must have been their best, picture. This film (or any of their others) could be used in a study of what motivates humor, or it can just be enjoyed for the classic comedy that it is. Rental from Films Inc. (as are most of the Marx comedies).

Night of the Hunter. 90 minutes. Black and white. Directed by Charles Laughton,

1955. This strange movie about a psychopathic, bogus preacher (with the words "love" and "hate" tattooed on his knuckles) who stalks two children down the Mississippi River for some stolen money stuffed in a doll was a failure in its time. The story unfolds as a kind of fable, partially narrated by Lillian Gish, and most of the action is from the children's point of view. It's all quite suspenseful and Robert Mitchum as the preacher is enough to give anyone nightmares. The screenplay was written by the late film critic James Agee. I have been informed that this film is in the process of being "discovered" by the film cultists. It is certainly absorbing melodrama. Rental from United Artists 16.

No Reason to Stay. 28 minutes. Black and white. National Film Board of Canada Production, 1965. An excellent short film about the irrelevancy of high school education. A young man decides to drop out of school because his teachers fail to recognize his zeal for learning. Over and over he is forced to conform to meaningless regulations. One teacher asks him to recite four reasons why Rome fell. The youth envisions his teachers being put before a firing squad, and in the end he does leave school (no cop out here). *No Reason to Stay* is an overstatement, but it is a thought-provoking commentary on modern education's communication gap. The film would be useful in teacher training, along with Frederick Wiseman's *High School*. Purchase or rental from Contemporary-McGraw-Hill Films.

No Way to Treat a Lady. 108 minutes. Color. Directed by Jack Smight, 1968. This is certainly not a great film. It may not even be a very good one. But

From the motion picture **Mutiny on the Bounty** (1962). Courtesy of Films Inc.—MGM

Rod Steiger's characterization of a schizophrenic killer with a mother complex is fantastic. Steiger charms his victims in a variety of disguises, actually assuming the personalities to match the costumes (a homosexual wig salesman, an immigrant plumber, a woman, an Italian waiter, etc.). The film becomes a sort of black comedy, and students may want to discuss the nature of this kind of humor. Rental from Films Inc.

Nobody Waved Goodbye. 80 minutes. Black and white. Directed by Don Owen, 1964. One of the National Film Board of Canada's rare features, this film is very similar in style and content to *Phoebe* and *You're No Good.* Two middle-class teenagers have an affair and are confronted with the value system of their elders. Like other films of its type, *Nobody* raises a great many questions about the problems of adolescents. The film is quite believable. Rental from Audio-Brandon Films.

No. 00173. 9 minutes. Color, and black and white. Directed by Jan Habarta (Polish), 1966. A fascinating futuristic short about how a butterfly almost succeeds in destroying the automated impersonality of society. This film could serve as an interesting motivator for discussion. Purchase or rental from Contemporary-McGraw-Hill Films.

The Nutty Professor. 107 minutes. Color. Directed by (and starring) Jerry Lewis, 1963. All right, laugh, but I cite this movie as proof that Jerry Lewis is a film-maker to be reckoned with. This carefully made take-off on Dr. Jekyll and Mr. Hyde is very funny and entertaining. It might even be useful in a unit dealing with the Robert Louis Stevenson work which implied there's a little of Jekyll and Hyde in all of us. Lewis' work is highly regarded in Europe, particularly France, and *The Nutty Professor* demonstrates that he has genuine talent. Rental from Films Inc.

Odd Man Out. 115 minutes. Black and white. Directed by Carol Reed (British), 1947. A classic film about the last hours of a fatally wounded Irish rebel hiding from the police. This film has much to say about revolutionary idealism (embodied in Johnny, the hero), but it is basically a dramatic character study. James Mason gives the greatest performance of his career as the dying rebel. *Odd Man Out* was recently remade as *The Lost Man* with Sidney Poitier and its situation was transformed to a group of Black Power militants in the United States. Interestingly, the remake was a failure, as critics maintained (as they had with *Up Tight,* the Black equivalent to *The Informer*) that the Irish and Black revolutions had little in common. *Odd Man Out* is available for rental from Janus Films; *The Lost Man*, from Universal 16.

Of Mice and Men. 108 minutes. Black and white. Directed by Lewis Milestone, 1939. This film version of John Steinbeck's famous Depression short novel about the relationship between an idealistic migrant laborer and his feeble-minded comrade looks its age. But the power of the story doesn't date as easily. The recent television play of this sensitive work proved that. Since that is not available for the classroom, the film version is still valuable. Rental from Contemporary-McGraw-Hill Films or Willoughby-Peerless Film Exchange.

Olympia 1936. Part I (100 minutes) includes the introductory ceremonies and track and field events; Part II (105 minutes) consists of gymnastic and aquatic competition as well as the marathon and decathalon events. Black and white. Directed by Leni Riefensthal (German), 1938. The most fantastic film about sports ever made. The great screen propagandist for the Nazis, Leni Riefensthal (who made *Triumph of the Will*), was commissioned to film the Olympic Games of 1936 in Berlin. Her film is not, however, propaganda. It is a celebration of the human athletic form. The cinematic techniques employed, especially in the god-like opening scenes in the Greek Parthenon where a runner receives the Olympic torch, and in the famous diving sequence where the photography makes the divers seem to be in eternal flight, are magnificent. *Olympia* is a great piece of history, considering the political nature of the Games in 1936 (it does include all of the great victories of Black American Jesse Owens, in violation of the Nazi racial ideal), and a brilliant motion picture. Students should see both parts in several sittings. However, the opening sequences, which celebrate the ancient ceremonies, are the most vivid. Rental from Museum of Modern Art, Contemporary-McGraw-Hill Films, and Audio-Brandon Films.

One, Two, Three. 108 minutes. Black and white. Directed by Billy Wilder, 1961. Another satirical comedy, and a brilliantly made one. James Cagney (in his last film to date) plays a Coca Cola representative in modern Berlin who would love to get an account with Soviet East Germany. When his boss' daughter visits him and elopes with an East German fanatic, his problems really multiply. I saw this film again recently, and much of its satire was blunted by the passing of time. Comic references to the Berlin Wall and Krushchev are no longer timely or funny. But *One, Two, Three* is so fast paced and stylishly produced that it is still worth seeing. Students interested in the foreign problems of the early Kennedy years may be especially interested in its dated satirical comments. Rental from United Artists 16.

Organizing for Power: The Alinsky Approach. Black and white. National Film Board of Canada Production, 1969. A series of five films examining the methods of organizer Saul Alinsky in unifying poor communities for political and economic action. The titles are:

> *People and Power.* 17 minutes.
> *Deciding to Organize.* 34 minutes.
> *Building an Organization.* 37 minutes.
> *Through Conflict Negotiation.* 46 minutes.
> *A Continuing Responsibility.* 43 minutes.

These films can be useful instructionally for students of grass roots political action. Each episode follows the dynamic Alinsky in his regular activities. He is shown working in two of his most noted organizations: the Rochester, New York, Community Action Group, and the Woodlawn Organization in Chicago. This series is also an interesting historical record of one of the most significant social reformers of our time. I suggest some enterprising film-makers similarly follow Ralph Nader. Purchase or rental of the entire series (or individual episodes) from Contemporary-McGraw-Hill Films or Films Inc.

Overture (Nyitany). 9 minutes. Color. Directed by Janos Vadasz (Hungarian), 1965. The embryo of an egg develops and hatches through time-lapse photography, orchestrated by Beethoven's Egmont Overture. A beautiful sample of film-making or a useful source for the biology class. Purchase or rental from Contemporary-McGraw-Hill Films.

Panic in the Streets. 96 minutes. Black and white. Directed by Elia Kazan, 1950. I just saw this film on television recently and despite its age it is still remarkably powerful. Several gangsters murder a man with a highly contagious disease. Unknowingly they become carriers of it, while hunted by the police and US Public Health servants. The direction is exciting as the film climaxes in a chase through a teeming New Orleans slum. A good example of provocative film-making. Rental from Films Inc.

The Passion of Joan of Arc. 77 minutes. Black and white. Directed by Carl Theodore Dryer (French), 1928. Silent (musical score sound track added). A classic silent film which is an intense, psychological study of the last days of Joan of Arc. The director pioneered many new film techniques in it. Primarily for students of cinema history. Rental from Audio-Brandon Films.

Patterns. 83 minutes. Black and white. Directed by Fielder Cook, 1956. One of the products of the "Golden Age" of television, this film (adapted by Rod Serling from his TV script) is still one of the few believable portraits of the operation of big business. The story deals with the rise of a young executive at the expense of an older man who is being "phased out." It looks a little dated, but its situations are, nevertheless, quite realistic. A younger Van Heflin and the late Ed Begley and Everett Sloane comprise the excellent cast. *Patterns* could be useful in a unit on the corporation man, since it is the best of its genre. Rental from United Artists 16.

Petulia. 105 minutes. Color. Directed by Richard Lester, 1968. The first time I saw *Petulia*, I was so fascinated by its visual effects that I felt I'd missed some of its plot. Recently I was able to see it again, and now I realize I didn't miss anything. This is one of those rare films (*A Man and a Woman* is another) that can get away with substituting cinematics for content. The story about a divorced doctor who falls in love with the kooky wife of a millionaire psychopath is well acted (George C. Scott, Julie Christie, Richard Chamberlain, Shirley Knight, and Joseph Cotton make a splendid cast), but it's still a soap opera at heart. Director Richard Lester's skill with flashbacks makes the film an intellectual puzzle, and students of technique should love it. Rental from Warner Brothers 16.

Phyliss and Terry. 36 minutes. Black and white. Directed by Eugene and Carole Marner, 1965. This cinema-verité style film records the discussion of two teenaged Black girls walking through the streets of Harlem. Their talk is candid, and it reveals, as does the roving eye of the camera, the "way it is" to live in a Black ghetto. The major problem with the film is that occasionally, due to the on-the-spot-sound recordings, the dialogue is unintelligible. Still, this is a valuable, honest portrait of life in the "inner city." Purchase only from Center for Mass Communications of Columbia University. Check local libraries for free loan.

Planet of the Apes. 112 minutes. Color (cinemascope only). Directed by Franklin Schaffner, 1968. A great fun movie. Spaceman Charlton Heston finds himself stranded on a strange planet where apes are the intelligent forms of life, and men live in cages. Loaded with tongue-in-cheek comedy, this film is highly entertaining. Its pseudoscientific ending, when Heston realizes he's back on earth after an atomic war has altered evolution, is worthy of some discussion, but *Planet of the Apes* is mainly a pop art comedy. Rental from Films Inc.

Popi. 113 minutes. Color. Directed by Arthur Hiller, 1969. A comedy with a heart and a message. Alan Arkin plays a Puerto Rican widower with two young sons. Trapped in the ghetto of Spanish Harlem, he dreams of a better life for his boys. After being mistaken for a Cuban freedom fighter, he gets the idea to have his sons pretend they are Cuban refugees so that they will be given special care by the American government. Naturally his scheme backfires. This blend of comedy and drama strains at times, but the film makes some valid commentary about this country's double standard towards its own poor. Rental from United Artists 16.

Pretty Poison. 89 minutes. Color. Directed by Noel Black, 1968. This strange film about a young psychotic who tries to impress a teenaged girl with violent tales only to discover that she, in fact, is a cold-blooded killer, is not for those with weak stomachs. Yet it is so well made and loaded with ironic twists that it becomes a kind of symbolic essay on our own violent society. Many critics applauded this film when it was released, and it is rapidly becoming an underground classic. Rental from Films Inc.

The Prisoner. 91 minutes. Black and white. Directed by Peter Glenville (British), 1955. An agonizing portrait of a prominent churchman imprisoned as a subversive in a Communist state. It literally wears the audience out watching Alec Guiness as the cleric resist his oppressive interrogator Jack Hawkins. The film is loosely based on the famous Cardinal Mindzenty case and was topical when released. Today it is simply a well-acted drama of a man's will to resist tyranny. Rental from Twyman Films or Swank Films.

The Quiet Man. 129 minutes. Color. Directed by John Ford, 1952. For those who like Irish nostalgia comedies, John Ford's famous film is the best. Pure entertainment and very well acted (John Wayne, Barry Fitzgerald, Maureen O'Hara, and Victor McLaglen). Rental from Films Inc.

Rashomon. 83 minutes. Black and white. Directed by Akira Kurosawa (Japanese), 1950. English subtitles. One of the great films in screen history. The story, set in the Middle Ages, concerns the murder of a nobleman and the rape of his wife by a bandit. After the bandit is captured, the event is viewed through four flashbacks, each representing a different interpretation of what actually happened. *Rashomon* makes a significant statement on the relativity of truth. As was the case with *The Magnificent Seven,* there is an American remake set in the old West called *The Outrage* (97 minutes. Black and white. Directed by Martin Ritt, 1964). However, the shallow cinematic style and poor acting make it merely a shadow of the original. Rental of *Rashomon* from Janus Films; *The Outrage* from Films Inc.

The Red Balloon. 34 minutes. Color. Directed by Albert Lamorisse (French), 1956. This beautiful fantasy about a little boy who dreams his balloon is alive is one of the best films ever made for children. It is also an excellent example of artistic cinema. Purchase or rental from Audio-Brandon Films.

The Red Shoes. 133 minutes. Color. Directed by Michael Powell (British), 1948. I have never been much of a ballet fan, and I don't think most high school kids appreciate it, but *The Red Shoes* is something special. Despite its rather ordinary backstage romance plot, the dancing scenes are superb. The camera and the art of the ballet perfectly compliment each other in this beautiful film. Rental from Twyman Films, Contemporary-McGraw-Hill Films, or Walter Reade 16.

The Revolutionary. 101 minutes. Color. Directed by Roman Polanski, 1968. All successful attempt at an intelligent portrayal of a revolutionary student. Based on Hans Koningsberger's novel, the film documents the conversion of a young scholar (simply known as "A") in a nameless country to the ideals of revolution. It's all done in a low-key (minus the hysteria of flops like *The Strawberry Statement*) and Jon Voigt is excellent as the young man. It ends inconclusively, however, and too often it is self-consciously copying the obscure symbolism of Kafka and Camus. Still *The Revolutionary* is the best of that genre so far. Rental from United Artists 16.

Rosemary's Baby. 136 minutes. Color. Directed by Roman Polanski, 1968. All jokes aside, Roman Polanski's film of Ira Levin's supernatural best seller is a splendid piece of horror. The well-known story of the young woman whose husband bargains to let the Devil impregnate her is beautifully filmed (the rape scene demonstrates some virtuoso cinematography and lighting). The dialogue and acting are so realistic that the horrifying situation doesn't come across as fantasy at all; it seems to be really happening. The film could be used in a unit with others of the horror genre to analyze what makes them so frightening. Rental from Films Inc.

The Russians Are Coming, The Russians Are Coming. 126 minutes. Color (cinemascope print available). Directed by Norman Jewison, 1966. A reasonably good comedy about a group of Russian sailors who are shipwrecked on a New England resort island. Most of the humor results from the panic of the American vacationers, fearing a full-fledged Soviet invasion. A sentimental, hands-across-the-sea type ending is a big let down, but most of it is quite funny. Alan Arkin made his screen debut as the kindly Russian lieutenant, and Carl Reiner, Paul Ford, and Jonathan Winters are perfect panic-stricken American fools. Rental from United Artists 16.

Satan's Choice. 28 minutes. Black and white. National Film Board of Canada Production, 1967. *Satan's Choice* is about a group of post-adolescents belonging to a Toronto motorcycle club. While not exactly an equivalent to California's Hell's Angels, these young men demonstrate their hostilities and desires to be free from society's standards. The film is an interesting portrait of group behavior, though it is too superficial to be an important sociological study. Purchase or rental from Contemporary-McGraw-Hill Films.

Saturday Night and Sunday Morning. 90 minutes. Black and white. Directed by Karal Reisz (British), 1961. An interesting character portrait of a lowerclass factory assembly-line worker, who wants no more out of life than "to have a good time." Part of that "good time" involves a torrid affair with a coworker's wife, whom he really doesn't care for. The point is that it's an exciting activity in his boring, routinized way of life. Naturally, he gets caught by his mistress' husband and is beaten within an inch of his life. Still, at the end of the film, he shows no signs of repentance. *Saturday Night and Sunday Morning* has a lot to say about the effects of our in-

creasingly mechanized society on the human personality. Rental from
Walter Reade 16.

Saul Alinsky Went to War. 57 minutes. Black and white. National Film Board of
Canada Production, 1968. An exciting documentary on the career of Saul
Alinsky, the noted organizer of the poor. This film contains some of the
highlights of the *Organizing for Power* Series (mentioned earlier), as well
as a candid portrait of the Alinsky-influenced Rochester Blacks confronting Eastman Kodak for increased job opportunities. This is a useful documentary for urban studies classes. Purchase or rental from Contemporary-
McGraw-Hill Films.

Sayonara. 147 minutes. Color. Directed by Joshua Logan, 1957. Seeing this film
for the first time recently on television was a wonderful experience for me.
The story of American airmen with Japanese brides confronting the prejudice of the military, which forbade such marriages, is still timely and relevant. The film is also a beautiful portrait of Japanese culture. Marlon
Brando (with a realistic Southern accent), Red Buttons, and Japanese
actresses Miko Taka and Miyoshi Umeki make up an excellent cast. *Sayonara*
definitely belongs in the classroom, though I have not been able to locate it
in 16 mm. Check local film exchanges for rental.

Scorpio Rising. 31 minutes. Black and white. Directed by Kenneth Anger, 1963.
One of the first of the so-called "underground" movies, this badly edited,
plotless film is still worth seeing. Its topic is a contemporary motorcycle
gang, but the images on the screen, including scenes of nudity and homosexuality, go beyond (or beneath) mere documentary technique. *Scorpio
Rising* should be mainly of interest to students of the underground film
genre (along with the Andy Warhol stuff), but it is visually fascinating.
Purchase from Rogosin Films, Inc. Check local film exchanges for rental and
libraries for free loan.

The Set Up. 72 minutes. Black and white. Directed by Robert Wise, 1949. To
date I have not seen this film, regarded by many critics as a minor classic.
Its story deals with an hour in the life of an aging boxer whose managers
have arranged for his last fight to be fixed. The camera work and editing
are supposed to be perfect examples of skillful technique. Rental from
Museum of Modern Art or Audio-Brandon Films.

Seven Days in May. 118 minutes. Black and white. Directed by John Frankenheimer, 1964. This film version of the best-selling novel is only partially
successful. The story of a plotted military coup d'etat against the United
States government begins believably, but gradually deteriorates into comic-
book melodrama. Still the idea behind it all is worth discussing. Frederic
March is excellent as the victimized President. Rental from Films Inc.

Shakespeare Wallah. 115 minutes. Black and white. Directed by James Ivory (British), 1966. This is one of those "oh so charming" films about the romance between a young English actress touring India with a Shakespearian troupe
(hence the title) and a wealthy Indian man. In the end, the differences between them are insurmountable and the girl returns to England. Critics generally loved it, although it's obviously not my kind of film. I mention it here
because everyone who saw it with me liked it and thought it would be valuable for teachers of world cultures. Rental from Walter Reade 16.

Shame (Skammen). 102 minutes. Black and white. Directed by Ingmar Bergman (Swedish), 1968. English subtitles. One of Ingmar Bergman's greatest films, *Shame* is an allegory on war's effects on men. A peaceful, music-loving couple live in a land surrounded by warfare. Somehow, they manage to shut it all out, concentrating on their music and their feelings for each other. But the war comes closer and closer (literally, as a battle engulfs their home) and ultimate, horrifying tragedy results. This is not a typical anti-war film in the tradition of those I've already dealt with. *Shame*, for me, is a shattering screen experience. Rental from United Artists 16.

The Shop on Main Street. 128 minutes. Black and white. Directed by Jan Kadar (Czechoslovakian), 1965. English subtitles. By far the best product of the "liberalized" Czech film industry. (After the Russian purges of the summer of 1968, many of Czechoslovakia's film-makers fled the country. Jan Kadar, the director of this film, now lives in the United States, where he has already made *The Angel Levine* and *Adrift*.) A bourgeois carpenter is appointed by the Nazis during World War II as Aryan administrator of a shop in a Jewish ghetto. Gradually, he gains respect for his neighbors (particularly the old woman who owns the shop) and he heroically risks his life to save them from the Nazis. *The Shop on Main Street* is a beautiful statement of man's responsibility to man. Rental from Audio-Brandon Films.

The Silent Spring of Rachel Carson. 54 minutes. Black and white. CBS TV News Production, 1963. The late Rachel Carson's book The Silent Spring was one of the first published warnings that America was destroying her natural resources. This television documentary takes Miss Carson's study and demonstrates its alarming accuracy through even more research, including interviews with leading experts on environment. In this time of tremendous ecological concern, the warnings of Rachel Carson to stop polluting our water and land with insecticides are particularly relevant. This film is a valuable synopsis of an important book and an early example of environmental study. Purchase or rental from Contemporary-McGraw-Hill Films.

Singin' in the Rain. 103 minutes. Color. Directed by Gene Kelly and Stanley Donen, 1951. I have never been a fan of screen musicals and except for *West Side Story* and the Busby Berkeley films, I've all but ignored this genre in the book. *Singin' in the Rain* is about the best of the standard Hollywood product, taking the form of a spoof on the early talking pictures. It's funny and mildly entertaining. Rental from Films Inc.

Some Like it Hot. 120 minutes. Black and white. Directed by Billy Wilder, 1959. Maybe the funniest American comedy of all, *Some Like it Hot* is a masterpiece of comic timing and slapstick. The plot about two musicians who disguise themselves as women and join an all-girl orchestra to hide from a bunch of gangsters is violent (in the early thirties gangster pictures tradition), but very, very funny. Tony Curtis, Jack Lemmon, and Marilyn Monroe are all in great form, and Joe E. Brown as a tipsy old playboy in love with Lemmon's feminine disguise is best of all. Rental from United Artists 16.

Soul. 27 minutes. Color. CBS TV's *Of Black America* Series, 1968. *Soul* is the second half of an hour program of this unique series. (The first half, *Body*, deals with the Black athlete concentrating on the proposed Olympic boycott of 1968, which never came off. It is now too dated to recommend.) Narrated by Ray Charles, the film documents the contributions of Black musicians and singers to American culture, using clips of performances by Charlie Parker, Dinah Washington, Count Basie, Duke Ellington, and Louis Armstrong. Charles also comments on the deep significance of music to Blacks as an outlet for the frustrations of poverty. A very useful film for the classroom. Purchase or rental from Bailey-Film Associates. Check local libraries for free loan.

Stalag 17. 120 minutes. Black and white. Directed by Billy Wilder, 1953. This famous comedy-drama about American prisoners-of-war in a Nazi camp is very entertaining. William Holden won an Academy Award as a cynical GI who ends up a hero. *Stalag 17* is little beyond good entertainment, however. Its melodramatics are not very realistic; in this sense I prefer *King Rat.* Rental from Films Inc.

Stolen Kisses. 90 minutes. Color. Directed by Francois Truffaut (French), 1968. English subtitles. Antoine Doinel (Jean-Pierre Leaud), the gritty little delinquent of Truffaut's *The 400 Blows,* grows up in this delightful comedy romance. Antoine has just been discharged from the army and sets out to find an occupation, since he has a lovely girlfriend he'd like to marry. After bungling as a private detective's assistant, he takes a job as a shoe clerk and ends up in bed with his boss's wife. *Stolen Kisses* is too light and comic to be considered a sequel to the serious *400 Blows*, but it demonstrates that director Truffaut is equally adept at comedy. Rental from United Artists 16.

Storm Over Asia. 115 minutes. Black and white. Directed by V. I. Pudovkin (Russian), 1928. Silent. V. I. Pudovkin has been primarily known to me as a great film theorist and his writings have been translated into many languages. This is one of his best known films dealing with the Soviet struggle to remove Western invaders from its Asian borders. The director's advanced editing techniques are displayed, which should be of primary interest to students of film history. Rental from Museum of Modern Art.

Summerhill. 28 minutes. Color. National Film Board of Canada Production, 1966. This is the only film to my knowledge dealing with A. S. Neill's legendary unstructured school. It shows a little of the teaching and living situations, but most of it consists of an interview with Neill. Anyone who has read the famous book should be interested in this brief, but interesting film. Rental only from Contemporary-McGraw-Hill Films. Purchase directly from National Film Board of Canada.

The Sundowners. 133 minutes. Color. Directed by Fred Zinneman, 1960. An exceptionally good film about a family of Australian sheepherders, *The Sundowners* provides a look at life in one of the world's last frontier environments. Its plot centers on the conflict between a husband who enjoys the freedom of roaming from job to job, living in a wagon (Robert Mitchum) and his wife (Deborah Kerr) who dreams of a permanent home for her children. Part comedy, part drama, the film succeeds as a portrait of modern pioneers. Rental from Audio-Brandon Films.

Sunset Boulevard. 110 minutes. Black and white. Directed by Billy Wilder, 1950. Billy Wilder's famous comedy-horror film about the weird existence of an ex-silent film queen (Gloria Swanson), her young, male "bodyguard" (William Holden), and the butler who was once her director and husband (Erich Von Stroheim). *Sunset Boulevard* is loaded with "inside" black humor about Hollywood, and young people might merely interpret it all as shocking melodrama. Still, it is skillfully directed and fascinating to watch. It might be a good companion piece for Robert Aldrich's popular *What Ever Happened to Baby Jane?*, to which it is far superior, in an analysis of the genre. Rental from Films Inc.

Sweet Smell of Success. 96 minutes. Black and white. Directed by Alexander Mackendrick, 1957. This is one of those neglected great films that passed virtually unnoticed when it was released. Clifford Odets and Ernest Lehman's screenplay about a power-mad syndicated columnist (Burt Lancaster), whose particular obsession is "Red baiting," came awfully close to portraying some real people of the 1950s (this may be why the film was unsuccessful). Tony Curtis gives an excellent performance as the columnist's "stool pigeon," whose morals have to be seen to be believed. This is not a pretty movie, but it is an important one. Rental from United Artists 16.

Tagore. 54 minutes. Black and white. Directed by Satyajit Ray (Indian), 1961. English narration. This documentary on the career of Rabindranath Tagore, a kind of Indian Leonardo Da Vinci, was commissioned by the Indian government on the hundredth anniversary of Tagore's birth. Consisting of a mixture of old newsreel clips and dramatizations, the film reveals the amazing artistic accomplishments of this genius (author, poet, painter, philosopher, educator, and musician). This film should be of interest for students of world cultures. Purchase or rental from Contemporary-McGraw-Hill Films.

A Taste of Honey. 100 minutes. Black and white. Directed by Tony Richardson (British), 1962. An excellent film version of the noted British play. The story of a lonely, homely young girl who has a brief affair with a Black sailor and ends up pregnant is believably developed. The girl (Rita Tushingham), deserted by her lover, leaves home and takes up with a young homosexual with whom she develops a friendly, platonic relationship. This film is an interesting statement about the problems of youth, and I think students will relate well to it. Rental from Walter Reade 16.

That's Me. 15 minutes. Black and white. Directed by Walter Stuart, 1961. A funny, thought-provoking short about the vast cultural gap between middle-class altruism and the poor. Alan Arkin (then of New York's improvisational Second City troupe) plays a young Puerto Rican who is confronted by a well-meaning but inept social worker (Andrew Duncan) about the need to get a job. In the end, it is Arkin who questions the social worker on the necessity of his job. Considering that all the dialogue is improvised, the confrontation makes some humorous comments about the meddling of reformers. Arkin's characterization later shows up again in the feature film *Popi*. Purchase or rental from Contemporary-McGraw-Hill Films.

They Came to Cordura. 123 minutes. Color. Directed by Robert Rossen, 1959. An interesting, if not always effective, film about the nature of heroism. A man branded a coward by his regiment (the American expeditionary force in Mexico seeking Pancho Villa in 1917) is assigned to escort six "heroes" home to receive medals. On the way he demonstrates quiet bravery while his comrades turn out to be criminals or cowards. Gary Cooper is excellent as the latent hero. Rental from Twyman Films or Swank Films.

The Thing. 87 minutes. Black and white. Directed by Christian Nyby (produced by Howard Hawks, who, critics maintain, was the real "auteur" behind the film), 1951. The scariest science-fiction thriller of them all. A group of Air Force researchers in the Arctic are confronted by a monstrous vegetable-man that lives on human blood. Getting rid of "him" becomes an almost insurmountable problem. Skillful directing makes the film work, and it can be studied for its ability to scare, even with such an absurd plot. Rental from Films Inc.

The Third Man. 93 minutes. Black and white. Directed by Carol Reed (British), 1949. This famous masterpiece of suspense is at the very top of its genre. The story about an American writer who arrives in postwar Vienna to discover that the old friend he's come to see is being buried, only to find out later he's not dead at all, is made suspenseful by some brilliant camera work and an eerie musical score played on a zither. *The Third Man* would be especially useful in a class on film-making, since it is a veritable textbook of technique. Rental from Walter Reade 16.

This Sporting Life. 126 minutes. Black and white. Directed by Lindsay Anderson (British), 1963. A blistering portrait of the career of an English rugby player and the violent world he lives in. (This "sport" is played virtually without protection for the players. Unlike American football, rugby players wear no padding or helmets, and are often brutally beaten as a result.) Richard Harris is excellent as the athlete, and the scenes on the playing field (including some slow-motion shots of players being stomped in agonizing pain) are brilliant. The subplot involving a romance between Harris and the troubled woman with whom he boards (Rachel Roberts) is less effective, but *This Sporting Life* is still a towering film about the violent games men play. Rental from Walter Reade 16.

Toys. 8 minutes. Color. National Film Board of Canada Production, 1967. Smiling children gaze in a department store window at some toys on display: tanks, toy soldiers, guns. Suddenly they seem to come to life. The guns fire, the tanks burn, and the soldiers drop as if they're dying (several are decapitated). The stunned children blink, and the objects appear to be toys again. This is a thought-provoking little film, making a significant commentary on the impact of war toys. Teachers ought to show it to young children around Christmas time. Purchase or rental from Contemporary-McGraw-Hill Films.

The Train. 113 minutes. Black and white. Directed by John Frankenheimer, 1965. A very unusual war film about a group of French underground agents who fight to save a trainload of rare works of art from being sent to Germany. The special effects are devastating, including the most spectacular train wreck in screen history. A good point for discussion might be to examine the motives for the Frenchmen's fanatical struggle to save those art treasures. Burt Lancaster, Paul Scofield, and Michel Simon head an excellent cast. Rental from United Artists 16.

The Treasure of Sierra Madre. 125 minutes. Black and white. Directed by John

Huston, 1948. One of the greatest American films, about a trio of men prospecting in Mexico in the 1920s, *Treasure of Sierra Madre* is both an adventure story and a statement on human greed. Humphrey Bogart gives an unforgettable performance as the paranoic "Fred C. Dobbs." The film won three Academy Awards. Rental from Films Inc., Contemporary-McGraw-Hill Films, or Audio-Brandon Films.

The Trial of Joan of Arc. 65 minutes. Black and white. Directed by Robert Bresson (French), 1962. An interesting, if unexciting, film based on the actual transcript of the famous witchcraft trial. The director, Robert Bresson, has been hailed by many critics and film-makers as France's best. This film demonstrates his cold, objective style, and it might be interesting to compare it to Carl Dryer's intense treatment of the same subject in *The Passion of Joan of Arc* (1928). Rental of the Bresson film from Contemporary-McGraw-Hill Films.

Tunes of Glory. 106 minutes. Color. Directed by Ronald Neame (British), 1960. A stagey but well-acted drama about the conflict between an older military officer and his "modern" thinking replacement in a Scottish regiment. It's all been done before, but the acting of Alec Guiness and John Mills makes it believable and rather exciting. Rental from United Artists 16.

Two Men and a Wardrobe. 15 minutes. Black and white. Directed by Roman Polanski (Polish), 1957. No dialogue. This sad little parable about two gentlemen who emerge from the sea carrying a large wardrobe and are refused entry wherever they go is a good conversation piece. It's too simple to be used in a conceptual unit, but it does raise some interesting discussion points about human callousness. Purchase or rental from Contemporary-McGraw-Hill Films.

The Two of Us. 86 minutes. Black and white. Directed by Claude Berri (French), 1968. English subtitles. Not unlike *The Shop on Main Street* (and not quite equal to it), *The Two of Us* is about an old anti-Semitic Frenchman under Nazi domination who learns about tolerance. A charming little boy comes to live with him, and he later discovers the child he's become so fond of is Jewish. The film avoids many of the sentimental clichés one might expect, and Michel Simon is great as the gruff old man. Rental from Columbia Cinematheque.

Two Women. 99 minutes. Black and white. Directed by Vittorio De Sica (Italian), 1961. English subtitles. A brutal condemnation of war. A woman and her 13-year-old daughter wandering through war-torn Italy are violently attacked and raped by some Moroccan soldiers (Allies!). Following the experience, the girl sells herself as a prostitute, and the rest of the film concentrates on her mother's search for her. Sophia Loren won an Academy Award for her performance as the grief-stricken mother. *Two Women* is a great film which a teacher can use effectively in a classroom for a number of purposes. Rental from Audio-Brandon Films.

Ulysses. 132 minutes. Black and white. Directed by Joseph Strick, 1967. James Joyce's controversial classic has been made into an excellent film (critic Bosley Crowther listed it as one of the 50 best of all time). The raunchy dialogue and explicit sexuality are all intact, as is the philosophical theme of the work. College classes in English literature should find great use for it. This film came out prior to the Motion Picture Production Code ratings, but it obviously would have been given an"X." Still, it is an important piece of cinematic literature and no film guide can afford to neglect it. Rental from Walter Reade 16 (currently at a very expensive rate).

Up the Down Staircase. 123 minutes. Color. Directed by Robert Mulligan, 1968. Bel Kaufman's popular teachers' notebook memoir makes a reasonably entertaining movie, but thus far no film realistically portrays the complexities of the classroom. Sandy Dennis as a young English teacher feeling her way towards communicating with students is too self-consciously undynamic. Her interpretation of a very feminine, compassionate teacher betrays her limits as an actress. (Her habit of deliberately stammering, for example, becomes quite annoying. Is this the only way she can convince the audience of the sincerity of the role?) Still, the on-location background of an old New York High School and some excellent juvenile actors make *Up the Down Staircase* the best film of its kind. Rental from Warner Brothers 16.

The Virgin Spring. 88 minutes. Black and white. Directed by Ingmar Bergman (Swedish), 1959. English subtitles. Bergman's film, based on a medieval Scandinavian legend about the rape of a virgin and the miracle that followed, is a somber and depressing tale of vengeance. A father stalks and brutally kills the herdsmen who raped and murdered his daughter. He then buries her body, vowing to build a cathedral on the spot. Following his prayers, a spring of pure, fresh water spurts from the grave site. The major interest the film has for me is its depiction of the medieval religious spirit. Rental from Janus Films.

War Games. 19 minutes. Black and white. Directed by Donald Richie (Japanese), 1963. No dialogue. American expert on the Japanese film, Donald Richie made this interesting little parable on war. Two Japanese boys play on a deserted beach. Gradually their play becomes conflict, as if to symbolize the aggressiveness of men at war. Rental from Audio-Brandon Films.

The Wild Child (L'Enfant Sauvage). 90 minutes. Black and white. Directed by Francois Truffaut (French), 1970. English subtitles. Truffaut's brilliant treatment of the efforts of a young nineteenth century doctor attempting to civilize a "wolf child" was the great critical success of the 1970 New York Film Festival. Reminiscent of *The Miracle Worker* (only more subtle and less hysterical), the film portrays the struggle between the doctor and the boy without oversentimentalizing it. The director acts the role of the sympathetic Dr. Jean Itard skillfully by underplaying it. And the boy, Jean-Pierre Cargol, is excellent. *The Wild Child* should make a superb classroom film. Rental from United Artists 16.

The Wild One. 79 minutes. Black and white. Directed by Laslo Benedek, 1954. Marlon Brando's prototype portrayal of a motorcycle gang leader has made this film almost legendary. A little dated now, the plot about a group of Hell's Angel types terrorizing a small town still has some important things to say about mob violence. Actually, the story is based on a true incident of the early fifties, and since motorcycle gangs are still very much around, the film is worth a look. Rental from Audio-Brandon Films or Contemporary-McGraw-Hill Films.

Witness for the Prosecution. 114 minutes. Black and white. Directed by Billy

Wilder, 1957. This is one of those great "fun" courtroom dramas, complete
with a breathtaking surprise ending. Based on an Agatha Christie play, a
teacher could justify a transmedia study, but it's simply exciting entertainment. Charles Laughton's portrayal of a wise old barrister is a droll delight.
The very best of its genre. Rental from United Artists 16.

Woman in the Dunes. 123 minutes. Black and white. Directed by Hiroshi
Teshigahara (Japanese), 1964. English subtitles. The most exhausting cinematic experience I've ever encountered. An insect collector becomes
stranded in a strange town. He is offered temporary lodging in the house
of a woman at the bottom of a sand pit. When he tries to leave, he realizes
that he was deliberately trapped there. The ladder that lowered him into
the pit is gone. Now he must work with the woman shoveling sand for the
townspeople in return for food. I'm not sure what it all symbolizes, but the
camera work and sound are so intense that watching it, I became physically
exhausted. Students should be fascinated by the whole experience, and
their discussion will be exciting. Rental from Contemporary-McGraw-Hill
Films.

The World of Apu. 103 minutes. Black and white. Directed by Satyajit Ray
(Indian), 1959. English subtitles. I have to admit that I have never been
able to appreciate Indian films. Despite certain obvious cinematic beauty
(especially in this film), they move too slowly for me. I realize that teachers
are interested in them as samples of the art of another culture, and so I
cite this third film of director Satyajit Ray's famous trilogy on growing up.
Rental of the *World of Apu*, as well as the other two parts of the trilogy,
Panther Panchali (112 minutes, 1956) and *Aparajito* (108 minutes, 1958),
from Audio-Brandon Films.

You're a Big Boy Now. 97 minutes. Color. Directed by Francis Ford Coppola,
1966. An uneven but very funny comedy about the sexual awakening of a
pampered adolescent. Peter Kastner (of *Nobody Waved Goodbye*) plays
the frustrated youth who moves away from his possessive mother (Gerald-
ine Page) and chases after a sexy, man-hating Go-Go girl. Parts of the film
are in bad taste (dwarf Michael Dunn as "Mr. Big"), but it's still a humorous
commentary on coming of age. Rental from Warner Brothers 16.

"Z". 128 minutes. Color. Directed by Costa Gavras (French), 1969. English subtitles. This pulsating suspense film with political overtones was the big "in"
movie of 1969. Extremely well made and a significant portrait of the evolution of the Greek police state, it, nevertheless, is guilty of some oversimplification. The villainous military men are portrayed as one-dimensional monsters, and this detracts from the film's sense of reality. (In one
scene, some reporters ask one of the evil colonels about to be tried for
treason if he believes he is a persecuted innocent like Dreyfus. He turns
and angrily replies, "Dreyfus was guilty!" A very well-timed, funny line,
but it merely underscores the oversimplification of the character.) Much
of the technique of *"Z"* is borrowed from *The Battle of Algiers*, which is a
much more believable film (the villainous colonel in that film was portrayed
as a human being). *"Z"* is not yet available in 16 mm.

Zero for Conduct (Zero de Conduite). 45 minutes. Black and white. Directed by
Jean Vigo (French), 1933. English subtitles. I have not seen Jean Vigo's
legendary experimental film, though I understand it is the ideological fore-

runner of Lindsay Anderson's *If.* . . . Set in a boys' boarding school, the film exposes the false values of the hypocritical teachers and ends with the students overturning the repressive system. Kind of prophetic for 1933. Rental from Audio-Brandon Films.

Zorba the Greek. 146 minutes. Black and white. Directed by Michael Cacoyannis, 1964. A great film of Nikos Kazantzakis' famous novel. The story of a wily, irresponsible old Greek whose great love for life infects those around him is too well known to summarize. Anthony Quinn's performance in the title role is now legendary. This is one of the most popular films in classroom study because kids respond so well to it. Rental from Films Inc.

BIBLIOGRAPHY

In recent years with the increasing interest in cinema as an art form, a number of books have been written on the subject. Despite the abundance of published works in the field, however, very few are of much real value for teachers of a celluloid curriculum. It seems the vast body of film writing is either highly technical and designed for aspiring film-makers or "auteur" cultists. This latter type of literature deals with analyzing the works of various motion picture directors and the individual artistry they bring to their products. Such studies are not biographical, nor are they very analytical. Unfortunately most of the "auteur" writers (a great many of whom are British though the theory originated among the French) don't study their subjects at all. Instead they spend page after page justifying the individual styles of directors ranging in skills from Orson Welles to Howard Hawks to Budd Boetticher (if you've never heard of him your only loss is that you've missed his output of grade "B" Westerns). This kind of overpraising hero worship isn't of much value for a teacher seeking an understanding of the medium.

Film history is another area that has seen an increase in publications recently. Sadly, too much of this is written by relatively uncritical men who are simply too much in love with film. Perhaps my own professional historical training has made me unsympathetic with the oversentimentality of most film histories, but I have yet to see any that would meet American Historical Association standards except for David Stewart Hull's Film in the Third Reich.

The following bibliography lists sources that I investigated, in one way or another, in preparation for this book. I have annotated those that I think will have exceptional value for teachers, and I have included the names of some prominent screen periodicals that may be of interest. I have also listed collections of critical reviews and published screenplays, both of which, in the long run, may be the best sources for teachers of a celluloid curriculum. (The asterisk preceding an entry indicates that a paperback version is also available.)

PERIODICALS

Cinema (tri-yearly). Subscription Department. 9667 Wilshire Blvd., Beverly Hills, Calif. 90212.

Film Culture (quarterly). G. P. O. Box 499, New York, N. Y. 10001.
Films in Review. 31 Union Square, New York, N. Y. 10003.
Film Quarterly. University of California Press, Berkeley, Calif. 94704.
Media and Methods. 134 N. 13th St., Philadelphia, Penna. 19107. An absolute
    must for **all** teachers interested in this field. The only teacher-oriented pub-
    lication of its kind. Subscription rate–$5 for ten issues–a bargain.
Show: The Magazine of Films and the Arts. P. O. Box 54996, Terminal Annex,
    Los Angeles, Calif. 90054. A slick, commercial journal, but loaded with re-
    views and insights on current films.
Sight and Sound (a British quarterly). 155 W. 15th St., New York, N.Y. 10011.

WORKS ON FILM FOR TEACHERS

*CULKIN, John. Film Study in High School. New York: Fordham Film Study
    Center, 1966 (pamphlet).
*FEYEN, Sharon *et al.,* Eds. Screen Experience: An Approach to Film. Dayton,
    Ohio: Pflaum Publisher, 1969. A comprehensive paperback, primarily for
    teachers, on film-as-art study. Includes much valuable information, though
    an obscure numbering code designed to apply various films to specific stud-
    ies makes it a little confusing to use.
*GESSNER, Robert. The Moving Image: A Guide to Cinematic Literacy. New
    York: E. P. Dutton, 1968. The best guide to film technique available. Ex-
    plicit, well-documented, and very useful.
*HODGKINSON, Anthony W. Screen Education. New York: UNESCO, 1968. A
    100-page pamphlet for film teachers.
KUHNS, William. Themes: Short Films for Discussion. Dayton, Ohio: Pflaum
    Publisher, 1968. A useful, loose-leaf arrangement of brief guides for the
    most popularly used short films.
*MALLERY, David. The School and the Art of Motion Pictures. Boston: National
    Association of Independent Schools, 1966. A very useful, how-to-do-it
    guide, loaded with film descriptions, by a giant in this field. Mr. Mallery is a
    pioneer in film study in secondary schools.
PETERS, J. M. L. Teaching About the Film. New York: UNESCO, 1961. A useful,
    if slightly dated guide for teachers of film language and technique. This was
    one of the first works of its kind.
*SCHILLACI, Anthony, and Culkin, John, Eds. Films Deliver. New York: Citation
    Press, 1970.
*SHERIDAN, Marion C. *et al.* The Motion Picture and the Teaching of English.
    New York: Appleton-Century-Crofts, 1965.
*SOHN, David. Film Study and the English Teacher (pamphlet). Bloomington:
    Indiana University, Audio-Visual Center, 1968. A very practical guide,
    available free from NET Film Service with catalogs. Highly recommended.
*STEWART, David, Ed. Film Study in Higher Education. Washington, D. C.:
    American Council of Education, 1966. Anthology.

COLLECTED CRITICISM

ADLER, Renata. A Year in the Dark: Journal of a Film Critic, 1968-1969. New
    York: Random House, 1969. Intelligent essays by the former critic for the
    New York Times.

*AGEE, James. Agee on Film, vol. I. New York: Grosset and Dunlap, 1969. Agee was one of America'a first serious film critics, and probably its best. This book is a collection of his reviews for *The Nation* and *Time* during the decade of the forties.

ALPERT, Hollis. The Dreams and the Dreamers (Adventures of a Professional Movie Goer). New York: The Macmillan Company, 1962. Interesting film essays by one of the *Saturday Review*'s critics.

*ALPERT, Hollis, and Sarris, Andrew, Eds. Film Sixty Eight to Sixty Nine. New York: Simon and Schuster, 1969. The most recent volume of the selected reviews of the National Society of Film Critics.

*BLUESTONE, George. Novels into Film. Berkeley: University of California Press, 1966. Useful critical analysis of the essence of novels as motion pictures.

*CRIST, Judith. The Private Eye, the Cowboy and the Very Naked Girl: Movies from Cleo to Clyde. New York: Holt, Rinehart and Winston, 1968.

CROWTHER, Bosley. The Great Films: Fifty Golden Years of Motion Pictures. New York: Putnam, 1967.

KAEL, Pauline. Going Steady. Boston: Little, Brown and Co., 1970. The most literate of film critics, Miss Kael's works are always worth reading. This, however, is the weakest of her three books, containing reviews of too many minor films.

*——. I Lost It at the Movies. Boston: Little, Brown and Co., 1965. Her first and best work.

*——. Kiss Kiss Bang Bang. Boston: Little, Brown and Co., 1968. Includes her famous essay on "The Making of the Group."

*KAUFFMAN, Stanley. World on Film. New York: Harper and Row, 1966. A collection of Kauffman's *New Republic* reviews from 1958-1965.

MACDONALD, Dwight. Dwight MacDonald on Movies. Englewood Cliffs, N. J.: Prentice-Hall, 1969. A compendium of the reviews (mostly negative) of one of the nastiest critics of all time.

The New York Times Film Reviews, 1915-1968. New York: Arno Press, 1970. A five-volume reprinting of all of the *Times* reviews. This collection is invaluable to students of film history.

ROBINSON, William R., Ed. Man and the Movies: Essays on the Art of our Time. Baton Rouge: Louisiana State University Press, 1967. A little known, but excellent anthology of film criticism by writers and scholars.

*SCHEUER, Steven H., Ed., TV Movies. New York: Bantam Books, 1968, and Matlin, Leonard, Ed., TV Movies. New York: Signet Books, 1969. A couple of useful synopses of most of the films currently run on television.

*SCHICKEL, Richard, and Simon, John, Eds. Film, Sixty Seven to Sixty Eight. New York: Simon and Schuster, 1968. An anthology of the best written reviews of members of the National Society of Film Critics in 1967-1968.

SIMON, John. Private Screenings. New York: Macmillan, 1967. Collected reviews of the most cynical, nastiest critic since Dwight MacDonald.

*WARSHOW, Robert. Intermediate Experience: Movies, Comics, Theatre and Other Aspects of Popular Culture. New York: Atheneum, 1970. A posthumous publication of the excellent essayist's evaluation of popular culture. Included are his famous essays "The Gangster as Tragic Hero" and "The Westerner."

WHITE, David M., and Averson, Richard, Eds. Sight and Sound and Society. Boston: Beacon Press, 1968. This anthology evaluating all media has a section devoted to film criticism. John Culkin's famous article is great inspirational reading.

PUBLISHED SCREENPLAYS

*AGEE, James. Agee on Film, vol. II. New York: Grosset and Dunlap, 1969. Agee's scenarios: The Bride Comes to Yellow Sky, Noa Noa, The African Queen, The Blue Hotel, and The Night of the Hunter.

*ANDERSON, Lindsay, and Sherwin, David. If. . . . New York: Simon and Schuster, 1969.

BERGMAN, Ingmar. Ingmar Bergman's Trilogy (Through a Glass Darkly, Winter Light, and The Silence). New York: Orion Press, 1968.

*——. The Seventh Seal. London: Lorrimer Publishing, 1960.

BUNEL, Luis. Three Screenplays (Viridiana, The Exterminating Angel, Simon of the Desert). New York: Orion Press, 1969.

CHAYEFSKY, Paddy. The Goddess. New York: Simon and Schuster, 1958.

*EISENSTEIN, Sergei M. Potemkin. New York: Simon and Schuster, 1968 (film originally released in 1926).

*FELLINI, Federico. Juliet of the Spirits. New York: Ballantine Books, 1965.

*FONDA, Peter, Hopper, Dennis, and Southern, Terry. Easy Rider. New York: Signet Books, 1969. Includes interviews with author-film makers and reviews.

GASSNER, John, and Nichols, Dudley. Twenty Best Film Plays. New York: Crown Publishers, 1943. A rare but extremely valuable collection of some of the top scenarios of the thirties and early forties (Grapes of Wrath, Rebecca, How Green Was My Valley, It Happened One Night, Make Way for Tomorrow, Fury, Stagecoach, etc.).

*KUROSAWA, Akira. Rashomon. New York: Grove Press, 1969.

*RENOIR, Jean, and Spaak, Charles. The Grand Illusion. London: Lorrimer Publishing 1968 (originally released in 1937).

*TRUFFAUT, Francois. The 400 Blows. New York: Grove Press, 1969.

*——. Jules and Jim. London: Lorrimer Publishing, 1968.

WORKS ON FILM TECHNIQUE AND ART

ARNHEIM, Rudolf. Film as Art. Berkeley: University of California Press, 1957.

*BAZIN, Andre. What Is Cinema? Berkeley: University of California Press, 1967. This translated collection of essays by the famous French critic and film theorist is valuable reading for those interested in the aesthetics of cinema.

*EISENSTEIN, Sergei M., Film Form and Film Sense. New York: Harcourt Brace Jovanovich, 1969. Jay Leyda's translation of two of the Russian film master's theoretical works is very difficult reading. Frankly, it confused me. Perhaps students of the technical aspects of the medium will appreciate it more.

HALAS, John, and Manvell, Richard. The Technique of Film Animation. New York: Hastings, 1959.

*JACOBS, Lewis, Ed. The Emergence of Film Art. New York: Lion Press, 1970. A good anthology, including some film criticism on the historical and technical development of the medium.

*—— Ed. The Movies as Medium. New York: Noonday Press, 1970. Recent anthology on film technique.

KRACAUER, Siegfried. Theory of Film: The Redemption of Physical Reality. New York: Oxford University Press, 1960.

*LAWSON, John H. Film: The Creative Process, 2nd ed. New York: Hill and Wang, 1967.

*LINDGREN, Ernest. Art of the Film. New York: Macmillan, 1963.

MANOOGIAN, Haig P. The Film-Maker's Art. New York: Basic Books, 1966.

*MAC CANN, Richard D., Ed. Film: A Montage of Theories. New York: E. P. Dutton, 1966. Anthology of some of the works of leading film theorists.

*PUDOVKIN, V. I. Film Technique and Film Acting. Edited by Montagu, Ivor. New York: Grove Press, 1970.

REISZ, Karel, and Millar, Gavin. Technique of Film Editing. New York: Hastings, 1967. A famous, standard work on the editor's role in film production, by a now well-known, British director (*Saturday Night and Sunday Morning*).

ROTHA, Paul *et al.* The Documentary Film, 3rd ed. New York: Hastings, 1964. The most authoritative work on the subject.

*SMALLMAN, Kirk. Creative Film-Making. New York: Macmillan, 1969. A well written, how-to-do-it-cheaply guide. Useful for teachers who want to use student film-making as a means of creative expression.

SPOTTISWOODE, Raymond. Film and its Techniques. Berkeley: University of California Press, 1951.

*STEPHENSON, Ralph, and Debrix, Jean R. The Cinema as Art. Baltimore: Penguin Books, 1965. One of the few books of this kind that helped me. A fascinating explanation of the nature of film technique.

*WOLLEN, Peter. Signs and Meaning in the Cinema. Bloomington: Indiana University Press, 1969.

FILM HISTORY (INCLUDING BIOGRAPHY)

*ANDERSON, Joseph L., and Richie, Donald. The Japanese Film: Art and Industry. New York: Grove Press, 1960. A well written scholarly history and analysis of the Japanese film. This is the best of all works on foreign film industries.

*ARMES, Roy. French Cinema since 1946, 2 vols., revised ed. New York: A. S. Barnes, 1970.

BARNOUW, Erik, and Krishnaswamy, S. Indian Film. New York: Columbia University Press, 1963. A well-researched history of the Indian film.

*BARRY, Iris. Film Notes: The Silent Film. New York: Museum of Modern Art, 1949.

*——. D. W. Griffith: American Film Master. Edited by Bowser, Eileen. New York: Museum of Modern Art, 1966.

*BAXTER, John. Hollywood in the Thirties. New York: A. S. Barnes, 1968.

BLUM, Daniel C. Pictorial History of the Silent Screen. New York: Grosset and Dunlap, 1953.

—. Pictorial History of the Talkies. New York: Grosset and Dunlap, 1958.

BOYER, Deena. The Two Hundred Days of 8½. New York: Macmillan, 1964. An incisive diary of a journalist-observer on the scene at the making of Fellini's masterpiece.

*BROWNLOW, Kevin, The Parade's Gone By. New York: Knopf, 1968. A nostalgic, readable history of the silent screen, brilliantly illustrated and punctuated with statements from retired silent film directors.

*BUTLER, Ivan. The Horror Film. New York: A. S. Barnes, 1967. The weakest of three works on this subject.

*CALDER-MARSHALL, Arthur. The Innocent Eye: The Life of Robert J. Flaherty. New York: Harcourt Brace Jovanovich, 1966. A well written biography of documentary innovator Robert Flaherty.

CARMEN, Ira H. Movies, Censorship and the Law. Ann Arbor: University of Michigan Press, 1966. Intelligent study of the problems of censorship.

*CHAPLIN, Charles. My Autobiography. New York: Simon and Schuster, 1964.

CLARENS, Carlos. An Illustrated History of the Horror Film. New York: Putnam, 1968. A solid, detailed study of this genre of films, though it tends to overpraise and overrate most of its subject.

COGLEY, John, Ed. Report on Blacklisting, vol. I. New York: The Fund for the Republic, 1956. See especially the section on "Communism and the Movies" by Dorothy P. Jones.

CROWTHER, Bosley. The Lion's Share: The Story of an Entertainment Empire. New York: E. P. Dutton, 1957. A history of MGM, now in need of updating in light of that company's current economic plight.

*DOUGLAS, Drake. Horror. New York: Macmillan, 1966. An interesting but cursory, undetailed history of the horror film.

DURGNAT, Raymond. The Crazy Mirror: Hollywood Comedy and the American Image. New York: Horizon Press, 1970.

EISNER, Lotte, H. The Haunted Screen: Expressionism in the German Cinema and the Influence of Max Reinhardt. Berkeley: University of California Press, 1969.

FENIN, George, and Everson, William K. The Western: From Silents to Cinerama. New York: Orion Press, 1962. The standard work on the genre, detailed but a little too nostalgic. It is updated in Everson's Pictorial History of the Western Film. New York: Citadel Press, 1969.

FRANKLIN, Joe. Classics of the Silent Screen: A Pictorial Treasury. New York: Citadel Press, 1959.

*GISH, Lillian, and Pinchot, Anne. The Movies, Mister Griffith and Me. Englewood Cliffs, N. J.: Prentice-Hall, 1969. A useful memoir of the noted actress, especially for her description of the early Griffith era.

GOODMAN, Ezra. The Fifty-Year Decline and Fall of Hollywood. New York: Simon and Schuster, 1961.

GRIFFITH, Richard, and Mayer, Arthur. The Movies, revised ed. New York: Simon and Schuster, 1969. A well illustrated but overly nostalgic "history" of the American film.

GRIFFITH, Richard. The World of Robert Flaherty. Westport, Conn.: Greenwood, 1951.

HALLIWELL, Leslie, Ed. The Filmgoer's Companion, revised 3rd ed. New York:

Hill and Wang, 1970. A detailed encyclopedia of most facets of cinema (actors, films, directors, cinematic terms, etc.), which can be a useful reference.

*HOUSTON, Penelope. The Contemporary Cinema. Baltimore: Penguin Books, 1967.

HUACO, George A.. The Sociology of Film Art. New York: Basic Books, 1965.

*HUGHES, Robert, Ed. Film, Book 2: Films of Peace and War. New York: Grove Press, 1962. A good anthology of pacifistic interpretations of war films. Includes complete screenplays of *Night and Fog* and John Huston's banned army documentary *Let There Be Light*. I have never seen Book 1 of this series, which deals with film art.

HULL, David S. Film in the Third Reich: A Study of the German Cinema, 1933-1945. Berkeley: University of California Press, 1969. By far the best cinematic history in print. Scholarly, well constructed, and significant.

*KNIGHT, Arthur. The Liveliest Art. New York: New American Library, 1959. A brief, readable screen history, period.

*KRACAUER, Siegfried. From Caligari to Hitler. A Psychological History of the German Film. Princeton, N. J.: Princeton University Press, 1947. A fascinating study on the German Film, though David Stewart Hull's work refutes much of its interpretation.

LAHUE, Kalton C. Bound and Gagged: The Story of the Silent Serial. New York: A. S. Barnes, 1968.

—. Continued Next Week: A History of the Moving Picture Serial. Norman: University of Oklahoma Press, 1964.

LEYDA, Jay. Kino: A History of the Russian and Soviet Film. New York: Hillary, 1960.

LIKENESS, George. The Oscar People. Mendota, Illinois: The Wayside Press, Inc., 1965. A well illustrated useful history of all phases of the Academy Awards, including synopses of winning features and shorts.

*MAC GOWAN, Kenneth. Behind the Screen: The History and Technique of the Motion Picture. New York: Delacorte Press, 1965.

MAYER, Michael F. Foreign Films on American Screens. New York: ARCO, 1965. A large, well illustrated book with detailed analyses of many of the popular European films of the early sixties. A bit dated now in its prediction of the censorship problems they would present for the future.

MICHAEL, Paul, and Parish, James R., Eds. The American Movies Reference Book: The Sound Era. Englewood Cliffs, N. J.: Prentice-Hall, 1969. A huge, expensive book ($29.95) that is supposed to be the last word in film scholarship. Considering its aspirations, it is *very* weak.

NOBLE, Peter. The Negro in Films. Port Washington, N. Y.: Kennikat, 1969; and New York: Arno Press. A good, scholarly study for films up to 1948.

*POWDERMAKER, Hortense. Hollywood: The Dream Factory (An Anthropologist Looks at Movie Makers). New York: Universal Library, 1950. A classic series of essays on the film industry of the late forties and an interpretation of its future potential.

RAMSAYE, Terry. A Million and One Nights. New York: Simon and Schuster, 1964. A not-too-detailed history of the silent screen up to 1925.

*RANDALL, Richard S. Censorship of the Movies: The Social and Political

Control of a Mass Medium. Madison: University of Wisconsin Press, 1970.

*RENAN, Sheldon, An Introduction to the American Underground Film. New York: E. P. Dutton, 1967. A useful book analyzing the development of the Andy Warhol end of the film industry.

*RICHARDSON, Robert. Literature and Film. Bloomington: Indiana University Press, 1969.

*ROBINSON, David. The Great Funnies: A History of Film Comedy. New York: E. P. Dutton, 1969.

RONDI, Gian Luigi. Italian Cinema Today, 1952-1965. New York: Hill and Wang, 1966.

*ROSS, Lillian. Picture. New York: Avon Books, 1969. This well-known record of the filming of John Huston's *The Red Badge of Courage* is a valuable behind-the-scenes source on the complexities of movie-making.

ROTHA, Paul and Griffith, Richard. The Film Till Now: A Survey of World Cinema, 3rd ed. New York: Twayne, 1967. An encyclopedic hodge-podge of film history which is too long and badly organized for skillful research. Typical of the state of much film scholarship.

*SCHICKEL, Richard. The Disney Version: The Life, Times, Art and Commerce of Walt Disney. New York: Simon and Schuster, 1968. An excellent analytical biography of one of the most complex and interesting leaders in the film industry.

—. *Movies: The History of an Art and an Institution.* New York: Basic Books, 1964. Brief and unspecific, but a very readable film history.

SCHUMACH, Murray. The Face on the Cutting Room Floor. New York: William Morrow, 1964. This enlightening study on all facets of movie censorship makes valuable background reading for teachers.

SNYDER, Robert L. Pare Lorentz and the Documentary Film. Norman: University of Oklahoma Press, 1968. This detailed biography of the noted documentary director of the thirties provides much useful data on Depression film-making, despite its dull format and colorless writing.

*SPRINGER, John. All Talking! All Singing! All Dancing! New York: Citadel Press, 1966. A pictorial history of the screen musical, for those who care.

*TALBOT, Daniel, Ed. Film: An Anthology, 2nd ed. Berkeley: University of California Press, 1966. A generally excellent anthology of film history.

THOMAS, Bob. King Cohn. New York: Putnam, 1967. This readable biography of the despotic former head of Columbia Pictures Harry Cohn provides some interesting insights into the film industry in the hey-day of big studios.

WAGENKNECHT, Edward C. The Movies in the Age of Innocence. Norman: University of Oklahoma Press, 1962. A general history of the early silent film.

*WALKER, Alexander. Sex in the Movies. Baltimore: Penguin Books, 1968. This timely history of censorship problems caused by the portrayal of sex on the screen is a handy guide for teachers surveying "controversial" films.

"AUTEUR" STUDIES (BOOKS THAT INTERPRET THE ART OF FILM DIRECTORS)

*AUSTEN, David. The Cinema of Stanley Kubrick. New York: A. S. Barnes, 1969.

*BOGDANOVICH, Peter. The Cinema of Alfred Hitchcock. New York: Museum of

Modern Art, 1962. Bogdanovich is the best of the writers of this genre. He thoroughly researches his material and provides many insights through interviews with his subjects. The other authors of works of this kind, unfortunately, are less skillful.

*——. The Cinema of Howard Hawks. New York: Museum of Modern Art, 1962.

*——. The Cinema of Orson Welles. New York: Museum of Modern Art, 1961. Currently being revised.

*——. Fritz Lang in America. New York: Frederick A. Praeger, 1969.

*——. John Ford. Berkeley: University of California Press, 1968.

*CASTY, Alan. The Films of Robert Rossen. New York: Museum of Modern Art, 1969. This is the only study I know of on the skillful director of *All the King's Men, Body and Soul,* and *The Hustler.*

*COWIE, Peter. Antonioni, Bergman, Resnais. New York: A. S. Barnes, 1964.

*DONNER, Joren. The Personal Vision of Ingmar Bergman. Bloomington: Indiana University Press, 1964.

*GEDULD, Harry M., Ed. Film-Makers on Film Making. Bloomington: Indiana University Press, 1969. A historical compendium of interviews including D. W. Griffith predicting sound would not be practical for movies. Also includes several recent directors.

*GELMIS, Joseph. The Film Director as a Superstar. Garden City, N. Y.: Doubleday and Company, 1970. This recent series of interviews with men like Mike Nichols, Stanley Kubrick, Arthur Penn, John Korty, and others is a very informative portrait of the relative independence of the director in today's films.

*GRAHAM, Peter, Ed. The New Wave: Critical Landmarks. Garden City, N. Y.: Doubleday, 1968. A study of the French cinema of the early sixties analyzing the works of key directors (Godard, Truffaut, etc.).

*KITSES, Jim. Horizons West (Anthony Mann, Budd Boetticher, Sam Peckinpah: Studies of Authorship Within the Western). Bloomington: Indiana University Press, 1969. Typical of this kind of writing, author Jim Kitses' adulation of his subject detracts from any scholarly contribution he may hope to make.

*LIVINGSTON, Don. Film and the Director. New York: Putnam, 1969.

*MC DONALD, Gerald D., Conway, Michael, and Ricci, Mark. The Films of Charlie Chaplin. New York: Citadel Press, 1965.

*PERRY, George. The Films of Alfred Hitchcock. New York: E. P. Dutton, 1965.

*PRATLEY, Gerald. The Cinema of John Frankenheimer. New York: A. S. Barnes, 1969.

*RICHIE, Donald. The Films of Akira Kurosawa. Berkeley: University of California Press, 1965. An exceptionally good work of this kind on the films of the noted Japanese director.

*SARRIS, Andrew. The American Cinema: Directors and Directions, 1929-1968. New York: E. P. Dutton, 1969. America's leading "auteur" critic, Sarris explains the theory and its limitations in this detailed reference book on the works of most American directors.

*——. Interviews with Film Directors. New York: Avon Books, 1969.

SHERMAN, Eric, and Rubin, Martin. The Director's Event: Interviews with Five

American Film Makers. New York: Atheneum, 1970. Interesting interviews with five directors who are very different from each other—Arthur Penn, Budd Boetticher (has any minor figure ever commanded so much attention?), Samuel Fuller, Abraham Polansky, and Peter Bogdanovich (the noted "auteur" critic made one film, an obscure thing called *Targets*).

*TAYLOR, John R. Cinema Eye, Cinema Ear. New York: Hill and Wang, 1964. Colorfully written essays by the film critic of the *London Times* on significant directors like Hitchcock, Fellini, Truffaut, Bergman, etc.

*TRUFFAUT, Francois. Hitchcock. New York: Simon and Schuster, 1967. The noted French director's adulatory interview of Alfred Hitchcock. Part history, part (mostly) hero worship.

*WOOD, Robin. Hitchcock's Films. New York: A.S. Barnes, 1965. Still another uncritical interpretation of the films of Alfred Hitchcock.

Index of Film Titles